THE CHILDREN OF IMMIGRANTS AT SCHOOL

The Children of Immigrants at School

A COMPARATIVE LOOK AT INTEGRATION
IN THE UNITED STATES AND WESTERN EUROPE

Edited by Richard Alba and Jennifer Holdaway

A joint publication of the Social Science Research Council
and New York University Press

NEW YORK UNIVERSITY PRESS

New York and London

www.nyupress.org

© 2013 by Social Science Research Council

Library of Congress Cataloging-in-Publication Data

The children of immigrants at school : a comparative look at integration in the United States and Western Europe / edited by Richard Alba and Jennifer Holdaway ; a joint publication of the Social Science Research Council and New York University Press.

pages cm

Includes bibliographical references and index.

ISBN 978-0-8147-6094-9 (cl : alk. paper)

ISBN 978-0-8147-6025-3 (pb : alk. paper)

1. Children of immigrants—Social conditions—United States. 2. Children of immigrants—Social conditions—Europe. 3. Children of immigrants—Economic conditions—United States. 4. Children of immigrants—Economic conditions—Europe. 5. Children of immigrants—Education—United States. 6. Children of immigrants—Education—Europe. 7. Social integration—United States. 8. Social integration—Europe. I. Alba, Richard D. II. Holdaway, Jennifer.

HQ792.U5C4325 2013

305.23086'912—dc23

2013017065

New York University Press books are printed on acid-free paper, and their binding materials are chosen for strength and durability. We strive to use environmentally responsible suppliers and materials to the greatest extent possible in publishing our books.

Manufactured in the United States of America

c 10 9 8 7 6 5 4 3 2 1

p 10 9 8 7 6 5 4 3 2 1

References to Internet websites (URLs) were accurate at the time of writing. Neither the author nor New York University Press is responsible for URLs that may have expired or changed since the manuscript was prepared.

Contents

Preface

The rich nations on both sides of the Atlantic are confronting a new set of challenges, arising from the large-scale immigrations they hosted during the second half of the twentieth century and the beginning of the twenty-first. Ironically, immigration in many cases was encouraged by governments and employers as a solution to labor-market problems, especially (but not exclusively) in filling slots at or near the bottom of the job hierarchy. But immigration imports its own set of dynamics, which are not easily controlled. In combination with the low fertility and aging of native populations in the wealthy countries, the swelling of youthful immigrant groups has produced profound, unanticipated shifts among the children of these countries. The share of children coming from immigrant homes has been increasing, and almost everywhere now, they account for substantial fractions of the young people in nurseries and classrooms. As these children grow up and enter adulthood, simultaneously with the departure of huge numbers of baby-boom natives from work and civic activity, an historic transition will take place toward much more diverse societies than could have been anticipated half a century ago. This transition will have far-reaching consequences. In effect, the future of the West in economic, cultural, and social terms—this is not too bold a formulation—will depend on how well immigrant-origin youth have been prepared to replace aging natives.

Many of these immigrant-origin youth—in most countries, the majority—belong to what in this volume we will call "low-status" immigrant groups. This means that they grow up typically in homes where adults have little education by the standards of the receiving society and work at low-skill jobs (or are unemployed) and where a language other than the mainstream one is in common use; and they and their parents belong to groups that are stigmatized in the new social context because of ethnic, racial, and/or religious differences from the native mainstream. This characterization applies to Turks in the multiple Western European countries where they have settled in large numbers and to Mexicans and Central Americans in the United States. The children from these groups begin school handicapped by substantial disadvantages rooted in their immigrant backgrounds, and their future contributions to the societies where they live and their ability to experience the full range of opportunities available there depend critically on their experiences in schools. If schools succeed in bringing them to parity with children in the native mainstream, then the transition to diversity will be made smoother; if schools do not succeed, then the challenges of coming decades will be that much more difficult. The project on which this volume is based, the Children of Immigrants in Schools (CIS), set out to find out how well schools are fulfilling this mission in the United States and five Western European nations—France, Great Britain, the Netherlands, Spain, and Sweden—and to identify features of educational systems that might possibly enhance the chances of children from immigrant homes.

The CIS project is a significant departure from the earlier and predominant focus of United States–based researchers such as ourselves on the American experience with immigration, presumed in the past to be unique. We believe that this exclusive focus is out of date and no longer justifiable, and that the immigration societies have much to learn from each other, since no one of them possesses a singularly successful formula for including immigrants and their children in the mainstream. In embarking in this direction, we join other US researchers, who are also embracing broader international and comparative perspectives. In "internationalizing" migration studies, some of them have looked into the origins of migrants who have settled in the United States and examined the implications of sustained transnational ties. Others have looked comparatively at the settlement and integration of immigrants into advanced industrial nations, including other countries formed by immigration, such as Australia and Canada, but also countries of prior emigration and now of immigration in Europe, such as Germany. To promote this geographic expansion of US immigration studies, organizations that support migration research are beginning to develop training for younger scholars along with research projects that are designed to promote international approaches.

When we initiated the CIS Project, one of our hopes was to develop a useful model of how international training and research could be organized and contribute to understandings of migration processes and outcomes. The project grew out of the Working Group on Education and Migration at the Social Science Research Council. Two workshops—one of which considered the interactions among institutions, policy, and agency in shaping the educational trajectories of children of immigrants within the United States, and the other comparing aspects of institutional and policy arrangements in the United States and Europe—provided the opportunity to explore possible analytical frameworks for cross-national analysis (see Holdaway and Alba 2009; Holdaway, Crul, and Roberts 2009). These discussions eventually broadened into a collaboration involving ten senior scholars—five in the United States and five in Western Europe—along with fifteen more junior ones, some of them in a postdoctoral phase, others working on their dissertations. Richard Alba, then director of the Center for Social and Demographic Analysis (CSDA) at the University at Albany, SUNY, took on the role of principal investigator, working in intellectual partnership with Jennifer Holdaway of the Social Science Research Council (SSRC). Both CSDA and SSRC provided essential infrastructural support. Funding came from two programs: the bulk was from the US National Science Foundation's Partnerships for International Research and Education (PIRE) program (grant OISE-0529921); in addition, the Nuffield Foundation in London gave us critical support to expand European participation by supporting six post-doctoral researchers (who could not be financed by the National Science Foundation because they were based outside the United States).

To best achieve the combination of international training and research, the research effort was organized into five teams, each led by two senior scholars, one from each side of the Atlantic, and staffed by younger scholars from the United States and Europe. Each team focused on a comparison of the United States to one of the European countries with a specific thematic emphasis (e.g., postsecondary education in the case of the UK-US comparison, or the transition from school to labor market in the case of France-United States). The younger scholars did much of the legwork of research but in close collaboration with the senior scholars. This organizational formula worked admirably.

Readers can see and evaluate for themselves the results in the ensuing pages, where the authorship of each chapter acknowledges the research contributions made by individual scholars. But here we want to recognize the extensive assistance by others that made the project work. At the National Science Foundation, we could not have managed without the help of Bonnie Thompson, along with her colleague, Patricia White. At the Nuffield Foundation, we are grateful to Anthony Tomei for seeing the potential of the endeavor and enabling it to become truly comparative by supporting the participation of six European postdoctoral fellows; to Catrin Roberts for her active engagement in the intellectual work of the program; and to Velda Hinds for assistance with logistics and finance.

At the Center for Social and Demographic Analysis, Walter (Chip) Ensel and Linda Lawrence made the administrative aspects of the project relatively painless, allowing Alba to spend as much time as possible on the research and training sides. Technical assistance on a number of fronts was provided by Dr. Ruby Wang. Jeffrey Napierala and Joseph Pereira (the latter at CUNY's Center for Urban Research) carried out the PISA analysis that appears in the first chapter. At the CUNY Graduate Center, Laura Braslow did a remarkable job of rendering complex educational system diagrams in a common visual vocabulary. At the SSRC we would like to thank the several program assistants who assisted with administrative matters and the organization of the numerous meetings and workshops associated with the program: Jeppe Wohlert, Samip Mallick, Wonny Lervisit, Eva Pepi, and Lauren Shields.

Richard Alba, Jennifer Holdaway, and Josh DeWind

CHAPTER ONE

The Integration Imperative: Introduction

Richard Alba and Jennifer Holdaway

Immigration is challenging the societies of North America and Western Europe in ways that could not have been anticipated several decades ago. The wealthy societies of the West have welcomed immigrants at key moments since the mid-twentieth century; and everywhere, immigration has been associated with increasing ethnic, racial, and religious diversity (Castles and Miller 2009). In societies such as Germany or Sweden, which previously thought of themselves as homogeneous, this diversity is a novel fact that they still struggle to absorb. In countries such as the United States, where immigration was already a part of the national story, ever-rising levels of diversity are setting off anxieties among the native majority about its grip on the levers of power and status.

All of the wealthy societies will confront a transition of enormous consequence over the next several decades (Alba 2011; Coleman 2006; Myers 2007). This transition involves a decline in the numbers of young people of "native" origins, however defined, and an increase in the numbers of their age mates from immigrant backgrounds. This shift will not unfold gradually and unobtrusively but rapidly and intensely because of another basic demographic fact: everywhere there was a spurt in the number of births in the decades immediately following World War II; and the baby boomers, who are overwhelmingly members of the native majority, will be retiring during the next several decades. The exit of this group, which occupies a disproportionate share of the most skilled and best-paying jobs, will create powerful churning in the labor market. The question that will have to be faced everywhere is: Who will replace the baby boomers?

One conclusion seems inescapable: these societies will have to rely more and more on young people of nonnative origins to sustain their economic, cultural, and social vitality. These young people will form not only an increasing proportion of the workforce in general, but they will have to make up a larger share of its upper tiers, where highly skilled positions with considerable authority over others are concentrated. The imperative is therefore to integrate young people from immigrant-origin minorities—Turks in Germany, North Africans in France, Mexicans and other Latin Americans in the United States. Integration implies that young people of minority origins are prepared to function in the work force in ways that are similar to those of well-trained natives. If integration falters or remains very incomplete, these societies risk losing their competitive position within the world economy, suffering a decline in the living standards of their populations, and perhaps failing to be able to support their growing elderly populations.

The imperative of integration follows not only from the utilitarian calculus of demographic and economic forces, but also from the moral logic of social justice. First-generation immigrants enter host societies that are more or less welcoming, but the new arrivals are not expected, and indeed do not always wish, to become full members of the national community. Their children, however, are generally citizens who should have equal rights to all the opportunities and public goods provided to the children of native parents. The processes endowing children with capabilities that unfold during adulthood are determined at levels beyond the reach of individuals and families (Sen 1999). Nevertheless, the children of immigrants are equally entitled to realize their full potential as individuals, workers, and citizens; and to do this they must acquire what James Fishkin (1997) refers to as "the essential prerequisites for adult participation in society." In this context, integration takes on a broad meaning and involves full and robust membership in the new society.

Obviously, the success of integration depends to a great extent on the performance of educational systems. The ability of schools in the United States and Western Europe to integrate children growing up in low-status immigrant homes is the concern of this volume. In the countries that have taken in large numbers of immigrants, such children pose a variety of challenges to schools: they frequently come from homes where an immigrant language, one other than the mainstream language of schools, predominates; and their parents typically have much lower levels of education than do parents of ethnic-majority students. Sometimes immigrant parents are even illiterate. While immigrant-origin students can reach the top of an educational system—in the United States, it is no longer remarkable when they are the valedictorians of their high schools—it is also common for them to be prominent among those at the bottom and, in fact, to leave school early, without credentials that have value in the labor market.

This book is founded on comparisons of six countries that have received substantial immigration since the middle of the twentieth century: France, Great Britain, the Netherlands, Spain, Sweden, and the United States. It takes advantage of variations across these countries in the organization and functioning of school systems. For example, the systems differ in their tracking schemes: some of the systems of northern continental Europe, like the Dutch one, shunt students at an early age along separate tracks heading toward different educational and labor-market outcomes, while the systems of France, Great Britain, and the United States hold students longer within comprehensive educational contexts, allowing them to keep their options open. The main question this book entertains is: What consequences do the varying features of school systems have for children coming from immigrant homes? Or, alternatively put, what can we learn from one system that can be usefully applied in another? We believe that there is much to be gained from a rigorous comparison of how immigrant-origin students fare in different contexts, and this is the major purpose of this volume.

The Second Generation

Observers have long recognized that the integration of immigrants is less determinative of the future of new racial/ethnic groups than is the integration of their children and the generations that come after. The term "second generation" is often taken in a broad sense to encompass children who grow up in immigrant homes, whether they are born in the receiving society or enter it at a young age; we generally use it in this sense throughout this volume. In the more precise language of social-science research, the term is reserved for those children of immigrants who are born in the host society, while the children who arrive at a young age and thus receive part or all of their schooling in the new society are called the "1.5" generation.[1]

Regardless of where they are born, children growing up in immigrant homes already constitute a large share of the child populations of rich societies, and the demography of these societies more or less guarantees that this proportion will continue to increase. Because the fertility of the native majority is lower than that of immigrant populations, in most wealthy countries, the native-origin population will shrink in relative, if not absolute, terms.

For example: in the Netherlands as of 2008, young people of immigrant origins account for almost a quarter (22.5 percent) of the Dutch population under the age of twenty-one (Statistics Netherlands 2009). This proportion is much higher in big cities such as Amsterdam and Rotterdam, where the immigrant population is concentrated. In those two cities, immigrant-origin children form the majority of students (Crul and Doomernik 2003). Those born in the Netherlands make up by now the largest share of immigrant-origin children, and the fraction belonging to the 1.5 generation is shrinking because of the restrictions on immigration and the growing weight of immigrants in the child-bearing population. Most immigrant-origin children, more than two-thirds overall, have non-Western origins, according to Statistics Netherlands (2009), meaning that their parents come from Morocco, Turkey, or one of the former Dutch colonies.

In Sweden, children of immigrant origins were one-quarter of all young persons under the age of eighteen in 2000 (Westin 2003). The bulk of the children growing up in immigrant families, more than three-quarters, were born in Sweden. Most of these Swedish-born children have parents who immigrated from neighboring countries, either in Scandinavia or elsewhere in Northern Europe (e.g., Germany, Great Britain), and thus face modest challenges in adjusting to Swedish schools. However, the majority of the 1.5 generation came from Eastern Europe (of whom a large number are refugees from the former Yugoslavia) or from outside of Europe. Many of them are facing considerable challenges in the school system.

In the United States as of 2009, almost one-quarter of all children (persons under the age of eighteen) come from immigrant families. The great majority of immigrant-origin children, more than three-quarters, belongs to the second generation in the strict sense of that term (Innocenti Insight 2009; Passel 2011). Reflecting the overall patterns of immigration, about half of the children are of Latin American origin, with parents from Mexico or Central and South America. Of these, children of Mexican origins constitute the majority. Another tenth come from Caribbean backgrounds, approximately half of whom have parents from the Spanish-speaking Caribbean (Cuba, the

Dominican Republic). A quarter of immigrant-origin children are of Asian background. The families of these children are very diverse in their national origins, though the largest groups are from the Philippines, Vietnam, India, and mainland China, in that order. The remainder has parents from Europe, Canada, and Africa.

In France, about one-sixth (17 percent) of all children are growing up in immigrant homes. Half of these children have parents who have come from Africa, almost all from countries that were formerly French colonies (Kirsz-baum, Brinbaum, and Simon 2009). The bulk of these immigrant parents hail from North Africa, but there are sizable contingents from sub-Saharan countries such as Mali and Senegal. Another third of immigrant-origin children have family roots elsewhere in Europe, mostly in nearby southern European countries, with the largest group originating in Portugal. The remaining children in immigrant families are predominantly of Asian backgrounds, and in this category the Turks form the largest group, followed by Southeast Asians.

In the United Kingdom, the proportion of all children who are in immigrant families is also about a sixth, and in this case, too, the immigrations from former colonies are preponderant. The biggest group among the immigrant-origin children, a plurality of about 40 percent, has parents from Asia, from Pakistan, India, Bangladesh, and China, in that order (Crawley 2009). Another 20 percent has parents from Africa, mostly from former colonies such as Ghana, Kenya, and Nigeria. Despite the visibility of the Afro-Caribbean migration to Britain, the children of these origins are a small group, just 5 percent. Most of the remaining children in immigrant families are of European background, with the Irish composing the single largest group in this category.

There are not yet Spanish data comparable to those enumerated above. However, we can get a glimpse of the changes underway among children from recent birth data. They show that in 2009, 24 percent of the babies born in the country had at least one parent who was a foreigner (INE 2010). The great majority of these parents came from outside of Europe, with Africa and South America the predominant continents of origin. Even among the Europeans, a large number of parents came from poorer countries of Eastern Europe, with Romanians alone accounting for more than 40 percent.

The Immigration Backgrounds of the Second Generation

All immigrations are not the same when it comes to the situation of the second generation. Some involve many individuals with advanced educational credentials—so called high human-capital immigrations—and produce second generations that frequently outperform native children at school. Others, especially those involving immigrants with low levels of schooling (and sometimes no schooling at all), lead to second generations whose members generally are not well prepared to excel in complex school systems, where sustained academic commitment and strategizing about educational choices are required to achieve the most favorable outcomes. In the United States, immigrants from several Asian countries, e.g., India, exemplify immigrations of the first type, and the academic achievements of their children are on average very high. Immigrants from a number of Latin American countries, e.g., Mexico, exemplify the second, and the relatively rates of high school dropout and low rates of university graduation for their children have long been a matter of concern (e.g., Telles and Ortiz 2008). If the nature of an immigration stream matters, it is also the case that the mix of these streams varies across receiving societies, and that the characteristics of the average immigrant received, say, by Sweden are not the same as those of the average new arrival in Spain. If we hope to disentangle the impacts of schools on the children of immigrants, we first have to sort out some key differences among the immigrant parents themselves.

When it comes to the educational inequalities between immigrant-origin and native children, migrations by low-skilled migrants seeking jobs in the bottom tiers of a rich society's labor market make up the most critical stream. Most of the subsequent essays in this volume focus largely or exclusively on the second generations from these migrations, typified not only by Mexicans in the United States but also by Turks in the Netherlands and Algerians in France. Generally large in size and usually coming from the countries of the global South, whose citizens are perceived to be culturally different from the mainstream of the countries of reception and frequently ethno-racially different, too, the labor migrations of the post–World War II era have created new minorities in many countries or expanded old ones (Portes and Zhou 1993). (Because of the multiple dimensions—socioeconomic and ethno-racial, above all—that distinguish these immigrants from majority populations in receiving societies, we will often refer to them as "low-status" immigrants.) Though often conceived as temporary by the governments that promote them, labor migrations generally lead to permanent settlement by some portion of the immigrant group, which finds the opportunities in the new society, however humble, preferable to those it would face upon return.

The governments and employers of the wealthy countries of the West had a major hand in the labor migrations of the second half of the twentieth century (Castles and Miller 2009). In the United States, the beginnings of the contemporary labor immigration can be spotted in the Bracero Program, which was initiated during World War II to fill the need for labor at a time when many American men were in uniform. In Europe, the labor needs that gave rise to large-scale labor migrations came after the war, during the rebuilding of damaged infrastructures and economies, when additional labor had to be imported because of the massive losses of manpower due to the war itself. France, for instance, established its office of immigration (ONI) in 1945. Germany had perhaps the exemplary program during the postwar period, recruiting so-called guestworkers, who were expected to come without their families and to work for predetermined periods and then return home (Bade 1994).

What started as temporary immigration initiated by the state often turned into permanent settlement. Family reunification has been the key policy provision that has played the role of catalyst in this process and allowed labor immigration to continue to grow in many countries. In the United States, a series of critical laws established family reunification as the primary principle that would govern legal admission. It was a centerpiece in the watershed 1965 act, which has shaped the landscape of immigration ever since its passage. In Europe, active recruitment of low-wage immigrants came to an end in most countries in the early 1970s when their economies were rattled by the shock of oil-price rises. However, immigrant populations have continued to grow as a result of the family-reunification parts of immigration law, which are found in all countries (although there have been some recent attempts to narrow them). Indeed, the end of active recruitment precipitated a process of settlement for many immigrant groups. The Turks in the Netherlands are a case in point: many of the guestworkers did not return home but found ways to stay and to bring their families. Family reunification accelerated with the official halt to guestworker recruitment in 1973, when the immigrants realized that entry into Western Europe would become more difficult. The Turkish population continues to grow through family-reunification immigration, which now often occurs in the form of marriages between second-generation Turks and partners from the home regions of their parents.

In both the United States and Europe, labor immigration also persists in unauthorized ways, with undocumented immigrants often receiving legal sanction after a period of residence and work through amnesties, which have occurred in the United States and in several Western European countries. In the United States, undocumented immigration appears to occur in roughly equal measure as result of clandestine border crossing, especially at the Rio Grande, and visa overstaying. As of 2010, the total number of the unauthorized has been estimated at eleven million, truly an astonishing figure in a nation with a population of just over three-hundred million—according to this accounting, about one of every thirty residents lacks the legal rights to live and work there (Passel 2006; Passel and Cohn 2008). The United States has had one amnesty, which was legislated in the 1986 Immigration Reform and Control Act and resulted in about three million grants of permanent residence to the previously undocumented. Whether and under what conditions the currently undocumented can gain legal status continues, as we complete this book, to be the subject of fierce debate in Congress and the media.

The unauthorized population is not as large in Western Europe, in part because a number of major European countries have more stringent internal controls than the United States does—e.g., the presentation of identity documents is required in many more situations. Its size is estimated at between five and seven-and-one-half million (Castles and Miller 2009, 238). Much of this population comes from the Mediterranean region, and a smaller share comes from sub-Saharan Africa. It is thought to be particularly large in the countries of southern Europe, including Spain, one of the countries in our study. Several of the European countries with sizable undocumented populations have had multiple regularizations—this is true of Spain, for instance, which in 2005 decreed a large-scale regularization that gave legal status to some 700–800 thousand immigrants, including many from Latin America (Arango and Jachimowicz 2005). In a number of countries, including France, Spain, and the United States, schools must at times address the problems of children whose parents are illegally resident or who are so themselves.

Complicating the reception of some labor migrants and their children is their origin in former colonies of the receiving societies. Postcolonial immigrations are initiated when former colonies gain independence. Simultaneous with independence, and to some degree after it, occurs an outpouring of former colonists and of the members of the native population who supported colonial rule or, at least, occupied relatively privileged positions under it.

Coming afterwards, often enough, are labor migrations, since citizens of the newly independent countries remain oriented toward the former colonizer, whose language they often speak and whose ways seem familiar. Algeria provides an example, since hundreds of thousands migrated to France after independence, in search of work.

The position of the second generation coming from postcolonial immigrations is affected by the "ethnic" status of its parents. The children of the former colonists are often seamlessly integrated into the societal mainstream—certainly, this appears to have happened to the children of the former Algerian colonists (Alba and Silberman 2002). The children of the immigrants who come afterwards as labor migrants are at best no different from the children of other Third World immigrants; at worst, they are confronted with more intense prejudice because of the stereotypes brought by white elites from their former colonies (Lucassen 2005; Silberman 2011).

If labor immigrants can be regarded on the whole as individuals who have "chosen" to leave their countries of origin and migrate abroad, usually in an effort to improve their economic situations and their children's opportunities, that is not true on the whole for another important immigration type that can play a role in second-generation educational inequalities. Refugees by definition are individuals who have been forced to flee their countries of origin because of imminent threat—often of a political, religious, or ethnic nature. Because they are usually unable to plan their departure and entry into the new society, refugees are typically extended significant financial support by the countries that receive them. Of the countries in our study, Sweden has the largest share of refugees among its immigrants—after migrants from neighboring Finland, for instance, those from the former Yugoslavia, admitted mostly during the civil wars that tore the country apart, are the most numerous (Westin 2006). Sweden has also admitted tens of thousands of Iraqis, either fleeing the regime of Saddam Hussein or uprooted in the wake of the US invasion.

How refugee groups subsequently fare is highly variable and depends on the trauma associated with their departure, the human and even financial capital they are able to flee with, and their reception in the host society. The United States exhibits the extremes in this regard. On the one hand, the Cubans, who fled their island home in several waves after the revolution of 1959, have been held up as a model of immigrant success. On the other hand, the Hmong, part of the refugee stream from Vietnam, have remained on the economic sidelines in the United States. Coming from a nonliterate society and suffering great trauma at the end of the war and during their departure because of their support for the US side, they remain unusually dependent upon social welfare a quarter century after arrival (Portes and Rumbaut 2006).

The second generation to come from such involuntary immigrations also exhibits great variation in its societal position and its progress through socioeconomic entryways to the mainstream. Where immigrant groups have had middle-class or elite origins, in whole or in part, or where they have managed to achieve some degree of economic independence in the immigrant generation, then the second generation has generally started from a favorable position. This has been true of Cubans in the United States, especially in the Miami area (Portes and Stepick 1993). However, this is probably the less common case. Where, by contrast, the refugees have remained dependent upon social welfare and economically marginalized, then the starting point for the new generation is obviously less favorable.

Immigrant-Origin Children in Schools

The education of the children of immigrants touches on a fundamental tension at the core of the educational mission. On the one hand, educational systems must provide students with an education appropriate to their adult lives. Operating within the context of highly differentiated labor markets and inequalities in earnings, school systems inevitably play a major role in determining how young people will be sorted across the socioeconomic spectrum. Since studies show that educational outcomes for all students reflect social origins to a greater or lesser extent, it is not surprising that schools also tend to reproduce inequalities, at least in the aggregate, between native and immigrant-origin students.

On the other hand, educational systems are charged with ensuring fair opportunities and the potential for social mobility for children coming from disadvantaged backgrounds. Many children growing up in immigrant families fit in this category—for example, those whose parents are low-wage workers with low levels of education when judged by the standards of the receiving society. In the most rudimentary sense, all the school systems of receiving societies do provide such opportunities: it is common for the second generation to make a large step beyond its parents in educational terms, if only because its members are growing up in societies where the legally mandated period of school attendance is far longer than in the societies from which immigrant parents came. But how far do these opportunities allow the children of immigrants to go?

In examining educational opportunities, we take as our point of departure the moral and practical imperatives for integration raised at the beginning of this introduction. In *Just Schools*, a detailed examination of contemporary American debates about multicultural education, anthropologist Rick Shweder argues that in liberal societies, four key values are both strongly held and potentially in conflict: autonomy and freedom of expression, "the merit-based allocation of benefits and fair assignments to statuses and positions in society," equal opportunity to "become qualified for valued positions in society," and "equal safekeeping from arbitrary or unfortunate harms" (Schweder 2008). While focused on the narrower question of how educational systems and policies shape educational opportunities for one particular social group— the children of low-status migrants—this volume also touches on the different ways in which the balance among these complementary but competing values is struck in different countries and with what results.

Achievements and Gaps: Students with Immigrant Parents from Countries with Low Average Levels of Education

In all of the countries we have examined, some of the students coming from immigrant families are doing remarkably well. Not at all uncommon are young people from families in which immigrant parents have primary-school educations (or less) who themselves have earned university diplomas; and many students from such backgrounds have achieved some degree of post-secondary education. Yet it is also true that in all of these educational systems immigrant-origin students on average are disadvantaged in at least some respects when compared with those coming from native families.

Disadvantages are found, moreover, in systems with very different structures and features. In order to maximize our chances of observing a link between system characteristics and the opportunities of immigrant-origin students, we have deliberately chosen systems with widely varying characteristics. We will shortly inventory the dimensions of these systems that may in principle be relevant to native/immigrant inequalities; but we exemplify the variation here. Consider the Netherlands, which possesses a formally stratified system, in which students are channeled starting at age twelve into different tracks, represented by different secondary schools and oriented toward different educational credentials and labor-market situations. The United States, by contrast, features a comprehensive system, which, though it has informal tracking, nevertheless houses students of different abilities in the same secondary schools, thus facilitating second chances through movements across tracks. However, the United States funds schools according to a system of mainly local and state-government financing, and this system permits a high degree of inequality among primary and secondary schools that correlates more or less with the social origins of students. France, like the United States, also maintains students in comprehensive school settings until near the end of secondary school. Unlike the United States, however, it features a more centralized system of financing that gives schools serving different groups of students a more equal funding base; furthermore, the French system has attempted to compensate for the social disadvantages of the students in some schools by giving these schools additional funds (through the so-called ZEP policy).

Our focus throughout is on children from immigrant groups that are defined by the low educational attainments of immigrant parents, the low-status occupations in which they are concentrated in the receiving society, and the ethnic-outsider status they occupy. Much greater urgency attaches to these children because their groups are typically viewed as problematic in terms of long-term prospects for successful integration into the mainstream. Moreover, a focus on the children from low-status groups is a way of controlling for the varying degree of selectivity in the immigration streams flowing to different countries. From the perspective of research design, this focus aids us in comparing different educational systems (as opposed to the character of the immigrant flow).

As an introduction to native/immigrant inequalities, we consider here inequalities in basic school-taught skills, i.e., those in literacy and mathematics, which are measured by the OECD PISA study, the Programme for International Student Assessment (OECD 2001, 2004, 2006, 2007). The PISA study tests these skills in students aged fifteen—in other words, at a point when they are nearing the end of secondary school and there is little chance left of erasing skills gaps.[2] Some data are shown in Table 1.1. In order to focus on the children of low-status immigrants, we limit the immigrant-origin group to children whose parents have not attained final secondary-school credentials;[3] we additionally restrict it to the second generation—i.e.,

TABLE 1.1. Average Scores on Basic-skills Tests in Reading and Mathematics for Native Students and Those of the Second Generation with Modestly Educated Parents, By Country, 2000–2009, PISA Studies

	France	Great Britain	Netherlands	Spain	Sweden	US
Reading						
second gen, parents lt secondary educ	451	470	472	450	457	444
children of native parents	511	514	525	483	521	508
difference	60	44	53	33	64	64
Mathematics						
second gen, parents lt secondary educ	460	465	487	450	451	428
children of native parents	520	513	551	489	517	492
difference	60	48	64	39	66	64

Note: Scores have been averaged across years.

immigrants' children born in the country of reception—to make certain that the education being assessed has taken place mainly in the receiving society.

The scores in Table 1.1 show a remarkably consistent picture given the overall variation of average scores on the PISA assessments across and within countries. In terms of literacy, the native students in all the countries save for Spain score on average within a narrow band from 505 to 525, and generally speaking the second-generation students score on average about 50–65 points less. The difference is smaller in Great Britain and Spain, in the latter case because the native students obtain a relatively low score. In general, the differences are large, given that a difference of about 70 points represents what the PISA researchers view as equivalent to a distinct proficiency level in literacy (of which there are a total of six).

The gaps in mathematics are, if anything, larger in terms of native/second-generation disparities in proficiency. In four of the six countries—again, Great Britain and Spain are exceptions—the difference is 60 points or more. For the mathematics scale, the proficiency levels identified by the researchers are defined in increments of slightly more than 60 points. Therefore, in France, the Netherlands, Sweden, and the United States, the average difference is on the order of a full proficiency level. In Great Britain, where the difference in Table 1.1 is about 50 points, it is a bit smaller. In Spain, it is smaller again, but as in the case of literacy the native students achieve relatively low scores. In should be noted that the scores of both native- and immigrant-origin American students are also low.

The native/second generation gaps would appear much smaller if we compared the second-generation students to native students whose parents were comparable to immigrant parents in educational terms. But it would not disappear, as a number of studies have shown (Buchmann and Parado 2006; OECD 2006). Nevertheless, we refrain from making this comparison for two reasons. The first is that the great majority of native students have parents who have attained at least the final secondary-school credential and are thus more educated than immigrant parents; in other words, the comparison is unrealistic in terms of the competition immigrant-origin students face in schools and the labor market. The second reason is that the commensurability of parental educations earned in very different educational systems (the Netherlands and Morocco, say) is very dubious. Almost all studies show that immigrants tend to be a selective group when compared to those who stay behind in the home country (e.g., Feliciano 2005). This implies that immigrants with low levels of education by the standards of the receiving society (or low occupational position) may have positive qualities, such as discipline and high aspirations for their children, that are not to be found among the equivalent group of native parents (Brinbaum and Kieffer 2005; Kao and Tienda 1995; Levels, Dronkers, and Kraaykamp 2008). Native fathers without high school diplomas in the United States, for example, are far more likely than immigrant men to have spent time in prison (Pettit and Western 2004). If our goal is to assess how school systems are faring in equalizing opportunity, then controlling for parental socioeconomic position risks producing unduly rosy results because of the unmeasured positive traits of immigrant homes.

In focusing here on the PISA data, we do not mean to imply that the academic skills measured by the PISA are the best or only way to evaluate the educational situations of immigrant-origin children. It is essential also to examine the native/immigrant-origin gap in terms of educational credentials earned, though this is more difficult than is the case with test scores because credentials are not easily standardized across countries. Nevertheless, credentials are undoubtedly more determinative of adult status than test scores. Moreover, even though the final outcomes of student careers are clearly correlated with academic skills, the relationship is not isomorphic. Studies have shown that some disadvantaged second-generation students persist for long periods on educational paths and eventually gain advanced credentials (Heath, Rothon, and Kilpi 2008). In the Netherlands, this phenomenon has become salient enough to garner a name—the "long route" (Crul and Holdaway 2009). That credentials earned after a longer-than-normative period in postsecondary education can still yield a payoff is demonstrated by research on the outcomes of the "open admission" program at the City University of New York (Attewell and Lavin 2007). Native-origin/second-generation differences in credentials earned, then, will be an important focus for the chapters that follow.

Dimensions of Inequality:
Features of Educational Systems That Matter

How should we think about the sources of such widespread inequalities between native and immigrant-origin students? One conventional approach is to look for factors within immigrant families and communities that may predispose their children to do less well in school than the children from native backgrounds. Such factors could include, as just noted, the generally weaker educational backgrounds of immigrant parents, or the more meager economic resources of immigrant families, or the divided linguistic practices that prevail in many immigrant homes (OECD 2006; Perreira, Harris, and Lee 2006; White and Glick 2009). However, the spirit of our enterprise is to look for differences across national contexts in the success of integrating immigrant-origin students through schools, and thus we turn outward, in the direction of the institutional context, rather than inward, into immigrant homes, in the search for critical factors.

Another approach targets national differences in integration models or philosophies and holds them responsible for disparities in the success of immigrant and second-generation integration (Brubaker 1992; Favell 2001). According to this perspective, countries like Canada and the United States where immigration has played a vital, acknowledged role in nation building are institutionally geared to promote integration, as indicated by the ease of access to citizenship, especially for the second generation as a consequence of the jus soli principle. Other countries, such as Germany, are reluctant to embrace immigrant groups as part of the nation, and the jus sanguinis principles in their citizenship laws (no longer true of Germany, since 2000) raise high barriers to integration, as do their other institutions (Brubaker 1992; Buchmann and Parrado 2006).

The story of different national models of inclusion grasps some interesting truths, but it is one that cannot be pressed very far in the service of understanding native/immigrant-origin inequalities. The reason seems plain to us: the integration of the children of immigrants plays out in specific institutional domains, such as the school system, whose main features in different countries were established well before the post-1950 arrival of immigrants. While in the case of schools a number of countries have introduced reforms intended to ease the scholastic adaptation of the children from immigrant backgrounds, such changes rarely alter the main structures of the educational system. In most countries, then, different institutional domains, such as the education system, were configured independently of immigration and cannot be comprehended within the framework of abstract integration models (Freeman 2004). There is no alternative to detailed investigation of how educational systems function and with what consequences for the children of immigrants.

Quite a different take on educational inequalities comes from theorizing now prevalent in the sociology of education. Called the theory of "maximally" or "effectively" "maintained inequality," its core idea holds that educational systems function in ways that preserve, on average, the cumulative advantages of middle- and upper-middle-class students (Alon 2009; Lucas 2001; Raftery and Hout 2003). Such an idea, it should be underscored, leaves plenty of room for individual mobility by students of lower origins, so long as it is not widespread enough to threaten the aggregate advantages of more privileged ones.

According to the theory, even when educational systems are altered by public policy to enhance opportunity for students from more humble origins, as is true for instance in France, which has tried to expand and democratize access to the *bac* (*baccalauréat*), the credential required for entry to higher education, the previous imbalance of educational opportunity is fairly quickly reestablished. The processes that, like a social gyroscope, restore the previous status quo are not spelled out by these theories; but, we observe, in democratic societies native middle-class parents influence what goes on in schools and are better equipped than working-class or immigrant parents to enlist the collaboration of school administrators and teachers. They are also in a better position to move among school districts, or to opt out of or supplement public provision through full- or part-time private education. Most of the time, their privileged position is maintained by the "normal" workings of the educational system; and the influence of these parents becomes visible only at moments of change when they intervene to make sure that their children retain their advantages in the face of efforts to level the playing field.

The thesis of maximally maintained inequality argues specifically that expansion of the higher tiers of an educational system, intended to create room for students from disadvantaged backgrounds to move upwards, also allows some students from more advantaged families to improve their educational outcomes. On net, then, there tends to be little change in the differentials separating students of different origins (Raftery and Hout 1993). In complementary fashion, the claim of effectively maintained inequality is that, as quantitative differences in students' educational outcomes (e.g., the numbers of years of education they attain) level off, qualitative differences become more consequential (Lucas 2001). Tracks within secondary schools and status differences among universities in Great Britain and the United States are examples of qualitative disparities that serve to maintain inequality in the aggregate even as opportunity ostensibly expands.

This vein of theorizing arose to explain the persistence of social-class-based inequalities in education. But the universality of the native/immigrant-origin inequalities in school-taught skills evident from the PISA studies suggests that it can apply equally well in this domain. It might seem then that this theorizing obviates the need for a study such as ours. If native/immigrant-origin inequalities are unyielding, alterations to school systems are unlikely to make much of a dent in them. However, we think otherwise for two reasons. For one, research on the link between socioeconomic origins and educational outcomes indicates that its strength varies from one national context to another; in other words, the degree of educational advantage of middle-class students is not constant across contexts (Breen and Jonsson 2005). These findings suggest that a comparative examination of the children of immigrants in schools may be able to identify features of educational systems that make a difference for their opportunities.

For another, there are historical cases of educational catch-up by disadvantaged groups, and their existence indicates that, under some circumstances, maximally and effectively maintained inequality may yield to other forces. One example is the mass assimilation in the United States of the children and grandchildren of Southern and Eastern European immigrants in the

1945–1970 period (Alba 2009). These groups were denigrated and excluded by native, middle-class white Americans during the first half of the century, and some of them—the southern Italians offer the best-documented case (e.g., Covello 1972)—lagged educationally far behind native norms, with high rates of truancy and early dropout. Yet, within a quarter century, their educational attainment accelerated, and they caught up to native white Americans in such key respects as college attendance and graduation. While the precise explanation for this postwar leveling can be debated, the expansion of the postsecondary system, which increased its capacity fivefold between 1940 and 1970, was clearly significant. Qualitative differences in the status of institutions attended were also ameliorated, as, for instance, when the quotas on the admission of Jews to elite, Ivy League colleges were lifted (Karabel 2005; Keller and Keller 2001).

The theory of maximally or effectively maintained inequality is extremely useful in drawing attention to the ways in which privileged groups manage to maintain their advantaged position in the context of efforts to expand opportunity. Yet the examples above demonstrate that educational systems are not governed entirely by zero-sum equations; inequality among groups is not inevitably frozen into their structures. Furthermore, the circumstances and needs of children of immigrants are somewhat different from those of working-class native youth and the mechanisms involved may work in different ways. Given this, there is a clear need for detailed cross-national analysis of the role of institutional arrangements and policies in curtailing or opening up opportunities for these children.

Comparative Research on the Children of Immigrants at School

Internationally comparative research on educational systems and their relevance to the integration of immigrant-origin children is in its beginning stages. Over the last decade, a number of such projects have shed some light on aspects of these complex subjects. On the broadest level, the PISA studies and similar data provide snapshots of school-taught skills at various points in schooling and enable a comparison of the second-generation and native-origin youth. The PISA data have been used also in attempts to more specifically relate educational outcomes for immigrant-origin youth to features of educational systems. Some major international surveys, such as those gathered by the EFFNATIS and TIES projects,[4] have been put to a similar use.

These comparative projects are helpful in thinking about the features of educational systems that matter. But while they are suggestive in many respects, their conclusions are rarely definitive. The PISA data, for example, must be used with caution because of the selectivity of the immigration streams flowing to different countries, which are implicated in the magnitude of native/immigrant-origin differences. It is typical to find that Australia and Canada stand apart from most other countries because of the parity between native and immigrant-origin students in these systems, a finding that is probably best attributed to the selective immigration policies of the two countries (OECD 2001) rather than to the functioning of their schools.

One salient conclusion from these comparisons, at least in the European context, is that native/immigrant-origin educational differences are greater in systems where tracking is formal and begins at an early age (Heckmann 2008). The paragon of such a system is the German one, where beginning typically after the fourth grade, students are separated among three types of schools, one of which, the *Gymnasium*, is destined for university education and another of which, the *Hauptschule*, channels students toward the bottom rungs of the labor market. In our study, the Netherlands comes closest to the German model, though tracking starts later than in Germany and there is more opportunity for students in all tracks to pursue postsecondary education.

Even this apparently well-grounded conclusion may need qualification insofar as the German system has been found to be quite effective in enabling second-generation youth to enter employment through vocational training and apprenticeships, even if it is less successful at preparing them for university. Intra-European comparisons reveal that the more open English and French systems allow more young people to attend university but are less effective in preparing them for employment (Crul and Schneider 2008; Crul 2011; Heckmann and Schnapper 2003).

The large-scale quantitative studies, though informative, are simply not fine-grained enough to determine precisely how the features of school systems are impacting on the life chances of immigrant-origin students. They give us the eagle's-eye view, high above the landscape and the day-to-day struggles on the ground. At a minimum, they need to be supplemented by studies, especially qualitative and in-depth survey ones, that are closer to the processes within educational institutions and to the experiences of different groups of students. But as a start we need to identify the key dimensions of educational systems that seem in principle to be implicated in educational inequalities. This is what we do in the remainder of this section, drawing on our previous reviews of relevant research (Alba, Sloan, and Sperling 2011; Holdaway and Alba 2009; Holdaway, Crul, and Roberts 2009). The dimensions we describe are the ones that readers should keep in mind as they peruse the research-based chapters that follow. In the final chapter, we will return to many of these dimensions to ask what we have learned from our comparisons and what recommendations appear to follow.

The Balance of Responsibility among Schools, Communities, and Families

In no system is all education conducted in schools—from the very first day, students come into the classroom with already developed differences in school-relevant skills, whether these involve the ability to sit still or to read some words. These initial skill differences are brought from homes and communities, outside agents that continue to play a crucial role throughout children's school careers.

This division of responsibility can be an important source of the disadvantages immigrant-origin students face in educational systems. Immigrant parents lack familiarity with the host society and its institutions, and many also had limited experiences in school in their home country. They often do not understand the ramifications of the decisions that must be made by them and their children (e.g., which curriculum to study in secondary school); they cannot help their children with their homework; and they cannot provide their children at home with the linguistic and cultural foundations for school success. Many studies have shown that students perform best academically when their parents are involved in their educations, meeting for example with teachers. But immigrant parents are handicapped in this respect by their lack of fluency in the language of the receiving society—they may not even be able to read the notices sent home from the school with their children (see, for example, chapter 3 on California and Catalonia).

The balance of responsibility among schools and other agents of education is not a constant but varies considerably across national contexts. Where the balance shifts in the direction of greater responsibility for families and communities, we can expect the disadvantages of immigrant-origin children to loom larger. One manifestation of the division of educational labor comes in the form of the length of the school day: children in the typical German elementary school, for instance, are sent home at lunch time to continue working there, helped by their mothers or older siblings. Over the course of the school year, they have only two-thirds of the contact hours with teachers that children in Dutch schools get (Crul 2011). Another manifestation is the length of the school year, and in this respect the United States stands out as exceptional: according to the TIMSS study of the OECD, as reported by *The Economist* (June 11, 2009), American children "have one of the shortest school years anywhere, a mere 180 days compared with an average of 195 for OECD countries. . . . Over twelve years, a fifteen-day deficit means American children lose out on 180 days of school, equivalent to an entire year" (see also National Center on Time & Learning: www.timeandlearning.org/resources). The long summer layoff in the United States has been shown repeatedly to be associated with a regression in learning, especially for poor and minority children. The evidence is strong, in other words, that the summer vacation period contributes to the inequalities among students at the beginning of each school year (Entwisle and Alexander 1992; Heyns 1979).

Another way that the overall balance of educational responsibility becomes manifest is through the age at which children enter school or school-like settings for the first time. This, too, varies significantly across national contexts. In France, the *maternelle* system of preschooling means that nearly all children are in educationally rich settings by age three; and in the Netherlands, children begin school at age four. In the United States, school typically begins at age five, and preschool is not universally available. Research shows that the children from some disadvantaged immigrant groups (e.g., Mexicans) are less likely to be in preschool than are native white children, principally because of the cost of such programs and the difficulties of access (Hernandez, Denton, and McCartney 2011). It should be obvious in general that, for immigrant-origin children whose families speak a nonmainstream language at home, the benefits of early entry into educational settings are especially strong because the children gain more fluency in the language that prevails in classrooms. This gain can be expected to be all the greater when these settings are able to mix minority-language children with those coming from mainstream-language homes, so that language learning occurs through play and other informal interactions.

Inequalities among Schools

Although the degree varies considerably, all educational systems demonstrate some inequality among schools. This inequality typically manifests itself in the qualities of teachers, physical facilities, curriculum, and material resources; and there is considerable evidence that children of immigrants tend to be concentrated in schools that are weaker in one or more of these respects. Inequality can appear at all levels from primary education through university. The nature and sources of inequality among schools vary across systems. But one critical factor is the system of school financing, which varies from one country to another in the extent to which it relies on local and regional sources versus centralized ones. In addition, school governance comes into play here because insofar as local and regional authorities control such matters as textbooks and school budgets, further inequalities can be introduced.

The United States stands apart as the paragon of a decentralized system (Goldin and Katz 2008). Because of the strength of its traditions of local control and of the constitutional role of the states in educational matters, the United States tolerates large disparities among schools. These disparities touch many aspects of school quality, from the physical condition of buildings, to the richness of the curriculum and the material resources brought to bear in teaching it, to the experience and credentials of teachers (Kozol 1991; Phillips and Chin 2004). Of these, the last may be the most critical for there is considerable evidence in the US context that the academic abilities of teachers affect the amount of learning that takes place in classrooms.[5]

For funding, the American system relies heavily on local and regional (i.e., state-level) sources, with the federal government accounting for less than 10 percent of the total K–12 budget (Hochschild and Scovronick 2003). The bulk then is paid in roughly equal shares by local taxes, mostly the property tax, and by states. This situation obviously contributes greatly to the stark inequalities visible among US primary and secondary schools. According to estimates presented by Hochschild and Scovronick, for 2001, the national average in spending per pupil was $7,800, "but some districts spent much more and some much less; between the highest-spending 5 percent of the districts and the lowest-spending 5 percent, there can be a variation of $5,000"— in other words, a two-to-one disparity. There can even be significant differences among the individual schools within a local system. These disparities are probably explicable in terms of the politics of local control, because the members of school boards are elected and often most responsive to more affluent, better-educated parents (Condron and Roscigno 2003; Kozol 1991).

In European systems, funding is typically more centralized and therefore more equal. France is the antipode to the United States in the sense that it is the paragon, insofar as practical realities permit, of a centralized system (Alba and Silberman 2009). There, for example, the budget for teachers in each school is determined by the national Ministry for Education and is therefore not subject to local control. In addition, there is a national curriculum, so that the content of education is standardized across schools. However, there is still room for wealthier areas to invest in their schools, in terms of school resources such as extra activities and the physical condition of buildings. In general, even where base funding from government is equal, wealthier parents will contribute additional resources for special facilities or activities that enhance their children's education. In all countries, the development of specialized schools, which are often eligible for extra funding, can become a way of marking particular schools as an elite tier, to which it is difficult for children of low-status immigrants to gain entry.

Everywhere the inequalities among schools are compounded by residential segregation, which, although more severe in some countries than in others, leads to educational systems in which students disadvantaged by their social origins tend to be concentrated in weaker schools. This conjunction of forces is particularly relevant for immigrant families, especially when the parents are low-wage workers, who tend to be concentrated in the poorer neighborhoods of cities or inner suburbs. The students from low-status immigrant families often cluster therefore in a relatively small number of schools, which must serve large numbers of children who need additional language and other preparation. In the United States, for example, Latino students, who represent the largest group among the children coming from immigrant families, have been found to be "the most segregated minority group in [the] nation's public schools." About 40 percent of Latino students are in "intensely racially segregated schools," where the fraction of majority white students is below 10 percent, and most Latino English-language learners attend largely minority schools (Civil Rights Project 2008; see also Orfield and Lee 2006). Poor conditions and extra workloads mean that the best teachers are often reluctant to teach in schools that serve a large immigrant population, further compounding the problem of school inequality. Efforts to reduce segregation through parental choice are not always successful when immigrant parents have little information about alternative schools or are reluctant to allow their children to travel outside their neighborhood.

In France and the Netherlands, policy attempts have been made to direct greater resources into schools with high percentages of immigrant students.

In France, Zones of Educational Priority (ZEP) have been created, designated in part on the basis of the number of immigrants living in them, and the schools in these zones are given extra funding by the government. The success of this program is, however, debatable (see chapter 5). In the Netherlands, additional funding was for a time attached to immigrant-origin students, and schools then received almost twice as much for each such student as they did for each student from a native Dutch family.[6] The significance of this policy is discussed in chapter 2.

Educating Students from Minority-Language Homes

One of the thorniest issues in the education of immigrant-origin students concerns their acquisition of an academic level of competence in the mainstream language, the one that is taken for granted as the language of instruction in schools. This issue arises for second-generation students who come from minority-language homes but also for immigrant students who, arriving after the age at which schooling begins, slip sideways into the educational system. Depending on the acquaintance with the mainstream language that students start with, it can take as long as five to seven years for them to acquire a language competence adequate to pursue their educational aspirations, according to Carola Suárez-Orozco, Marcelo Suárez-Orozco, and Irina Todorova (2008).

There is a remarkable degree of variation among the systems under study in how they address the educational needs of students from minority-language homes. In some systems, few explicit measures are taken, but other features of these systems have positive consequences for these youngsters. That is, most countries emphasize mainstream-language learning through immersion, but they also offer additional instruction in the mainstream language, especially during the primary-school years, to students who come from families where another language is spoken (see chapter 5 of OECD 2006). Immersion does not mean that the needs of these students are neglected. In France, for example, the nearly universal attendance of preschool provides ways for minority-language children to learn French informally. In the Netherlands, primary schools have in the past received additional funding for every immigrant-origin child they educated; and schools with many such children were therefore able to decrease class size, or increase the ratio of teachers to students, so that students received more individual attention.

In the United States, there has been has been experimentation with various forms of bilingual education, in which some degree of instruction takes place in the mother tongues of children whose first language is not English. Bilingual education has stoked considerable controversy, while a large-scale research effort has attempted to establish the basic facts about it. Despite all the attention, much remains murky (for a good recent overview, see Goldenberg 2008). The research has established that there is an advantage for minority-language students when schools strengthen their proficiency in their mother tongues and provide some subject instruction in it, but the advantage is modest in magnitude. And many facets of this advantage remain to be clarified—for example, whether it is specific to some kinds of minority-language students or holds broadly. So far, there is little comparative literature on bilingual instruction and practices (an exception is McAndrew 2009).

Selection and Tracking Mechanisms

All of the educational systems of the advanced economies involve some form of tracking—that is, separating students hierarchically at some stage according to their presumed talents. Tracking is often seen as appropriate for reasons of educational efficiency given the varied academic abilities of students or because of the responsibility of schools to prepare students for the different positions they will occupy in the adult world (Van de Werfhorst and Mijs 2010). However, tracking takes on quite distinct forms in different systems and, in particular, varies according to its *formality,* the degree of separation among different streams of students, and *rigidity,* the degree to which students are unable to change tracks. Also consequential is the age at which tracking begins.

In the more formalized tracking systems—as already mentioned, Germany is the most extreme example—students may be separated at an early age into different schools and taught different curricula, preparing them for distinct educational endpoints and labor-market destinations. The desires of students and their parents may play only a minor role in these track assignments, despite the fatefulness of them. The bottom track typically corresponds with a vocational education that prepares students to take less-skilled blue-collar jobs at the end of secondary school, while the top track is intended for students who will eventually attend universities and enter the professions. It can be difficult to change tracks, and especially to move from a lower to a higher one.

Tracking is consequential for the children of low-status immigrants for some of the same reasons that cause them to be at a disadvantage in systems dependent on a large family and community role. Broadly put, immigrant parents lack the cultural and social capital in the mainstream that would enable them to strategize and assist their children's school careers. In addition, immigrant-origin children, coming from disadvantaged, typically minority-language homes, are usually not able to demonstrate quickly their academic abilities in mainstream classrooms and may therefore be consigned to lower tracks, further disadvantaging them. Finally, the judgments of teachers and school administrators about the abilities of these students, which often play a critical role in track assignments, may be influenced by stereotypes. For all these reasons, immigrant-origin students are overrepresented in lower tracks, with typically powerful impacts on their academic outcomes.

Of the countries in this study, the Netherlands represents the most formalized tracking system, one that is fairly typical for Northern Europe. At the age of twelve, children take a standardized test and, on the basis of their results and the recommendations of their teachers, they proceed along one of several tracks. These include: two academically oriented tracks where students prepare for university entrance or for other professional training; and two more vocational tracks, the lower of which heads straight to low-wage employment, while the other leads to a lengthy period of training for higher-level paraprofessional or technical work, with university entrance possible thereafter. The advantages native children hold in terms of Dutch language skills and cultural capital over their immigrant-origin age mates are generally sufficient to ensure that the majority of the natives directly enter the university or higher vocational education tracks. However, our research also demonstrates that some students initially placed on the vocational track pursue what is known as the "long route" and ultimately complete university degrees (see chapter 2 in this volume).

France is an intermediate case. As part of the democratization reforms, the age at which students are separated into formally distinct tracks has been postponed to the high school level. Today, only a minority of students enters the "professional" *lycées*, which offer a vocational training. The majority begins together in schools that offer general academic and technological curricula but its members choose more specialized curricula at the end of the second year. A response to the democratization reform has been increasing differentiation by prestige among the specialized curricula: even the students on academic tracks specialize in terms of scientific, literary, or economic and social subjects, each of which has its own *baccalauréat*, associated with a distinct level of prestige in the hierarchy among the different academic *baccalauréats*.

In the United States, with the exception of some elite high schools that select students by examination, most public secondary schools are comprehensive. But their quality, as discussed above, varies considerably due to patterns of residential segregation and inequities in school funding and teacher quality. Graduation rates and test scores are highly correlated with the social origins of the students. Informal tracking generally occurs as early as primary school through devices such as ability grouping. At the secondary level, students are also separated into different tracks within schools, through gifted and talented programs and enriched course offerings at one end, and remedial and special education programs at the other. Distribution across these programs also follows predictable patterns according to social origins, which have persisted despite efforts at educational reform. These patterns occur in part because the high schools attended by poor and minority students often do not offer the full range of academic options, especially at the enriched end of the spectrum.

The private school system also plays an important role in many parts of France and the United States, especially in areas where there is a large Catholic school system. For example, in New York, over a third of native children attend private and Catholic schools, using them as an exit option from the public system. Although some immigrant families attempt to use the same strategy, the expense involved means that few can afford to send their children to Catholic schools for the whole of secondary education (Louie and Holdaway 2009). In the United States, new voucher programs, which allow parents to opt out of poor local schools, offer some choice to parents, but the number of places in high-quality institutions is too small for this to be a solution to the problems facing the public schools, in which the majority of students continue to be educated.

In Britain, a few areas retain a formal selection process, with students taking an exam at the age of eleven that channels them into academic (grammar) or vocational (secondary modern) schools. But 90 percent of students attend comprehensive schools. However, informal tracking into ability streams still occurs, and there is also considerable variation in school quality that correlates with the social background of students. Religious schools also receive state funding, and some parents choose them as offering stricter discipline and more rigorous instruction.

The consequences of selection and tracking mechanisms for the children of immigrants are critical for any evaluation of how well educational systems are meeting the challenges of the integration imperative. The completion of a secondary-education credential that indicates adequate mastery of the compulsory educational curriculum and allows the option of proceeding into the tertiary system should be considered the minimum bar for achieving "the essential prerequisites for adult participation in society." By this standard, one can question whether any of the systems we consider is succeeding on a mass scale for young people from disadvantaged immigrant backgrounds.

Postsecondary Education

The sector of higher education is internally diverse in all the systems considered here, producing very disparate outcomes for students who participate. The dimensions of internal diversity concern above all:

- the formal differentiation within the system, with all countries offering, at the lower end, some forms of vocational and paraprofessional training and, at the higher, education that leads to professions such as law and medicine; and

- the informal stratification of postsecondary institutions, which is greatest in the United States, whose system of baccalaureate-granting institutions ranges from the most prestigious of the world-class universities, to large campuses of state-funded institutions, to small and frequently underfunded private colleges. The continental European systems, which are more dominated by institutions funded by the national government, are much "flatter" as a consequence—hence, the specific university a student attends has less impact on his or her subsequent life chances. The British and French systems are intermediate cases.

There are also clear-cut differences among the postsecondary systems in different countries. One concerns the barriers to entry, with the United States placing the bar especially low in comparison with European countries, which are more highly selective. Another relates to the cost, which tends to be much greater in the United States than elsewhere, with the consequence that some students from poorer families are unable to afford to achieve their academic aspirations, though they have demonstrated the ability to do so (Goldin and Katz 2008). In addition, the length of time required to achieve the most advanced credentials differs; the United States is unusual in forcing many students to study a general curriculum for four years before allowing them to specialize in their desired professional training. Finally, there is the question of the labor-market value of partially completed postsecondary training, as many students leave universities without earning degrees.

Each system in our study presents, it seems, a unique configuration of elements, with implications for the chances of immigrant-origin students to acquire valuable credentials. In the United States, a high percentage of students begin some form of postsecondary education, since the requirement for entry is set low: a high school diploma or General Equivalency Development (GED) diploma, a supposed equivalent that can be earned by examination. However, this high percentage entails a large number of dropouts, students who fail to complete any postsecondary credential (College Board 2010).

Moreover, the American students are distributed across two broad tiers with major consequences for the quality and labor-market significance of the education obtained: two-year or community colleges provide, on the one hand, a vocational education leading to various types of certification and, on the other, an academic preparation intended for transfer to a four-year institution; and four-year colleges offer a range of bachelor's-degree programs and sometimes also postbaccalaureate and professional degrees. Within each tier, the quality of the institutions varies enormously. Some of the better two-year institutions provide helpful internships and act as bridges to four-year institutions, while others offer mostly terminal certificates and associate degrees, with few students continuing their education further.

The children of low-wage immigrants tend to be concentrated within the two-year colleges, where rates of dropout are frequently high and the chances of ultimately gaining a baccalaureate or a professional degree are low. In addition, within each broad tier there is further sorting of students by social origin, and the children of low-status immigrants tend to be clustered in particular institutions. For example, of the children of Dominican immigrants in New York who attended a four-year college, fewer than 5 percent went to a national tier-one university, compared with 28 percent of native whites. The children of immigrants are instead concentrated in the colleges of the municipal university system and disproportionately in its weaker schools (see chapter 2 in this volume).

In the Netherlands, there is a much sharper distinction between vocational and academic postsecondary education. Entry into university is possible only to students who have attended academic high school (VWO) or who have first completed higher vocational education (HAVO). The latter is the "long-route," and children of immigrants who manage to get to university often do so this way. Although access to university is more limited in this system, the quality of universities is more uniform. Higher-level vocational education also provides training for many careers that would be accessed through four-year degree programs in the United States, including teaching, social work, and many technical occupations. In the Netherlands, postsecondary education is free, and the financial penalty for students who take the long route is not heavy.

The situations in France and Britain fall somewhere between these two poles. In Britain, postsecondary education used to be sharply divided between academic programs offered in universities and vocational and paraprofessional certification offered at technical colleges and colleges of further education. The lines are now much more blurred, as former polytechnics have been turned into universities, and greater numbers of students attend higher education. However, this opening has gone hand in hand with a clearer stratification of universities, in which children of immigrants are overrepresented in the newer, generally less prestigious institutions (see chapter 4 in this volume). In this respect, Britain resembles the United States, but it differs (and more resembles European systems) in also offering a range of occupation-specific qualifications—for example, Higher National Diplomas. In France, by comparison, the quality of the universities is more uniform, but a critical distinction lies between the university sector and the *grandes écoles*, which provide an elite form of training. Anyone with a *baccalauréat* diploma is entitled to enter a university, but admission to a *grande école* is secured only by successful completion of a stringent selection process that includes additional years of post-*lycée* education and the passing of a rigorous examination. Few children from immigrant homes embark on this process, and very few enter the *grandes écoles*.

Given the variations among, and the complexities of, these systems, it is perhaps less easy than with secondary-education systems to identify all the implications of these arrangements for immigrant-origin children. What can be said with certainty is that in all of them, children of low-status immigrants are clustered at the lower end of the spectrum, and their career opportunities are therefore limited compared with those of native peers. To a considerable extent, this clustering should be viewed as the accumulation of the numerous disadvantages that accrue to immigrant-origin youth on their way through the prior stages of education. It is also clear that students from immigrant homes who do manage to get to universities often take longer to complete their degrees, such as the Dutch students who pursue the "long-route" and the US students who pass first through community colleges. In all systems, the percentage of children of low-status immigrants who complete the postgraduate programs necessary to enter the highest paid professions (such as law and medicine) is extremely low.

The Children of Immigrants in Schools Study and the Plan of the Volume

The book that follows reports the main results and conclusions from a four-year international study of how host-society educational systems and processes impact on the children of low-status immigrants (whom we describe below also as "immigrant-origin" children or as children "from immigrant homes" and whom we contrast with "native" children, meaning children growing up in homes headed by parents who are part of the native mainstream of the receiving society). This study, which was funded mainly by a Partnership in International Research and Education award from US National Science Foundation, was designed around focused comparisons that would help to illuminate potentially critical aspects of the US educational system for the second generation. A grant from the Nuffield Foundation of Great Britain enhanced the international character of the study.

The study was organized in terms of thematically driven binational comparisons conducted by teams of American and European researchers. Each team was led by two senior scholars—one from the United States and one from the European country—and staffed by three predoctoral and postdoctoral scholars, two from the United States and one from Europe. There was disciplinary and methodological diversity among the teams: although sociologists predominated overall, the comparison of California to Catalonia was staffed by anthropologists, who carried out ethnographic research; and the comparison of New York City international high schools to comparable schools in two Swedish cities was led by a US researcher trained as a psychologist and a Swedish scholar of education.

The teams provide full reports of their studies and findings in the following five chapters. We begin with the Netherlands and the United States. Chapter 2, written by Maurice Crul, Jennifer Holdaway, Helga de Valk, Norma Fuentes, and Mayida Zaal, specifically considers the ways in which school systems in New York City and Amsterdam shape the educational trajectories of two groups of relatively disadvantaged immigrant youth: the children of Dominican immigrants in New York and of Moroccan immigrants in Amsterdam. The study is based on two unusual surveys, the Immigrant Second Generation in Metropolitan New York (ISGMNY) study (Kasinitz, Mollenkopf, Waters, and Holdaway 2008) and the Amsterdam component of The Integration of the European Second Generation (TIES) study (Crul, Schneider, and Lelie 2012). Both surveys involve large samples of second-generation young adults, who were asked in detail about their experiences growing up, in schools and outside of them.

One might in principle expect children of immigrants in Amsterdam to be attaining significantly better educational results than those in New York. In terms of public policy, the United States and the Netherlands have taken quite different approaches toward the integration of immigrant students, with the Netherlands actively seeking to promote integration, for example, by providing additional funds for immigrant-origin students and special programs to serve their needs, while the United States has taken a more laissez-faire stance. However, the structures of the educational systems are also quite different, since the Netherlands, as noted, is the most formally stratified of the systems in our study. The evidence is clear that immigrant-origin students in Amsterdam tend to be concentrated in the lower tracks of the secondary system. Tracking also affects Dominican and other immigrant-origin students in New York City, who are concentrated in the weaker secondary schools of a system that is undoubtedly more unequal than that in the Netherlands.

Both groups of immigrant-origin youngsters achieve relatively modest levels of educational attainment. Neither educational system does an adequate job of serving them. Not surprisingly, given the lower levels of education in the first generation and early tracking, Moroccans are less likely to complete compulsory education. However, they attend university in almost equal numbers to their Dominican counterparts, and are more likely to complete higher vocational education. The study also suggests ways that some immigrant-origin students can succeed. For instance, some Moroccan students in the Netherlands take advantage of the "long route," ultimately attaining university credentials after beginning secondary school in a vocationally oriented track. Dominican young adults also appear to have benefited from their location in a city with a well-developed public university system.

The next research chapter also compares two subnational systems, those of Catalonia and California. Written by Margaret Gibson, Silvia Carrasco, Jordi Pàmies, Maribel Ponferrada, and Anne Ríos-Rojas, chapter 3 focuses especially on the exclusionary processes in schools that affect linguistic minorities, Arabic- and Berber-speaking children of Moroccan descent in Catalonia and Spanish-speaking children of Mexican descent. In contrast to the previous chapter, the research in this study, conducted by a team of anthropologists, relies principally on participant observation within schools and thus helps to demonstrate the general robustness of our findings about persisting inequality, which are supported by both quantitative and qualitative forms of evidence.

In fact, like the chapter that precedes it, this study arrives at the conclusion that, although the educational systems differ in important ways, immigrant-origin children appear to be similarly disadvantaged. Differences might be expected to favor the Mexican-descent students in California, if only because the United States has so much more experience in integrating the children of immigrants. Immigration to Spain is a very new phenomenon in a country that previously had seen itself as a source of immigrants, to Latin America and, in recent years, to other parts of Europe. Moreover, Moroccan immigrants and their children may be viewed through the national narrative, in which they are cast as the Muslim "other," whose final defeat and expulsion in 1492 laid the foundation for the Spanish Catholic nation. (To be sure, Mexican immigrants in California are also residing on territory that was wrested from their ancestors by conquest [Massey, Durand, and Malone 2002].)

This study asks why the discourse of welcome extended to immigrant-origin students, found in both systems, is so contradicted by educational practices. The construction of bright boundaries between native students, often middle-class, and immigrant-origin students, often poor or working-class, occurs across schools and within them. The immigrant-origin students are concentrated within the weaker schools in both settings, and within schools, they are segregated to some extent within separate classrooms, such as those serving minority-language students who are learning the mainstream language. On a symbolic plane, the hierarchy of languages and ethnic cultures is sharply drawn—amounting to a "hidden" part of the curriculum—and the languages of the immigrant students are treated as deficits rather than assets. The consequences include the frequent placement of immigrant-origin students in special classes that are not nearly as challenging as those offered to the average native student and a discouragement of their identification with academic processes and achievements.

Chapter 4, by Mary Waters, Anthony Heath, Van C. Tran, and Vikki Boliver, extends the story through a closer examination of immigrant-origin groups in postsecondary education in the United States and Great Britain. The analysis, which is quantitative and takes advantage of comparable large-scale data sets from the two countries, pivots on the distinction between primary and secondary effects on education. Among educational sociologists, primary effects are viewed as the impacts of the home environment, and social background more broadly, on educational performance, while secondary effects determine differences in subsequent attainments among those who are equivalent in performance at the end of a particular stage of education.

In both countries, the profile of primary and secondary effects is sharply different and in some similar ways. Taking test scores at the end of secondary school as a measure of performance, the researchers find that the primary effects associated with ethnic/immigrant background are large and, for the most part, disadvantaging, though in both countries some Asian groups such as the Chinese avoid them. However, the secondary effects associated with ethnic/immigrant origin are quite different, with minority groups as or more likely to persist past secondary school than is the majority, once test scores are controlled for. In short, the disadvantages evident in the primary effects have largely disappeared in the secondary ones.

These two systems are alike in offering many second chances to students, and the findings suggest that this feature may provide enhanced educational opportunities to some young people of low-status immigrant origin. Nevertheless, there is one difference of huge consequence between the systems: in Great Britain, many of the most disadvantaged minorities, such as the Bangladeshis, have caught up to their majority counterparts in terms of the overall rate of acquiring university credentials; nothing similar can be said about the United States. Whether this is primarily due to features of the British system, such as its lower cost to students and their families, or to a lack of educational mobility in the working-class white British population, is difficult to say but deserves further research.

One other way in which the two systems are similar to each other (but different from the continental university systems) seems consequential: higher educational is internally quite differentiated, containing great inequalities of status and credential value between various tiers. This differentiation provides another opportunity for the advantages associated with majority status to express themselves, and they do. In both systems, minority students are underrepresented in the elite tiers and overrepresented in the bottom ones. The consequences of this form of inequality of chances need more investigation, according to the authors.

Chapter 5, by Richard Alba, Roxane Silberman, Dalia Abdelhady, Yaël Brinbaum, and Amy Lutz, is the one of our studies that examined the transition from school to the labor market. It focuses on the situation of Mexicans in the United States and North Africans, or Maghrebins, in France.

The first part of the chapter examines how the educational systems in the two countries impact on children coming from immigrant homes. As in most other comparisons, the differences between the systems stand out. The French system has a more egalitarian thrust than the US one, since, for example, school financing is much more uniform. Moreover, France has implemented policy reforms in recent decades that are intended to improve equality of opportunity; one crucial example concerns the expansion of access to the *baccalauréat*, the indispensable credential for entry to the university system. Yet the educational outcomes for Mexicans and North Africans are broadly similar, especially when viewed in terms of their distance from the mainstream educational norms of each society.

Explaining how this similarity arises involves an examination of the mechanisms in each system that reproduce inequality. Here there are important similarities. One, certainly, is the powerful role that tracking plays in each society: tracking takes place both within schools, as children of different social origins are distributed unequally across instructional streams moving at different speeds and entailing different degrees of rigor and complexity, and between schools. The concentration of students of immigrant background in certain schools in each society is a function of residential segregation, combined with complex systems of school choice that require considerable parental knowledge to navigate. In France, an additional burden on families arises from the large number of different credentials that can represent the final secondary-school outcomes for students. Immigrant families are less able to assess the value of these credentials; and many of their children complain about the poor advice they receive from guidance counselors.

The transition to the world of work plays out differently in the two societies, largely because the labor markets are so different. Youth unemployment has been much higher in France, though the Great Recession starting in 2008 has narrowed the gap. Oddly, the chances of immigrant-origin youth are also affected by unemployment in the older generation, which is also higher in France. The interviews revealed that Mexican American youth with no more than a high school diploma could readily find jobs with the help of relatives and friends, but the same was not true for their North African counterparts because many of their older relatives are unemployed. Hence, they were more dependent in their job search on formal methods of application, which also rendered them more vulnerable to discrimination. To be sure, while Mexican Americans more readily find jobs, these are often low-wage, dead-end positions; and the study is not able to evaluate longer-term trajectories.

In the final research chapter, Carola Suárez-Orozco, Margary Martin, Mikael Alexandersson, L. Janelle Dance, and Johannes Lunneblad ask whether schools that are successful with immigrant-origin students employ educational practices that have the promise of usefulness elsewhere. Their examination focuses on two US high schools, both in New York City, and two Swedish high schools, also in large cities.

Perhaps the most important difference between the four schools and conventional high schools in both countries is the approach to educating immigrant-origin students. The authors characterize it as a "preparation agenda," in contrast to one defined by compensatory thinking. That is, rather than regarding immigrant-origin students as bearing deficits and deficiencies because of the homes and communities in which they have been reared, administrators and teachers in the four schools see them like all other students, as needing help in preparing for the challenges to be faced by twenty-first-century adults, and try to build on the foundations that the students bring to school from their backgrounds. As the chapter notes, the preparation agenda requires a different sense of mission on the part of teachers, who must be capable of seeing themselves reflected in their ethnically different students.

These schools, it appears, are continually innovating to serve the individual needs of the students. Despite innovation, they do share a number of practices that appear to benefit immigrant-origin students. For instance, all of them feature integrated, rigorous curricula, where instruction is thematically organized and interdisciplinary. Classrooms tend to emphasize cooperative learning—that is, students are encouraged to collaborate with one another. Multiple, flexible methods are used to assess students, giving them different ways to show progress and excel.

The biggest challenge in educating immigrant-origin students can be bringing them to academic proficiency in the mainstream language. As is often noted, children can quickly acquire oral competence in a new language, but literacy at a level that allows them to do well in school is a more difficult achievement that can require 5–7 years. All of the schools studied by this team avoid some conventional ways of helping mainstream-language learners, such as segregating them in separate, less rigorous classes. Their strategies involve combinations of ways of assisting these students as they become integrated into regular classrooms, such as using all content areas for language learning and encouraging mentoring relationships among students sharing the same linguistic background.

At the end of the book, we return to the issues we have laid out here in order to describe what we have learned as a result of this project and what we would recommend in order to meet the integration imperative, which all of the countries in our study will face in the coming quarter century.

Notes

1. Decimal designations (e.g., 1.5, 1.25) for the foreign born who came as young children were invented by the sociologist Rubén Rumbaut.

2. Another international study of school-taught skills is provided by TIMSS (Trends in International Mathematics and Science Study). The TIMSS study is carried out by the International Association for the Evaluation of Educational Achievement. Its data assess the mathematics and science knowledge of fourth and eighth graders, thus potentially giving a picture of how skills inequalities evolve. (A related data program, PIRLS [Progress in International Reading Literacy Study], collects data on reading skills.) However, the TIMSS data do not include all the countries we are studying, and findings about immigrant/native student differences are not a focus of investigation (though it appears to be the case that the requisite questions are asked of students).

3. It is not possible in the PISA data to be more specific about origins because of a lack of consistency across countries in the way that immigrant origins are measured (Levels, Dronkers, and Kraaykamp 2008).

4. The EFFNATIS (Effectiveness of National Integration Strategies toward Second Generation Migrant Youth in Comparative European Perspective) project was undertaken with field surveys carried out in Germany, France, and Britain using a common questionnaire and with country reports based on secondary analysis of existing data in Sweden, the Netherlands, Switzerland, Finland, and Spain. The TIES (The Integration of the European Second Generation) project is a large-scale collaborative survey of second-generation young adults whose parents came from Morocco, Turkey, and the former Yugoslavia and are living in Austria, Belgium, France, Germany, the Netherlands, Spain, Sweden, or Switzerland.

5. There is a substantial tradition of this research, but the most recent and perhaps the most convincing entry is the analysis of the adult outcomes of the Tennessee STAR experiment, which appears to demonstrate far-reaching effects of the quality of kindergarten teaching (Leonhardt 2010).

6. This policy changed around 2006 to one that provided a smaller subsidy for students whose parents had low levels of education; such a policy still targets immigrant-origin students disproportionately (De Jong 2010).

CHAPTER TWO

Educating the Children of Immigrants in Old and New Amsterdam

Maurice Crul, Jennifer Holdaway, Helga A.G. de Valk,

Norma Fuentes, and Mayida Zaal

Because many migrants to the United States and Europe have limited formal education, school systems are challenged to avoid the reproduction of inequality in the second generation and to enable the children of immigrants to enjoy the opportunities available to their native-born peers. This study assesses how well two school systems meet this challenge by considering the experience of second-generation Moroccans in Amsterdam and Dominicans in New York City (originally known as New Amsterdam)—two groups that differ in terms of ethnicity and religion, but who share a similar socioeconomic position. The parents in both cases are predominantly low-wage labor migrants with modest levels of education, and second-generational educational outcomes are low compared with the children of native-born parents, raising concerns about labor market prospects and social inclusion.

This study focuses on two cities. A comparison at the municipal level has certain advantages. It enables us to avoid problems of regional variation, especially problematic in the US context, by limiting ourselves to single school systems. And it means that the populations studied face the same set of constraints and opportunities in terms of education and the labor market, which is not always the case with national studies (Reitz and Zhang 2011). At the same time, because major metropolises tend to share certain characteristics—including a high density of educational institutions offering a diverse range of programs—it also means that the findings may not be generalizable to all areas of the countries concerned.

This study does not focus solely on explaining how two school systems contribute to low educational outcomes for these students, which are to be expected given their parents' low levels of education and limited family resources. We also explore how patterns of achievement are distributed across the two groups and how those differences can be explained. In particular, we look at the ways in which students are tracked onto different educational pathways that have implications for their future trajectories into higher education and the labor market, and at the resources available to immigrant families in navigating this process.

The study draws on both quantitative and qualitative data. We take advantage of two data sets on second-generation attainment in New York and Amsterdam. For the Dominicans, we use the Immigrant Second Generation in Metropolitan New York (ISGMNY) study. This includes a telephone survey that was carried out in 1998–2000 with 3,415 respondents aged eighteen to thirty-two living in the Greater New York metropolitan area, including second-generation young adults from five different immigrant and three later-generation groups. The sample includes 428 Dominicans. Since educational attainment is very high among whites who move to the New York region for employment, we consider only those who grew up in the region in our comparative analysis. We use the Dutch data from The Integration of the European Second Generation (TIES) survey conducted in 2007. This study sampled eighteen- to thirty-five-year-old second-generation Moroccan and Turkish as well as Dutch young adults of native parentage in the cities of Rotterdam and Amsterdam. In the analyses for this chapter, we include the total sample of five hundred second-generation Moroccans living in Amsterdam or Rotterdam.

The chapter presents several main findings. Compared with children of native-born parents, children of low-wage labor migrants in both countries are concentrated in the lower levels of the educational system, but both systems nonetheless allow for some mobility. A considerably higher percentage of students of Moroccan than of Dominican descent are leaving school with no useful credentials, which is not entirely surprising considering their lower starting point in terms of family resources. A more unexpected finding is that second-generation Moroccans are doing comparatively well at the higher end of the educational ladder. Roughly equal percentages of both Moroccans and Dominicans are enrolled for or had attained the equivalent of a bachelor's or master's degree, but a considerably higher percentage of second-generation Moroccans are enrolled in a program for or have attained the equivalent of an associate degree. Meanwhile, more second-generation Dominicans have only a high school level education.

This polarized outcome for second-generation Moroccans has been stressed in previous research (de Valk and Crul 2008) but appears in a new light when contrasted with the United States, which is generally assumed to provide a more positive reception than Europe for immigrant families. While this finding calls for further research, we explore some possible explanations, including the impact of more active efforts in the Netherlands to provide financial resources and other educational support to students from immigrant families.

Interestingly, multivariate analysis reveals that family background characteristics, and in particular parental education, are much less able to explain differences in outcomes among children of immigrants of either second-generation group than they are for the students of native-born parents. This suggests that the variables commonly used in the sociology of education may not adequately capture the factors that make a difference in determining educational success or failure for immigrant youth. Although this is another question that will require further investigation, the qualitative analysis conducted as part of this research points to some possible lines of inquiry.

Background

We chose to compare the experiences of second-generation Moroccans and Dominicans because, although they differ in some important ways—most notably, religion—there are strong similarities in their social situations. Both are the children of poor labor migrants with low levels of education who arrived in the host country at a time when manufacturing employment was on the decline. Both groups also are racially stigmatized and stereotyped. As such, their experience is a useful test of the effectiveness of different education systems in serving the most disadvantaged students.

Although Mexicans are by far the larger immigrant group on a national level in the United States, Dominicans make up the single largest national-origin group of immigrants in New York City. The earliest arrivals were mostly political supporters of the dictator Rafael Leonidas Trujillo, who was overthrown in 1961. An American-assisted coup against the left-wing government that replaced him led to a further flow of labor activists and dissident students (Grasmuck and Pessar 1991; Pessar 1995). In the years that followed, foreign debt, rising oil prices, and limited employment opportunities for growing numbers of college-educated Dominicans led to high rates of emigration. The first to leave were middle-class, relatively educated people from Santiago and other urban areas, who were later joined by rural migrants (including both wealthy landowners and poor agricultural laborers) and by working-class relatives of the original migrants. Although the majority of Dominicans entered the United States legally, a significant but unknown number entered on tourist visas that they subsequently overstayed, or came through nearby Puerto Rico without valid papers. The Dominican population in New York grew rapidly, exceeding 200,000 by 1990. The 2000 census counted 407,473 people of Dominican ancestry in New York, or about 5 percent of a population of just over eight million, although researchers considered this an underestimate (Logan 2001). By 2006, the Dominican population was estimated at 609,885, according to the American Community Survey of the US Census Bureau (Fuentes-Mayorga 2011). Dominican immigrants initially settled mostly in Manhattan's Lower East Side but over the course of the 1960s many moved to the outer boroughs, to neighborhoods including Bushwick and Willamsburg in Brooklyn, Corona in Queens, or Washington Heights on the northern tip of Manhattan. Washington Heights in particular became a lively ethnic community where Luis Guarnizo estimated that, in 1992, there were more than 1,500 Dominican-owned enterprises, including travel agencies, bodegas, and gypsy-cab operators (Guarnizo 1994).

The first Moroccan labor migrants went to the Netherlands at the beginning of the 1960s, often after brief spells working in Belgium or France. The continuing demand for low-skilled workers in the Dutch textile and metal industries triggered a process of chain migration by relatives and friends from their home countries. In 1964, the Netherlands signed official agreements on labor migration with Morocco. Dutch industry needed low-skilled labor, and the majority of these first-generation Moroccan "guestworkers" were drawn from the lowest socioeconomic strata in their home country. Labor recruitment was aimed only at men, and women began to come only much later, in the early 1970s, mostly to join their spouses. The peak of labor migration occurred between 1970 and 1974, when official migration was halted (Crul and Doomernik 2003).

Amsterdam-West is the "capital" of the Dutch Moroccans in the Netherlands. In 2004, about 8 percent of the Amsterdam population was of

Moroccan descent (Crok et al. 2004), making it the second-largest national-origin group in the city. It is also the fastest growing group; more than half belong to the second generation, and more than 40 percent are younger than nineteen years old (Crok et al. 2004).

Family Characteristics and Resources

Clearly the resources that families have to support their children's education are important in shaping outcomes. These include family size, the parents' level of education and income, the presence of adults in the home to provide financial and emotional support, and the quality of the neighborhood in which young people grow up. Although Dominicans and Moroccans are both disadvantaged relative to mainstream groups in the two cities, there are nonetheless still significant differences between them, with Moroccans on the whole having fewer resources.

Both Moroccan and Dominican young adults grew up in families that were big compared to those of their peers in the Netherlands and the United States. But Moroccan families were considerably larger. The survey data show that second-generation Moroccans had an average of 4.9 siblings, and second-generation Dominicans an average of 4.1 siblings. This difference becomes even larger when we look at the number of siblings that respondents actually grew up with, which is 4.1 for second-generation Moroccans in Amsterdam but only 2.4 for second-generation Dominicans in New York. These actual family sizes are related to the fact that Dominican young adults are also more likely to have grown up in a single-parent household or to have experienced a parental separation or divorce. Slightly more than half of them (52 percent) have parents who are no longer together. Far fewer Moroccan young adults, or only 14 percent, living in Amsterdam/Rotterdam have parents who have separated.

Language acquisition is generally regarded as a key factor shaping the school performance of second-generation youth and it is often assumed that growing up with a different language in the home than is spoken in the host society will have a negative effect. Three-quarters of the second-generation Dominicans in the ISGMNY study said that Spanish (probably along with English) was the main language they spoke at home. For Moroccan young adults we know the language they currently speak with their mothers, and we can assume that this was not very different when growing up. A small

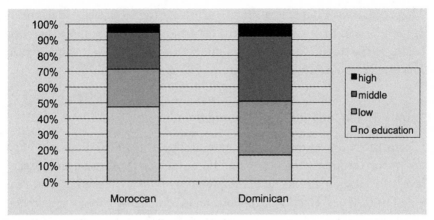

Figure 2.1. Educational Levels of Moroccan and Dominican Mothers

Source: TIES and ISGMNY data

majority (51 percent) say they more often or mainly speak their mother tongue rather than Dutch with their mothers.

In native-born families, parents' level of education correlates strongly with that of their children, and is especially relevant in understanding the degree of social mobility across generations. Parents of second-generation Dominicans and Moroccans have low levels of education overall, but there are significant differences between them. As Figure 2.1 shows, Dominican mothers in particular are more educated, with considerably more having a middle level of education and far fewer having no formal education. In contrast, 70 percent of Moroccan mothers have a primary education or less. A similar difference exists for fathers, although their level of education is slightly higher than that of mothers.

Another factor that might affect the educational achievement of young people, albeit in different ways, is the labor force participation of their parents. Having parents who are employed not only improves the family's financial circumstances but also brings greater knowledge of the host society and, by implication, its educational system. However, there may also be negative effects. Parents who work long hours may have less time to spend with their children, to engage with their schools, and to supervise their homework. The consequences of unemployment might also be quite different depending on whether immigrant parents have access to social welfare programs such as unemployment benefits, healthcare, etc.

The survey data on labor force participation show that both the fathers and mothers of second-generation Dominicans were more likely to have been employed than the parents of second-generation Moroccans. Only just over half of the Moroccan fathers (55 percent) versus 83 percent of the Dominican fathers had a paid job when the respondents were young, and the contrast is even larger for the mothers. Three-quarters of the Dominican mothers worked compared with only 16 percent of the Moroccan mothers. Because many first-generation Moroccan men became unemployed as the result of industrial restructuring or occupational disability, they received social benefits that provide a minimum income.

Both groups are known for their strong relationships with family and relatives in the home country. In addition to shaping identity, this strong transnationalism has implications for educational attainment in the second generation. The fact that one parent often migrated first means that some families were separated when the children were growing up, causing tension and lack of communication within the family (Pessar 1995; see also Levitt 1991). And if children return for long spells, their education can be disrupted. At the same time, while remittances may be an important source of support for relatives at home, those funds are not available for investment in the future of the family in the United States or the Netherlands. If, as in New York, the quality of schooling received is highly dependent on the neighborhood, and rents and house prices in neighborhoods with good schools are high, immigrants who split their resources between two countries can be at a disadvantage relative to those who concentrate their resources in New York or Amsterdam (Kasinitz, Mollenkopf, Waters, and Holdaway 2008).

Although both groups have strong transnational ties, it appears to be more common for Dominican second-generation youth to spend a significant amount of time in their parents' country of origin. Survey respondents were asked whether they stayed in the home country for more than three months (Moroccans) or more than six months (Dominicans). Only a minority (11 percent) of the Moroccan second generation had spent more than three months in Morocco, and the percentage is lower among those of school age: almost a third of those who are older than twenty-seven years of age stayed in Morocco for three months compared to only 2 percent of the eighteen- to twenty-two-year-olds. In contrast, almost a quarter of second-generation Dominicans had spent six months or more in the Dominican Republic, and this percentage is stable across age groups. Because of the wording of the question, which asked about stays of six months for Dominicans and only three months for Moroccans, the actual difference may be even greater. The survey also suggests that the Dominican second generation has stronger transnational financial ties. More than a third of Dominican young adults (35 percent) compared to 19 percent of Moroccans had recently sent remittances to their parents' country of origin.

In addition to family resources, the educational attainment of children of immigrants is also affected by the kinds of educational opportunities open to them, and there are important differences in the two cities. The quality of schools, more so in the United States than in the Netherlands, is related to the socioeconomic status of the neighborhood and the degree of ethnic segregation—factors that sometimes, but not always, overlap. Dominicans are one of the most segregated communities in New York. In 1990, the Index of Dissimilarity from Whites (the percentage of a group's population that would have to move to achieve a residential pattern that reflects the group's percentage of the population in the city) was 82 percent, and it had fallen only 2 percentage points by 2000 (Logan 2002). Later research has documented the growing spatial and racial isolation of Dominicans in New York (Fuentes-Mayorga 2011). In the last two decades, census estimates reveal that the group has experienced greater segregation than other Latinos, and that it is the most spatially isolated group in New York City after blacks. This residential clustering leads to concentrations of immigrant-origin children in particular schools.

Moroccans are also the most segregated of all ethnic groups in Amsterdam, but segregation has a totally different flavor in Amsterdam than in New York. The segregation index from persons of Dutch descent (39 percent) is much lower (Musterd and Deurloo 2002), and Moroccan neighborhoods are less dominated by a single ethnic group, although the other residents are often also immigrants (mostly Turkish). In combination with "white flight" (parents of Dutch descent sending their children to schools outside their own neighborhood), this segregation also results in schools with a majority of children of immigrants. The quality of education in these schools, referred to as black schools,[1] is generally lower than in other neighborhoods. Differences in quality, however, are not as great as they are in New York, as we discuss in more detail below.

Both groups are concentrated in areas with high crime rates. Neighborhoods in Amsterdam with a concentration of Moroccan inhabitants have become known for "troublemaking youth." Reported crime rates show a dramatic overrepresentation of Moroccan adolescents and young men

(Junger-Tas, Cruyff, van de Looij-Jansen, and Reelick 2003; Komen 2002; Martineau 2006). Similarly, the New York City neighborhoods in which Dominicans settled, particularly Washington Heights, have become known for the prevalence of drugs, and although only a very small minority of the population is involved in the drug business, many more are affected by it. Forty-three percent of Dominican respondents in the ISGMNY study said that drugs were a problem in their neighborhood, and many complained about the pervasive stereotype of Dominicans as drug dealers.

This kind of stereotyping reflects one aspect of the discrimination that both Moroccan and Dominican second-generation youth encounter, which affects their educational careers and prospects in a number of complex ways. For Dominicans, discrimination is primarily related to skin color. Although many first-generation Dominicans in particular resist being identified as black, which they see as a characteristic of Haitians—the group with which they uneasily share their home island of Hispaniola—many other New Yorkers regard them as black and discriminate against them on this basis (Candelario 2007; Itzigsohn and Dore-Cabral 2000; Lopez 2003; Pessar 1995). The ISGMNY study found that, after native blacks and West Indians, Dominicans were most likely to say that they had been discriminated against by the police, in public spaces, and at work. Men consistently reported considerably higher rates of discrimination than women (Kasinitz et al. 2008).

Moroccans are more likely to feel that they are discriminated against because of their religion. Tolerance toward the Muslim population among the Dutch majority population has declined dramatically in the past decade, and there is a strong negative discourse about Muslims in the media that has also gained considerable political support. Figures indicate that Moroccan youth, especially Moroccan boys, suffer the most discrimination of all visible ethnic minority groups in the Netherlands in the labor market and in public spaces. In one study, 50 percent of Moroccans, and 70 percent of the younger cohort, reported serious incidents of discrimination or racism in the last year (Boog et al. 2006). That is twice as high as among the Surinamese Dutch, who are of African or Indian descent. A third of Moroccans who went for a job interview in the previous year were sure that discrimination was the reason that they were not chosen, and a quarter suspected it. According to the same study, Moroccan pupils with a middle vocational education had 30-percent less chance of being invited for a job interview than pupils with Dutch-sounding names.

The expectation of discrimination in the labor market can affect motivation in different ways. Some young people may be less motivated to study if they feel their efforts will not be repaid, but others may push themselves further because they know they will need even higher qualifications to succeed in the unequal competition with majority peers. The ISGMNY study found evidence of this two-track effect. The survey data shows that 60 percent of Dominicans said that their parents had spoken to them about discrimination against Dominicans, and 19 percent said that their parents told them they would have to work harder than whites to get ahead. In-depth interviews found that respondents did indeed react in different ways to the expectation of discrimination, with some becoming discouraged, while others were motivated to try harder (Kasinitz et al. 2008).

Educational discrimination is multifaceted, and includes both individual and institutional aspects. Students may be most aware of discrimination by individual teachers and other pupils, which, as chapter 3 of this volume illustrates, can take both very direct and very subtle forms. But less visible, structural discrimination that limits them to low-performing schools can have an even more profound effect on their educational trajectories. We found little evidence of the first kind of direct discrimination in schools in the Dutch case. Only 6 percent of the second-generation Moroccan youth in the TIES study said that they were regularly confronted with discriminatory behavior in schools. Similarly, although some Dominican respondents asserted in interviews that teachers had low expectations of them and were sometimes overtly rude or disrespectful, only 14 percent reported being discriminated against in school (Kasinitz et al. 2008). However, this may be partly because these young people mostly attend very segregated schools where they do not encounter many white Dutch or American peers. This situation in turn reflects the structural discrimination exerted through the tracking system, which is discussed in some detail below.

This consideration of the social resources of Dominicans and Moroccans has shown that the two groups are similar in some basic ways. In both cases, the second generation grew up in poor households in highly segregated neighborhoods, and their parents have low levels of education. For different reasons, both groups are also subject to considerable discrimination. In light of this, it is not surprising that their educational attainment is significantly lower than that of native-born white students in both countries. Overall, Moroccans are somewhat more disadvantaged in terms of family background and might therefore be expected to perform less well in school than Dominicans. A comparison therefore offers a good opportunity to see how effective the education systems in the two countries are in reducing this preexisting disadvantage.

The Characteristics of School Systems in Amsterdam and New York

Children of Moroccan and Dominican families enter school systems that differ considerably both in their overall structure and in their specific policies toward children of immigrants. One of the pillars of the Dutch educational system has always been the freedom to choose the school of one's own religious or ideological preference without extra cost. All schools teach the same curriculum, and school fees are very low or nonexistent. However, although in principle immigrant parents can send their children to a primary school in an upper-class neighborhood without additional cost, in practice, they generally send them to schools in their own neighborhood (de Valk and Crul 2008). Most Moroccan parents do not send their children to schools in better-off neighborhoods because they usually do not have information about them.

Another important characteristic of the Dutch school system is the extra funding that primary schools receive for the children of immigrants. Since the 1980s, primary schools with many children of immigrants have received extra funding under the Educational Priority Policy. At the time of our study, schools received nearly twice as much funding for a child with an immigrant background as they did for a child of native-born parents from a middle- or upper-class background.[2] Through this mechanism, hundreds of millions of euros were invested in primary-school education for the children of immigrants during the last twenty-five years (Crul and Doomernik 2003). The funding scheme for disadvantaged students was changed, however, in 2006, and schools now receive the additional funding—which is no longer so ample—based on the socioeconomic/educational position of the parents irrespective of origin. The new system still tends to concentrate the supplemental funding in schools attended by the children of low-wage immigrants.

A child officially enters primary school in the Netherlands when he or she turns four. Primary school consists of eight grades, so children usually leave at age twelve. At the end of primary school, all children have to take a national examination (the CITO test) that is crucial for their further education in secondary school. Based on their test results and the recommendation of their teacher, they will be assigned to different tracks in the secondary school system. At the time when the young adults in our study were in school, Prevocational Secondary Education (VBO) was the lowest and least attractive stream of secondary education, and it is where children with the lowest recommendations from primary school were assigned. Then and today, children with higher recommendations usually go to comprehensive schools that have multiple streams. At that time, these included: Junior General Secondary Education (MAVO, now part of the VMBO track), and two streams preparing children for tertiary education: Senior General Secondary Education (HAVO) or Pre-University Education (VWO). (See Figure 2.2 for a diagram of the current educational system.)

In the first two years of comprehensive school, it used to be the case that all children studied together regardless of their recommendations from primary school. This meant that selection for most children was postponed for two years, and there was the possibility for some to move up to the more prestigious streams (HAVO and VWO). However, more and more schools have since moved toward a system of two homogenous tracks, one for VBO/MAVO pupils (VMBO in the present system) and the other for HAVO/VWO pupils. Most children continue to study after they have gained their secondary-school diplomas. The children who had a VBO or MAVO diploma could continue in Middle Vocational Education (MBO). This could mean a two-, three-, or four-year course, either full time or part time. A three- or four-year course gives students the right to continue to the University of Applied Sciences (HBO), but most students take shorter courses and leave school to look for a job. Pupils with a HAVO diploma can go on to the University of Applied Sciences, and pupils with a VWO diploma go on to university. (These usual directions of movement are not indicated by arrows in this and subsequent system diagrams, but by the vertical placement of stages.)

Another characteristic of the Dutch school system is that pupils can move from one stream to the other. In principle, one could start at the bottom and move up step by step to the highest stream, taking what is called the "long route" through the educational system. The long route takes between one and three years longer, but many children of immigrants have moved up the educational ladder in this way. This is possible in large part because tuition fees for higher education in the Netherlands are low, and students can receive a

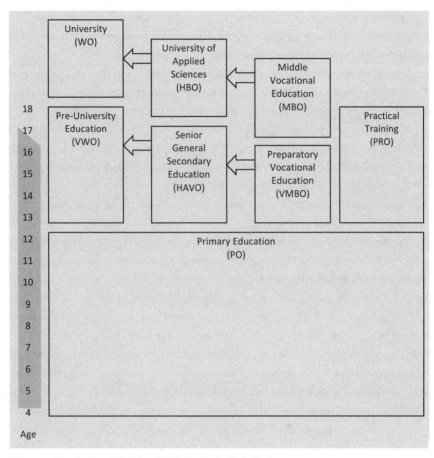

Figure 2.2. Organization of the Education System in the Netherlands

Note: Shaded ages indicate compulsory education. Arrows indicate a possible movement; in addition, students who complete one track can move to the one directly above it.

Source: *EURYDICE.*

study grant and get an additional loan from the government, so there are few financial costs for taking the long route beyond foregone earnings.

In New York, the education system is characterized by extreme variation in the quality of schools. Residential segregation and the underfunding of urban schools have been the subject of considerable attention in the US literature (see, for example, Anyon 1997; Hochschild and Scovronick 2003; Kozol 1991), and recent research has begun to focus on where the children of immigrants fit into this picture. The ISGMNY study shows that patterns of residential settlement and different levels of parental information regarding schools mean that the children of different immigrant groups attend quite different schools on average (Kasinitz et al. 2008).

The diversity of educational provision is accompanied by a lack of formal tracking mechanisms or a clear connection between educational programs and the labor market (Rosenbaum 2001). Children begin school at age six (though many attend preschool before that), usually attending the elementary school in their neighborhood. From there, they move to middle school at age twelve, and then to high school at fourteen. Although high school continues until age eighteen, legally required education in New York State ends at age sixteen, and some students leave early with or without a diploma. (See Figure 2.3 for a system chart.)

At the end of high school, students who plan to attend college generally take the SAT test, which is used by most university admissions committees to assess candidates' reading, math, and writing skills. Although the No Child Left Behind Act passed during the George W. Bush administration (and discussed in more detail in chapter 6) has introduced an element of standardized testing into the system for children in earlier grades, unlike many other countries, the United States has no uniform national test that measures educational attainment at the point of graduation from secondary school. The high school diploma and the General Educational Development (GED) diploma (which is earned after or outside high school) are undifferentiated, and the quality of education offered in different high schools varies considerably. The completion of certain courses, including honors and Advanced Placement courses, will improve students' chances of college acceptance and success. Although a high school diploma opens up the path to higher education, students who fail to graduate are generally left with no qualifications at all (Kerckhoff 1995). New York does have a number of vocational high schools that prepare students for particular careers, but the majority of schools are comprehensive. Overall, while tracking methods are much more informal than in the Netherlands, as we will show in the more detailed discussion on tracking, students are still effectively channeled from a very young age onto very different and unequal educational trajectories.

Policies and Programs for Immigrant Students
In addition to differences in the underlying structure of the education systems, the opportunities open to immigrant students are also affected by

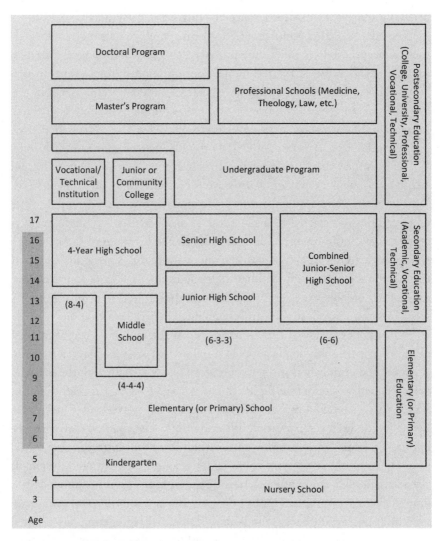

Figure 2.3. Structure of Education in the United States

Note: Shaded ages indicate compulsory education. Adult-education programs, while not separately delineated above, may provide instruction at the elementary, secondary, or higher education level. Chart reflects typical patterns of progression rather than all possible variations.
Source: US Department of Education, National Center for Education Statistics

various policies and programs designed to assist them in particular or to more generally address the difficulties faced by disadvantaged students.

The educational trajectories of Moroccan pupils are strongly shaped by their concentration in inner-city primary schools with many children of immigrants. Because of the residential concentration of immigrants in certain neighborhoods, a few schools have had to absorb many children of immigrants (including both Moroccans and, for example, children of Turkish immigrants) over a short period of time. Over a five- to eight-year period, primary schools in Amsterdam neighborhoods like Indische buurt, de Pijp, Bos en Lommer, and Baarsjes changed from having a mostly Dutch-descent clientele to having a predominantly Moroccan and Turkish student body. Whenever the number of children of immigrants passed 40 percent, families of Dutch descent started to avoid these schools. This white flight accelerated the concentration of children of immigrants. Freedom of school choice thus provided Dutch parents with the opportunity to escape schools in their neighborhoods with many children of immigrants, but local policy makers did not act on this for a long time because they feared that forced mixing would cause them to lose votes from the Dutch majority population.

When policy makers finally took action, at the end of the 1990s, almost all inner-city neighborhoods adopted a policy that allowed parents freedom of school choice only within their own neighborhood. Although the measure was intended to stop white flight, this is not what happened. Either native Dutch parents found a way around the rule, or they moved out of neighborhoods with a high concentration of immigrants. The result was that neighborhood schools became more, rather than less, concentrated, and at the same time, immigrant parents could no longer send their children to schools outside their own neighborhood. In the end, then, the combination of demographic change (more than half of children under twelve in Amsterdam are now from immigrant backgrounds) and residential segregation has resulted in a great number of schools with 70 percent or more children of immigrants (the threshold for being labeled as a "black" school). In an increasing number of schools, there are no children of native Dutch parents.

Especially in the 1980s, when schools were confronted in a short period of time with a large influx of students of Moroccan and Turkish descent, they were unable to provide sufficient help and support to these pupils. During this period, most of these primary schools developed ad hoc policies and were basically in a state of crisis management. Teachers complained that it was impossible to teach adequately because of the wide variation within the classes in terms of age, abilities, and years of Dutch schooling (de Jong 1986). Schools with a high concentration of children of immigrants still perform worse even after adjustment for parental socioeconomic status, although the difference has decreased. Qualitative differences are evident in mathematics and language scores. The poorer quality of "immigrant schools" is partly a consequence of lower standards applied to immigrant pupils there. Because teachers believe that many pupils cannot handle the full study load, they consciously or unconsciously lower their standards. The mechanisms involved here were reported by the national education inspectorate, which monitors schools on a regular basis (Crul 2000).

Alarmed by numerous reports about the problems in primary schools, in 1985 the government launched the Educational Priority Policy. The cornerstone of the policy was support for primary schools with a high percentage of immigrant children, which would receive almost twice (1.9 times) as much funding for each immigrant child as for a middle-class or upper-class native Dutch child. The extra funding in the first years of this policy change was spent mostly on creating smaller classes, but this did not bring the results hoped for (de Jong 1997). The idea was that the teacher would be better able to provide individualized help and support, but the percentage of immigrant children in these schools continued to rise to the point where more than 70 percent of children in some schools were from immigrant backgrounds, outweighing the benefits of smaller classes.

Slowly, the schools also found out that second-language acquisition was not the only problem. The class background of the immigrant parents posed equally big challenges. The children were often the first in the family to go to school on a regular basis. Many parents had only minimal formal education themselves, so they were often unable to give their children much practical help. Language and cultural barriers also made contact between parents and teachers problematic. A major complaint from teachers in the 1980s and 1990s was that Moroccan and Turkish parents seldom attended teachers' contact evenings and were generally less involved in the school careers of their children. Parents' interactions with educators were likely affected by cultural and social norms from their country of origin that position teachers as the experts who should not be questioned, and perhaps also by a sense that immigrants were not welcome at the school.

Schools increasingly started to focus on new teaching methods, especially those aimed at second-language education. The new teaching methods and books were financed with extra grants from the city of Amsterdam (made available to the larger cities through the national budget). As a result, conditions in schools with many children of immigrants have improved. The classes in these schools are often smaller now (ten to fifteen fewer pupils than in a class with mainly children of native Dutch parents), and they often have an extra teaching assistant, the newest teaching methods and books, and the best facilities in terms of classrooms and available space.

Recognizing that Moroccan parents are not often able to help with homework or give advice about educational choices, Amsterdam, like other cities in the Netherlands, has also introduced mentoring programs, which are discussed in more detail below.

These programs have resulted in gradually improving academic results for most children of immigrants. National test scores at the end of primary school show that children of immigrants are slowly closing the gap with children of native-born parents. In eight years (1994–2002), Moroccan pupils managed to close 30 percent of the gap with their peers on the national test (Gijsberts and Hartgers 2005). With the extra funding that allows for smaller classes and a curriculum that focuses on special (language) support for Dutch as second language, some of their disadvantage seems to have been overcome.

Better results in primary school mean that more Moroccan pupils are able to take intermediate classes that give them a chance to continue to HAVO or VWO. If we compare the position of Moroccan pupils in the third year of secondary school in 1995–1996 and in 2001–2002, we see a more than twofold increase (from 8 percent to 19 percent) over six years in the percentage of Moroccan students in these more prestigious tracks (Herwijer 2003), which give access to higher education. More and more Moroccan pupils were able to avoid selection into a vocational track at the end of primary school.

A similar pattern of residential segregation shaping educational opportunity exists in the United States, and of course has a longer history, rooted in slavery and the "separate but equal" school system that persisted long after slavery was abolished. The landmark case *Brown v. Board of Education* in 1954 undermined the legal basis for separate schools but the problem of how to integrate them has never been resolved. In the early 1970s, court-ordered bussing in many states met with fierce opposition from whites, fueling their move to the suburbs, and by the 1990s, the policy of achieving integration by moving students ended in most cities. Without explicit efforts to stop it, and with residential concentrations continuing to underpin it, school segregation has been on the increase in many states (Orfield and Lee 2006; Orfield and Yun 1999), creating growing numbers of schools with high concentrations of low-income, and often English-language learner, students.

More recent efforts to bring about equity in education have focused on funding and the quality of education provided rather than on the race and ethnic mix of the students. Increasingly, the issue is framed in terms of parental choice. But choice only helps if there are enough places available in "good schools," and one group of researchers estimates that there are up to thirty applicants for every seat in the better New York schools (Teske, Schneider, Roch, and Marschall 2000). Parental choice also works to the advantage of families with the most information about the system, and the time and skills to advocate for their children, which most immigrant parents lack. With the exception of Chinese parents, few take advantage of opportunities to send children to school outside of their own neighborhood (Kasinitz et al. 2008; Lipsit 2003).

As a result, the quality of the K–6 grade school (primary school) that a child attends is still largely determined by where the family lives. New York City has thirty-two community school districts, each of which is divided into zones, and students go to their zone school unless their parents apply for a waiver, which is known as a "variance" (Cookson and Lucks 1995). Although they are part of the same school district and receive the same funding, the quality of education in these local schools varies enormously. These differences in quality overlap strikingly with patterns of residential concentration. For example, analysis of data from the New York City Board of Education shows that the percentage of elementary and middle school students performing at grade level in English in 2001 ranged from as low as 26 percent in the predominantly black and Latino Highbridge/South Concourse neighborhood of the Bronx to 76 percent in the Bayside/Little Neck area of Queens, where residents are mostly white and Asian. There was a similar range for student performance in math. Low-performing schools have worse facilities and higher percentages of teachers who are uncertified or not qualified to teach the class subject (Mei, Bell-Ellwanger, and Miller 2002).

Recent data show some improvement, with four-year graduation rates for the entire 2006 student cohort (graduating in 2010) rising to 71 percent for women and 60 percent for men (from 54 percent and 40 percent, respectively, in 2005). The gap between Hispanic and white students also narrowed from a 33-percentage-point difference for the 2001 cohort to a 27-point difference for the 2006 cohort. However, Hispanic males continue to have the lowest four-year graduation rate (52 percent compared with 75 percent for white males, and 53 percent for blacks), and the lowest percentage earning Regents Diplomas (39 percent compared with 65 percent for white males) (NYSED 2011a).

Most of the support for children of immigrants in the United States has taken the form of language education. Although some states introduced formal instruction in the home language of immigrants—particularly German—as early as the 1830s, and many others provided dual-language instruction on an informal basis, bilingual education was more or less abolished during World War I. It reappeared only in the context of the civil rights movement in the 1960s and when a new influx of immigrants made it clear that it was not possible to leave them to "sink or swim" in English-only classrooms. The Bilingual Education Act of 1968 (eliminated in 2001 by No Child Left Behind) provided federal funds to encourage states to provide some form of dual-language instruction for immigrant students; and following a Supreme Court ruling and several lawsuits at the state level, the Equal Educational Opportunity Act was passed in 1974, mandating schools to overcome linguistic barriers for students' equal access to the curriculum. This legislation did not, however, stipulate how this should be done, and debate has subsequently raged over the role that the heritage languages of children of immigrants should play in schools (see for example, Goldenberg 2008; Olsen 2009).

Whereas other states have pulled back from bilingual education, New York continues to maintain a comprehensive program, with most of the city's schools offering some kind of bilingual or English as a second language (ESL) program. If students entering school score lower than 41 percent on the Language Assessment Battery test, they are designated English-language learners (ELLs) and are obliged to enroll in either bilingual or ESL classes until their score is over the cutoff point. Elementary schools that have more than fifteen ELL students speaking a common mother tongue over two consecutive grades are required to create a bilingual program in that language (for high schools, it is twenty students). Bilingual programs include short-term transitional programs that aim to transfer students to English as soon as possible, maintenance bilingual programs that aim to develop academic proficiency in both English and the parents' language, and dual-language programs that include both ELL students and native English speakers. In New

York, short-term transitional programs predominate. Despite investment of $123.3 million annually, more than one-quarter of the system's more than four thousand bilingual teachers are not certified, and even fewer are specifically certified as bilingual or ESL teachers (New York Department of Education 2008).

Another source of additional funds comes from the federal government in the form of support for supplementary programs under the Department of Education's Title I. These funds are disbursed to school districts based on the number of low-income families identified in the census, and their use is determined by school boards and includes after-school programs, tutoring, parent information, and training. The funds available to any given school in New York City will therefore depend on the number of students enrolled and also on the percentage of students who come from low-income families. Charities and foundations also support educational programs, sometimes with substantial contributions. Although they occasionally support institutional reform, as with the William B. Gates Foundation's small-schools initiative, foundation contributions are often targeted toward after-school and other supplementary programs for disadvantaged students. Some of these funds go directly to schools while others are channeled through community-based organizations, including some, like the Allianza Dominicana, that work with particular immigrant groups. These are discussed in more detail below.

However, although some supplementary education programs do exist, there has been no comprehensive effort in New York to identify and address the specific needs of children of immigrants—for example, through the kind of mentoring programs in place in Amsterdam. Of course this is partly because questions of educational equity are framed in a very different context than in Europe. On the one hand, the primary concern in the United States has been with overcoming enduring racism and improving the educational opportunity and achievement of African Americans. Given that native-born blacks (and later Puerto Ricans, who are also US citizens) are similarly concentrated in poorly resourced schools and have much lower educational outcomes than whites, it would be difficult to justify targeting children of immigrants for special programs while excluding other low-income students who might also benefit. On the other hand, immigrants to the United States are more diverse in their educational backgrounds than those in most European countries. As a result, migration status in itself is not a good indicator of educational disadvantage in the way that it is in the Netherlands. The children of some immigrant groups, in particular Indians and Chinese, in fact regularly outperform whites in terms of educational attainment.

Tracking in the Two Systems

The early educational experience of the children of Moroccan and Dominican immigrants means that they are generally behind at the point of selection into secondary school. In the Dutch system, this is a very clear turning point in a student's school career. A good school recommendation at the end of the primary years is critical for getting into the more prestigious tracks in secondary school. The TIES study shows that at the end of their primary schooling, about 30 percent of Moroccan pupils are tracked into the lowest streams of secondary education (see Figure 2.4). Many boys get a recommendation for a technical school, and many girls are directed to a vocational school. This means that they are not able to go to an intermediate class in secondary school and are sent directly into the vocational streams. By age twelve, their future school careers are already pretty much determined.

Fifty-six percent of children of Dutch descent get into an intermediary class that gives access to academic tracks compared with only 43 percent of the children of Moroccan descent. In some cases, the outcome is determined by the performance on the CITO test, but if we compare youngsters of Moroccan and Dutch descent with the same school recommendations, we see still-considerable differences. Around 92 percent of Dutch-descent children with somewhat above average recommendations get into these classes but only three-quarters of children of Moroccan descent do. This may be because Dutch parents are more active in advocating on behalf of their children, or because they are more successful in doing so. Dutch parents may also be more aware of the importance of this tracking point for the educational careers of their children. Additionally, teachers' perceptions of students' ability to perform in a higher track can also contribute to these disparities.

The concentration of children of immigrants in vocational schools in Amsterdam has increased rapidly in the last five to ten years, and the same problems faced by the primary schools can now be found in vocational schools. These schools furthermore are also facing the additional challenge of educating immigrant children between the ages of twelve and fifteen who

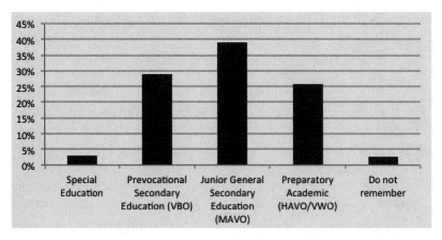

Figure 2.4. First Track in Secondary School for Second-Generation Moroccans in Amsterdam and Rotterdam

Source: TIES survey

have just arrived in the Netherlands. Dropout rates in the vocational schools are high, and the school climate is often not conducive to school success. In the TIES study, 16 percent of the second-generation Moroccans who started a lower vocational track dropped out without a diploma.

Another 40 percent or so of second-generation Moroccans in Amsterdam enter a middle-level track (MAVO then, VMBO now) in secondary school directly after primary school, or after two intermediary years (see Figure 2.4). The school climate on this middle track is in general considerably better than in the lowest level, where the likelihood that a Moroccan child will drop out of school without a diploma is three and one-half times higher (Tesser, Merens, and van Praag 1999). About one-quarter continue at the highest levels in secondary school (HAVO or VWO, the preparation tracks for tertiary education).

Those who finish the lowest or middle level usually go to Middle Vocational Education (MBO). They are either placed in short tracks of one or two years, or they are given access to the three- or four-year tracks. Most of those who went to a middle-level track in secondary school go the three- or four-year tracks that give access to skilled blue- or white-collar jobs. A diploma from a four-year MBO track also gives access to higher vocational education. This long route to higher education means that students have to study three years more than they would if they took the direct route through secondary school (see Figure 2.2) and only those who are very persistent are able to stay the course. Nonetheless, about 40 percent of the second-generation

Moroccans in the TIES study who finally entered higher education did so through the long route. Two-thirds of them are female. The existence of the long route plays an important role in explaining educational success among second-generation Moroccan youth.

A smaller group enters short one- and two-year tracks after secondary school. These programs are especially designed for those who finished secondary school at the lowest level or who left secondary school without a diploma. There is a concentration of pupils with learning and behavior problems on these tracks, and dropout rates in some schools are as high as forty percent. At best, these short programs lead to unskilled jobs, but many young people who take them are unemployed long term.

Taking the long route to higher education of course requires considerable persistence and support. In the TIES study we found, as in earlier research (Crul 2000), that older siblings can play a pivotal role by providing advice, and practical and emotional support, to their younger siblings. This support seems especially effective if an older sibling is already in higher education (see also de Valk and Baysu 2011). Fifty out of the fifty-nine respondents in the TIES study who have an older highly educated sibling stated that this sibling was (very) important for their educational career, and it seems that educated siblings often take over the advisory role that would be played by parents in Dutch-descent families.

In the United States, students usually move on to middle school after fifth or sixth grade and then to high school after eighth grade at the age of fourteen (see Figure 2.3). Middle schools, or junior high schools as they are also called, were introduced shortly before World War I. In addition to providing the last few years of education to those who then left for the labor market, they also had the goal of sorting the students who were continuing their education into the two high school tracks available at that time—vocational and college preparatory. Today, most tracking takes place within rather than across schools. Most high schools are comprehensive, but sorting by ability already takes place in most middle schools, in the form of "smart" classes or special programs for "gifted and talented" students (Oakes 1985). Because middle schools rely on residential catchment areas, they also vary widely in their quality, which is crucial in determining the type of high school to which students can hope to gain entry.

Although most New York high schools are comprehensive, students can take a test for entry into one of five magnet high schools. These schools

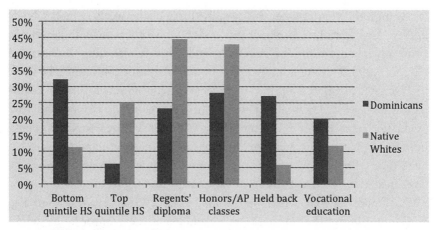

Figure 2.5. High School Experience of Dominican Second Generation Compared with Whites

Note: Only whites who grew up in New York City are included. Percentages for high school are of those attending public school.

Source: ISGMNY

provide an enriched curriculum, and some are more selective than Ivy League colleges. Selective magnet and specialized programs are also available at certain other high schools. However, few students who attend weaker primary and middle schools pass these highly competitive tests. If their parents cannot afford private or parochial school fees, they will then go to locally zoned high schools.

Although there is no formal hierarchy, the city's general high schools differ enormously in terms of measures of quality and performance, and the worst of them are very bad indeed. Children of Dominican immigrants are concentrated in the low end of the system (see Figure 2.5). Less than one percent of Dominican students in the ISGMNY study went to the three most prestigious public secondary schools in New York (Stuyvesant, Bronx Science, and Brooklyn Tech), only 6 percent went to schools ranked in the top 20 percent of the public system, and nearly a third went to schools in lowest-performing 20 percent of the school system, which only 11 percent of native-born white students in the public system attended.[3] Sixty percent attended schools ranked in the lowest two quintiles in terms of performance, compared with about 40 percent of the West Indian second generation, 50 percent of native blacks, and 55 percent of Puerto Ricans. In fact, Dominicans on average attended worse schools than any other group even when parents' level of education and other factors were controlled for.

As an indication of what this means, thirty of the weakest high schools in New York City had four-year graduation rates of less than 30 percent in 2000, when many of the ISGMNY respondents were attending (Balfanz and Letgers 2004). Despite improvements in overall graduation rates since then, high schools in which Dominican students are concentrated, such as Washington Irving High School in lower Manhattan, continue to have four-year graduation rates of only 55 percent (42 percent under the new standards being introduced that require Regents Diplomas for graduation), and they are fed by middle schools in which low percentages of students are achieving grade level on standardized tests (NYSED 2011b).

As Figure 2.5 indicates, Dominicans in the ISGMNY study were also much more likely to be held back a grade and to have been in vocational tracks in high school than were white students. They were much less likely to have earned Regents Diplomas, or taken honors or advanced placement courses, which expose high school students to college-level material. In short, the secondary education they experience limits them significantly in terms of their options for postsecondary education and employment. Many respondents in the ISGMNY study who had attended poor high schools and did manage to attend college reported being unprepared academically for college-level work (Kasinitz et al. 2008).

There is no significant difference in the schools attended by Dominican men and women, but boys are significantly more likely to be held back than girls (39 percent compared with 19 percent), and to have been in special education classes (11 percent compared with 3 percent), while girls are more likely to have taken honors courses (31 percent compared with 24 percent). This indicates that even within the same schools, Dominican boys are less able to make educational progress than their sisters. The complex factors within and outside the school context that shape these gendered educational trajectories are discussed in more detail by Nancy Lopez (2003).

Although we do not have as detailed an account of school career paths in the ISGMNY data as in the TIES data, there are also many indications that Dominican students are both taking a longer time to complete their education than white students and graduating from programs that offer much more limited career opportunities. This can be seen partly from the rank of the postsecondary institutions attended by the Dominicans who go beyond high school. Whereas 28 percent of college-bound whites attended universities ranked in the first tier nationally by *US News and World Report*, fewer than 5

Maurice Crul, Jennifer Holdaway, Helga A.G. de Valk, Norma Fuentes, and Mayida Zaal percent of Dominicans did so. Dominican students were instead concentrated in the local City University of New York (CUNY) system and, within that, in the schools with the poorest academic reputations. A quarter of those attending college were at regional tier-four institutions, compared with less than 5 percent of whites. Until recently, access to the public university system was quite open, and many students in the lowest-ranked colleges spent a considerable amount of time taking remedial courses to compensate for their inadequate high school preparation, a situation that questions whether this should count as college-level education. This has now changed with the institution of stricter acceptance criteria for CUNY schools. It is not clear yet what the impact of these stricter entrance requirements will be on the enrollment of children of immigrants, but it is likely that many of those with weaker preparation, including many of the Dominican second generation, may now find it harder to gain admission.

In order to control for the fact that Dominicans in the ISGMNY sample were younger on average than whites, and to capture the speed with which they move through the system, Figure 2.6 shows the level of education completed at various ages. It indicates that over time, most Dominicans do complete their high school education, and more than 60 percent enter some kind of postsecondary institution, even if it is mostly quite lowly ranked.[4] This is an impressive achievement in light of their parents' educational background. However, fewer than half of those who started higher education obtained a bachelor's degree, even in the twenty-eight to thirty-two age group: only 34 percent, compared with 56 percent of whites, 11 percent of whom have already attained a postgraduate qualification by this age. Only 10 percent of Dominicans ever obtain a postgraduate qualification, which is the gateway to most professional jobs, compared with over a quarter of the whites. Since educational attainment is very high among whites who move to the New York region for employment, we only consider those who grew up in the region in this and other comparisons.

Comparing Outcomes and Explanatory Factors

The preceding account has given a broad picture of the backgrounds of the two groups and the educational system with which they interact, as well as some preliminary outcomes. Now we move toward a comparison of the two groups in terms of educational outcomes and the factors that seem to

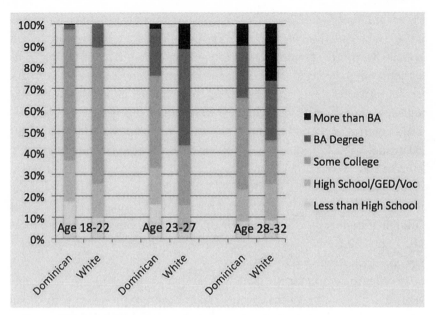

Figure 2.6. Educational Attainment by Age, Dominicans Compared with Whites
Source: ISGMNY

be important in shaping attainment. The data imposes certain limitations. Both surveys included questions covering a wide range of issues, including family background, education, work, neighborhood, partner relations, identity, and discrimination. But despite the overall similarities in the questionnaires used in the two cities, not all information was gathered in both surveys nor are all the variables easily comparable due to the specific situations in New York and Amsterdam. Therefore separate analyses were performed on the two datasets to test for context-specific influences on the school careers of the two groups.

In addition to the quantitative data, we draw on qualitative data collected as part of the Children of Immigrants in Schools project. Norma Fuentes conducted in-depth interviews, focus groups, and ethnographic work with Moroccan families in Amsterdam during 2006–7. Her study focused on the role of mothers in shaping the educational expectations and school careers of second-generation Moroccan young women, on the role of siblings and birth order, and on how family and school environments affect the different school trajectories and mobility of Moroccan girls. She interviewed twenty-three second-generation women and ten mothers, and conducted ethnographies with two families. Mayida Zaal studied the experiences of twenty-two Moroccan youth (ages eleven to eighteen) who participated in six different youth programs throughout the city of Amsterdam. She conducted participant observations, focus groups, and in-depth interviews to understand the types of support Moroccan youth received from the youth programs in which they participated. To understand the range of services offered and the challenges these programs faced, she interviewed twenty-five adults representing thirteen youth-serving organizations including three schools. The findings of this fieldwork are considered in light of earlier interviews conducted with the Dominican second generation as part of the ISGMNY study.

In order to gain a picture of educational attainment and patterns of achievement in the two countries, we grouped respondents into four categories: (1) early school leaver (no high school diploma / lower secondary dropout, or at most a lower secondary diploma); (2) secondary school diploma only and no longer enrolled (graduated high school / one- or two-year MBO); (3) postsecondary vocational education (associate degree completed or enrolled / three- and four-year MBO tracks or HAVO/VWO); and (4) university (graduated or enrolled in BA program / HBO or university).

At the lower end of the spectrum, Dominicans in New York are doing better than Moroccans. Only 12 percent of those aged twenty and above had failed to attain a high school degree, compared with 24 percent of Moroccans (Figure 2.7). While a high school dropout rate of over ten percent is surely a reason for concern, the situation is clearly much more worrying in Amsterdam, where almost a quarter of Moroccan students are failing to obtain the most basic educational qualification.

At the higher end, however, the results for the two groups look remarkably similar, with about 30 percent of both groups enrolled in higher education programs or having completed a BA or MA program. Given that university-completion rates are much higher in the Netherlands, it is likely that a higher percentage of those who are enrolled will eventually finish. This is impressive when considering how many Moroccans grow up in families where the parents have almost no formal education.

The middle of the range also presents an interesting picture. Although Dominicans are graduating from high school at higher rates than Moroccans, fewer of them are finding their way into associate-degree programs, with a high percentage achieving no more than a high school degree. It is not clear

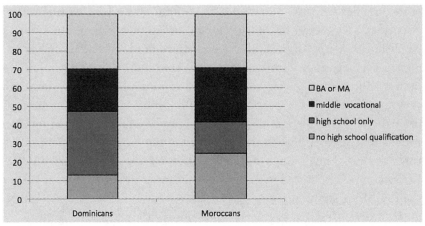

FIGURE 2.7. Educational Attainment/Enrollment of Second-Generation Dominicans and Moroccans
Source: ISGMNY & TIES data

whether this reflects differences in the labor market (with more low-skilled positions available in New York than Amsterdam) or the fact that the fees for postsecondary education in Amsterdam are low. Most likely it is some combination of the two.

In order to assess the factors that shape these outcomes, we conducted ordinal logistic regression analysis for each of the two datasets separately, with the four-category scheme for the highest educational level attended as the dependent variable.[5] The impact of demographics, family background, and school-related characteristics on attainment was studied with a stepwise analysis. Because it was not possible to match all the relevant variables, the findings are presented separately for the two datasets on New York and Amsterdam/Rotterdam. As before, we distinguished four possible levels of educational attainment in each case (see below for more detail). The results are shown in tables 2.1 and 2.2.

Dominicans
The analysis shows that some demographic characteristics of the family are important: respondents growing up with more siblings, as well as those in a one-parent family, do less well than those in smaller families and living with both biological parents. However, other characteristics of the parental home, including in particular the parental level of education and the language spoken at home (not shown) were not significantly related to educational

TABLE 2.1. Logistic Regression Coefficients for Highest Level of Educational Attainment/Enrollment of Dominican Second Generation (Aged 20 and Over)

	B	SE	B	SE	B	SE
gender	0.271	0.202	0.363~	0.204	0.192	0.213
age	0.142***	0.030	0.141***	0.031	0.122***	0.032
currently enrolled	2.752***	0.256	2.757***	0.259	2,777***	0.266
number of siblings			-0.144*	0.062	-0.072	0.064
educational level parents			0.193	0.122	0.140	0.126
parents were working when young			0.201	0.193	0.218	0.200
lived with both biological parents			0.476*	0.220	0.251	0.232
Catholic school					0.662**	0.236
held back in school					-0.725**	0.243
time spent on homework					0.169 ~	0.090
ESL classes					-0.450 ~	0.236
pseudo R2	0.35		0.39		0.43	

~p<.10 *p< .05 **p <.01 ***p<.001
Source: ISGMNY N= 369

attainment. This is quite surprising given that parents' educational attainment is a generally such a strong predictor of children's attainment and, as discussed in the introduction to this volume, therefore key to theories about the reproduction of inequality across generations.

We also examined a number of school-related variables. Attending Catholic schools turned out to be a positive factor, as did doing more homework, while being in English as a Second Language classes and being held back a grade were negative. Of course, these last three aspects of the educational experiences cannot easily be disentangled from academic aptitude or teachers' influences, but they nonetheless suggest that these aspects of educational provision play an important role.

Moroccans

Similar analyses were performed for the Moroccan young adults living in Amsterdam. As with Dominicans, we do not find much effect of the socioeconomic position of the family of origin on the level of education attained. (In the final model, parental education is marginally significant, at p < .10.) Unlike the Dominican case, however, living in a two-parent family was not significant, but this may be because most Moroccans in the survey grew up in intact families, so there is not much variation on this characteristic.

What is more surprising is that family size was not important. The TIES survey has more detailed information about siblings than the New York data, and provides additional evidence of their role in the educational career of second-generation Moroccans. Having a sibling with a higher education diploma is positively related to attainment, whereas having a sibling who dropped out shows a negative association. Further evidence of the influence of family networks and support is demonstrated in the finding that having a mother who participated in the labor market is related to better educational outcomes,[6] as is having parents who helped with homework. At the same time, transnational ties appear to exert a negative effect. The small percentage of respondents who spent three months or longer in Morocco have significantly lower levels of educational attainment (not shown) and, regardless of whether the time spent abroad is significant in itself, presumably differ in some important ways from those who remained continuously in the Netherlands.[7]

The TIES data also contains quite detailed information about respondents' school careers. Looking at these, it is surprising that we do not find effects of attending preschool, changing primary schools, repetition of classes, or having remedial/special teaching in secondary education (not shown). However, we find a positive association between attending a school affiliated with a religious denomination and higher educational attainment. The association is particularly strong for second-generation Moroccan women. In terms of the ethnic composition of the primary school (not in table), we find that men who attended schools where more than 25 percent of the students were of immigrant origin do less well than those where this percentage was lower, and the imbalance increases as the percentage of immigrant students rises.

In the Dutch educational system, the recommendation at the end of primary education is of major importance in determining students' future educational opportunities. On the basis of this recommendation, students are tracked into different levels of secondary education. As the recommendation is not an exogenous variable with regard to educational level, we cannot meaningfully include this variable in our models. Nevertheless, bivariate

Maurice Crul, Jennifer Holdaway, Helga A.G. de Valk, Norma Fuentes, and Mayida Zaal

TABLE 2.2. Logistic Regression Coefficients for Highest Level of Educational Attainment/Enrollment of Moroccan Second Generation (Aged 20 and Over)

	B	SE	B	SE	B	SE	B	SE
gender	.347~	.194	.359~	.197	.317	.200	.316	.203
age	.039	.029	.033	.029	.052~	.031	.049	.032
currently enrolled	1.904***	.236	2.010***	.242	2.070***	.246	2.063***	.249
number of siblings			-.045	.037	-.057	.038	-.014	.041
parents ever separated			.131	.287	.133	.291	.291	.300
educational level parents			.241*	.117	.256*	.125	.217~	.129
mother working when 15			.244	.163	.256	.166	.407*	.173
parents helped with homework					.227*	.101	.236*	.102
parents talked about school and education					-.374**	.115	-.334**	.118
held back							.314	.246
Catholic/Protestant primary school							.540**	.208
sibling dropout							-1.051***	.246
sibling with HS diploma							.502*	.244
pseudo R²	0.21		0.25		0.27		.320	

~p<.10 *p< .05 **p <.01 ***p<.001
Source: TIES N=366

exploratory analyses support the notion that this recommendation is related to Moroccans' persistence in school and ultimate educational outcome.

Comparative Insights from the Quantitative Analysis

From the factors shaping attainment in the two cities, certain patterns emerge, some of them predictable but others quite surprising and worthy of further investigation. Of course, the small sample size complicates detailed multivariate analysis and limits the possibility of generalizing from the results. However, the comparison confirms the importance of certain variables across the different contexts, while at the same time suggesting that different mechanisms are at work in the two cities.

In terms of the impact of family characteristics, it is interesting that in neither case does parental education have much of an impact on the educational attainment of the children. This is remarkable given that this variable often explains as much as 30 percent of the variance in studies of students in general (as it also does for the control groups in these two studies) and, also, that "controlling for class" often makes the difference in attainment between native-origin and immigrant-origin children disappear. By contrast, the family background model is weak in its explanatory power, and the variables that are most significant for students overall explain very little for the children of immigrants. This suggests that we are failing to capture many of the important differences in financial, human, and social capital that explain intragroup variation in educational attainment, a question to which we return below.

In comparing family background characteristics, the one difference between the two groups that stands out is that larger family size seems to be a more negative factor for Dominicans than for Moroccans. This may be one way in which the issue of school funding is surfacing. In New York, where the quality of the school that children attend is very dependent on the neighborhood, families must either be able to afford to buy a house or rent in districts with better schools, or pay tuition fees to send their children to Catholic schools. In this context, family size becomes a serious constraint on opportunity. In Amsterdam, where education for children of immigrants is more subsidized and there is less variation in the quality of schools, being one of a larger number of siblings is not such a disadvantage.

The comparison also shows that school tracking is important in both contexts, although it takes place in different ways. In both cases we see that certain types of educational experience are highly correlated with high or low outcomes. In the New York case, attending ESL classes and being held back a grade are early warning signs of poor later outcomes, suggesting that more attention should be paid to providing greater assistance to students who show these early signs of problems. In the case of honors classes, which are associated with better outcomes, the problem is not only that Dominican students are less likely to be assigned to them, but also that these classes are less available in weaker high schools, a situation that raises the more general problem of the segregation of Dominican students in lower-quality schools. However, the fact that enrollment in such classes varies quite substantially by gender indicates that even within the same school context, boys are choosing, or being steered onto, different tracks from girls.

Insights from the Qualitative Data

The qualitative fieldwork conducted by Norma Fuentes and Mayida Zaal, as well as previous fieldwork by Maurice Crul and the qualitative interviews from the ISGMNY study, shed light on some of the factors that shape immigrant families' capacity to navigate the school system and some of the differences in the resources available to immigrant families that are not well captured by most quantitative analyses. These include factors that influence aspirations and access to educational resources, as well as the ways in which families navigate the school system.

Fuentes's work, which focused on the relationship between mothers and daughters, shows how family dynamics and the integration experience of the first generation can shape educational aspirations and attainment for children of immigrants. It also helps to explain the shift in the gender gap in educational outcomes in favor of women. She found that many young women pursued education as a means of avoiding the isolated, dependent existence that they felt their mothers had been forced to lead both in Morocco and in Amsterdam. In fact, their aspirations were often expressed as a negative emotion. When asked, "What did you not want to be when you grow up?" one respondent instantly replied, "Not like my mother! I don't want to be like her, she did not study; did not work; never left the home; she was like a prisoner all her life! Whatever I do, I know it will not be that!" (twenty-five-year-old MBO student).

Although labor force participation was much higher among first-generation Dominican women in New York, the second generation showed a similar desire to avoid being limited to the opportunities open to their mothers, which were primarily factory and domestic-care work. As one woman put it: "My Mom, she didn't have papers. So she was working under the table, cleaning, ironing for people. That's like a Hispanic thing, you know? It was a way of getting through the tough times. . . . I wouldn't want to. Because I was raised here, you know? I speak very good English" (twenty-four-year-old Dominican woman). Avoiding early marriage was another incentive for young women in both groups to stay in school. In a context where early marriage and childbearing are common for women in the home country, and pressure to marry mounts as they hit their twenties, education provides a reason to delay. The tension between education and marriage was evident among second-generation Dominican women in the ISGMNY study (Kasinitz et al. 2008), and, as a successful Moroccan young woman explained, "For me it was like an escape. If I had stopped after the MAVO, I'd have had to find a job, and if I had been working that means I would have been ready for marriage, and I didn't want that" (twenty-seven-year-old university student).

Fuentes's research indicates that Moroccan families encourage education and have high aspirations for their children, but they have little information about the workings of the educational system and are wary of taking certain risks, such as sending children to schools outside the neighborhood. These factors, combined with the lack of good programs within neighborhood, lead students not to realize their potential. As one young woman who eventually took the long route explained to Fuentes, "I did not know the difference between vocational and academic programs. In my time, we had MAVO, HAVO, and VWO. And VWO prepared you for the university. I had HAVO recommendation, but there was no HAVO in the neighborhood; so, I had to go to MAVO and stay in the neighborhood, because my parents did not allow me to take a bus. . . . I resented that for a very, very long time, because it held me back for a lot of things . . . for years I was thinking, if I had done the HAVO, then I could have gone to the VWO. It took me three years longer to achieve my goal, or finish my HBO. I was so angry. When I talk about it, I am still angry sometimes" (thirty-four-year-old MAVO graduate).

In this context, siblings' educational and labor-market experiences also play an important role in providing the benefit of having an educated, "proxy" parent whose experience with the system could be transferred to younger siblings. Although research has shown that having numerous siblings can place a burden on family resources, particularly when it comes to paying for private education in New York, the problem in Amsterdam seems to be more that the burden of housework and childcare falls to older girls, limiting the time they have available to concentrate on schoolwork.

At the same time, siblings can also be a resource for younger children in the family and for parents. As pioneers, their experience provides lessons for those following them through school. In her analysis, Fuentes found that girls who were middle siblings, usually 1.5-generation youth, were more likely to delay marriage and stay in school longer, and less likely to be on vocational tracks. Siblings offered both concrete examples of the implications of following particular educational pathways and practical advice about how to navigate the system. Zaal's respondents also reported relying on older siblings for support in choosing a secondary school that offered their track. In the ISGMNY study, in-depth interviews likewise showed that Dominican parents were generally unable to give much advice about educational choices for their first child but were able to make more informed choices about the education of later children, having learned more by this point about the variation in school quality (Kasinitz et al. 2008).

It is generally assumed that families will want their children to attend the best schools available, and that their low representation in better institutions is the result of residential segregation, but this is not always the case. Families make choices within the limited circumstances in which they find themselves and may see attending a lesser school as preferable to other potential risks (Maira and Soep 2005; Opotow 2005). Quantitative analysis cannot easily detect the influence of self-selection or self-protective factors on educational trajectories, but the qualitative data from TIES and the ISGMNY study shows that these factors should be taken into account.

As we have seen, immigrant families are often wary of sending their children out of the neighborhood, particularly if this involves significant travel on public transportation. And young people themselves are also sometimes unwilling to attend schools where they will be in the minority. Fuentes describes a Moroccan woman who opted to switch from a five-year physical-therapy program within the HBO track to two-year training as a doctor's assistant within an MBO health education program. She blamed the isolation she had felt in the mostly Dutch program and the attitudes of the senior peers responsible for her daily training and supervision: "They [her Dutch peers] were just cold; they would smile at you and then gossip behind your back. They would give me good daily evaluations and tell my supervisor I was doing fine; but, then I would hear from this Turkish girl how they were always talking about me behind my back. It got to a point that I was really unhappy and decided to leave." Similarly, the young participants in Zaal's study reported instances of feeling excluded as a result of their ethnic origin or their religious affiliation. They expressed concerns about the prevailing negative stereotypes of Muslim (specifically Moroccan) youth in Dutch society that could lead to them being excluded and shunned in school, in the playground, and in the labor market. As Musa, a twelve-year-old boy attending an after-school homework group expressed the worry, "I really don't want . . . [them to] think negative about me . . . otherwise I will be refused job applications or something, and, uh, friendships."

Some participants in both Fuentes's and Zaal's research reported choosing to attend schools in which they would not be a minority, even though they had tested into higher tracks. For example, Hamid, a high-achieving fourteen-year-old Moroccan student, who had been placed in a high academic track (HAVO/VWO), hoped to switch to a lower HAVO track in a more diverse school for his second year to avoid the older bullies who often teased him and the French teacher who told him and his classmates that they would never amount to more than discount-supermarket store clerks. Dominicans in the ISGMNY study reported similar feelings of self-doubt and anxiety about discrimination. Asked why they did not take the test for the specialized high schools even when their teachers recommended it, several said that they preferred not to go to a school where they would be in a minority, or worried that they would be unprepared academically (Kasinitz et al. 2008).

Mentor and Homework Project Programs

In the Netherlands, efforts have been made to replicate the positive sibling effect through mentor projects in which successful students of immigrant descent mentor younger pupils from their own ethnic group in high school. The methodology and effectiveness of mentoring in the Netherlands have been described in various research projects (Crul 2001; 2003; Crul and Akdeniz 1997; Crul and Kraal 2004); and over the last three years, the number of such projects has increased rapidly. One of the biggest projects working with Moroccans is Stichting voor Kennis en sociale Cohesie (SKC, the Foundation for Knowledge and Social Cohesion), which supports over 1,400 pupils in Amsterdam from the last year of primary school into the first years of secondary school (Crul et al. 2008). The first programs were started by Moroccan and Turkish student organizations but over the past years many educational institutions have also taken the initiative to start student mentor projects for migrant youth. Oranje Fonds, the foundation of the Dutch royal family and one of the biggest foundations in the Netherlands, spent six million euros in the last 4 years to develop a national mentoring scheme in 24 cities.

Zaal studied six mentoring programs, ranging from the city-wide SKC, which serves over a thousand students, to smaller programs for fifty students in particular neighborhoods. All of the programs had limited paid staff and most part-time mentors or instructors were volunteers, but the ratio of youth to instructors was quite low (5:1 or 7:1), allowing adults to give young people individualized attention. Most of the funding came from the Dutch state (local and/or national) and the EU, and some programs received private grants.

The ideas behind the programs show a complex and sometimes contradictory mix of social, political, and economic motives, with many employing multiple approaches including remedial/enrichment, preventative/preparatory or reactive/proactive service (Cordero-Guzman, 2005; Nettles 1991; Noam and Rosenbaum Tillinger 2004; Woodland 2008; Zhou and Kim 2006). The more preventative and reactive approaches, for instance, respond to fears about the potential radicalization of Muslim youth. Enrichment and preparation-based programs focus on developing youth's academic skills, exposing them to cultural institutions, and introducing them to potential career tracks. Both types of program are funded by the state, and the choice between taking a proactive stance over a reactive one was not always clearcut. Sometimes programs were compelled to apply for funding for prevention (even if they thought this was opposed to their program goals) in order to offer young people the preparation they needed. These tensions created difficulties for the young people and the adults who worked with them, and meant that the programs had positive effects but also limitations.

Zaal found that the primary benefits for Muslim youth who participated in these programs were that they received mentoring and support from engaged adults in environments that felt like safe havens. The participants discussed the importance of having Moroccan mentors with whom they could interact, and described feeling understood by mentors in terms of their culture, traditions, and languages. For instance, being able to speak slang, Moroccan Arabic or Tamazight (the Berber language) added to their sense of belonging. Several of the students explained the significance of having Moroccan mentors who could speak to their parents. However, while the cultural background of their mentors was not irrelevant, it was not crucial to young people's experiences of feeling respected, safe, and tolerated. Young people repeatedly said that what mattered more than their mentors' ethnic background was how open, welcoming, and accepting they were. This finding reinforces the benefits of the mentoring pedagogy.

Young people who received direct academic support and instruction from the programs they attended described feeling more engaged in school and prepared for the CITO test. They also described being more willing to answer questions and participate in class after reviewing content matter with their instructors and/or their peers. As in other studies, their level of engagement and willingness to participate were correlated with feeling safe and respected by the adults who worked with them (Noam and Rosenbaum Tillinger 2004; Woodland 2008). Youth described the programs as *gezellig*, meaning cozy and comfortable. It helped that most of the program facilities were roomy, modern, well-lit spaces enhanced with bright colors. Rania, a twelve-year-old participant, explained how she perceived her place in the program she attended as compared to her place in the outside world: "With the organizations, it's mostly that they see you as equal to others. They think it doesn't matter to them whether you are a foreigner or uh, just Dutch and mostly on the street it's like, uh, that does matter."

Samira, a seventeen-year-old participant, talked about the level of respect she experienced in terms of her religious beliefs: "I respect everyone and my organization does too, . . . Like others respect my religion so I respect theirs. . . . If they didn't I wouldn't be here; I would notice that." Like Samira and Rania, other participants distinguished between how they felt in the comfortable and safe microcosm created by the youth program they attended and the world outside.

Equally important was the youth programs' connections to schools and to the participants' families. This included the advocacy function that some programs served in their capacity as liaisons between families and schools. The extent to which programs connected with and included parents in their activities varied. Some held periodic meetings with parents or sent reports home. Others organized community events, presentations, or performances of children's work to which parents were invited, creating opportunities for parents to participate in their children's education.

Several of the programs supported young people by serving as liaisons between teachers and families. In one outstanding example, mentors attended the parent/teacher conference where the children received their recommendations for secondary school. This is a highly anticipated and significant milestone in the context of Dutch schooling. Making sense of a child's recommendation and what it means in terms of choosing a school can be quite complex and overwhelming for parents of any background. For immigrant parents, unfamiliar with the Dutch school system, the challenge is compounded, and they find it hard to advocate for their child. In contrast, mentors of Moroccan descent who had been educated in the Netherlands had greater Dutch fluency and were familiar enough with the system to ask questions about how the decisions were made and challenge them if necessary.

Although the primary area of need that youth identified in terms of navigating the school system was receiving assistance with choosing a secondary school (once they received their recommendation), surprisingly almost none of the mentoring programs offered explicit support with this process. Therefore, youth were left to rely on the limited information they received in primary school. Those in vocational tracks also expressed the need for assistance in securing paid internships to help mitigate the ethnic and religious discrimination many faced when entering the labor market, and they were frustrated that they did not have anybody helping them navigate this obscure process.

While there were many reported benefits, program coordinators were often limited in what they were able to offer. Staffing concerns and funding trends and requirements also presented potential restrictions. In some instances, the programs' reactive approaches (e.g., offering only remedial services and not enough enrichment opportunities) limited their scope. Many of the programs (intentionally or unintentionally) reproduced the dominant discourses about Moroccans and/or Muslim youth; there were, however, those programs that found ways to resist the dominant ideologies and provided counternarratives that challenged the status quo.

While New York City is not without after-school and other programs offering support for students, there is currently nothing on the scale of the Amsterdam mentorship programs that focuses on improving the academic achievement of children of immigrants. Those programs that identify the children of immigrants as the target population generally offer English language instruction and little more. Other youth programs that focus on academic help through community-based organizations in the Washington Heights area of New York City are not explicitly geared toward the children of Dominican immigrants, though they effectively serve that population.

Youth programs through Dominican community-based organizations are the primary means through which the children of Dominican parents can receive extra academic help or learn to effectively navigate the school system. For example, the Youth Enhancement and Self Development Program (YES) at the Asociación Comunal de Dominicanos Progresistas offers entrepreneurship seminars that simultaneously sharpen math, reading, writing, and oral skills. Tutoring for homework help is available to the participating students. Other after-school programs that serve the children of Dominican immigrants in New York do not identify academic enrichment as their primary purpose. They are designed primarily to keep the children occupied after school. In a 2009 survey of household attitudes toward after-school programs in New York State, most parents listed having fun, improving social skills, and staying out of trouble as important features for participants in after-school programs, with academic enrichment a less prominent goal.[8]

Most after-school programs are municipally funded. In addition to support from the NYC's Department of Education and the Department of Youth and Community Development, many community-based organizations have benefited from the financial and programmatic support of nonprofit organizations like The After School Corporation (TASC) to design, implement, and assess programs.

Conclusion

This comparison of Amsterdam and New York has shown that although the two systems differ in many ways, they produce quite similar outcomes. In the end, the formal tracking process in the Netherlands and the more informal mechanisms that sort students onto different educational pathways in the United States both serve to channel children of Moroccan and Dominican immigrants into the lower reaches of the educational system. Considerable numbers of both groups are failing to obtain even the most basic educational qualification.

In comparing educational policies and their results across the Atlantic, we can detect both positive and negative elements in both systems. The extra investments in elementary school in the Netherlands have had the effect of enabling more second-generation Moroccans to continue into postsecondary education over time. The effects of the investments in elementary schools are, however, constrained by the Dutch educational system's early selection of students at age twelve into vocational or general academic programs and, unfortunately, have been reduced since a policy change in 2006. The

Moroccan second generation has been slowly narrowing the gap (in Dutch language abilities and math scores) with children of native parentage over the years in elementary school, but it is hard for them to catch up before this crucial turning point. In New York, formal selection takes place much later, but the lack of resources in schools results in a persistent or even growing gap between students over time. In an ideal situation, children would get enough support to close the gap with their mainstream peers, and be given sufficient time to do so before having to prepare for decisive tests.

At the same time, a substantial number of students do manage not only to complete high school but also continue onto higher education at the bachelor's or master's degree level—around 30 percent in both cases. This represents a high degree of social mobility, especially when one considers that many of the Moroccan parents had almost no formal education. Yet the higher education their children obtain is not equivalent to that of native-born white students. The Moroccan second generation in Amsterdam often enters higher education via the long route through middle vocational education, taking on average three years longer than if they entered postsecondary education through the college-preparation track and delaying their entry into the labor market. Because in the Netherlands the tuition fees for higher education are low and there is not much variation in quality, the cost of the long route is mainly time and lost income. Dominicans in New York also take longer than their native-born peers to complete college, and retention rates are low. Because they must pay considerable tuition fees, this often leaves them burdened with debt. Since they are also concentrated at the low end of a highly diversified higher education system, the college education they receive does not prepare them for occupations similar to those that their white native-born peers who attend more prestigious institutions. These factors, in combination with the more open labor market in the United States, may partly explain why fewer Dominican youth continue into higher education.

The success of the long route to college, like the occasional self-selected downward school mobility of second-generation students initially placed in higher tracks, is itself a demonstration of the detrimental effects of early selection in the Dutch system. However, the fact that so many immigrant students persist and eventually succeed in completing higher education proves that they have the ability to do so. It therefore seems necessary to consider how more of them could be supported to enter the direct track to college and complete their education in a shorter time frame.

The high dropout rates in the Dutch case also demonstrate that extra investment by the state does not automatically translate into good prevention schemes for at-risk youth. The Dutch educational priority programs have primarily targeted youth in preschool and elementary school, but this is clearly not enough. Vocational schools with youth in the most vulnerable and difficult school ages (around puberty) have hardly received any extra funding. For schools to keep these youngsters (often from families with multiple social problems) aboard is a task that goes far beyond their resources.

This analysis has shown that although family background characteristics, like educational level of parents, may explain much of the difference in educational attainment between the native born and the children of immigrants, they do little to explain the considerable variation within second-generation groups. Rather than their parents' education, the success of children of immigrants seems to depend more on factors related to their social capital and to their experiences within the school system, both of which can help or hinder them from accessing the higher reaches of the system. In particular, the presence of educated siblings or mentors appears to be particularly helpful.

Interestingly, the government of the Netherlands seems to have grasped the potential of community-based organizations to serve as bridges between immigrant communities and schools. In contrast, although the United States is usually seen as having a strong civil society compared with Europe, it has yet to draw fully on community organizations as partners in efforts to improve opportunities for children of immigrants. This is but one of the ways that the United States, despite its rich history of successful immigrant-group incorporation, can be schooled by the developments taking place in countries with more recent records of large-scale immigration, like the Netherlands. Old Amsterdam still has something to teach New Amsterdam.

Notes

The authors would like to thank the members of the CIS team for their helpful comments, and Lauren Shields for research assistance.

1. In the Netherlands, a school is identified as a "black" school (*zwarte school*) "if more than 70 percent of its pupils have low-skilled or non-Western parents" (Ministry of Education, Culture and Science 2007).

2. For native children of working-class families, schools received 1.5 times more funding.

3. Measured by the school system on a scale that includes the percentage of students performing at grade level, teachers' qualifications, and so forth.

4. It should be noted that this is inferred from cross-sectional data rather than longitudinal data relating to individuals.

5. Ordinal logistic regression was used because the level of education the student attained is an ordinal variable in which there is a clear order in the levels but the distance between them is not necessarily the same. Only respondents aged twenty or over are included in the analyses in order to get the best possible measure of final educational level. The analyses were conducted for men and women separately as well, but as patterns were similar for both sexes, only the combined analyses are presented here. The analyses were conducted using a stepwise model in which the explanatory variables were added in blocks in order to better estimate the relative importance of each of the main individual, parental, and school characteristics. More information on the analyses or models not presented in the chapter can be obtained from Helga de Valk at valk@nidi.nl.

6. This question asked whether parents were employed when the respondent was age fifteen.

7. At the same time additional analyses reveal that it is less common to spend time in Morocco among the younger cohorts compared to the oldest cohorts of the second generation (not in table).

8. "New York after 3PM Fact Sheet," The Afterschool Alliance. *America after 3PM* was conducted for the Afterschool Alliance and sponsored by the JC Penney Afterschool Fund.

CHAPTER THREE

Different Systems, Similar Results: Youth of Immigrant Origin at School in California and Catalonia

Margaret Gibson, Silvia Carrasco, Jordi Pàmies, Maribel Ponferrada, and Anne Ríos-Rojas

The United States and Spain have very different immigration histories as well as education systems and policies, yet there are many similarities in the school experiences of students from immigrant families. Despite official goals to include youth of immigrant origin socially and academically, both systems operate in ways that deny these youth equal educational opportunities. In both countries serious disparities exist in academic achievement between native middle-class students and students from the largest immigrant groups, i.e., children of Mexican descent in the United States and children of Moroccan and Latin American descent in Spain.[1] Although differing in their structures, policies, and practices, in both settings immigrant-origin students encounter systematic forms of exclusion that shape their patterns of academic engagement and, in the long run, their educational futures.

We draw our findings from field research conducted in six high schools: three in Catalonia and three in California. The aim of this chapter is to describe the contradictions between discourse and practice, on the one hand, and immigrant students' actual experiences in school, on the other. Our analytic frame builds directly from prior research detailing how school practices simultaneously welcome and unwelcome immigrant youth, thereby creating "an inclusionary-exclusionary process that in the end place[s] immigrant students on the margins of school life" (Gitlin, Buendía, Crosland, and Doumbia 2003, 92). As Gitlin and other scholars (Foley 1996; García Sánchez 2009; San Miguel and Valencia 1998) remind us, history plays a direct role in how these processes unfold and how the identities of immigrant-origin youth come to be socially constructed as "other."

In the US case, California was taken by force from Mexico as part of the terms of the Treaty of Guadalupe Hidalgo following the US-Mexican War (1846–48). Although the treaty guaranteed Mexican Americans the right to maintain their language, their culture, and their lands, the reality has proved very different. California passed its first law prohibiting the use of Spanish in public schools in 1870. By the 1890s, courses that focused on Mexican heritage and history had been eliminated from the public schools and replaced by a more Anglocentric curriculum. Most of the schools that Mexican American children attended at that time were inferior and segregated. Some children managed to do well academically, but they were the minority (San Miguel and Valencia 1998).

In the Spanish case, economic and historical links with its former colonies have been the main triggers for recent immigration flows from Morocco and Latin America. Moroccans, furthermore, have a tangled history with Spain that includes the Moors' occupation and rule of different parts of the Iberian Peninsula for over 700 years (from 711 until 1492), coupled with their lasting and important influence on Spanish art and culture. This long and contested history mediates Spain's integration approaches, with immigration bringing these existing historical tensions to the fore. Conflicts over multiculturalism have been debated largely in relation to the Muslim community, and notions of Spanish identity have, in part, been formed through a negative perception of "the Muslim," the Moroccan in particular (Zapata-Barrero 2010).[2] In the specific case of Catalonia, the politics of self-government, questions of Catalan national identity, and the place of the Catalan language are intimately bound to the politics of immigration. The arrival of new immigrants has served to reactivate "old questions" related to religious, cultural, and linguistic pluralism (Zapata-Barrero 2010).

The current status and experiences of Moroccan and Latin American youth in Catalonia and of Mexican youth in California are caught up in these histories, and youth from North Africa, Latin America, and Mexico are among the most disparaged groups in each country. To understand the processes that have led to the marginalization of these immigrant youth, we also draw from research on the political salience of ethnic borders and boundaries (Alba 2005; Barth 1969; Erickson 1987; Phelan, Davidson, and Yu 1997). As Alba (2005) observes, the majority group imposes social boundaries between itself and immigrant minorities, but the nature and terms of the boundaries vary from one societal context to another, "brighter" in some societies and more "blurred" in others. Alba's concept of bright (rigid) and blurred (more porous) boundaries and his question about the conditions that give rise to one or the other are similar to the questions raised by Erickson (1987) regarding why minority youth are more able to cross social, cultural, and linguistic boundaries with comparative ease in some school settings while in others differences become politically charged and are not easily transcended. In the sections that follow, we explore the ways in which cultural, social, and linguistic borders are structured, experienced, and negotiated and how the politicalization of borders directly impacts immigrant-origin students' access to resources in school, their sense of membership within the school community, the nature of their participation in school activities, and ultimately their school persistence and achievement.

Two central questions guide our work. First, how do schools through their structures, policies, and practices influence the social and academic integration of immigrant youth? And second, how do immigrant youth perceive and negotiate their social and academic integration? Findings are presented in four sections, beginning with an overview of immigration and education in each country. Next, we describe the six high schools where we carried out fieldwork. We then turn to the treatment of cultural and linguistic diversity within the schools, focusing on contradictions between rhetoric and practice and the ways that differences are turned into hierarchies. The final section focuses on the actual experiences of immigrant-origin students in different settings in order to further highlight ways in which school structures and practices are contradictory, yielding results that fall short of their stated goals or intentions.

Methods

Our overarching methodology has been one of ethnographic research, carried out at the six sites. Fieldwork included intensive participant observation of classes, programs, activities, events, and meetings in the schools, and in the neighborhoods where the students and their families were living. At each school, we conducted extensive case studies with at least six immigrant students, carried out focus group interviews with additional students, native as well as immigrant, and gathered survey data from a still-wider group of students to help contextualize emerging findings. We also conducted interviews with school administrators, teachers, education authorities, community members, and parents, and we obtained academic and archival data from school and community documents. At the outset we centered our attention on fifteen-year-old students—ninth graders in California and those in third ESO (*Educació Secundària Obligatòria*)[3] in Catalonia. In Catalonia, this is the year before compulsory schooling ends and a point when one's academic performance can have a determinative impact on future educational options. In California, ninth grade can also be a critical transition point, a time when students face the sometimes difficult shift from middle school to high school and the added academic pressures that high school can bring.

We selected field sites that represented three types of public high schools in terms of the student populations served: the first had a high concentration of working-class, immigrant-origin youth mainly of the same ethnic background (Mexicans in California, Moroccans in Catalonia). The second had a mix of students, both immigrant and native, from middle-class and working-class families. In the third type, native students formed the majority, mostly from advantaged backgrounds, but each school also included a significant population of working-class, immigrant-origin youth. In each country we had one school of each type. The field research in Spain was conducted in Catalan and Spanish; in the United States it was conducted in English and Spanish.

The schools in Catalonia were urban in their locations, all three within greater Barcelona, a densely populated metropolitan area that includes the city proper as well as neighboring villages and towns.[4] The California schools, located along California Central Coast with mountains to the east, the Pacific Ocean to the west, and rich farmlands nearby, were more rural in their surroundings. Although we recognize that there are structural and cultural differences between "urban" and "rural" settings, we believe these to be of less significance in advancing this chapter's specific arguments than are other characteristics of the six schools. We also question whether a conceptual approach that positions urban and rural at opposite ends of the spectrum hides more than it reveals about the dynamics of ethnic/race relations and the impact these have in mediating the education of immigrant students. Our analysis aims to extend beyond the urban-rural dichotomy to examine the various ways in which different social formations manifest in schools with differing minority/majority compositions. Each of the schools is described more fully in a following section.

Research was carried out by Pàmies at Berryville High School in California, by Ponferrada at Field High School in California, and by Ríos-Rojas at IES de la Vall in Catalonia (fieldwork took place in 2006 and 2007). The fact that these researchers were conducting fieldwork in what for them were foreign countries enriched their ability to provide a comparative perspective on the two school systems and immigrant students' experiences at school. The field research at the other three schools was completed earlier—by Carrasco and her team at IES del Cim and IES del Mar in Catalonia (Carrasco, Pàmies, and Bertran 2009; Carrasco, Pàmies, Ponferrada, Bertran, and Ballestín 2009; Pàmies 2006; Ponferrada 2008), and by Gibson and her team at Hillside High School in California (Gibson and Bejínez 2002; Hurd 2004, 2008; Koyama and Gibson 2007). All names of schools, school districts, towns, teachers, and students used throughout this chapter are pseudonyms.

Immigration and Education

Catalonia

Unlike the United States, which is often described as a nation of immigrants, Spain had no history as an immigrant-receiving country until the early 1990s. However, at the time of our fieldwork, Spain had become the second country in the world after the United States in the overall number of immigrants received annually, with the immigrant share of the population increasing from 1.6 percent in 1998 to 11 percent in 2006 (del Barrio 2007). This sharp growth in immigration has resulted from Spain's rapid economic and social development following its becoming a part of the European Union (EU) in 1986, its location on Europe's southern border that makes it a major gateway for immigrants from Africa, and the ease of incorporation expected by immigrants from Latin America migrating to the former "mother country." Moroccans and Ecuadorians form the largest non-EU immigrant groups.[5]

The fact that our focus within Spain is Catalonia adds additional complexity to the immigration picture. In contrast to other regions of Spain that have long histories of exporting workers, Catalonia has been an important destination for workers from the rest of the country since the beginning of the nineteenth century due to its early industrialization and comparative affluence. Over the past two decades, it has also experienced intense flows of international migration. As of 2008, 15 percent of Catalonia's population of 7.35 million was foreign born (INE 2008).

Catalonia has its own education system within the framework of the Spanish national education law (see Figure 3.1 for a diagram of the Spanish education system). Most children (97 percent) begin preschool at age three. Compulsory schooling begins at age six and continues until age sixteen, or the fourth year of ESO. The three preschool years (ages three to six) plus grades one through six are housed together in primary schools (*Centres d'Educació Infantil i Primària*). The four years of ESO (equivalent to grades seven to ten in the United States) are located in Institutes of Secondary Education (*Instituts d'Educació Secundària* or IES), which also house postcompulsory academic and vocational programs. In both public and private schools in Catalonia the teacher-student ratio averages 1 to 12.3, a far more generous ratio than found in California schools.

At the start of each school year in Catalonia, secondary school students are assigned to a class group or section, and they take all their classes, apart from a few electives, together with this group. Students who graduate from fourth ESO may either attend the two-year *Batxillerat* program, which prepares them for university admission (comparable to grades eleven and twelve in the US system), or they may enroll in one to four years of vocational or technical training (*Cicles Formatus de Grau Mijtà* and *Cicles Formatius de Grau Superior*), leading directly to jobs or less frequently serving as an alternate but longer path to university. University admission is based on a student's record in *Batxillerat* and on his or her scores on the university entrance exam (*Selectivitat*), although some technical colleges or specific degree programs will admit students based solely on their records in *Cicles Formatius* and a special exam. Students who finish four years of ESO without satisfying all the requirements for a diploma receive a certificate of completion, which enables them to attend vocational training but not *Batxillerat*.

In 1998–99, less than 2 percent of students in compulsory education in Catalonia were the children of immigrants. By 2007–08, the immigrant share had mushroomed to 15 percent. There are significant differences, however, between the public and private sectors in immigrant enrollments. Forty percent of Catalonia's students attend private schools, 34 percent in schools that receive state funding and 6 percent in elite schools that receive no state funding and operate independently of state mandates. Several studies since the mid-1990s have drawn attention to the ghettoization of newcomer immigrant students attending public schools in working-class neighborhoods, as well as the efforts of some local councils to redistribute students to avoid this sort of

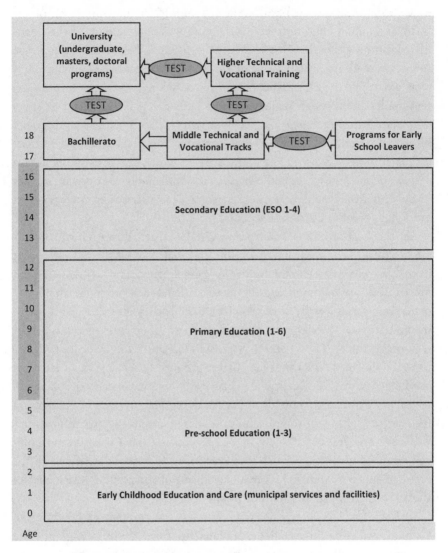

Figure 3.1. Structure of the Education System in Spain

Created by: Silvia Carrasco

Source: Ministerio de Educación, Gobierno de España

ghettoization (see Carbonell, Simó, and Tort 2005 on "the Vic model"). In general, however, levels of segregation within the public schools are rising, in part because private schools, including those receiving state funding, have not been required to accept the same percentage of immigrant students as the public schools, thus allowing both working-class and middle-class Spanish parents to compete for places in the private schools (Carrasco 2008; Ferrer, Valiente, and Castel 2008; Síndic de Greuges 2008). In 2008, just 7 percent of students attending private high schools were immigrants compared to 22 percent of those attending public high schools (Departament d'Educació, Catalunya 2008).

As an autonomous community, Catalonia has some educational provisions particular to its region including Catalan as the language of instruction and a multilingual policy that requires the study of Spanish and English, in addition to Catalan, beginning in the primary grades. An elective fourth language, usually French, is introduced at the secondary level. Language policy in Catalonia needs to be understood within the context of the region's historic struggle to maintain its own cultural and political identity. Catalonia was incorporated into Spain as part of the Reino de Aragón, an independent kingdom under a common royal rule in the sixteenth century. Early in the eighteenth century it lost the right to its own language, leading to a century-long decline in the use of Catalan until Barcelona's industrial bourgeoisie turned to its heritage as a strategy to oppose the authoritarian centralist rule. Catalan regained its status as the region's official language during the ephemeral democracy of the Second Republic (1931–39), but it was repressed again during Franco's regime from 1939 to 1977.

In 1983, as part of official policy to recover, protect, and promote Catalan culture and language, Catalan was reestablished as the language of instruction. Non-Catalan-speaking children, almost all of whom at that time were native Spanish speakers, were offered Catalan immersion classes. The common roots between Catalan and Spanish, both of them Romance languages, together with the fact that most teachers were bilingual, facilitated the transition. More recently, studies have shown that some of the Spanish-speaking children from Latin America, especially those from middle- and upper-middle-class families, perform as well academically as native Catalan-speaking students even though they must learn Catalan on entering school. However, a middle-class background and knowledge of Spanish do not necessarily pave the way to social and academic integration. Ecuadorian children in Catalonia, for example, generally perform poorly in school even when their parents' educational levels are higher than the average for native-born residents in the neighborhoods where they reside (Carrasco, Bertran, and Gómez-Granell 2005). Educational difficulties have also emerged among the increasing numbers of newcomer children who have no background in Catalan, Spanish or another Romance language (Vila 2006). Special provisions, including "welcome classes," have been set up for these students to accelerate their learning of Catalan.

Although the Catalonia Department of Education does not publish ESO graduation rates disaggregated by student nationality or country of origin, we have been able to access some data comparing the ESO graduation rates for Moroccan and Latin American students attending public schools (49 percent and 52 percent respectively in 2007) with those of native students (78 percent).[6] Several other indicators shed light on achievement disparities: first, more immigrant students than native students have to repeat a grade during ESO, and more immigrant students are tracked into "adapted" classes (classes with a curriculum geared toward "lower ability" students), which effectively prevents them from continuing on to *Batxillerat*. Further, dropout rates from ESO are much lower for native students than for immigrant students (Serra and Palaudàries 2007), and a higher percentage of native students continues from ESO to postcompulsory education. For example, of the Moroccan youth who graduated from ESO in 2005, it appears from the data available that less than 25 percent continued on to any type of postcompulsory education and just 5 percent enrolled in *Batxillerat* (Carrasco, Ballestín, and Borison 2005; Pàmies 2006), compared to 60 percent of native students continuing to postcompulsory education, with 36 percent attending *Batxillerat*. Postcompulsory continuity rates for Latin American immigrants who graduated from fourth ESO were better than among Moroccans but still low, e.g., less than 50 percent among Ecuadorians (Carrasco, Ballestín, and Borison 2005). It is not yet possible to determine higher education enrollment patterns for the children of immigrants because large-scale international immigration to Catalonia is too recent. However, there are indications that the rate of university attendance is far lower among immigrant-origin students than native students.

California

With 12 percent of the US population, California is the most populous state in the nation. It is also the state with the largest immigrant population.[7] In 2008, 27 percent of Californians were foreign born, more than double the national rate of 12.5 percent (MPI 2010). Nearly half of the state's immigrants are from Mexico, with most of the rest coming from Asia and other countries of Latin America (Public Policy Institute of California 2008).

California offers free public education from kindergarten, which students begin at age five, through grade twelve, the final year of high school. Schooling is compulsory from age six until a student graduates from high school, or until age eighteen. Due in large measure to immigration, the overall number of K–12 students in California has grown dramatically over the past thirty years, to nearly seven million, 92 percent of whom attend public schools (California Department of Education/CDE 2008a, 2008b). During this same period, the ethnic makeup of California schools has shifted from 56 percent non-Hispanic white, 26 percent Latino, 10 percent African American, 7 percent Asian American, and 1 percent American Indian (1981–82) to 49 percent Latino (mostly of Mexican origin),[8] 28 percent non-Hispanic white, 11 percent Asian American, 7 percent African American, 1 percent American Indian, and 4 percent in an Other category (2007–08) (CDE 2006, 2008a).

Unlike Catalonia, California has no publicly funded system of prekindergarten or preschool for children ages three and four, and preschool fees are prohibitively expensive for many families, often costing over $1,000 a month per child. Although some subsidies are available based on family income, only one-third of the children whose families earn less than $33,000 per year attend preschool, and among low-income immigrant Latino families, the attendance rate is even lower (Children Now 2007). The lack of preschool enrollment leads to a "disparity at the starting line" for many children of immigrants (Wyner, Bridgeland, and DiIulio 2007).

Fully half of all California K–12 students today have at least one immigrant parent, more than double the national average of 22 percent, and half of these children live in low-income or economically disadvantaged households. Most also come from families where a language other than English is the primary language spoken at home. These children generally start school with limited proficiency in English. They are what Ofelia García has aptly termed "emergent bilinguals" (García, Kleifgen, and Falchi 2008), more commonly labeled English-language learners (ELLs). According to this conception and terminology, one in four California students is an ELL, the overwhelming majority (85 percent) of whom speak Spanish at home (CDE 2008c).

Test results reveal huge within-state disparities between ELLs and native English speakers, between Latinos and non-Hispanic whites ("whites" hereafter), and between students who are socioeconomically disadvantaged and those who are not. In 2006, just 27 percent of California's Latino students compared to 60 percent of its white students scored at the "proficient" or "above proficient" levels in English-language arts (CDE 2008d). The gap, although smaller, remains significant when comparing Latino and white students who are *not* socioeconomically disadvantaged. Disparities also exist in high school graduation rates, college readiness, and college attendance. Only 60 percent of Latinos receive a high school diploma after four years compared to 77 percent of white students. Of those who do graduate, only 20 percent of Latinos compared to 38 percent of whites have completed the coursework required for admission to a four-year California college or university. Latino students are particularly underrepresented at the University of California, California's flagship public university.

There are also disparities in how resources are distributed. Schools located in middle- to upper-middle-class neighborhoods tend to have more resources than schools with high concentrations of immigrant children, English learners, and children living in poverty (Oakes 2002; Rogers, Terriquez, Valladares, and Oakes 2006). At least half of all Latino children in California live in low-income households, one in three is an English learner, and one in four attends a school where at least 90 percent of the students come from an "underrepresented group" (UCLA/IDEA and UC/ACCORD 2007). Ten percent of California high schools are of this type, including Berryville High. Over half of California's Latino children attend a school where from 50 to 89 percent of the students are from underrepresented groups. Field High School is of this type. Only one in four Latino students attends a school that is majority white or white and Asian American. Our third California school, Hillside High, is characteristic of this type. While the disparities in educational opportunities and outcomes are more extreme in highly segregated, high-poverty neighborhoods and in schools with high concentrations of English learners, serious achievement gaps exist in other types of schools as well, including well-resourced suburban high schools (Ferguson 2002).

In California, the achievement gaps, or opportunity gaps, that exist are in part a product of a long history of devaluing Mexican culture, the repression of the Spanish language, and segregated schooling (San Miguel and Valencia 1998). Unfortunately, a negative and deficit view of Mexican American students' abilities has persisted to the present time. Although academic outcomes have improved significantly for children of Mexican descent, wide disparities remain. In 2008 California Superintendent of Public Instruction Jack O'Connell described the achievement gaps as "pernicious" and "pervasive" (CDE 2008e), and in 2009 he warned that "without more money California will ensure a two-tiered education for its students," with "white, Asian and wealthier students far outperforming[ing] students who are black, Hispanic and poor" (Williams 2009). California's funding for K–12 public education is well below the national average and only half that of some states. California also ranks forty-ninth of the fifty states in terms of its teacher to student ratio, currently 1 to 21 (Luckie 2009), a sharp contrast to Catalonia's teacher-student ratio of 1 to 12.

The Six High Schools

Catalonia

The Catalonia schools where we conducted our fieldwork are public high schools or institutes. All three have experienced major transformations in recent years, but there are also important social, cultural, and linguistic differences among them.

IES del Cim   Prior to 1995, IES del Cim was an institute for technical and vocational training whose students were mostly males and mostly the children of industrial workers who had migrated to Catalonia from Andalusia and other parts of Spain during the late 1960s and early 1970s. When compulsory secondary education was introduced in 1995 the institute was required by law to add ESO 1–4. With this change del Cim started to receive as many girls as boys, as well as increasing numbers of immigrant students, most of them from Morocco.

In 2004–5, del Cim had an enrollment of about 400 including 125 students attending ESO, 55 in *Batxillerat*, and 150 in *Cicles Formatius*. Del Cim presents itself as a school committed to the educational success of all its students. As set forth in its mission statement, the school seeks to respect the diversity and plurality of individuals, foster feelings of belonging to the school community, and promote a sense of solidarity and cooperation. Teachers were initially excited by the 1995 education reforms, seeing them as an opportunity to attract "good students," which they defined as those "interested in school learning." However, del Cim rapidly became pegged as a high school for immigrant and academically weak students. This was the case even though nearly 60 percent of the students in fourth ESO continued on to *Batxillerat*.

To guard against their school becoming a magnet for Moroccan youth, the staff initially refused extra resources designated for immigrant support. In the period covered by Pàmies's research on del Cim (2000–2005), tracking was implemented, initially as a temporary experiment, and Moroccan students quickly became overrepresented in the lowest tracks. At the same time, a committed head teacher instituted a community outreach effort that came to be known as *El Barri Educa* (the neighborhood educates). The welcome class teacher also worked hard to increase the participation of newcomer students in mainstream school activities.

IES del Mar   Prior to the 1995 reforms, the second school, IES del Mar, was very similar to IES del Cim in the social origins of its students, mostly working-class Spanish children whose parents had migrated to Barcelona from other parts of Spain. However, unlike del Cim, it offered only the prestigious *Batxillerat* program, and it prided itself in playing an important role for neighborhood students with aspirations to a university education and the economic mobility that would bring. After 1995, like all other high schools throughout Catalonia, del Mar was required to offer ESO 1–4, which it did in addition to *Batxillerat*. At the time of Ponferrada's research (2001–5), the large majority of del Mar's 450 students continued to be working-class Spaniards, but one-fifth of the student body was immigrant, originating from Morocco, Ecuador, China, and Bangladesh, and mostly attending ESO; only a few immigrant students were enrolled in *Batxillerat*.

Although enrollments were stable, there was among students as well as teachers a growing sense that academic standards were on the decline. Student doubts were reflected in such comments as "I don't know if we are well educated" or this is a "shitty school." Some teachers described del Mar as "the periphery of the periphery," but others viewed it as an "island" of excellence within an increasingly problematic neighborhood. Many teachers were nostalgic for the "old days" when del Mar was a top-rated selective institute, and they worried about how to prevent the school from becoming stigmatized as a "ghetto" school. Paradoxically, this concern was reflected in their continuous refusal to accept special resources earmarked for immigrant students, fearing, much like the teachers at del Cim, that this would encourage more immigrant youth to attend.

Following the practice of other Catalonia secondary schools, immigrant students assigned to del Mar's welcome classroom were referred to as *nouvingut* (the Catalan term for newly arrived). Once immigrant students transferred into regular classes they were no longer referred to in any specific way in an effort to avoid perpetuating their "foreigner" status. In spite of this official practice, Ponferrada observed that references to students' racial and/or ethnic backgrounds increased as their numbers at the school increased.

IES de la Vall   The third Catalonia school is located in a small affluent town on the outskirts of Barcelona where most of the residents are natives of Catalonia, as are most of the students who attend IES de la Vall. Schools such as this are increasingly rare in Catalonia since most middle- and upper-middle-class families transferred their children to private schools following the 1995 educational reforms, which effectively ended selective public high schools. Bucking this trend, de la Vall has succeeded in retaining students whose parents typically hold professional jobs or are academics, business owners, or artists. A growing number of immigrant working-class families have also moved into the area, most of whom work in construction or in jobs such as municipal cleaners, lawn maintenance, restaurant workers, domestic servants, and caretakers for young children and the elderly; an increasing although still-small number of their children were attending de la Vall at the time that Ríos-Rojas carried out her fieldwork there (January to December 2007).

Since 1995, IES de la Vall has had to shift from being an elite selective *Batxillerat* institute to a high school that is more comprehensive and inclusive; its 510 students are now divided between the ESO and *Batxillerat* programs. At the level of official discourse, de la Vall expects students to continue to *Batxillerat* and on to university, and the research projects of the *Batxillerat* students hang prominently in the front hallway along with posters announcing foreign exchange programs and courses offered at local universities. However, like del Cim and del Mar, along with many other Catalonia high schools, de la Vall has recently instituted curricular tracking. Immigrant youth, together with working-class Spanish youth, are overrepresented in the lowest tracks, while native Catalonian students are mostly found in the higher tracks. All students, moreover, had to contend with teacher comments about the "ideal student" of the past. "Only the best came here," one teacher commented. "Now we have kids that don't belong here, . . . that should be working," confided another.

Student demographics for the three schools are presented in Table 3.1. The "non-national" category includes the children of immigrants from both EU and non-EU countries. Some of these students were born in Spain, as the

TABLE 3.1. Student Demographics for the Three Catalonia High Schools

Year	2004–05	2004–05	2006–07
	IES del Cim	*IES del Mar*	*IES de la Vall*
Enrollment in ESO (N)	125	320	371
Nationals	59%	75%	82%
Non-nationals*	41%	25%	18%

* The non-national category includes students from EU and non-EU countries; it also includes second-generation students if they have not yet obtained Spanish nationality.

children of immigrants retain their parents' foreign nationalities until they, or their parents if they are minors, apply for Spanish citizenship. At del Cim, 30 percent of the students were "foreigners"[9] in 2001, all of them from Morocco, but by 2005 half of the foreign students were from other countries, mostly from Latin America. Likewise, at de la Vall half of the foreign students were from Latin America, with Ecuadorians representing the largest group. At del Mar the foreign students came from a wide array of Asian and Latin American countries, as well as from Morocco.

California

Like the schools in Catalonia, the three California schools have all experienced rapid demographic shifts in recent years. The California schools are much larger than their Catalonia counterparts, ranging in size from 1,400 to 2,200 students in 2007. Each offers a wide range of classes to students in grades nine through twelve, and the emphasis is on college preparation for all, a clear contrast to the schools in Catalonia. Two of the schools, Berryville High and Hillside High, are located in the same county and are part of the same school district. Field High is located in a different county and is part of a small rural school district that has only one high school.

Berryville High School   Over the past forty years, due to the rapid growth in Berryville's Latino (largely Mexican origin) population, the student body at Berryville High has shifted from 34 percent Latino to 94 percent Latino. Severe overcrowding at the high school led in recent years to a decline in academic standards, an increase in student conflicts, and a high degree of student truancy. As a result, many middle-class families, including most of the white and Asian American families, removed their children from the school. Berryville High today fits the profile of other intensely segregated schools that also serve high concentrations of low-income students, many of them English learners. A large percentage of Berryville High students are also the children of migrating agricultural workers and thus qualify for support through the federally funded Migrant Education Program.

With the opening of a third high school in the district in 2004, overcrowding was alleviated, truancy declined, and the campus grew safer. Under the leadership of a new principal, Berryville High introduced a set of academic reforms designed to raise academic standards. The school website in 2007 highlighted advanced placement, honors, and accelerated classes, and the official discourse was one of academic success and opportunity. As one teacher explained, "The school is a good school in itself," reflecting a shared belief among the staff that "opportunities are there for anyone who wants to accept them." Students in the top academic tracks do well for the most part, and many continue directly to four-year colleges. However, poor standardized test results and low graduation rates reflect the school's ongoing academic shortcomings. In 2007, only 28 percent of Berryville High students scored "proficient" in English and only 33 percent "proficient" in math, compared to the statewide average of 48 percent and 50 percent respectively.

Hillside High School   Until the opening of the third high, up to 700 students from Berryville, mostly of Mexican origin and mostly low income, were bussed ten miles to Hillside to attend Hillside High. Elsewhere we have described Hillside High as a "bimodal high school," not only because of the ethnic and economic differences that characterized the student population but also because of differences in academic preparation prior to high school, the educational performance gaps that persisted through high school, and well-defined social divisions on campus between the two major student groups (Gibson and Bejínez 2002). More than half of the white parents had four-year college degrees. In sharp contrast, most parents of Mexican origin were immigrants who had had little opportunity in Mexico to attend school beyond the primary or junior high years. At the time of Gibson's field research at Hillside High (1998–2002), the class of 2002 was almost equally divided between white students and students of Mexican descent. Half of the Mexican-descent students received free- or reduced-price meals and half were classified as English learners; two-fifths had parents who worked as agricultural laborers.

Hillside High has a reputation for its solid academic program, excellent cocurricular activities, and strong teaching staff. However, in spite of the school's notable accomplishments and its goals to "accept, value, coach and encourage diversity," academic performance patterns at the time of our research revealed disturbing and persistent gaps between the grades received by white and Mexican-descent students, and in college preparatory courses taken by each group. Just 21 percent of the Mexican-descent students who graduated from Hillside High in June 2002 had completed all the courses required for admission to one of California's public universities, compared to 68 percent of their white classmates.

Field High School   The rural community where Field High is located has experienced some out-migration in recent years among both middle- and working-class families, Mexican and Anglo alike, due to the greater availability of jobs and the lower cost of housing in a nearby inland city. The high school has also experienced a shift in its student population from 53 percent white, 40 percent Latino, 27 percent low income, and 11 percent English learner in 1998 to 31 percent white, 63 percent Latino, 42 percent low income, and 15 percent English learner in 2008. Despite these demographic changes, Field High has maintained a reputation for high academic expectations and strong academic outcomes compared to schools serving similar populations.

The school district's goal is for all students to be responsible learners, for all to finish high school, and for all to be prepared to attend college. The district views itself as innovative and as representing the rich diversity of its community. The exploration of cultural differences is a designated part of the curriculum, and the promotion of bilingualism is an explicit goal. Field High teachers commented on the "good atmosphere" at the school and the "good rapport" between teachers and students. Although some student conflicts were noted, these were, according to teachers, "far fewer than in other schools" with similar student populations. The school also prided itself for its emphasis on group work and project-based learning, and teacher discourse was generally one of academic success and opportunity. On several occasions the state has recognized Field High for its outstanding programs and the high graduation rate of its Latino students. Still, like the other two California school, test results for low-income students of Mexican-descent were disappointingly low.

Table 3.2 displays student demographics at the three California high schools for 2000–2001 and for 2006–7 in order to capture recent changes at each school.

TABLE 3.2. Student Demographics for the California High Schools

Year*	2000–01	2006–07	2000–01	2006–07	2000–01	2006–07
Enrollment	Berryville 3,216	Berryville 2,169	Field 1,453	Field 1,387	Hillside 1,978	Hillside 1,433
Latino	88%	94%	44%	57%	39%	28%
White	9%	5%	50%	35%	55%	66%
Low-income	43%	55%	31%	40%	24%	18%
English Learners	46%	37%	13%	14%	12%	6%

Language and Culture: From Differences to Hierarchies

The linguistic complexities of the California and Catalonia regions underpin the ways in which educational programs for the children of immigrants are structured, although each region takes a different approach—the former more monolingual and the latter more multilingual. In both areas, however, the emphasis placed on immigrant youth attaining a certain level of proficiency in the primary language of instruction, be it English or Catalan, before they can share classes with mainstream peers or enroll in advanced academic courses, serves as a major impediment to these students' academic and social integration. The barriers extend far beyond those related to language proficiency. Although official school discourse appears to embrace diversity and/or cosmopolitanism, the reality is that language and cultural differences are constructed as hierarchies. Certain students' languages, as are their speakers, are only reluctantly included in each school's self-portraits, instructional programs, and communication systems. As a consequence, and as we shall detail, immigrant students often ended up marginalized and silenced when speaking their home languages at school. Likewise, their less than "perfect" use of the host language became cause for ridicule.

The Treatment of Cultural Diversity: From Rhetoric to Practice

Although all six schools declared their support for cultural diversity, their actions often contradicted their espoused goals either by restricting expressions of difference or through elitist and tokenistic practices that essentialized[10] students' identities and cultures. Several examples illustrate these points. IES de la Vall portrayed itself as a school that welcomed students from other countries. As in other high schools with a predominantly native Catalan staff and student body, a particular nationalist discourse emerged that prided itself in the lack of racism and discrimination, as these were seen to be un-Catalan. Yet this discourse contradicted the everyday lived experiences of isolation and racialized discrimination among the newcomer students from non-EU countries. For example, Jie, a student who had arrived from China the previous year, was often laughed at by his Spanish classmates, and no one would sit near him in class. Teachers generally attributed the mocking to typical adolescent behavior, or they framed such incidents in individualistic and power-neutral terms. Jie was simply "too shy," a boy who had difficulty making friends. Yet students in Jie's newcomer class had a very different understanding. "He doesn't go near anyone," one classmate explained, "but then nobody goes near him unless it's to laugh at him or to imitate the way he talks!"

At IES del Cim, and in direct contrast to de la Vall, there was no website applauding the diversity of the student body. In fact, there was little mention at all of the students' national or ethnic backgrounds even though one-third of the students were of immigrant origin, mostly Moroccans. Further, although teachers accorded high value to the Moors' influence on Spanish architecture, art, and language, they shared far less favorable impressions of contemporary Moroccan culture. During the late 1990s, when only a handful of girls were enrolled at the school, little notice was given to the headscarves worn by the Moroccan girls or to these girls' dress and customs. Attitudes changed markedly, however, as the number of Moroccan students increased and after the March 2004 bombing of three Madrid train stations by terrorists, including several of Moroccan descent. Especially revealing was an episode during a computer web class where several Moroccan students tuned into a program on Al-Jazeera. The teacher, seeing this as indication of Islamic fundamentalism taking root in the school, immediately reported the boys' "suspicious" behavior to the vice-principal.

We found similar unease with Moroccan students at IES del Mar. Several teachers had organized an intercultural event, held in the welcome classroom after the official school day had ended. As is typical at such affairs, students were asked to bring "traditional" food and music and to show off "traditional" dances. Parents were invited to participate, and a few of the Moroccan mothers who attended were wearing headscarves. Assuming that headscarves indicated support for a patriarchal culture and the oppression of women, the principal and teachers decided not to hold the event again, believing it sent the "wrong" message to students.

In California, school events designed to celebrate cultural diversity and recognize Mexican holidays often ended poorly. Far from promoting cross-cultural understanding, the celebration of Mexican Independence Day (*16 de septiembre*) generated overt backlash from some of the white students at Hillside High, who ripped off the Mexican flag from cards they were given that displayed the Mexican and American flags side by side. When asked why they did this, one of the offenders replied: "Mexico sucks. It's all about the United States." *Cinco de Mayo* celebrations at Hillside High prompted similar conflicts, with some white students feeling Mexican culture was being forced on them and many Mexican students disheartened that their history and culture were being disrespected.

Field High also celebrated *Cinco de Mayo* but the activity as structured did nothing to educate the wider school community about this piece of Mexican history, and it also failed to make the recently arrived Mexican students feel included since all activities were in English and run by second-generation Mexican-origin students. The celebration was organized by the Migrant Student Association and held late in the afternoon after most nonmigrant students had left campus. While this avoided the types of tensions that had erupted at Hillside High, it also communicated a limited interest in and possibly limited acceptance of the event by the wider school population.

We observed a different and more intentional celebration of Mexican culture in the newcomers' class at Berryville High, where the teacher evoked images of a glorious Mexican past. Similar to what Spivak (1990) has referred to as a "strategic essentialism" employed by oppressed groups to navigate unequal power relations, the teacher, a Mexican American man, sought to bolster students' pride in their heritage and identity by telling them that they were "descendants of emperors." His aim was to strengthen students' pride in their Mexicanness in a school and larger societal context where this identity was denigrated. However, he did so in a way that seemed at times to neglect the fluidity and constantly expanding nature of students' hybrid identities. When a student whose given name was Francisco wrote the name Frank on one of his poems, the teacher held up the paper and asked the class: "Who is Frank?" A small and usually quiet boy slowly, and it seemed reluctantly, raised his hand. Smiling at the boy, the teacher said: "Did you write this poem? And this person who signed the name Frank, is that you? Who is this Frank? Your name is Francisco and your name will be Francisco until you die! Until the day you die you will be Francisco. You must be proud of being Francisco."

Efforts to encourage students to take pride in their Mexican identity usually took place in English Language Development (ELD) classes, the newcomers' classroom, or in activities run by the Migrant Education Program. Although images such as a glorious Aztec past were in part fiction, often idealized and representing static views of culture, our research at Hillside High suggests that this type of support helped to engage and motivate Mexican-descent students academically as well as socially, bolstering a sense of cultural pride within a larger and sometimes hostile school environment (see Gándara 1995 for a similar point). However, while intended to bolster a sense of belonging among Mexican-origin students, the images, albeit unintentionally, also contributed to a conception of Americanness that positioned these youth as "foreign" and outside the bounds of American citizenship. Moreover, the activities appeared to have little impact on the negative images that some mainstream teachers had of Mexican students, their abilities, and their possibilities. Nor did they help later-generation Mexican American students, or those from other ethnic backgrounds, get to know their Mexican-immigrant classmates or counteract the very real acts of subordination and harassment that these youth experienced in school.

At all three California high schools, immigrant Mexican students were subjected to jokes, humiliations, and even direct physical assaults by the "Americans," a group that, depending on the context, might include US-born students of Mexican descent who were also seeking to carve out their place within US cultural and ethnic hierarchies. One Field High student explained, "When you're from Mexico, you feel like you're inferior." Another student, from Hillside High, noted that "American" students "think that Mexico . . . doesn't have the value that the United States does, or [that] what Mexico does isn't the right thing."

In Catalonia, similar processes were played out through the "prescribed" national identities that newcomer students were consistently expected to perform in their classes, subjecting them to one or another of their teachers' stereotypical and narrow ideas about their home countries and cultures. At IES de la Vall, as part of a class project on agriculture, two newcomer students were asked to prepare posters dealing with agriculture in their native countries. The teacher assumed that the students came from rural areas when in fact one was from Beijing and the other from Havana, and she attributed to them an expert knowledge of rice crops and tobacco cultivation, enterprises neither student had any direct experience with. Moreover, the teacher believed that in making this assignment, she was inviting the students to work on topics that would interest them and offer them an opportunity to teach their nonimmigrant peers about their "cultures of origin." In actuality, the students were frustrated by the assignment and others like it, having repeatedly been asked to take on a confining essentialized identity that further marked their outsider status.

Unfortunately, this sort of commodification of culture, resulting from teachers' clichéd understandings of students' backgrounds solely in terms of "traditional" customs, foods, and dress, occurs too often in the very classes set up to welcome and support them. In their promotion of simplistic and oftentimes erroneous identifications, teachers inadvertently stereotyped the immigrant students' countries and in the process reinforced notions of immigrants as perpetual foreigners coming from "backwards" cultures bound by tradition. The ways in which the schools approached diversity also led some immigrant students to internalize negative perceptions of their native countries and placed unnecessary pressure on them to mold their physical and behavioral styles to those more acceptable within the ethno-racial and gendered hierarchies of their schools.

Language Ideologies, Power Relations, and Students' Rights

The manner in which languages are represented, and the place they occupy in schools, reflect existing power relations between groups and reinforce the status position of their speakers. Whether implicit or explicit, language ideologies impact students' attitudes about their own language and about learning and using new languages. Some students' home languages are only reluctantly included in instruction or other school activities, and if included it is usually for specific pragmatic purposes and without connection to a school's declared commitment to multilingualism and multiculturalism (Carrasco 2001).

In Catalonia, as earlier noted, the primary language of instruction is Catalan, in keeping with the government's official commitment to promote and protect this endangered language. Spanish language and literature are taught during two or three periods each week, these classes being structured with the assumption that students are already orally proficient in Spanish. English is also taught for three periods a week starting in the primary grades.

Students are strongly encouraged to study an additional foreign language during high school.

All three Catalonia high schools followed this official curriculum, but there were clear differences in the ways in which language hierarchies were enacted at each site. At del Cim all official school documents were written in Catalan, as was most information sent to families. This was the case even though many of the teachers spoke Spanish as their primary language, as did most of the native-born students, and Spanish was the language they used when chatting among themselves. English was viewed as the prestige international language. Arabic, on the other hand, even though it was the native language of a majority of the immigrant students, was considered completely out of place in the curriculum or in conversation.[11] During his three years of fieldwork at del Cim, Pàmies observed only one instance when a letter was sent home in Arabic. The letter, an invitation to a school event, resulted in a massive attendance by Moroccan parents. The use of Arabic in letters to Moroccan parents was never repeated, and teachers persisted in complaining about the Moroccan parents' "lack of interest" in their children's education (Carrasco, Pàmies, and Bertran 2009).

Linguistic hierarchies were in full force in other school settings at del Cim and the two other Catalonia schools. For example, a proposal to offer Arabic classes in after-school hours was roundly opposed by the del Cim faculty, who noted that it was not the school's job to promote Arabic (Pàmies 2004). "That's all we need," one teacher sarcastically commented. Others noted that students who wanted to study Arabic should take classes "at the mosque," linking the teaching of Arabic with the study of the Koran, thus rendering it an inappropriate activity for a secular public school. At del Mar, where Catalan was the native language of most of the teachers and the language they used among themselves, English and French were viewed as having academic value, but not Spanish. This was the case even though the large majority of students were themselves native Spanish speakers, either the children of migrants from other parts of Spain or immigrants from Latin America. Rather than embracing and promoting proficiency in Spanish as well as Catalan, the teachers reacted as though Spanish were a threat (Ponferrada 2008).

At IES de la Vall the use of multiple languages was officially embraced, including the use of Spanish. However, none of the languages of the non-EU immigrant students was given any academic position at the school, and students were judged on the basis of their academic and social proficiency in

Catalan, the latter being the most important. Yet social acceptance rested on more than mastery and use of Catalan. Students from Chile and Argentina were viewed as different from other immigrant youth, "more European" and "more like us" according to one teacher, who also noted that "they tend to learn more quickly, and with Catalan they pick it up almost immediately!" Her implicit assumption was that those who were "more European" were also those who "learn more quickly." Ecuadorian and Bolivian students were not included in the "more-like-us" category.

We also observed a clear difference between the treatment and status of international exchange students and newly arrived, or even not-so-newly arrived, immigrant students. At de la Vall an exchange student from the United States was praised for her command of English, her efforts to learn Catalan, and the wealth of knowledge she could share with her peers. Yet a student from Morocco, who spoke some French as her second or third language after Arabic and Berber and before Catalan and Spanish, was told that it would be too difficult for her to take French as her elective. At Field High in California we observed a similar differentiation between exchange students and immigrant students. Like all students for whom English was not the home language, the foreign exchange students were tested for their proficiency in English. However, rather than placing the exchange students whose English proficiency was judged "limited" into ELD or sheltered English classes, they were placed directly into regular classes. "Their parents are not paying a lot of money to see their children placed in sheltered English classes with the Mexicans," one teacher explained. Seemingly, what was viewed as best for the children of Mexican families, mostly from working-class backgrounds, was not considered best for middle-class exchange students from Spain and other European countries.

In all six schools the treatment and use of Spanish clearly reflected the enactment of social hierarchies having to do with the status of those for whom Spanish was the home language. In spite of the very large proportion of native Spanish speakers at each of the California high schools, almost all communication (written and oral) was in English. It was, in fact, one of the major contradictions of the three California schools that opportunities to promote Spanish/English bilingualism were consistently overlooked. This was the case at Field High even though the promotion of bilingualism was an official school district goal. At Berryville High, even though the large majority of students were native Spanish speakers, there was almost no recognition of these students' bilingualism or any serious efforts to promote the maintenance of Spanish. The information given to students was almost exclusively in English. The use of Spanish was restricted to Spanish language classes, the newcomer class, the Migrant Education Office, and to documents that non-English-speaking parents needed to comprehend. This led to a dual paradox. On the one hand, newcomer students were excluded from knowing what was going on in the school because the information was only available in English, and, on the other, they were subjected to an accelerated unlearning of their mother tongue through sometimes quite incomprehensible translations of English texts into Spanish.

Contradictions between Discourse and Practice: The Students' Experiences

In exploring how the contradictions between discourse and practice play out in the lives of immigrant youth, we focus in particular on students who were recently arrived or were still mastering the language of instruction, be it English or Catalan. We also center attention on the special classes and instructional programs provided to newcomers and second-language-learners and to the contradictions and shortcomings of these programs. A primary interest is how the schools' policies, programs, and practices were at different moments and in different spaces both welcoming and unwelcoming, leading students either to a sense of belonging and school engagement or to feelings of nonbelonging, disengagement, and even withdrawal.

Classes for Newcomers and Second Language Learners (SLLs)

California's Department of Education states two basic goals for English learners: first, that they acquire proficiency in English as rapidly and effectively as possible, and second, that they meet state standards for academic achievement. In their efforts to meet these goals, California high schools typically provide some extra support for ELLs until they have attained the level of English proficiency considered necessary for success in regular classes with classmates who are fluent in English. This support generally includes a combination of ELD, sheltered English, and in some cases instruction offered in the student's home language.

ELD classes seek to provide English-language learners with the competencies in English that native speakers already possess. Students with the lowest levels of English proficiency generally receive two periods of ELD instruction daily. More advanced students have one period. Sheltered English is a special methodology designed to make academic instruction in the various subject areas (e.g., math, science, history) understandable and accessible to English learners. Instruction is entirely or largely in English and the goal is for ELLs to develop their subject matter knowledge in addition to furthering their skills in English. Students are "sheltered" in the sense that they do not compete academically with native English speakers since classes include only ELLs.

All three schools also offered subject matter classes in Spanish to ELLs while they were learning English. Such classes have been greatly restricted in California schools since the 1998 passage of Proposition 227, or the English Language in Public Schools initiative. This initiative, which required that all public school instruction be conducted in English (except in those circumstances where parents have signed waivers requesting an alternate instructional technique), had limited impact on the classes offered at the three high schools in our study because none of these schools had robust bilingual education programs prior to 1998. Yet beyond actual curricular offerings, Prop. 227 clearly has had a chilling effect on the promotion of bilingualism and on the use of Spanish in school, including in the three schools studied. This proposition, and the wide support it garnered, reflected a nativist uneasiness toward the rise of the immigrant population in California, Mexicans in particular, and their presumed threat to "American" culture and identity. As Galindo and Vigil (2006) have noted, language discrimination, such as that reflected in Prop. 227, can serve as an acceptable method of discrimination against a particular group without resorting to race.

In addition to ELD, sheltered English, and the subject matter classes in Spanish offered to the ELLs, Field High and Berryville High also offered newcomer classes whose chief aim was to help newly arrived students settle in socially as well as academically. Students placed in a newcomers class were frequently behind age mates academically, or perceived to be so, due to limited or interrupted schooling prior to immigrating to the United States. It merits noting that not all ELLs are newcomers or even recently arrived. At Hillside High, for example, 35 percent of the students assigned to ELD classes had been in the United States for six or more years. These "long-term ELLs" could speak English, often quite well, but they had not passed the tests that demonstrated their academic English skills. Since the ELD classes were not geared to these students' needs, many, the boys in particular, responded by misbehaving in class or losing interest in school.

Apart from the long-term ELLs, most of the students felt comfortable and welcome in both the ELD and newcomers classes. We observed students rehearsing songs for an upcoming festival, debating who would get which role in a play, and joking with one another about the latest games in the Mexican soccer league. We also saw students from previous years returning to these classrooms during their breaks to socialize with friends. Moreover, as one teacher explained, "The children look for protection in my classroom at lunch time." It was, he said, because "They don't feel connected. They are looking for a refuge. They don't feel part of the system." Other teachers shared that they kept their classroom doors open during breaks so that immigrant youth would have safe places to gather. Echoing teacher comments, immigrant students themselves described the ELD and newcomer classrooms as the places on campus where they felt comfortable and "safe."

Teachers at the California schools frequently brought up the subject of gangs, and there seemed to be general agreement that newcomer students needed protection from gang members. Gang labels, moreover, were commonly tossed about by students and teachers alike, although in reality most gang members no longer attend school during their teen years (Vigil 2004). Still, many Mexican-origin students, including students in the schools studied, identify with and even loosely affiliate with either a *Norteño* or *Sureño* identity, gang "wannabes" "who participate in the symbolic display of gang culture (e.g., by writing gang slogans or graffiti on their school notebooks, or by wearing baggy clothes) but who, for the most part, have little to do with any committed aspects of gang affiliation" (Mendoza-Denton 2008, 57).

In Catalonia, high schools serving newly arrived immigrant students, including all three schools in our study, have instituted welcome classes for students who speak neither Catalan nor Spanish. These classes focus, in theory at least, on the intensive teaching of Catalan, instruction in core academic subjects, and enrichment activities. For a portion of each day, welcome-class students also join mainstream classes for subjects such as art and physical education (PE) that do not require strong Catalan proficiency. After attending a full year in the welcome class, students are moved into regular classes, but their placement is often in an "adapted class" or another lower-track section of their grade. Welcome classes, thus, frequently became the first rung of a tracked system, rendering it almost impossible for recently arrived high school–aged immigrant students ever to be prepared for *Batxillerat* when they graduate from ESO.

Immigrant students from Morocco also face the additional challenge of mastering a new system of writing, if they have not taken French in their previous schooling, since the direction and logic of written Arabic is completely different from Catalan. There were other hurdles for Catalan learners, particularly for those who didn't already speak Spanish. Even though Catalan was officially the language of oral instruction and of textbooks, some teachers spoke to the immigrant students in Spanish in the belief that this was helpful. Paradoxically, this tended to make learning more difficult. As one Moroccan student explained, "In the morning we are in the welcome class learning Catalan and everything is in Catalan, and in the afternoon the teachers talk to me in Spanish." Another student described how learning Catalan was hard "because the teacher explains it in Spanish and the book is in Catalan."

Segregated and Shortchanged

Beyond matters of curriculum and instruction, a further rationale given by teachers in both countries for placing newcomers and second language learners into separate classes was the fact that students in regular classes were often impatient with classmates who didn't speak English or Catalan/Spanish well and who needed "extra" help from the teacher. Mainstream teachers themselves often also had misgivings about having second-language learners in their classes if they couldn't keep up academically without special assistance. As a result, recently arrived immigrant students usually remained in segregated classes for some or even most of the day, separated from and it seems "protected" from fluent speakers of English or Catalan/Spanish.

While newcomers appreciated the extra support, at least initially, it was also clear that many students believed that they learned little in these classes after the initial settling-in period. In general, they viewed the classes as less rigorous and often less interesting than mainstream classes. One California student referred to his sheltered English classes as the "low expectations" classes. Students in ELD classes reported similar feelings, noting "We never do anything," or "We always do the same thing—watch movies," or "The teacher learns more Spanish than we learn English."

There were exceptions, of course, and students readily admitted that much depended on the teacher. When teachers had strong preparation in second-language acquisition, students responded positively and learned a lot. English-language learners in California shared with us that they also liked having teachers who could speak Spanish and could explain course material to them in Spanish if they were having trouble grasping the ideas in English. In general, however, students in the ELD classes had little opportunity to engage in project work either on their own or with others, and ELD teachers tended to overemphasize the use of worksheets with a focus on the repetitive drill of grammar and vocabulary, sometimes in combination with infantilizing activities such as coloring and cutting up pictures. In many cases, the academic behaviors expected in these classes contrasted notably with those valued in high-track mainstream classes, where active participation was expected and student opinions were regularly elicited on a wide variety of topics including those requiring a high degree of abstraction. Moreover, except for some of the long-term ELL boys in California, who were quick to crack jokes in English, usually at the expense of the teacher or some classmate, students actually spoke very little English in their ELD classes. Nor did they practice English outside of class either with their ELL friends or with their more English-proficient peers. In fact, at all three California schools we found that the ELLs almost never engaged socially in English with other students. Even in integrated classes, like PE, or in school-wide activities, they stuck to themselves, usually off to the side.

By contrast, we saw a stronger pedagogy within the welcome class at IES de la Vall than in many of the mainstream classes there, including one-on-one attention and help with understanding what was going on in the mainstream classes they attended. The teacher-learner relationship was also less authoritative and more cooperative in de la Vall's welcome classroom, and it was a space where we saw second-language learners having ample opportunities for input and sharing. However, in all the Catalonia schools, we also observed contradictions and dilemmas between the desire to support and protect newcomers and the actuality of segregating them in separate classrooms. There was a strong feeling expressed by teachers at each school that newcomers were the responsibility of the welcome-class teacher rather than students who needed to be integrated into the larger school community. Even the physical placement of the welcome classroom contributed to the segregation. Del Cim teachers resisted having the welcome classroom near the entrance to the school, fearing that highly visible "non-prestigious" students would undermine school prestige. Similarly at del Mar, when teachers finally agreed to having a welcome class, they placed it far from the center, arguing that this location would "protect" newcomers from the youthful outbursts of energy of the rest of the students, which they expected the newcomers would find "intimidating."

This segregated approach to teaching newcomers meant that the newcomers had little opportunity to practice Catalan with native speakers. Nor was the oral practice of Catalan emphasized by the welcome-class teachers at del Mar and del Cim (de la Vall was the exception) even though acquiring proficiency in Catalan was a primary rationale for instituting these classes. Moreover, on those few occasions when a welcome-class teacher arranged for the newcomer students to present their work to their native-born classmates, the result was sometimes contradictory to what was intended. Efforts were largely tokenistic and in reality did little to bring immigrant students into the mainstream of school life.

The language programs for second-language learners at all six schools fell short in many of the same ways that have been described in the literature on second-language learning in the United States (Gándara and Rumberger 2006; García, Kleifgen, and Falchi 2008; Hurd 2004; Valdés 1998) and in Spain (Martín Rojo 2003; Nussbaum and Unamuno 2006; Vila 2006). Curriculum materials tended to be unchallenging and boring in their construction, disconnected from students' lives, and instruction generally failed to build on what students already knew. In California, the ELD classes were frequently too large for effective second-language instruction and often included students at very different levels of English proficiency. Classes taught in Spanish also suffered from inadequate curriculum materials and from teachers who, although bilingual in English and Spanish, often lacked subject-matter training in Spanish (Valdés 2004). This meant that they were expected to teach history or biology in Spanish but they had only studied their discipline in English. It was paradoxical, as well as contradictory to instructional aims, that the students in the Spanish-language subject-matter classes often had trouble understanding the lessons due to the poor translation of curriculum materials into Spanish or the teachers' lack of specialized vocabulary in Spanish. Likewise, teachers in the ELD and welcome classes, although generally very dedicated to their second-language-learner students, in the main lacked adequate preparation in second-language acquisition. Moreover, some (not all) unwittingly conveyed to their students a message of low academic expectations. Furthermore, and quite ironically, these special classes provided too little opportunity for students to practice oral English or oral Catalan. Because the second-language learners were segregated for much of the school day and often marginalized when in classes with mainstream students, they also had little opportunity to learn the new language from fluent English or Catalan speakers apart from their teachers.

Outside of class, Latin American students in Catalonia tended to stick with Spanish unless they had arrived during primary school and had been included in Catalan-speaking friendship groups. However, at de la Vall—the only school in our study with large numbers of native Catalan speakers—such friendships were rare, due at least partially to the tracked nature of the classes. The Ecuadorian students, for example, were generally assigned to the adapted classes, which were largely taught in Spanish rather than Catalan, and thus they were more resistant to speaking Catalan outside of class and less likely to form friendships with their native Catalan peers. At del Cim we observed some Moroccan students speaking to one another in Arabic in order to assert their identity in the face of assimilationist pressures, but more typically these same students would speak to one another in Spanish (but not Catalan) when no teachers or native students were around and thus when they felt no need to make a public statement by using Arabic.

In California, ELLs shared with us that they were embarrassed to speak English because other students made fun of them when they made errors. The put-downs were sometimes made by US-born Mexican-descent peers who generally spoke only in English. As one newcomer student explained, "They don't speak Spanish because they are ashamed of Spanish." Some of these students had never learned Spanish at home; others had stopped using it due to assimilationist pressures and anti-Spanish attitudes not only at school but in the larger US society. Some, whose Spanish was less than perfect, were embarrassed to speak it in front of fellow Mexican-origin schoolmates whose Spanish was strong. At all three schools there was a clear language hierarchy in which English dominated. Although the value of bilingualism was often touted, the actions of each of the schools sent quite the opposite message. It is not surprising, therefore, that some Mexican American students who spoke Spanish, some even very well, refrained from speaking it at school and even pretended not to understand it.

Although attitudes about bilingualism are far different in Catalonia, the experiences of immigrant students when they moved outside the safety of their protected classes were remarkably similar. When newcomer students joined regular classes, they usually sat in the back, out of sight of the other students. This was the case at IES del Cim when students from the welcome class joined the mainstream classes for an hour or two each day. Moreover, while newcomer students initially worked hard in the mainstream classes, their attitude and participation levels shifted when teachers failed to integrate them into the larger class, overlooked their questions, and continued to give them the same type of dull work sheets week after week, as was too often the case.

The staff at each of the Catalonia schools recognized that the needs of newcomer students were not being met but there seemed no adequate resolution. Moreover, the efforts that were made appeared only to reinforce in everyone's mind, including the newcomers themselves, that they were "less able." Simply placing newcomers into regular classes did little to overcome their social isolation. Neither did it give them a real chance to engage in mainstream class activities, however peripherally. Too often the immigrant students, including some who had been in Spain for many years, had to cope not only with their marginalization in mainstream classes but also with harassment by some of their native peers. At del Mar, we observed a Spanish student come up to two Moroccan girls, Halima and Mouna, and shout: "Let's see your papers," imitating a policeman asking a foreigner for documents. Then, as if this were not intimidating enough, he hit the nearby table with an imaginary truncheon like those carried by the police. The Moroccan girls looked downwards while he spoke, waiting for him to go away. He repeated his command several times until the researcher intervened. Later, with tears in their eyes, the two confided, "It has happened many times." They hadn't said anything, they explained, not wanting to be viewed as snitches.

Discussion and Implications

In spite of their different immigration histories and systems of education, we have found many similarities between Catalonia and California in terms of the schools' treatment of immigrant-origin youth and in terms of these youths' school participation patterns, academic achievement during high school, and preparation to continue on to higher education. Both systems have laudable goals with respect to meeting the needs of the children of immigrants, but both are falling short. Although there is official rhetoric of integration, cosmopolitanism, multiculturalism, and equality of educational opportunities, immigrant youth in the end are being shortchanged. In both countries and across the different types of high schools we found systematic contradictions between discourse and practice. The systems operate in ways that seek to welcome and include but paradoxically end up with school structures and practices that are unwelcoming and exclusive and that serve to marginalize and segregate immigrant youth.

The major questions then become: Why do these patterns exist? Why are they so similar in spite of the many differences between the two countries? And what might we propose based on our findings in terms of how the two educational systems can do a better job of meeting the needs of immigrant youth? We have suggested that the patterns that get played out within the schools relate to the existence of historically entrenched linguistic and cultural hierarchies that perpetuate the privileged status of the native students and contribute to the subordination and "othering" of the immigrant youth. These hierarchies also contribute to the teachers' inability to recognize and build on the social and linguistic capital that immigrant-origin students bring with them, which in turn contributes to teachers' low expectations for these youth and the denigration of their languages and cultures.

In many cases, perhaps most, the teachers and the native students are unaware of the impact these hierarchies have on the daily lives and opportunities afforded to immigrant youth. They do not see how rigid and politicized the boundaries are. Nor do they see, on the one hand, the ways that they pressure immigrant youth to assimilate and, on the other, how they contribute to the essentializing of their supposed differences. What the educational systems do quite effectively is to maintain the privileged position of the native students and the ascendancy of their languages and cultures. In this way the educational systems in both countries serve to reproduce ethnic, racial, and class hierarchies.

All too often immigrant students' home languages and ways of knowing are defined as deficits or problems, something to be remedied rather than rewarded or treated as the assets that they are. Thus, when immigrant youth perform poorly in school, their difficulties are seen as intrinsic to them or their families or their neighborhoods rather than recognized as related to shortcomings within school structures and policies. Recently arrived immigrant youth are placed in special classes intended to speed their social and academic integration, but in the process they end up segregated and isolated for much of the day with unchallenging classes and little opportunity to mix with native students or to use the new language that they know they have to learn.

Outside of class the immigrant youth also end up spatially separated, most commonly residing on the periphery of school life physically as well as socially. Once they move out of special classes for newcomers and second-language learners, they often find themselves placed into the lowest academic tracks with little opportunity to meet college-entrance requirements. Even when they are placed in higher-track college-preparatory classes, they often feel unsupported, marginalized, and silenced, their knowledge and talents unacknowledged. Although extracurricular activities appear to be arenas that promote participation and belonging for all students, these activities rarely are organized in ways that encourage immigrant students' participation as full and equal members of the school community.

It need not be this way. Teachers and other staff members should be provided with the kinds of professional preparation, preservice and in-service, that will enable them to understand, reflect upon, and find ways to dismantle the cultural, social, and linguistic hierarchies that operate within their schools. As noted at the outset, linguistic and cultural differences provide opportunities for conflict, but they also provide opportunities for students to learn from one another and to acquire the skills that will be needed to operate successfully in an increasingly globalized world (Gibson and Ríos-Rojas 2006). Teachers, as well as students, need to move beyond frameworks that construct immigration as a problem and that insist upon "repairing" immigrant students' alleged deficits. An important step in moving forward rests in the ability to shift the focus from immigrant children's supposed "deficiencies" to their "funds of knowledge" (Moll, Amanti, Neff, and Gonzalez 1992) and to recognize the value of "additive" forms of acculturation (Gibson 1988, 1995) as an alternative to rigid and oftentimes coercive assimilationist practices that serve to exclude rather than include.

As noted by Fine and colleagues, young people, perhaps immigrant youth in particular, need spaces where both old and new identities can be "tried on, played with, and tossed off" (Fine, Weis, and Powell 1997, 253) and where questions of difference are engaged explicitly and within a historical framework of power. They need such spaces both as physical sites and as sets of relationships that serve to nurture their evolving identities and provide access to the kinds of institutional support required for school success. More than at any other time in history, schools need to prepare children for a globalized world. To do this, teachers need not only to view multicultural competencies as an asset but also to support their development among students, native and immigrant alike. However, in seeking to do this, educators must attend carefully to how schools themselves through their unequal relations of power and their reproduction of linguistic and cultural hierarchies provide differential access to the cultural knowledge and competencies that are valued and rewarded within schools (see Goodenough 1976).

Notes

We are deeply grateful to the students, parents, educators, and community members who participated in this study. We wish also to extend our gratitude to the agencies that helped to fund the research, including the US National Science Foundation's Partnerships for International Research and Education (Award #OISE-0529921), the Nuffield Foundation, the Spencer Foundation (#199900129), the US Department of Education/OERI (#R305T990174), and the Spanish Ministry of Science and Innovation I+D Project SEJ-2005–09333.

1. The authors recognize that categories such as "native" and "immigrant" are contestable and imbued in each country with particular social and political meanings. In the Spanish context, by "native" we are referring here to Spaniards of Spanish origin. The terms immigrant, immigrant origin, and children of immigrants are used interchangeably throughout the chapter. As used most commonly in Spain, these terms refer to children whose parents have immigrated to Spain from the developing countries of the world. In the US context, we focus on the children of immigrants from Mexico, both US and foreign born.

2. In the aftermath of the 9/11 and 3/04 attacks in New York and Madrid, respectively, negative portrayals of the Muslim and Moroccan community in Spain have been all the more palpable in both popular and political discourses (European Monitoring Centre on Racism and Xenophobia 2006).

3. Terms related to schooling in Catalonia are written in Catalan.

4. Altogether, five million of the eight million inhabitants of the Autonomous Community of Catalonia reside in the city of Barcelona or the greater metropolitan area.

5. Romanians were the largest non-EU immigrant group until they joined the European Union in 2008.

6. Graduation rates for immigrant-origin students disaggregated by ethnicity and/or national origin were not available for individual schools. However, in the three Catalonia high schools where we conducted our field research, we observed that fewer Moroccan and Latin American students graduated from ESO than native Spanish

students. Based on data we gathered, graduation rates for native students were 60 percent at IES del Cim, 68 percent at IES del Mar, and 88 percent at IES de la Vall.

7. As used here, the category "immigrant" refers to all persons resident in California who are foreign born, including those who have become naturalized citizens.

8. In California, state and school statistics include students of Mexican origin within the broader category of "Latino," i.e., of Latin American origin, the overwhelming majority of whom are children of Mexican descent.

9. As used in Catalonia and in the rest of Spain, the category "foreigners" (or "foreign students") includes second-generation students if they have not yet obtained Spanish nationality. In actuality, most of the students in our study were first generation (i.e., foreign born).

10. Reducing a culture, people, or group to what are presumed to be its essential characteristics, and in so doing creating caricatures that deny the agency, fluidity, and diversity of group members (e.g., this is how women are, or Spaniards, or baseball players, or hockey fans).

11. The Moroccan community in the neighborhood surrounding IES del Cim is predominantly Arabic speaking, although in Catalonia as a whole 60 percent of Moroccan residents are Amazigh or Berbers, the indigenous non-Arab population of North Africa. Most of them speak Tamazight, the main Berber language.

CHAPTER FOUR

Second-Generation Attainment and Inequality: Primary and Secondary Effects on Educational Outcomes in Britain and the United States

Mary C. Waters, Anthony Heath, Van C. Tran, and Vikki Boliver

The children of immigrants whose parents have low levels of education face a daunting task. In a time of growing inequality, postsecondary education holds the key not only to a better job, but to a host of other desirable outcomes, including better health, a more stable family life, and better overall happiness (Hout 2012). Yet children whose parents do not have a postsecondary education are at a disadvantage in accessing higher education. An immigrant background adds a host of other impediments, including the learning of a new language, the possibility that some students began their educations in a different educational system, as well as the possibility of ethnic and racial discrimination in local schools and neighborhoods. To what extent are children of immigrants able to overcome these barriers and achieve a postsecondary education? To what extent does their academic ability get recognized by different educational systems? Do children of immigrants make the transition to higher education at lower or higher levels than children of natives? And if we can control for prior academic achievement, are we able to find evidence of a second-generation penalty or advantage over the natives?

In this chapter we examine these questions by assessing the educational careers of young people in the United States and England at four points—performance scores at age sixteen, completion of secondary education, completion of tertiary education, and the type of university attended among those who go to university. Using these four data points we can compare the fortunes of the children of immigrants in both countries on two theoretically important but different aspects of schooling—the primary and secondary effects of social background on educational attainment. *The primary effects* of social background are usually conceptualized to include the effects of the home environment, particularly parental help and encouragement, that contribute to success on attainment tests during the period of compulsory schooling. So our first question will be whether there are differences between immigrant and native children in test scores at ages of fifteen and sixteen, and whether those differences persist when we control for parental education.

The secondary effects of social background on attainment are those that determine whether, among children of equal attainment, some are able to continue or not. Here it has been customary to think of the decisions that young people and their families make. The key decision in both Britain and the United States, in both of which schooling is compulsory until age sixteen, is whether to drop out or to continue at that point. A second key decision is whether to attend university or some other postsecondary school. A third decision is which university or college to attend. In both England and the United States, students have many universities to choose from and these vary a great deal by selectivity and social prestige. When we examine these secondary effects, we will ask whether children of immigrants compared to children of natives *who share the same educational achievement as measured by test scores* vary in the decisions they make at these crucial points in their educational careers. We do this in each country by comparing the children of immigrants to the third- and later-generation children of native whites, while controlling for social class of parents.

The theory of effectively maintained inequality (described in the introduction to this volume) posits that as more young people attend university, the variation in outcomes among students will shift toward *qualitative* distinctions among the types of universities attended and away from merely the *quantitative* amount of education each student achieves. Using novel sources of data from both the United States and Britain, we are able to examine this question. We analyze below whether the ethnic origins of children of immigrants and natives affect the prestige of the university they attend.

We use panel data in the United Kingdom and longitudinal data in the United States that allow us to examine these outcomes while controlling for the social class and migration background of parents. These data sources are the Youth Cohort Survey in Britain and the National Longitudinal Study of Adolescent Health (Add Health) in the United States. At the tertiary level we use data from the Immigrant Second Generation in Metropolitan New York study, which gathered detailed data on the quality of the universities attended by the second generation and the Universities and Colleges Admissions Service data in the United Kingdom that provides data on ethnicity, generation, and selectivity of college and university attended.

Our findings on the primary effects of ethnic background on education show strong and similar effects in both countries. The children of low-skilled labor migrants from the black Caribbean, Pakistan, Bangladesh and Africa in the United Kingdom and the children of Mexicans, West Indians, and Puerto Ricans in the United States perform significantly lower than third- or later-generation native whites. Higher-status immigrant groups such as Filipinos in the United States and Asian Indians in Britain score better than native whites. In the United States, the native minority groups of African Americans and Puerto Ricans score significantly lower than native whites. In both countries, Chinese youth show very high performance scores, despite the fact that many of them have parents with very low levels of education. These ethnic differences persist even after controlling for social class. These findings on the primary effects of ethnicity are similar to the findings of other scholars working on these issues in both countries. They also echo the conclusions of scholars investigating social-class effects on educational outcomes who find that parental educational attainment has a strong effect on test scores at age sixteen.

Our findings on the secondary effects of ethnic background on educational outcomes are more complex and novel, and depart from the established findings in the social-class literature. In Britain, while the children of labor migrants such as black Caribbeans and Pakistanis are less likely to complete secondary education than native whites, Bangladeshis have caught up with the British majority group. In the United States, African Americans and second-generation Mexicans are much less likely than native whites to complete secondary school but the children of black immigrants have almost caught up with the majority group. When we control for performance scores at age sixteen and ask whether young people with the same scores are more or less likely to finish secondary school, we find that in both countries the ethnic coefficients are positive. Comparing majority and minority students with similar performance scores, the ethnic minorities are at least *as* likely as or *more* likely to finish secondary school than native whites.

At the level of tertiary education we find strong differences between the United States and Britain. In Britain, the ethnic minority groups are considerably more likely to complete university education than native whites with similar GCSE (General Certificate of Secondary Education) scores. Yet in the United States, African Americans, Puerto Ricans, and second-generation Mexicans are *much less* likely to complete university than native whites with similar test scores. This difference is all the more remarkable since many American colleges and universities practice some form of affirmative action in admissions to create more racially and ethnically diverse student bodies than would happen based on grades and test scores alone, while British universities have no such programs.

Finally, we find that in both Britain and the United States there is a relatively unrecognized source of inequality—the sorting of different ethnic groups into institutions of differing status and quality. In both countries we find that native whites are much more likely to attend the most selective and highest-status universities and the children of low-status immigrants are concentrated in less selective and less prestigious institutions. This finding is consistent with predictions of effectively maintained inequality and is a prime example of the "reactivity" of educational systems evident in all of the countries studied in this volume and highlighted in the conclusion to the volume (Lucas 2001; Raferty and Hout 1993; Alba and Holdaway, this volume).

In the pages that follow we first describe the major immigrant groups and their histories in Britain, as well as the British educational system. We then present our substantive findings on ethnic differences in attainment scores at age sixteen, completion of secondary education, completion of college or university education, and attendance at institutions of lesser or higher prestige and selectivity. We conclude the chapter with a discussion of some of the more surprising patterns in the data—the better outcomes for the children of low-skilled immigrants in terms of university attendance in Britain as opposed to the United States, and the previously unexamined inequality in the type of university attended by different ethnic groups in both countries.

Comparing the United States and the United Kingdom

The United States and the United Kingdom are more similar to one another than to other Western European countries on a number of dimensions important to understanding the pattern of immigrant integration. (See for example Heath and Cheung 2007 for detailed comparisons of the labour-market situations of migrants and their children in these two countries with a range of other European countries.) Britain and the United States have similar citizenship regimes (civic, not ethnic), similar welfare states and social benefits (especially when compared with more generous European welfare systems), similarly flexible educational systems that provide more opportunities for second chances and less early tracking into vocational education (especially when compared with other West European nations such as Germany and France), some overlaps in the national origins of immigrants (including sizable numbers of Caribbean blacks, Indians, and Chinese), and similar attention to race as an important source of division in society.

It is perhaps this attention to race and the definition of groups as ethnic and racial minorities in both the United States and Britain that most differentiates them from other Western European countries coping with integration of immigrants and their descendants. The United States has classified post-1965 immigrants in racial terms, based on a system of classification and social identification that arose out of internal population dynamics owing to a long history of slavery and to the conquest of American Indians and Hispanics in the Southwest and Puerto Rico (Waters 2008). When Asians started to arrive as immigrants in the late nineteenth century, they were racially classified by the federal government and a racial exclusion of them was ultimately enshrined in American immigration law until the 1950s. In an ironic turn of events, the classification of the population by race, developed in order to discriminate and exclude, was officially enshrined in our federal statistical system after the civil rights movement resulted in legislation designed to prevent and prosecute discrimination, and is now most vigorously defended by racial minorities themselves.

This attention to race and the development of antidiscrimination legislation was also incorporated into British society. Modeled after the US race and civil rights laws, Britain has developed a policy based on multiculturalism and antiracism to integrate immigrants and their descendants. Thus, while Britain and the United States often perceive their "immigration" integration issues as race-relations issues, this is very different from other Western European countries. For example, France explicitly forbids collecting data on race and in Germany the sharp divisions that surround immigration are about birthplace, citizenship, and ethnic belonging rather than skin color.

Yet this common language of race as an organizing principle of social distinction in Britain and the United States can obscure some real differences between them in the meaning of "race," the social construction of ethnicity, and the drawing of group boundaries. One possible difference has to do with what W. E. B. DuBois (1903) famously called the "color line." In the United States there is a vigorous debate occurring about where to locate this fundamental cleavage (Foner and Fredrickson 2004; Gans 1999). This debate centers on whether American society divides whites from nonwhites or blacks from nonblacks. The question, in other words, is whether Asians and Latinos are being incorporated onto the "white" or the "black" side of "the color line." Before the civil rights movement and mass immigration from Asia, Latin America and the Caribbean, the position of Latinos and Asians was closer in many ways, even legally, to African Americans, than to whites. Recently, many scholars have argued that the high rates of intermarriage and residential integration of Asians and light-skinned Latinos have meant that the serious ramifications of race for life chances in the United States are concentrated among those socially identified as blacks, not as nonwhites, in general (Bean and Stevens 2003; Kasinitz 2004; Waters 2008).

In the United Kingdom, the key distinction can be more clearly drawn between white British and nonwhites. Patterns of acceptance and social identification continue to posit a common "minority" experience, encapsulated in the term BME, or blacks and minority ethnics. In addition, blacks are not uniformly more separate from whites than Asians are in Britain. Indeed, on certain key indicators including intermarriage and residential integration, black Caribbeans and black Africans are more integrated with whites than are Pakistanis and Bangladeshis.

The countries also have other important differences—a much longer and more prominent historical role for immigration in the American case, the presence of a large population of native African Americans in the United States, the much greater role of Muslim immigrants in Britain, the significance of European Union membership for the British case, and the role of the long land border with Mexico and the predominance of Latino immigrants in American immigration flows. Indeed, the most pressing and complex immigration issue facing the United States today is the presence of eleven million undocumented immigrants, approximately seven million of whom are Mexicans (Passel 2006). While Britain also has an undocumented population, it is much smaller, both relatively and absolutely. In 2005 the Home Office estimated the number of undocumented immigrants in Britain at somewhere between 310,000 and 570,000 (Casciani 2006). While the United States has been a magnet for immigrants from many different countries, Britain drew most of its immigrants in the latter half of the twentieth century from former colonies. This colonial legacy was quite important in shaping expectations among immigrants of full inclusion in the society and in shaping the immigration laws and bureaucratic directives that allowed people into the country. In recent years Britain has begun receiving immigrants from Eastern Europe, especially Poland, and asylum seekers who may not come from former colonies, perhaps leading to different kinds of accommodation among immigrants in the future (Vertovec 2007).

Immigration to Britain

The United Kingdom of Great Britain and Northern Ireland is a relatively new state, dating only to the 1922 partition of Ireland. The United Kingdom is a multiethnic state composed of the English, Scottish, Welsh, and the Northern Irish. When the Irish Free State was formed, citizens of the Republic of Ireland were given free entry into the United Kingdom. Migration between the two states has been large and the Irish have become Britain's longest-established minority.

Modern migration to Britain is often dated to the arrival of one ship from the Caribbean, the Windrush, in 1948. The people who debarked were not framed as "immigrants" because as subjects of the British Empire they already possessed citizenship and the right to move to Britain. The 1948 British Nationality Act gave an unrestricted right of entry to the 800 million people who were citizens of the colonies or Commonwealth. The first group to take advantage of this were the Caribbeans. There was active recruitment by the British Government of nurses to work in the National Health System and of less skilled workers to work in the London Underground. Until recently, the source countries of most international migrants to Britain were former colonies—in the Caribbean, South Asia, and Africa.

Afro-Caribbeans faced widespread discrimination in all walks of life. There were race riots in Notting Hill in London in 1958 and a number of subsequent incidents involving police harassment of young black men. Anti-discrimination legislation was passed in 1965 and extended to employment in 1968 and to indirect discrimination in 1976. As immigration and conflict increased, the government introduced successively more restrictive immigration legislation, beginning in the 1960s. This was the time when the other countries such as Canada, Australia, and the United States were lifting their restrictions on immigration. Acts in 1962, 1968, 1971, and 1981 gradually reduced rights of Commonwealth citizens to enter, but entry vouchers were given out fairly liberally.

Indians were the next large group to arrive. They came beginning in the 1960s, mainly from northern India. They were a relatively educated group, including doctors recruited to work in hospitals. The group includes Sikhs, Hindus, Muslims, and Christians and a variety of language groups so that it is difficult to generalize to an "Indian group." This group also includes Indians who had first migrated to other countries in the British Empire (East Africa, South Africa, Caribbean, Fiji, and Malaysia) and had become economically successful. Africanization policies of newly independent countries of sub-Saharan Africa, especially Kenya and Uganda, led to the expulsion or migration of many Indians from East Africa. Despite UK legislation designed to restrict immigration, it proved impossible to limit entry in practice. These "twice migrants" have been Britain's most successful immigrant group.

Pakistani Muslims also began to arrive in the 1960s, many recruited to low-skilled jobs in the textile industry in the north of England. They are generally less-skilled migrants, often from rural areas and possessing limited English language proficiency. Bangladeshi migration has been relatively recent. Immigrants have come from rural areas of Sylhet and have very low levels of education and very little knowledge of English language.

There has been a long tradition of Chinese immigrants, especially concentrated in particular occupational niches such as restaurants and laundry. This low-skilled group was joined in the 1990s by the immigration of many highly educated Chinese from Hong Kong, with a major influx in the run-up to Hong Kong's return to China in 1997. In the past decade, there has also been a growth of African immigrants to Britain, especially from Nigeria. They tend to be highly educated and fluent English speakers. Many are students who come for university educations and then stay, some without legal permission to be in the country.

Beginning with the arrival of the Caribbeans, the differences between these new groups and established citizens were framed around race rather than citizenship—and in the 1960s managing "immigration" came to be seen as managing "race relations." Thus, immigrant groups are ordinarily referred to as "ethnic and racial minorities" rather than as first-, second-, or third-generation migrants. And immigration policy has always been intertwined with race policy in Britain; as Joppke (1999, 100) puts it: "the peculiarity of

British immigration policy is that it is directed not against aliens, but against former co-nationals." Without citizenship to draw the line between those the British society and government wanted to let in and those they wanted to keep out, "British immigration policy had to operate on a proxy. This proxy has been race." Much of recent British discussion of immigration and citizenship acquisition has been covering new territory and inventing new policies and approaches as sources of immigrants have changed dramatically in the 1990s and 2000s to include Eastern European migrants and asylum seekers from around the globe.[1]

Table 4.1 gives the ethnic distribution of the population in England and Wales. There are large differences among the groups in levels of intermarriage and residential segregation (Muttarak and Heath 2010; Peach 1996). The Chinese are the least residentially segregated and the Bangladeshis the most. Caribbeans have relatively low levels of residential segregation and the tendency is toward less segregation over time. The extent of residential segregation is much lower than in the United States for all groups.[2] There are also large differences in the rates of intermarriage and the sizes of the resulting "dual-heritage" or "mixed-race" populations. The Chinese and Caribbeans have the highest rates of intermarriage, approaching 50 percent of the second generation who mainly intermarry with white British. The lowest rates of intermarriage are for Bangladeshis and Pakistanis, some of whom still have arranged marriages with spouses brought over from South Asia.

The Educational System in England

Figure 4.1 provides an overview of the British educational system. There are large differences in the structure of schooling in different parts of Great Britain, which includes Wales, Scotland, and Northern Ireland. Because of this, we focus only on England in our analyses. England has a largely comprehensive system of education (although a number of selective grammar schools coexist alongside comprehensive schools) with compulsory schooling from age five until age sixteen. Some students complete their education at this age, and many have an additional two years of education in secondary school (or at a further education college) until the age of eighteen, at which point they either continue to university or enter the labor market. At age sixteen, students take a public examination (General Certificate of Secondary Education

TABLE 4.1. Total Population by Ethnic Group: England and Wales in 2009

Ethnic Groups	Total population	Percent
White: British	45,682,100	83.35
White: Irish	574,200	1.05
White: Other White	1,932,600	3.53
Black: Caribbean	615,200	1.12
Black: African	798,800	1.46
Black: Other	126,100	0.23
Asian: Indian	1,434,200	2.62
Asian: Pakistani	1,007,400	1.84
Asian: Bangladeshi	392,200	0.72
Chinese	451,500	0.82
Asian: Other	385,700	0.70
Mixed: White and Black Caribbean	310,600	0.57
Mixed: White and Black African	131,800	0.24
Mixed: White and Asian	301,600	0.55
Mixed: Other Mixed	242,600	0.44
Other	422,500	0.77
Total	54,809,100	100.00

Source: Office for National Statistics (UK). 2011. "Population Estimates by Ethnic Group 2002–2009." Statistical Bulletin May 18, 2011. Retrieved on March 29, 2012 at: http://www.ons.gov.uk/ons/publications/index.html

or GCSE exams), and many students leave schooling at this point. Those who continue on then take another set of examinations—General Certificate of Education Advanced Level Examination (or GCE A Levels), which is the usual entry qualification for university.

England has had an ostensibly unitary system of higher education since 1992 but there are sharp status distinctions between different universities—Oxford and Cambridge are at the top of the status hierarchy, followed by established older universities (often referred to as the Russell Group) and then newer, less selective higher education institutions. There are also a number of part-time study and subdegree programs available in Britain, similar to the United States. These provide second chances for students to return to university after time in the labor market or to combine work and study.

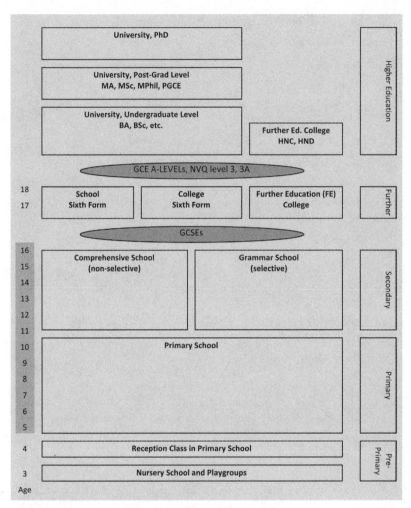

Figure 4.1. The Educational System in England and Wales

Note: Oval areas indicate mandatory exams/tests.

HNC = Higher National Certificate; HND = Higher National Diploma

Source: Schneider (2008), as amended by Vikki Boliver

There have been major changes to student-funding regimes in higher education, with a withdrawal of grants that paid living expenses for students in the 1980s and 1990s, the introduction of student loans in 1990, and the introduction of tuition fees (initially 1,000 pounds) since 1998 and variable fees (maximum 3,290 pounds in 2010). This is still a small fraction of what students pay to attend private universities in the United States and a lower cost than is found at most public universities there. In September 2012, fees have increased markedly to a maximum of 9,000 pounds a year, above the cost at most public American universities. This has been met with widespread consternation among students, and protests in the streets.

A key difference between the United States and England is the high-stakes testing that occurs at age sixteen in England. This sort of examination has a long history in Britain and goes back to the old selective system of education that existed before 1965. The United States does not have such a national exam (the SAT is neither universal for high school students, nor required by all universities). This structural difference has implications for the position of a sixteen-year-old in the labor market in the two countries.

While a sixteen-year-old in the United States who leaves school is a high school dropout, a sixteen-year-old who leaves school after the GCSE in Britain has some qualification and is better off than someone who leaves school before then with no qualifications. Britain thus has a much higher proportion of the population that fails to complete secondary education (51 percent compared with 13 percent in the United States), in part due to this option to leave school at age 16 with a qualification that helps in the labor market (Rothon, Heath, and Lessard-Phillips 2009).[3] One implication of this difference is that among students who complete secondary education in Britain, a higher proportion (over one-third) actually go on to complete a degree, whereas in the United States, the proportion of high school graduates who go on to complete a university degree is less than one-third.

Primary and Secondary Effects on Educational Outcomes

Our focus in this first empirical section of the chapter is on the educational careers of the second generation in Britain and the United States. Following the classic traditions on both sides of the Atlantic in the sociology of education, we visualize the educational career as a series of stages with decision points as to whether to stop or continue to the next stage (Halsey, Heath, and Ridge 1980; Mare 1980).

Sociologists of education have found it very helpful to make a distinction between the *primary* and the *secondary* effects of social origin on educational attainment (Boudon 1974). All over the world, sociologists have found that there are large effects of social background (indexed by parents' social class or parental education) on test scores at this age (primary effects). Results of the Programme for International Student Assessment (PISA) studies for example show that, both in Britain and the United States, social background has a major influence on test scores (Marks 2005). These effects are usually attributed primarily to processes of socialization within the home although of course they may also reflect the types of schools students have attended, peer-group pressures, and the type of curriculum (Alba and Holdaway, this volume). In general, though, we can say that these primary effects tend to reflect how children have been treated in their early years at home and school.

We next examine the secondary effects of social background—the decisions that young people and their families make about whether to continue schooling. Standard approaches suggest that, inter alia, a major factor in these decisions is how successful young people have been in their education up to that point. The standard rational-choice theories of educational decision-making posit that the decision of whether or not to continue will depend in part on the perceived probability of success at the next stage. So students who have performed badly might be quite rational if they were to decide not to continue. Of course, the issue is much more complex than that since students' decisions about how hard to work in lower secondary education might be influenced by their eventual plans for education in upper secondary or tertiary education (see Cameron and Heckman 1998; Morgan 2005), and there are many other factors apart from earlier educational achievement that influence continuation decisions. But educational research has always found a strong relationship between performance scores at age sixteen and continuation decisions. And we therefore expect to find that inequalities (whether class or ethnic) at later stages of the educational career will tend to reflect those found at the earlier stages.

However, in addition to perceived chances of success, the family economic position (its income and assets) may be crucial in determining whether a child can afford to stay on at school or must enter the labor market in order to contribute to the household income. For example, Boudon (1974) claimed that, even among children with similar test scores (and presumably with similar probabilities of educational success in upper secondary schooling), social background tended to have a strong association with continuation. He termed these the secondary effects of social background and he argued that they may well be larger than the primary effects.[4] It is also worth making the point that these secondary effects may be easier for policy-makers to influence than the primary effects—as shown for example by the recent Labour government's introduction of Educational Maintenance Allowances in Britain for upper secondary education (now replaced by a bursary scheme in England), a policy directed specifically toward ameliorating the secondary effects of social background.

European sociologists of education have tended to focus on the primary and secondary effects of social-class background, and recent research suggests that the effects are cumulative. Thus, middle-class children tend to have higher test scores than working-class children and, while children from all social classes have higher continuation rates the higher their test scores, middle-class children have been found to have even higher continuation rates than working-class children with the same test scores. Heath and Brinbaum (2007) have applied these ideas to ethnic origins as well as to class origins. However, they make the important point that the mechanisms explaining ethnic inequalities, both the primary and the secondary ones, in education may be rather different from those explaining class inequalities. Whereas the primary and secondary effects of social class may be cumulative as one moves through the educational system, the effects of ethnic background may be reversed at different stages. For example, because of factors such as discrimination in the labor market, the "opportunity costs" of leaving school may be higher for minorities than they are for members of the white majority group, and minorities may thus persist in educational systems at higher rates than the majority group. (The anticipated discrimination argument depends upon expected ethnic-specific returns to continued education: if minorities believe that discrimination is greater against the more highly educated, then this would counteract the opportunity cost argument. In practice the reverse is probably true.) Other possible reasons why there might be positive rather than negative secondary effects of ethnicity are that minorities might have higher aspirations (reflecting the positive selection of their immigrant parents) or greater family and community support (especially among groups such as Punjabi Sikhs).

We begin therefore by establishing the primary effects, looking at ethnic differences in performance scores during the period of compulsory schooling. We then move on to the subsequent stages of the educational career, looking at completion of secondary education, tertiary education, and the type of tertiary institution attended.

Performance Scores at Age Sixteen

In Table 4.2, we report results for Britain and the United States, drawing on the Youth Cohort Study (YCS) for Britain and the National Longitudinal Study of Adolescent Health (Add Health) for the United States (Harris et al. 2008). For Britain we present the scores on the GCSE examinations, the public examinations taken around the ages of fifteen and sixteen that have a crucial bearing on whether students can continue in education. For the United States, we give scores on the Peabody vocabulary test that was administered as part of the Add Health survey in Wave 1. In both cases we have standardized the scores, setting the average score of the white majority group to zero. Positive scores therefore indicate that the minority in question has higher performance scores than the majority, while negative scores indicate that the minority is doing less well at this stage of their educational career.

Our identification of the ethnic groups by immigrant generations was guided by ethnic demographic profiles and data availability in each country. The second-generation category includes the 1.5 generation (those who migrated before the age of twelve) along with those born in the receiving country to immigrant parents (the more usual and stricter definition of the second generation[5]) whereas the third-generation category is restricted to those with two native-born parents. In the United Kingdom, we were able to separate the children of West Indian immigrants from those of African immigrants whereas such division was not possible for the United States because of the relatively smaller sample size in Add Health. That said, given the demographics of black immigration to the United States, the majority of individuals identified as second-generation blacks should be West Indian. In addition, three South Asian groups (Indian, Bangladeshi, and Pakistani) and one East Asian group (Chinese) were identified in the UK data whereas the major Latino groups (Mexican, Puerto Rican, and Cuban) and two Asian groups (Chinese and Filipino) were identified in the United States. The Central/South American category includes a range of smaller Latino groups (Columbian, Ecuadorian, Peruvian, etc.) that share important human capital characteristics and residential settlement patterns in the United States. Finally, "other" is a residual category that captures all of the other small ethnic groups.

Since we are measuring rather different outcomes, we should be cautious in comparing the actual scores between countries. However, it is quite

TABLE 4.2. Performance Scores of Second-Generation Groups in Britain and the US

Britain		USA	
Ethnic origins	Standardized mean GCSE score at ages 15 & 16	Ethnic origins	Standardized mean PVT[1] test score at ages 15 & 16
THIRD OR HIGHER GENERATION		THIRD OR HIGHER GENERATION	
White	.005	White	.000
		Black	-.347
		Puerto Rican	-.196
		Mexican	-.232
		Other	-.178
SECOND GENERATION		SECOND GENERATION	
		White	-.009
Black Caribbean	-.459	Black	-.256
Black African	-.145	Puerto Rican	-.187
Pakistani	-.226	Mexican	-.369
Bangladeshi	-.117	Cuban	-.187
Chinese	.496	Chinese	.204
Mixed	-.046	Filipino	-.008
Indian	.234	CSA[2]	-.114
Other	.092	Other	-.087
N	16,459		7,739
Age range/selection	15–16		15–16

Sources: YCS (2000) and Add Health Wave 1 (1994-1995).

1. Add Health used the Peabody Picture Vocabulary Test (PVT) which was designed primarily to measure a subject's receptive (hearing) vocabulary for Standard American English. The PVT standardized scores range from 9 to 141 and resemble scores in a traditional IQ metric. Because PVT scores are sensitive to age, adolescents were first classified into 3-month age intervals. For each age group, raw scores were standardized to a mean of 100 and standard deviation of 15 before models were developed to predict smoothed scores from raw PVT score. These scores were first computed using the Wave I model relating the unsmoothed standardized score to age and Wave I raw scores. They were then standardized based on the mean value for the "third-generation white" category. This provides an easy interpretation for the scores of the other ethno-racial groups, with positive scores suggesting better performances than 3rd-generation whites and negative scores suggesting worse performances.
2. CSA indicates Central/South Americans.

striking that the range of scores does seem to be greater in Britain. On this criterion, ethnic inequalities do appear, at this stage of the school career, to be greater there than in the United States. We are on somewhat safer ground when we compare which ethnic groups do worse and which do better than the comparison group (the white majority group) in each country. The key points are as follows:

- In both countries, the Chinese are the most successful minority group, outperforming the majority group by a considerable margin.

- In Britain, they are followed by the Indians (who are also a very successful group in the United States, though their sample size in Add Health sample is too small to give them a separate category).

- The lowest performing groups in Britain are the black Caribbeans, the Pakistanis, the black Africans, and the Bangladeshis.

- Black groups are also among the lowest performing in the United States, although the lowest performers of all are second-generation Mexicans.

- Other groups fall in between and are closer to the respective majority comparison groups.

These are relatively familiar results and will not come as a surprise to scholars in the field.[6] There is also a huge literature attempting to explain these ethnic inequalities, which emphasizes factors such as social-class background and parental education, parental aspirations, and immigrant optimism, as well as the roles of ethnic social capital and of oppositional culture. Broadly speaking, there are major social-class differences in performance scores in both countries, which certainly contribute to these ethnic differences. Controlling for social class, some ethnic differences remain significant, especially the Chinese and Indian success and the black disadvantage. These results are also consistent with findings from a recent analysis of academic performance for ethnic groups in the United Kingdom (Jackson, Jonsson, and Rudolphi 2012). Hence, ethnic-specific explanations are needed in addition to the standard social-class ones.

All these suggested explanations are to varying degrees controversial. For example, social-class background as measured by parental education is problematic in the case of children of immigrants, and we may be comparing apples and oranges when we compare their social-class background with those of white majority students. As Alba and Holdaway point out in chapter 1, the first generation was educated in very different school systems than are found in the destination country and (perhaps because of discrimination, foreign qualifications, or origin-country-specific human capital) may well have been forced to take menial jobs there, even if they had relatively high levels of education and occupation in the country of origin. The home environments that they can provide to their children may thus be rather different from those of white majority parents in the same menial occupations.[7] However, our focus in this chapter is *not* on explaining these cross-sectional differences in school attainment but in exploring *change* over the course of the educational career. In particular, we can ignore factors that are largely time-constant (such as social class) since these drop out of the analysis in an analysis of progress.

Completion of Secondary Education

We turn next to progress in upper secondary education. We are not able, from the data sources available, to investigate continuation decisions per se, but we do have data that enable us to look at the rates of completing upper secondary education, which are in many ways the key outcome for young people. Table 4.3 shows these completion rates. Completion in the British context is defined as attainment of a level-three qualification such as A-level, whereas in the US context it is defined as attainment of a high school degree or a GED equivalent.

Table 4.3 shows much higher rates of completion of upper secondary education in the United States than in Britain. As we have indicated, this difference is well known. There are some important theories in the sociology of education suggesting that educational expansion is the key to reducing inequalities (Halsey, Heath, and Ridge 1980). One theory is that expansion per se is the key to reducing inequalities. Another argument is that it is only when saturation levels are achieved by advantaged groups that expansion will begin to show progress for disadvantaged groups. In other words, once the advantaged groups such as the white majority group or the middle class have reached a point where all the children who wish to are obtaining a particular level of education, then disadvantaged groups such as minorities or the working class will be able to catch up.

Yet expansion of education may not reduce inequality at all. For example, Raftery and Hout (1993) have argued that inequality will be maximally

TABLE 4.3. Proportion Completing Secondary Education in Britain
and the US

Britain		USA	
Ethnic origins	%	Ethnic origins	%
THIRD OR HIGHER GENERATION		THIRD OR HIGHER GENERATION	
White	60.5	White	89.0
		Black	84.6
		Puerto Rican	84.1
		Mexican	80.0
		Other	83.6
SECOND GENERATION		SECOND GENERATION	
		White	89.0
Black Caribbean	45.6	Black	88.1
Black African	51.6	Puerto Rican	88.1
Pakistani	51.6	Mexican	74.9
Bangladeshi	62.7	Cuban	93.6
Chinese	73.9	Chinese	98.6
Mixed	61.7	Filipino	92.5
Indian	71.0	Central/South Americans	75.0
Other	69.3	Other	92.4
N	7,738		8,928
Age range/selection	18–19		18–22

Sources: YCS (2001) and Add Health Wave 1 (1994-1995)

maintained because those from more-privileged backgrounds will be the first to take advantage of new opportunities. This is the idea of Maximally Maintained Inequality (MMI). Lucas (2001) argues that inequality is effectively maintained (EMI) through new sources of stratification—qualitatively different educational tracks, for instance, rather than just more years of schooling. In other words, when applied to ethnic inequalities, these arguments suggest that, even if inequalities are small at educational levels where 'saturation' has been reached (such as completion of upper secondary education in the United States), they will reemerge either at higher educational levels such as tertiary education (the MMI thesis) or through qualitative differences (the EMI thesis), for example, by the white majority group monopolizing opportunities in more prestigious educational tracks or in more prestigious institutions. We return to these issues in more detail when we consider higher education later in this paper.

However, focusing on completion of secondary education for the moment, Table 4.3 shows that the rank order of the various minority groups is largely unchanged in both countries. Thus:

- The Chinese are once again the most successful minority group, out-performing the white British or American majority group by a considerable margin.

- In Britain they are followed by the Indians.

- The lowest-performing groups in Britain are once again the black Caribbeans, the Pakistanis, and the black Africans although the Bangladeshis have now caught up with the white British majority group.

- African Americans continue to be among the lowest performing in the United States, and the lowest performers remain the second-generation Mexicans; but the second-generation blacks in the United States have now almost caught up with the majority group.

- In the United States, second-generation Cubans and Filipinos also seemed to have moved ahead of the majority group, while Central and South Americans have fallen behind.

As we had expected, therefore, there is considerable (although far from perfect) continuity in the patterns of ethnic inequality at ages of fifteen and sixteen as well as seventeen and eighteen. However, it is quite hard to compare the percentage completion rates in Table 4.3 with the standardized performance scores in Table 4.2. A simple technique that we can use to facilitate the comparison is probit, which enables us to transform the completion rates into the equivalent of standardized performance scores. Essentially, probit is a technique for analyzing binary data using the assumption that there is an underlying normal distribution that can only be observed at a single cut point. We use this technique in Table 4.4, where we are thus able to compare these two stages of the educational career using equivalent metrics.

The very striking result here is that in Britain the relative performance of the ethnic minorities has not deteriorated. If anything, the gaps have tended to close slightly. For example, the coefficient for black Caribbeans has moved from -0.54 at age sixteen to -0.38 at ages of seventeen

TABLE 4.4. Performance Scores at Age 16 and Completion
of Secondary School

	Britain			USA	
Ethnic origins	GCSE scores	Probit of Completion	Ethnic origins	PVT scores	Probit of Completion
THIRD OR HIGHER GENERATION			THIRD OR HIGHER GENERATION		
White	0	0	White	.13	0
			Black	-.24	-.22*
			Puerto Rican	.07	-.23
			Mexican	-.15	-.33*
			Other	-.03	-.28
SECOND GENERATION			SECOND GENERATION		
			White	.15	-.05
Black Caribbean	-.54***	-.38**	Black	-.09	-.05
Black African	-.27*	-.23	Puerto Rican	-.11	-.07
Pakistani	-.26***	-.23*	Mexican	-.30	-.58**
Bangladeshi	-.09	.06	Cuban	-.09	.22
Chinese	.69***	.37	Chinese	.28	.96**
Mixed	.06	.03	Filipino	.08	.19
Indian	.13*	.29***	CSA[2]	-.08	-.58*
Other	.01	.24	Other	.03	.20
N	7,712	7,712		7,351	7,351
Age range/ selection	17–18	17–18		18–22	18–22

Notes: In order to make strict comparisons, because of sample attrition, the results in this table are restricted to respondents who remained in the panel studies at both time points.
*p < .05; **p < .01; ***p < .001
Sources: YCS (2001) and Add Health Wave 3 (2001–2).

and eighteen. In other words, there is gradual convergence with the white majority group. This further has the clear implication that continuation and completion rates for minorities, conditional on their performance at age sixteen, is little different from that of the majority group. This is a very different story from the one for social class. Whereas studies of social class show major secondary effects with the gaps widening as one progresses through the educational system (Jackson, Erikson, Goldthorpe, and Yaish

2007), our results suggest that there are no secondary effects of ethnicity: in other words, the major disadvantage that minorities experience, at least in Britain, comes in their lower secondary (and primary) education rather than at later stages of the school career.

The picture is not quite so straightforward in the United States, with rather different patterns emerging for different groups, some minorities tending to move ahead while others such as the Mexicans appear to be falling behind. One interpretation for the relatively low attainment among Mexicans would be that it takes them *longer* to finish secondary education, so some of them are not quite done with their high school education by age 22. There is some evidence to support this because among second-generation Mexicans between the ages of twenty-three and twenty-six, the proportion having a high school diploma went up to 83.1 percent from 74.9 percent among those between the ages of eighteen and twenty-two, though that is still the lowest of all groups. But, exactly as in Britain, there is clearly no general tendency for minorities to fall behind the white majority group.

We can verify this provisional conclusion by carrying out a more detailed analysis in which we use probit to investigate completion of secondary schooling controlling for performance scores. This is the key analysis that needs to be done in order to check whether there are secondary effects of ethnicity in the same way that there are secondary effects of social class. This is done in Table 4.5.[8]

Here we see a very clear story, one that is remarkably similar in the two countries. First of all, we see that performance scores at ages of fifteen and sixteen have a very powerful relationship with eventual completion of secondary education. In both countries the coefficients for standardized test scores are highly significant and substantively large, indeed of very similar magnitude.

Second, we can see that, with only one or two exceptions, almost all the ethnic coefficients are positive in both countries. In other words, comparing majority and minority students with similar test scores, we find that ethnic minorities generally have higher likelihoods of completing upper secondary education. In many cases these positive coefficients are not significantly different from zero, partly reflecting the small sample sizes for specific minorities. But the key point is that, unlike the negative primary effects of ethnicity in Table 4.2, there is generally speaking an absence of negative secondary effects.

Table 4.5. Probit of Completion of Secondary School

Ethnic origins	*Britain* Probit with GCSE scores control only	Probit with gender & social background		*USA* Probit with PVT scores control only	Probit with gender & social background
THIRD OR HIGHER GENERATION			THIRD OR HIGHER GENERATION		
White	0	0	White	0	0
			Black	.26**	.25*
			Puerto Rican	-.08	-.04
			Mexican	.02	.10
			Other	-.09	-.03
SECOND GENERATION			SECOND GENERATION		
			White	-.07	-.04
Black Caribbean	.23	.36*	Black	.27	.19
Black African	.04	-.01	Puerto Rican	.18	.18
Pakistani	.08	.13	Mexican	-.07	.09
Bangladeshi	.21	.26	Cuban	.60	.68
Chinese	-.49*	-.35	Chinese	.79	.73
Mixed	.00	.00	Filipino	.23	.27
Indian	.26*	.28*	CSA²	-.34	-.25
Other	.37*	.35*	Other	.36	.38
Standardized test score	1.35***	1.29***	Standardized test score	1.32***	1.20***
Includes test score control	Yes	Yes		Yes	Yes
Include gender and social background controls	No	Yes		No	Yes
N	7,712	7,712		7,351	7,351
Age range/ selection	17–18	17–18		18–22	18–22

Sources: YCS (2001) and Add Health Wave 3 (2001–2)

Notes: Social background controls include father's and mother's education. *p<.05; **p<.01; ***p<.001

This is completely different from the situation with respect to social class. In its case we find that, again in much the same way in both countries, lower socioeconomic groups have lower test scores at age sixteen (i.e., negative primary effects), and, controlling for test scores, lower likelihoods of completing secondary education as well (i.e., negative secondary effects). This confirms findings from previous research on the primary and secondary effects of social class. However, ethnic processes work very differently from class processes when we come to upper secondary education. While we cannot explain the source of this difference with these analyses, it is possible that the positive outcomes among the children of immigrants reflect what Kao and Tienda (1995) described as "immigrant optimism" or what Kasinitz, Mollenkopf, Waters, and Holdaway (2008) described as the "second-generation advantage." In both cases these authors point to the selectivity of migrant parents and the special circumstances of ambition and family loyalty that characterize many immigrant families.

Completion of Tertiary Education

We now move on to the tertiary level of education. While it would be ideal if we could follow up the same individuals and see how many started college and how many eventually completed tertiary education, we cannot do this with the British data as the YCS only follows people to age eighteen.[9] For Britain therefore we have to use alternative data sources, which only permit us to look at completion of tertiary education and acquisition of a degree-level qualification. We do this in Table 4.6 using the Longitudinal Survey (LS), a dataset that links results from the 1991 and 2001 censuses. This dataset links individuals who were present in the 1991 census to the data collected about them ten years later in 2001. The results in Table 4.6 are based on a restricted sample of individuals who were born in Britain, aged fourteen to eighteen in 1991, and living with their families at that time. We are able to measure what proportions from each ethnic group had achieved tertiary qualifications by 2001 when they were aged twenty-four to twenty-eight.[10]

Table 4.6 shows a remarkable picture for Britain with most of the ethnic minority groups actually overtaking the white majority in the completion of university education. In Table 4.3, for completion of secondary education we found that several minority groups in Britain—notably black Africans, black Caribbeans, and Pakistanis—were lagging behind the majority group; we

TABLE 4.6. Probit of Completion of First Degree

Britain			US		
Ethnic origins	Percentage completing first degree	Probit	Ethnic origins	Percentage completing first degree	Probit
THIRD OR HIGHER GENERATION			THIRD OR HIGHER GENERATION		
White	28.8	0	White	23.0	0
Other minority		0.01	Black	11.7	-.45**
			Puerto Rican	22.7	-.01
			Mexican	6.5	-.78**
			Other	14.9	-.30
SECOND GENERATION			SECOND GENERATION		
White	17.5	0.08	White	26.7	.12
Black Caribbean	41.7	0.37**	Black	17.5	-.20
Black African	41.4	0.37*	Puerto Rican	5.6	-.85**
Pakistani	32.0	0.11	Mexican	9.1	-.60**
Bangladeshi	22.0	-0.19	Cuban	6.1	-.81**
Chinese	64.3	0.98***	Chinese	80.4	1.59***
Mixed	32.6	0.23	Filipino	21.8	-.04
Indian	54.7	0.69	CSA	21.4	-.06
Other	57.4	0.79***	Other	32.5	.29
N	24,285	24,285		5,521	5,521
Age range/selection	24–28	24–28		23–26	23–26

Notes: *p < .05; **p < .01; ***p < .001

Sources: LS (1991–2001) and Add Health Wave 3 (2001–2002)

now find that they either match (in the case of the Pakistanis) or have over-taken the white British, although the Bangladeshis appear to have slipped behind. We can also see that the Chinese and Indians (as judged by the probit coefficients) have actually moved further ahead of the white British.

These are such important and remarkable results, and in some cases are based on rather small sample sizes, that we have replicated them with an alternative, completely independent, data source (the pooled Labour Force Survey or LFS for 1994–2004). For most groups, the picture is almost identical in the two sources. Thus, whereas the LS shows 29 percent of white British from this age group with tertiary qualifications, the LFS shows 27 percent. For Chinese the figures are 64 percent in both sources, for Indians the figures are 55 percent in both sources, for Pakistanis they are 32 percent and 30 percent respectively and for black Africans they are 41 and 46 percent respectively. However, there are bigger discrepancies for black Caribbeans (much lower in the LFS) and for Bangladeshis (much higher in the LFS dataset), so we have to be more cautious about these results. Our best guess is that these two groups are probably about on a par with the white British. (This suspicion is reinforced by a third data source that we use below for examining the prestige of the institution attended.)

However, the American results are different, and there do appear to be some very large gaps between the minorities and the majority group. On the one hand, the Chinese exceed the majority group (as they have done all along), although by an even larger margin than before. Several other groups, as in Britain, have achieved or maintained parity with the majority—for example, third-generation Puerto Ricans, second-generation Filipinos, second-generation Central and South Americans, second-generation whites and second-generation "other" all match or slightly exceed the white majority, while second-generation blacks are slightly lower, but not significantly so.

On the other hand, we also see some very large and statistically significant negative coefficients for third-generation blacks, third-generation Mexicans, second-generation Puerto Ricans, second-generation Mexicans, and most surprisingly second-generation Cubans. Furthermore, these negative coefficients are the largest that we have seen so far, suggesting greater inequality at the tertiary stage than at earlier stages. However, a quick look at data from the Current Population Survey for the same age group suggests that, whereas we get basically the same figure for whites—23.7 percent, the figure for Cubans is actually higher at 29.9 percent.[11] So this is similar to the British results in that two sources yield very different figures for Bangladeshis.

Before drawing any strong conclusions, we need to remember that even statistically significant coefficients can arise by chance, and different data sources (with different patterns of response bias, different minority oversampling strategy, and the like) can also show very different results for the same group, as we saw in the cases of black Caribbeans and Bangladeshis in Britain. So we do need to be somewhat cautious. Our results should be regarded as provisional. More importantly, there are institutional differences between Britain and the United States that may be highly relevant here. In particular, it is much more common in the United States for students to work their way through college, to take breaks in their studies, and in general to take longer to complete higher education. Hence, the Add Health data, while providing a valuable picture, may not fully reflect the sample's eventual educational achievements. It may well be that some of the groups such as second-generation Mexicans or Cubans will take longer to obtain their degrees but will eventually narrow the gap. To be sure, the fact that they need to take longer is itself an important source of inequality and ethnic stratification.

Stratification in Higher Education

Another crucial point is that tertiary education in both countries is now highly stratified, ranging from public community colleges to private elite universities. So the apparent success of the British minorities may be largely illusory if they are concentrated in low-status institutions with poorer labor-market prospects. This essentially is the core of the EMI thesis of Samuel Lucas: minorities may have caught up or even overtaken the privileged majority group in quantitative terms, but qualitatively, in terms of the status of the institutions they attend, they are still some way behind.

However, we are also aware that the pattern of stratification might be more pronounced in the United Kingdom than in the United States. One key difference between the two countries is that the United States has a much more open and flexible system of higher education. Moreover, both community colleges and four-year public colleges in the United States are quite affordable, providing good opportunities for college attainment and subsequent life successes (Hout 2012). For example, the City University of New York—the largest urban public institution in the country, with eleven senior colleges and seven community colleges—has been instrumental in providing affordable education to students from racial-minority backgrounds. In their longitudinal analyses of data on women who enrolled at CUNY in the 1970s, Attewell and Lavin (2007) find that 31 percent of the women who entered a junior college ended up completing a four-year degree. Furthermore, they find that women with credentials from CUNY reported earnings that were on par with those with similar background and experiences in national data, and that the socioeconomic boost of a college education—regardless of the institutional type—extends into the second generation (i.e., their offspring).

Very few datasets contain detailed information that will allow us to systematically examine the stratification in postsecondary education. However, the Immigrant Second Generation in Metropolitan New York (ISGMNY) dataset does contain the required information. Specifically, the colleges and universities that respondents in the ISGMNY attended are broadly representative across a range of American higher education institutions and not limited geographically to the metropolitan New York area, as many respondents in the sample did attend college outside of New York. The project asked about the names of the colleges that respondents went to and then recoded this information based on the *US News and World Report* ranking into various tiers (Kasinitz et al. 2008). We also have access to data from the Higher Education Statistics Agency (HESA) and the British Universities and Colleges Admissions Service (UCAS), which contain the ethnicity of students at different types of university. By relating these data to the size of the relevant age groups, we can produce results comparable to the ISGMNY data.

In this analysis, we distinguish three tiers of universities in each country. In Britain we have the elite, highly selective research universities that form the so-called Russell Group. Next we have the "old" universities; many of these are not that old and were established in the 1960s but all are traditional universities offering high-status courses in traditional academic subjects and are relatively selective in their intakes. The lowest tier includes the "new" universities (sometimes called the "post-1992" universities), which used to be locally based polytechnics offering largely vocational courses. In the ISGMNY data, we have a very similar categorization, although the distribution is somewhat different with a larger proportion falling in the middle category.

Before turning to the ethnic inequalities that these tables reveal, it is worth emphasizing that both tables look at enrollment not completion. Consistent with this we find much higher enrollment percentages in the United States than in Britain. In Britain, as shown in Table 4.7, the enrollment rates are not much higher than the completion rates shown in Table 4.6, whereas in the United States there is a much bigger gap between enrollment and completion. This is a critical problem facing American higher education. Until the 1980s, the United States led the world in the number of young adults aged twenty-five to thirty-four with a university education. It is now ranked twelfth among thirty-six developed nations. The decline is not due to access to higher education, which has remained high overall. Almost 70 percent of graduating high school seniors attend college or university within two years of graduation. The problem is that many who start college never finish. Only

TABLE 4.7. University Attendance by Ethnic Group in Britain

Ethnic Origins	% at elite (Russell Group) universities	% at other "old" universities	% at "new" universities (former polytechnics)	% not enrolled in college or universities
White	8.6	8.6	20.8	62.0
Black Caribbean	2.6	6.6	35.8	55.0
Black African	7.5	14.3	51.2	27.0
Indian	13.0	15.1	43.0	28.9
Pakistani	6.1	10.5	32.4	51.0
Bangladeshi	4.4	8.3	26.4	60.9
Chinese	14.1	10.8	24.2	50.9
Mixed	10.4	9.6	20.1	59.9

Sources: HESA (2001–2) and UCAS (2001)

Notes: Figures are derived from Connor et al. (2004) and Boliver (2005).

TABLE 4.8. University Attendance by Ethnic Group in the US

Ethnic Origins	% enrolled in top-ranked (elite) universities	% enrolled in middle-ranked universities	% enrolled in lower-ranked universities	% enrolled in community colleges	% not enrolled in colleges	N
White	16.7	32.6	21.1	10.3	19.3	408
Black	2.6	11.6	23.0	19.7	43.1	421
Puerto Rican	1.2	8.6	20.3	16.6	53.3	433
Chinese	14.2	44.8	14.8	10.5	15.7	607
CEP	2.2	25.1	16.7	26.4	29.6	402
Dominican	2.1	16.4	16.8	25.5	39.2	428
Russian Jews	8.4	41.4	19.4	11.9	18.9	309
West Indian	2.7	13.0	23.6	23.8	36.9	470

Notes: CEP includes Columbians, Ecuadorians, and Peruvians. All respondents were between the ages of 18 and 35. Whites, blacks, and Puerto Ricans are third-generation in the ISGMNY study whereas all remaining groups are second-generation.

Source: ISGMNY (1999)

57 percent of those who enroll in a four-year bachelor's degree graduate six years later, and fewer than 25 percent of those who begin in a two-year community college get an associate's degree as of three years later (Lewin 2010). It remains to be seen whether the large increases in student fees in Britain will also lead to a lower graduation rate there over time.

In both countries we see a very high degree of ethnic stratification in higher education. In Britain, for example, all the ethnic minorities exceed the white British majority group in their overall enrollment rates, but many minorities are concentrated in lower-status universities and are substantially underrepresented in the elite institutions (Vasagar 2011). In fact, the picture at elite universities looks remarkably similar to the one we started with in Table 4.2 when we looked at performance scores at age sixteen. Thus, just as at age sixteen, Chinese and Indians outperform the majority group and all the other minorities lag behind, especially the black Caribbeans who fare least well in the competition for elite education, just as they did at GCSE.

In the United States—strictly speaking, metropolitan New York—we again see a high level of ethnic stratification. Once again, the Chinese (and Russian Jews) are the most successful minorities, with the other second-generation minorities some way behind, confirming previous findings from the New York study (Kasinitz et al. 2008). However, in New York, unlike Britain, all the minorities, except for the Chinese, have lower rates of access to the elite institutions. In other words, third- and higher-generation whites are unambiguously at the top of the ethnic hierarchy in New York whereas that is no longer true for Britain. In line with this, we find that the probit coefficients for the United States are substantially larger than the comparable ones for Britain, and are all negative. As we would expect, the probits for elite universities are quite similar to those for overall enrollment and for tertiary completion. They are also substantially larger than any we have seen at earlier stages of the educational career.

Over the last few decades, community colleges have become an increasingly common entry point to higher education in the United States. For example, 42 percent of undergraduates begin their education at a community college according a recent estimate (Dougherty 2002). For many students in the American context, community colleges not only provide an important starting point for higher education, but also serve as a prerequisite for subsequent attainment, with about a third of the enrolled students successfully transferring to four-year institutions (Attewell and Lavin 2007, 169). Those for whom the associate's degree was also their terminal degree reported earning 7.5 percent more than high school graduates of similar background (Attewell and Lavin 2007, 170). Therefore, the value of an associate's degree is not trivial, even though its holders generally earn substantially less than those with a bachelor's degree (Hout 2012).

For ethnic and racial minorities, community colleges from California to New York—with their open access policy—represent an important venue of postsecondary education. Examining community colleges in the larger context of stratification in higher education is also important because recent research has shown that students who are least likely to attain a college education are also most likely to benefit from it (Brand and Xie 2010), and these benefits extend beyond the students themselves into their offspring and the next generation (Attewell and Lavin 2007).

At the other end of spectrum, researchers have also documented the greater return to a college education from selective and elite institutions. Graduates from the most selective universities benefit from significantly higher investments while in college (Hoxby 2009) and earn significantly more money than graduates of other universities (Black and Smith 2006; Dale and Krueger 2011). That said, the debate on whether the relationship between college selectivity and earnings is causal or spurious is ongoing (Dale and Krueger 2011, 2002; Black and Smith 2006) and unmeasured individual traits are an obvious concern. In other words, individuals admitted into elite institutions might possess personal traits or characteristics that might make them successful in general, independent of the selectivity of the colleges they attended. (See Hout 2012 for a recent review of this literature.)

The ISGMNY data provide a unique opportunity to explore how enrollment at community colleges varies across ethnic groups. Distinguishing between two- and four-year colleges is particularly important in the context of New York City, where the City University of New York has played a central role in the education of immigrants and their children for decades (Attewell and Lavin 2007; Kasinitz et al. 2008). Table 4.8 shows that Hispanics and blacks are more likely than whites and Chinese to start in the lowest tier. On the one hand, South Americans and Dominicans reported the highest community-college enrollment rates (26.4 percent and 25.5 percent), followed by West Indians (23.8 percent). On the other hand, native whites, Chinese, and Russian Jews are least likely to enroll in community colleges (10.3 percent, 10.5 percent, and 12.0 percent). These differences not only reflect major disparities in academic preparation received by different groups in elementary and high schools, but also provide a window into how this early-stage stratification perpetuates inequalities in educational attainment across groups, both in terms of quantity and quality.

However, there are many reasons for supposing that New York provides a rather different environment from the national one. In particular, the third-generation whites in New York may be an unusually selective group and they may thus be the true outliers, as they include significant numbers of Ivy League graduates from across the country who arrive in New York City every year to take on positions in the city's financial, legal, and cultural industries (Kasinitz et al. 2008). However, New York also disproportionately attracts highly educated young adults from a variety of other ethnic/racial backgrounds. Therefore, the advantage among third-generation whites, though a potential concern, is also reflective of broader patterns that have been documented in other studies drawing on national data (Brand and Xie 2010; Dale and Krueger 2011).

For these reasons, we are very cautious about drawing any strong conclusions from the cross-national comparison in Table 4.9. Metropolitan New York does show greater ethnic stratification across postsecondary institutions than does Britain. But the key point is that in both contexts, there is greater ethnic stratification at elite institutions than overall, and in Britain the contrast is particularly stark with positive coefficients for overall enrollment in universities transforming into much reduced, and generally negative coefficients, for enrollment at elite institutions. Only the Chinese are able to buck this pattern. But even the Chinese, who throughout all stages of the educational career appear to outperform the white majority in Britain, find that their advantage is smallest when it comes to access to elite universities. That said, we recognize that these privileges are only applicable to the small proportion of whites in the United Kingdom who have access to elite education. It is nonetheless the case in both countries whites continue to occupy the higher end of the educational hierarchy—a fact that has implications for the overall patterns of ethno-racial inequality.

Conclusions

Let us first comment on some of the parallels between Britain and the United States.

TABLE 4.9. Probit of University Enrollment: Overall and Elite

| Ethnic origins | Britain | | Ethnic origins | USA | |
	Overall university enrollment	Enrollment at elite universities		Overall university enrollment	Enrollment at elite universities
THIRD OR HIGHER GENERATION			THIRD OR HIGHER GENERATION		
White	0	0	White	0	0
			Black	-0.92	-0.88
			Puerto Rican	-1.08	-1.18
SECOND GENERATION			SECOND GENERATION		
Black Caribbean	0.18	-0.58	West Indian	-0.89	-1.03
Black African	0.92	-0.07	Dominican	-0.97	-1.09
Pakistani	0.28	-0.18	CEP	-0.78	-1.10
Bangladeshi	0.03	-0.34	Russian Jews	-0.05	-0.39
Chinese	0.28	0.29	Chinese	0.04	-0.13
Mixed	0.05	0.11			
Indian	0.86	0.24			
N=76,512			N=905		
Age range/ selection	23–26	23–26	Age range/ selection	23–26	23–26

Sources: UCAS (2001) and ISGMNY (1999)

- In both the United States and Britain we find ethnic inequalities in test scores at ages of fifteen and sixteen.

- In both countries we find that test scores at ages of fifteen and sixteen are very powerful predictors of completion of upper secondary education.

- In both countries, when we control for test scores, we find that minorities have high continuation rates into upper secondary education; when they can choose whether to stay on or leave, they are just as likely to stay on as are the white majority group members with similar test scores.

- In both countries, minorities have high rates of attending and completing tertiary education, in many cases (though in the United States not all) matching or exceeding the rates of the white majority.

- In both countries there are very substantial inequalities in access to elite education.

- In both countries the ethnic hierarchy is rather similar, with Chinese (and Indians) being the most successful minorities, blacks (and Mexicans) the least successful.

The differences are less striking but are instructive about variation in the way education works in these two societies. We would like to highlight two important differences between the United Kingdom and the United States that most definitely complicate our comparisons. First, leaving secondary education is different in the two countries. Even though both the United States and the United Kingdom have compulsory schooling only until age sixteen and students are expected to complete secondary education at age eighteen, there is a large difference in what it means to be a sixteen-year-old who leaves school in the two countries. In the United States a sixteen-year-old who leaves before high school graduation is a dropout with dismal labor force prospects. In Britain a sixteen-year-old who leaves school after taking the GCSE exam but before completing secondary school has a qualification that is recognized in the labor force. Indeed, the reasons given by young people in Britain who leave school at age sixteen are mostly about getting a job and earning a wage (Connor 2001; Helmsley-Brown 1999; McGrath and Millen 2004). In particular, working-class whites could be more likely than minorities to have the right connections to get a decent job at age sixteen— either in the construction industry or other well-paid blue-collar occupations; this might contribute to the relatively lower rate of white participation in higher education. The different levels of secondary-education completion in the United States and the United Kingdom are therefore not directly comparable, and the much lower levels of completion in the United Kingdom for all of the ethnic groups discussed here will not necessarily translate into the same kinds of disadvantages in the labor force on both sides of the Atlantic.

The second issue troubling our comparison is the nature of the reference population for evaluating second-generation attainment. While at first it might appear that third- and later-generation whites are the correct comparisons for immigrant-origin groups in both countries, there is a historical difference between the United States and the United Kingdom that complicates this. The true "native born" population in the United States includes both native whites and native blacks, with African Americans having much lower levels of test scores, high school completion, and university completion than native whites. There is a comparable group to African Americans in some ways in the United Kingdom—working-class whites. Inequalities in test scores and educational attainment by social class are very strong in the United Kingdom, with working-class whites very underrepresented in higher education. Indeed, the discourse about educational inequality in the United Kingdom has been about social-class differences, while in the United States it has primarily been about racial differences. By comparing ethnic minorities in the United Kingdom to native whites, we set the bar quite low in terms of educational outcomes. In fact one could argue that the native comparison group in the United States ought to contain both native whites and blacks to make an equivalent comparison group with the native whites of Britain. Following research conventions, we did not do that in this chapter but the conceptual case for such a comparison deserves to be considered for future analyses.

The main, very tentative, difference seems to be that ethnic inequalities are larger in Britain than the United States at the ages of fifteen and sixteen but end up being smaller in Britain at the completion of tertiary education or in access to elite universities. But the big story is that ethnic inequalities are most marked when students are being tested or selected; they are least marked when students are choosing whether to persist. The underlying distinction between *what is done to students* and *what they choose to do themselves* is even more powerful than we had anticipated. It is when students are tested or selected that the inequalities are most apparent. In a recent analysis of ethnic inequalities in academic performance for England and Sweden, Jackson, Jonsson, and Rudolphi (2012, 172) reach a similar conclusion: "choice-driven educational systems are to the advantage of ethnic minority students."

To be sure, in both countries and educational systems, there is a great deal of emphasis on meritocracy. Formal testing is used for example by elite institutions when selecting their students, and so this gives an appearance, and perhaps some reality, of fairness in admissions procedures. These findings are even more significant when we take into account the fact that elite universities in the United States still have affirmative action programs in which they admit minority students with lower average test scores than white applicants. This is a highly contentious policy issue that is being battled in the courts and that is interpreted and applied in different ways across different universities. In an important 2003 US Supreme Court case, the court said that a state university, the University of Michigan Law School, could take diversity into account in deciding on admissions, but the recognition of race in admissions had to be one of many factors weighed and the university could not just set a lower numerical score for minority students (*Grutter v. Bollinger* 2003). Meanwhile, several states (including Arizona, California, Florida, Michigan, Nebraska, Texas, and Washington) have passed laws prohibiting the use of race in college admissions. After the law was passed in California, the enrollment of black students plummeted at the elite University of California at Berkeley (Hinrichs 2012), suggesting that without the policies in effect at many of the elite private universities to take into account race in university admissions in order to increase diversity, there would be much less ethnic and racial diversity at these institutions. Similarly, a recent study also documented a positive impact of *Grutter v. Bollinger* on racial minority students' enrollment in graduate and professional school in Texas (Garces 2012). As of this writing, *Fisher v. University of Texas*, a case involving affirmative action, is currently before the US Supreme Court. The case was brought by Abigail Fisher who allegedly claims that her race was held against her in the admission process at the University of Texas at Austin. Once decided, the case has important ramifications for affirmative action policy, as it is currently applied to university and college admission across the country in the spirit of *Grutter v. Bollinger* (Liptak 2012).

It is also important to recognize that much of the inequality may arise because students from minority backgrounds simply do not apply to elite institutions. In the United Kingdom, Boliver (2004) has shown that the ethnic gap in access to Oxford can be largely explained by lack of applications rather than discrimination at the point of application. However, Heath and Zimdars (2005) (see also Zimdars, Sullivan, and Heath 2009), using different data, do show very clear evidence of "ethnic penalties" in admissions decisions at Oxford. In the United States, Brown and Hirschman (2006) have also shown that the passage of Initiative 200, a ballot measure that eliminated affirmative action in Washington state in 1998, led to a decline in college enrollment among minority students, though this decrease was due less to changes in admission rates and more from declines in applications from these underrepresented groups. Indeed, many versions of affirmative action emphasize the importance of outreach activities targeted at minority candidates[12] as well as the signaling of an institutional welcoming environment to minority students in order to attract them as applicants.

The findings here suggest that perhaps the United States would look even worse in this comparison were it not for affirmative action. While both countries show marked stratification at the college level, the secondary effects of ethnicity on enrollment and completion of higher education are less in Britain than they are in the United States. In the United States, ethnicity affects the rate of college completion, once test scores are controlled for.[13] In Britain, the children of immigrants are more likely to complete education than native whites. If there were affirmative action in Britain, presumably we would see less stratification in the quality of higher education institutions young people would attend, and more representation of minority students in the most selective and prestigious institutions. Without affirmative action, the sorting of the children of immigrants and other minorities into lower-status institutions in the United States would be even higher. Since those institutions have lower completion rates, it could be that the completion of higher education net of test scores would look even worse. (The opposite argument could also be made. Perhaps ethnic minority students would be more likely to complete college without affirmative action programs because they would be placed in institutions where their credentials would make them more competitive with white students).

The other changing policy that might shape these outcomes in the future concerns the funding of higher education in Britain. Just at the moment when in the United States the crushing debt young people and their families face in paying for university is taking on more prominence in policy discussions, Britain is following the American model of vastly increasing and privatizing the cost of university education. This may have the consequence of decreasing access for minority students from immigrant backgrounds who may until now have outpaced their American counterparts in educational attainment precisely because of the greater affordability of education in Britain.

Our overall findings lead to both optimistic and pessimistic perspectives on reducing inequality in the education of the children of immigrants. The optimistic story is that, even though ethnic minorities in both countries do less well on performance scores than native whites, they show ambition and a commitment to education. Thus, when we control for social class and for performance scores in adolescence, minorities are more likely to get postsecondary education than comparable native whites, especially in Britain. This would seem to us to be an argument for the kinds of flexibility and second chances that the United States and Britain have in their educational systems, which do not close off the possibility of higher education based on tracking and test scores at a younger age.

The pessimistic story in our findings is that as a greater proportion of the population attends higher education and this education is opened up to minority students, the type of institution attended and degree awarded are the sites where inequality is also being reproduced. It is very important for scholars to better measure this stratification in the educational system. It appears that in both the United States and Britain middle- and upper-class native whites maintain the dominant positions in the most elite universities and the increased access to higher education that has occurred is disproportionately located at less elite institutions. If there is a greater return to a university education from a more selective and prestigious institution, then the stratification within higher education is another mechanism by which native whites are maintaining a privileged position in society.

Notes

This work contains statistical data from the UK Office for National Statistics (ONS), which is Crown copyright and reproduced with the permission of the controller of HMSO and Queen's Printer for Scotland. The use of the ONS statistical data in this work does not imply the endorsement of the ONS in relation to the interpretation or analysis of the statistical data. This work uses research datasets that may not exactly reproduce National Statistics aggregates. Copyright of the statistical results may not be assigned, and publishers of this data must have or obtain a license from HMSO. The ONS data in these results are covered by the terms of the standard HMSO "click-use" license. This work also uses data from the US National Longitudinal Study of Adolescent Health (Add Health) a program project directed by Kathleen Mullan Harris and designed by J. Richard Udry, Peter S. Bearman, and Kathleen Mullan Harris at the University of North Carolina at Chapel Hill, and funded by grant P01-HD31921 from the Eunice Kennedy Shriver National Institute of Child Health and Human Development, with cooperative funding from twenty-three other federal agencies and foundations. Special acknowledgment is due Ronald R. Rindfuss and Barbara Entwisle for assistance in the original design. Information on how to obtain the Add Health data files is available on the Add Health website (http://www.cpc.unc.edu/addhealth). No direct support was received from grant P01-HD31921 for this analysis. The authors also acknowledge Philip Kasinitz and John Mollenkopf (co-PIs with Mary C. Waters) of the Immigrant Second Generation in Metropolitan New York (ISGMNY) project. That study was funded by grant 5RO3HD044598–02 and 990–0173 from the NICHD and with grants from the Russell Sage, Mellon, Ford, Rockefeller, and MacArthur Foundations.

1.   The UK government has passed five major pieces of legislation related to immigration—in 1993, 1996, 1999, 2002, and 2004.

2.   The only exceptions might be Bangladeshis and Pakistanis, who are quite segregated from white British.

3.   At the lower end, the proportion of British students who completed at least a single pass at a low grade increased from 92.2 percent in 1996 to 99 percent in 2010, which means that virtually everyone who left school at age sixteen in the United Kingdom has some minimal form of qualifications. At the upper end, the proportion of British students who completed five good passes (i.e., passes at grades A* to C) also increased from 44.5 percent to 74.8 percent during the same period. In reality, the students at the lower end are least prepared for the labor market whereas those at the upper end are more qualified to undertake a vocation.

4.   As it happens, British research has tended to suggest that the primary and secondary effects are of roughly equal magnitude. See Jackson, Erikson, Goldthorpe, and Yaish (2007).

5.   The results do not change substantially when we restrict our analyses strictly to only the second generation, so we conducted the analyses on both 1.5 generation and second generation to boost the sample size by ethnic group.

6.   See Rothon (2007), DfES (2005), Connolly (2006) for Britain and Lutz (2007) for the United States.

7.   See Kao and Thompson (2003) on the United States and Heath, Rothon, and Kilpi (2008) for Europe.

8.   Full results for Table 4.5 are available upon request—mcw@wjh.harvard.edu.

9.   This means that the YCS will only record information on tertiary education for those who enter university at the traditional age, but will miss mature students and those who take a gap year.

10.   These will thus be an older group than the individuals who form the basis of Tables 2–5, who were around ten years younger. So, unlike the Add Health data, we are not actually tracing the same birth cohort through the educational system. However, other evidence suggests that the relative ethnic inequalities are unlikely to have changed much between the two birth cohorts involved.

11.   The relatively low attainment data for Cubans seems specific to the Add Health sample and might be due to selective attrition between Wave 1 and Wave 3.

12. In Northern Ireland, for example, it is not antidiscrimination measures and lawsuits that have reduced Protestant/Catholic inequalities in access to jobs, but mandatory outreach policies aimed at overcoming the "chill factor." See McCrudden et al. (2009) for reviews of findings in the United Kingdom, and Dobbin and Kalev (2007) for similar findings in the United States.

13. We also recognize that other factors beyond test scores could affect college completion, including the opportunity cost of attending college. For example, the second generation from minority background might leave school to enter the labor force earlier than their native counterparts because of necessity (i.e., the need to support oneself or one's family) or lack of affordability (i.e., the inability to pay for tuition or other related expenses). However, adjudicating between these competing explanations goes beyond the scope of our chapter.

How Similar Educational Inequalities Are Constructed in Two Different Systems, France and the United States: Why They Lead to Disparate Labor-Market Outcomes

Richard Alba, Roxane Silberman, Dalia Abdelhady, Yaël Brinbaum,
and Amy Lutz

The France-United States comparison is intriguing because of the complex profile of similarities and differences it involves. In terms of incorporation regimes, these two countries are generally viewed as positioned toward the assimilationist end of the spectrum because their citizenship rules allow relatively easy access by immigrants and, based on the jus soli principle, grant citizenship automatically (or, in the French case, quasi-automatically) to immigrants' children who are born on the national territory (Weil 2002). Both countries also encourage assimilation to the mainstream, though both are largely tolerant of cultural difference.

Yet there is little doubt that major inequalities along lines of ethnic origin are salient in both societies. How they are constructed intergenerationally is the question, and here is where the differences between France and the United States become more intriguing, for the two differ systemically in their educational systems and in the functioning of their labor markets. In broad brush strokes, the differences would appear to favor greater equality in educational outcomes between native and immigrant-origin children in France than in the United States, whereas the differences in the labor markets, by contrast, have led to greater employment for the children of immigrants in the United States than in France, albeit often in low-wage jobs. In this paper, we lay out in some detail the basis for these statements and examine the empirical degree of inequality between the children of natives and of immigrants associated these differences. The groups we consider are the Mexicans in the United States and the Maghrebins, or North

Africans, in France, both low in status. What we find, stated very briefly, is that the two educational systems, despite their manifest differences, produce broadly similar educational inequalities, but the labor-market outcomes for the children of immigrants, at least in terms of employment, have been more favorable in the United States. Whether the Great Recession there that started in 2007–08 will erode this difference must remain for now an unanswered question.

Differences in Educational Systems

In terms of the fundamentals of its organization, the US educational system would appear much less equipped than the French one to redress the inequalities that children bring into the classroom from their homes and communities. Most significantly, the US system varies considerably from one location to another, while the French system is organized to be more uniform across space. Among rich nations, the funding of American public schools rests to an unusual degree on locally and regionally raised taxes, while the national government plays a limited role. This system contributes to marked inequalities among schools in resources and in the characteristics of teachers (e.g., Hochschild and Scovronick 2003; Kozol 1991; Orfield 2001). These inequalities impact negatively on minorities, both native and immigrant, because of residential segregation and their concentration in places that are relatively impoverished. From the perspective of its organizing principles—we are not yet speaking of its operation in actuality, which is moreover disputed—the French system treats schools more uniformly, reducing (but not eliminating) the opportunities for affluent areas to provide their schools with greater resources.

Moreover, the French government has tried to counteract the impact of social inequalities on education. In 1981, it put in place a policy, the ZEP (for Zones of Educational Priority), to provide additional funding to schools in difficulty according to criteria that include the percentage of immigrants in the catchment area. The French system has also undertaken a major "democratization" in recent decades, with the aim of opening up pathways for working-class and immigrant students to the *baccalauréat*, the indispensable credential earned at the end of the high school years that leads to higher education. One sign of this democratization has been the successive postponement since the 1950s of the moment in the educational career when students are separated between vocational and academic tracks (Merle 2002; Prost 1968); simultaneously, long-sequence vocational tracks have been established at the upper level. These developments have especially affected the short-sequence vocational curricula (Silberman and Fournier 2006a), which were previously the fate of many immigrant students and ended in an early departure from school and entry into the labor market (Tribalat 1995). These separate curricula were formerly institutionalized in distinct middle schools (collèges), which sealed the separation of the students on different tracks and also the destiny of those in vocational programs; now students attend comprehensive middle schools that house various programs.

Another major element of democratization has been the creation of new types of baccalauréat, deemed "professional" or "technological." The latter allows students who are not willing, or allowed, to commit themselves to the classical curriculum of the traditional baccalauréat, and who take an educational track that prepares them for a career, to continue into the university system (Merle 2002). The explicit goal of the democratization was to bring 80 percent of French students to the point of preparing for one or another baccalauréat, although by 2003 only 70 percent of a cohort was attaining this level. Moreover, even though there has been an important increase over thirty years in the proportion of students obtaining the academic baccalauréat, only 33 percent do so.

Another feature of the French system that could benefit some children of immigrants is the preparation for schooling through maternelles, which many children begin to attend at the age of three and which educate nearly all four- and five-year-olds in the country. The maternelles, by providing a common preparatory foundation to nearly all children and introducing children from immigrant homes into a French-language environment, are one way that the French system attempts to overcome the very different endowments they receive in their families. One study of differences in the educational attainments of the children of Turkish immigrants in different European countries credits the maternelles with the somewhat more favorable outcomes achieved in France (Crul and Vermeulen 2003); other studies, however, suggest that in general improvement does not last beyond the end of the primary school (Oeuvrard 2000).

In a similar vein, the systems differ in the way that their public and private portions relate to one another. Both have well developed private systems. In the United States, almost 10 percent of students are attending private schools in any given year (and an additional 2 percent are educated at home [US Census Bureau 2008]); in France, the comparable figures are 14 percent at the primary level and 20 percent at the secondary, and one estimate is that about a third of students spend at least a year in the private system by the time they have completed their secondary-school years (Langouët and Léger 1997). In both countries, the private system is frequently used as a refuge by students from middle-class circumstances whose families want to avoid public schools with many minority and poor students. However, in the United States, the private system is truly separate, which means that, at its elite levels, it can provide a level of educational resources well above that attainable in the public schools. In France, by contrast, the private system, which consists mainly of religious schools (along with some well-known nonreligious schools), is much more integrated with the public one. As long as the private schools, mostly Catholic (Héran 1995), agree to teach the national curriculum and accept the same constraints as the public schools (e.g., number of students by class), they receive state funding for the teaching staff, which mostly has the same qualifications found in the public schools. So, from the parents' perspective, the main differences from the public sector remain the limitation of contact with socially inappropriate children (since the private schools have the freedom to select and expel students) and more severe in-school discipline. French private schools tend to be much less expensive than American ones, and this allows a few immigrant families to send their children to private schools.

These are not the only major differences that might matter for the children of immigrants. US schools have made more deliberate efforts than those in France to meet the educational needs of students coming from minority-language homes, though these efforts, especially when based on bilingual strategies, have been contested and uneven (Gándara and Rumberger 2009). The US system is also one that offers second chances to an unusual extent: access to postsecondary education is potentially open to the large majority of each cohort, since the only requirement is a high school diploma (which can even be earned through an equivalency test). The postsecondary system is highly stratified, with colleges and universities recognized as having varying quality and thus leading to different ultimate outcomes. But positive discrimination at the university level enhances the access of immigrant minorities, especially to the elite tier of the university system (Bowen and Bok 1998; Massey, Charles, Lundy, and Fischer 2002).

Differences in the Transition to the Labor Market

The differences in the way the labor markets work in both societies are complex. One key difference lies in the way that the educational system articulates with jobs. In the United States, that articulation is unusually loose, for the educational system produces, at least below the level of professional education, few distinct degrees and diplomas. For instance, the high school diploma, the certificate bestowed upon the completion of secondary school, exists in just a few varieties and is the credential required by a wide range of jobs. Accordingly, much of the training specific to particular jobs is acquired at work rather than in school. By contrast, the many degrees and certificates of the French system should articulate better to the labor market, a vision inherited from the post-war "planification" period (Tanguy 1986). Even at the secondary-school level, a number of key distinctions exist and a variety of vocational diplomas can be earned to provide qualifications for different occupations. To be sure, both systems produce youth, especially from immigrant origins, who have no credential at all and thus fall to the very bottom of the labor market.

However, a countervailing difference has been in the availability of jobs, especially for youth and low-wage workers. In this respect, the United States is usually depicted as toward the laissez-faire end of the spectrum—that is, regulating the labor market with a light hand that allows wage inequalities in particular to grow, while France is viewed as typical of the more highly regulated labor markets found in continental Europe (Blau and Kahn 2002; DiPrete, Goux, Maurin, and Quesnel-Vallee 2005; Gautié and Schmitt 2010). In France, the conditions of employment are stipulated by employer/employee contracts that are regulated by law and, in the majority of cases, guarantee indefinite periods of employment that can be terminated only with difficulty by employers; wages are mostly set within frameworks established by collective-bargaining processes (even though, ironically, few French workers belong to unions) and constrained at the bottom by the state-determined minimum income (SMIC); and the more generous benefits afforded workers, and the social-welfare net more generally, require substantial employer contributions to the state. This degree of wage and employment protection, it is argued, makes it more costly for French employers to add new jobs. The greater flexibility of the US market is shown by its more rapid generation of jobs during periods of prosperity (such as the years of the mid- and late 1990s) and by the higher rates of employment of individuals of prime working ages. In 2000, the percentage of persons fifteen to sixty-four who were employed was 61 percent in France, while the equivalent figure was 74 percent in the United States. The OECD average was 66 percent in that year (Estevão and Nargis 2005). To be sure, the rate of employment in the United States has fallen because of the economic stagnation initiated by the recession starting in 2007, and as we write this chapter, it is not apparent whether the lower rate establishes a "new normal" for the US economy or it will eventually return to a prior level.

France has adapted to the slow growth of the full-time labor force by the introduction of short-term employment contracts, which over time have come to account for a larger share of the work force, particularly for young people, under twenty-five years old, of whom one-third were in short-term contracts according to the 2010 Labour Force Survey. These contracts, which legally bind the hands of employers as well as employees and rigidly limit the term of employment (typically, to no more than eighteen months), allow job insecurity to permeate selectively into the ranks of the employed; that insecurity is in turn strongly associated with age, as young workers, especially those without any postsecondary education, are strongly affected. For many young people, the search for a permanent job is an all-consuming task during the first few years after leaving the educational system. According to DiPrete et al. (2005), about 50 percent of young French workers, between eighteen and twenty-eight years old, were either unemployed or worked in temporary positions in 2001. Given the scarcity of "good" jobs, young people draw not just on their human capital but also on the social capital that they and their families possess in order to find an appropriate position. This reasoning suggests that ethnicity and other social characteristics could factor into an emergent job rationing system. In other words, youth from immigrant families, especially those of disparaged origins such as the Algerians, may face some degree of labor-market discrimination, assuming that employers, mostly belonging to the native majority population, are likely to favor those like themselves in a tight labor market.

Part I: The Construction of Educational Inequalities

The Degrees of Inequality
Remarkably, given the differences between the educational systems, the educational outcomes that on average separate second-generation students, of Mexican origin in the United States and North African origin in France,

		No qualification/ No secondary- school diploma	Secondary- school diploma	Some post- secondary, no credential	"Low" Post-secondary credential	"High" Post-secondary credential
France						
2nd gen. Maghrebins	Men	27.4	30.1	10.8	15.6	16.1
	Women	20.5	32.0	14.2	16.7	16.5
Mainstream population	Men	12.5	36.4	10.1	17.5	23.5
	Women	12.2	31.9	7.6	22.5	25.7
United States						
U.S.-born Mexicans	Men	20.5	34.3	24.7	7.2	13.0
	Women	16.3	29.1	28.1	8.7	17.9
Mainstream population	Men	8.0	28.2	23.0	8.4	32.5
	Women	5.8	21.1	23.0	10.3	39.8

Notes: French data come from INED's *Trajectoires et origines* survey (2008–9) and are restricted to individuals who attended school in France and are in the ages 26–35. The lowest category includes individuals who left the system without any diploma or earned only the BEPC, a middle-school credential. The two highest categories include, respectively, individuals who earned a technological or other diploma requiring two years beyond the *baccalauréat*, and individuals who completed a more advanced diploma. The mainstream population is defined as the French-born children of French-born parents.

    The American data are tabulated from the Census Bureau's 2005–9 American Community Survey file and are restricted to individuals in the ages 26–35. The two highest categories include, respectively, individuals who earned an associate's degree, and individuals who earned at least the baccalaureate degree. The mainstream population is defined as U.S.-born non-Hispanic whites.

from those of the ethno-racial majority are broadly similar. Since the immigrant parents of the second-generation students typically have very low levels of education by comparison with the mainstream norms of the receiving societies (Hernandez, Denton, and McCartney 2006; Tribalat 1995), it is also true that the second generation in both cases makes major strides beyond its parents. Yet the gap from the average levels of educational attainment of majority students remains large and is especially noticeable at the lower and upper ends of the educational distribution, when students exit from school without any credentials that are meaningful in the labor market, on the one hand, or emerge from a lengthy school career with postsecondary credentials that position them favorably in the labor market, on the other.

    Consider the data in Table 5.1. In the US case, the data are drawn from 2005–9 American Community Survey and cannot be limited to the second generation (because of the absence of a parental nativity question in census data); however, considerable research shows that, in cross-sectional data such as these, there is not much difference between the educational attainments of the second and the third and later generations (Farley and Alba 2002; Telles and Ortiz 2008). The educational distribution of the US born is therefore a suitable proxy for that of the second generation. The French data come from the 2008–09 *Trajectoires et origines* survey, a sizable national survey that compared immigrants and their descendants with the native French mainstream. In this case, the data are for immigrants' children who were educated in France, a group that includes some in the 1.5 generation (individuals who immigrated as young children). In both data sets, we have narrowed the tabulations to age groups that have recently exited from the educational system in order to capture as much as possible current inequalities in life chances between native- and immigrant-origin groups.

The ratios between the rates for second-generation and majority youth tell the basic story. At the lower end of educational attainment, 15–20 percent of young Mexican Americans have left high school without a diploma. These percentages are two-and-a-half to three times the rates among non-Hispanic whites (i.e., Anglos). The proportion of the Maghrebin second generation that leaves school without a useful diploma is also high, despite the democratization of the French school system during the closing decades of the last century.[1] Nevertheless, the ratio of disparity in relation to the native French is not quite as large as its equivalent in the United States—among Maghrebin men, the percentage without a useful diploma is twice that among the native French; among women, the Maghrebin percentage is two-thirds higher. But the absolute values are higher than for Mexicans in the United States, with more than a quarter of second-generation men having no diploma to present to prospective employers. All in all, there is a rough similarity in the disparities at the lower end.

At the upper end, the disparities are smaller in France. It is noteworthy that about half of Mexican-American students and nearly as many Maghrebin students now go beyond secondary school. They are therefore positioning themselves to qualify for jobs that are in the middle class, broadly construed. In both countries also, there is little difference between the second generation and the mainstream when it comes to two-year diplomas and degrees such as the associate's degree in the United States or the BTS (*Brevet de technicien supérieur*) in France, though these are much more common as the final credential in France. Gaps in relation to the mainstream widen when we consider more-advanced credentials, such as the baccalaureate in the United States or the *licence* in France (the latter requiring three years of university study).

Thus, in the United States, native whites earn these more-advanced credentials at more than twice the rate of Mexican Americans. The situation is somewhat more favorable in France: The rate at which Maghrebins earn these credentials is about the same as for Mexicans, but the gap from the mainstream is smaller. Still, French natives hold sizable advantages: for men and women, the native rates exceed the Maghrebin ones by about 50 percent. If we narrowed our focus to the most disadvantaged of the Maghrebin groups, the Algerians, then the disparities would rise substantially and resemble those noted in the United States.

Overall, then, the profiles of outcome inequalities between the two societies are similar but not identical, and the American one is more extreme, as one should expect. Yet we place our emphasis on the similarity between them, rather than the difference, because what strikes us as most noteworthy is that systems so different in their formal organization produce basically equivalent inequalities. Thus, it seems useful then to consider how they arise in two different systems.

Primary School

We begin where formal schooling begins, with the primary school, where some important similarities between these systems appear despite formal differences. (For a diagram of the French system, see Figure 5.1.) Studies in the United States show the consolidation of inequalities in school-relevant skills before the end of primary school. For instance, according to the assessments of the National Center for Educational Statistics (NCES) for "The Nation's Report Card" (2005), there is a sizable gap in average reading scores between Anglo and Hispanic (as well as African American) students by the end of the fourth grade, though there is also good news because over the nine-year period between 1998 and 2007 the gap narrowed significantly (from 32 to 26 points on the NCES scale).

The first important similarity concerns the connection of inequalities in spatial location to those among schools, for there is substantial segregation of second-generation children from middle-class majority-group children. In both countries, this is largely a function of well-entrenched residential segregation according to social class and ethno-racial origin. This segregation involves

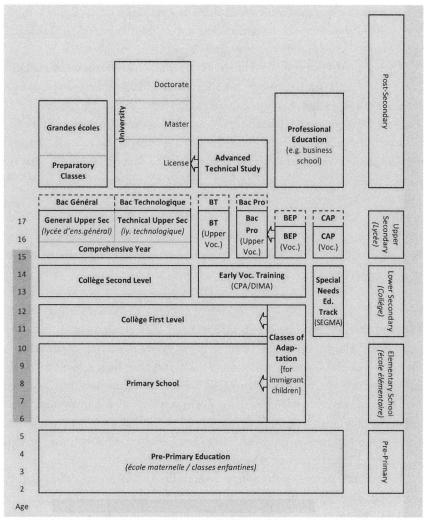

Figure 5.1. The Current Structure of the Education System in France (2012)
Note: Areas enclosed in dashed lines indicate mandatory exams/tests.
Source: Ministry of Education

concentrations of minority and majority families in different jurisdictions, as much as it involves segregation by neighborhood within the same city. In the United States, European-American families with school-age children tend to be found in mostly white suburbs, while minority families are more often located in large cities or inner suburbs (Alba et al. 2009); these spatial placements are nearly the reverse of those in France, where immigrant minorities are concentrated in specific suburbs (*banlieues*) around major cities (Guillon 1990; Préteceille 2009). Since in both countries most children attend local primary schools, the impact on school segregation is probably equivalent.

Recent analyses from the United States demonstrate that Latino children, along with black children, are increasingly likely to be found in heavily minority elementary schools, partly due to the declining proportion of European American children in school-age cohorts and especially in the portions of those cohorts in public schools (Orfield 2001; cf. Logan, Oakley, and Stowell 2008). We have no comparable systematic data on school segregation from France, but a study of Bordeaux reveals school segregation based on class and ethnic origins (Felouzis 2005).

In the United States, in comparison with France, the inequalities in funding across jurisdiction and school stand out. School funding disparities frequently complement other disparities among schools serving socially diverse populations (Hochschild and Scovronick 2003). That is, schools with many socially disadvantaged students are faced with a series of other disadvantages that would require substantial additional funding to overcome; needless to say, they rarely if ever receive this. Observing that predominantly minority schools are also highly likely to serve areas where poverty is concentrated, Gary Orfield and Chungmei Lee (2006, 29) note that such schools are typically beset by a variety of problems that impede learning: "less qualified, less experienced teachers, lower levels of peer group competition, more limited curricula taught at less challenging levels, more serious health problems, much more turnover enrollment," and they could have added more serious levels of threat to the safety of students.

Inequalities in school funding are more limited in France, though they exist and have increased in recent years. Since the end of the 1990s, the national government has decentralized an increasing share of the financing of, and decision making about, local schools (Henriot-Van Zanten 1990; Louis 1994). It has nevertheless retained the budget for, and allocation of, teachers, the single most important factor determining the level of inequality. The financial support provided for the teaching staff in a school is, moreover, a function of the numbers of students and classes, and the Ministry of Education strictly controls the number of students per class. The ability of even school principals to exert an influence over the teaching budget remains limited. Nevertheless, the rules governing teacher allocation, which give some choice to more experienced (and better paid) teachers, reinforce inequalities and even produce, as a secondary effect, lower public spending on schools serving disadvantaged areas because the least experienced teachers are concentrated in them.

There has been an attempt to compensate for inequalities by some increase in funding for schools in areas with social problems. The so-called ZEP policy, initiated in 1981 and revised several times since, provides supplementary support for the teaching staff at such schools, with an aim of reducing the number of students per class. Eleven percent of the primary schools are under the ZEP, but little data exist to establish the extent of the reductions in class size due to the policy, which is almost certainly small. In any event, the pressures to reduce class size are also powerful on the schools serving more affluent areas, since the parents there signal to school administrators that it is a major factor in their decision about whether they will send their children to the public school. They can find justification, if they need it, in a recent study that seems to demonstrate an improvement in school achievements when classes at the primary level are reduced by two children (Piketty and Valdenaire 2006).

In both systems, school choice is limited. In the United States, the default principle determining where a child is educated at public expense is still that of the "neighborhood school." The No Child Left Behind Act of 2001 does allow parents to transfer their children out of underperforming schools, but what data there are suggest that this option is selected by few parents (and that it brings little benefit to the children who transfer; see Zimmer et al. 2007). In France, the government has increasingly restricted school choice in recent decades, imposing a mapping of addresses to schools (*carte scolaire*). This was in fact an attempt to constrain the ability of more affluent families to avoid local schools with many poor and/or immigrant students and thus to encourage the mixing of students from different backgrounds, but at the same time it implies as a matter of policy that school composition will reflect the local resident population and thus that schools will be segregated in the way that neighborhoods are. For those affluent parents who find that the *carte scolaire* will send their children to the socially "wrong" school, the private schools are always an option in case they cannot manage to find a place in another school, for instance, near their work place.

In both countries, the "richness" of the educational programs differs across schools in ways that reflect the social origins of the students. While curricula in the United States are to some degree standardized across schools—at least in the sense that states define minimal standards that must be met for different subjects in each grade, and the No Child Left Behind legislation, along with the testing movement, has further strengthened the role of standards—schools that are more resource-rich and serve middle-class populations are able to offer their students many supplements to the minimum standards, so that differences in learning grow over time (Kozol 1991). In France, despite the more limited control of local authorities over finances, they have nevertheless played a role in financing supplementary activities and functions (Dutercq 2000). Thus, they are responsible for the supervision of children during school vacations (which are numerous in France) when their parents are unable to take care of them during the workday. These periods of supervision have taken on more and more of a pedagogical character (e.g., trips to the theater) and play an increasing part in the access of children from poor or immigrant families to cultural resources. Families sometimes send their children to the vacation supervision even when a parent is at home, since the cost is modest. Similarly, the primary schools offer after-school care, generally for two extra hours, for which parents have to pay a modest fee, which they can request the local authorities to subsidize. Since the 1970s, some schools have tried to use these supplementary hours (les "études") to help students with their homework, with the aim of reducing socially based inequalities. The development of educational inequalities from supplementary school activities is furthered by the so-called nature classes (classes de nature). These involve excursions with a pedagogical character and even exchanges with other countries, the latter often connected with instruction in foreign languages (mainly English), which now begins in the maternelles. The expenses associated with these classes are partly financed by local authorities and partly by parents, thus placing children from poor families at a disadvantage (although limited numbers of "scholarships" [bourses] are generally available). The schools in the more affluent areas organize such activities more frequently because of the pressures of parents to provide this form of cultural and educational enrichment and their willingness to pay the extra costs (Glassman 2001).

One respect in which the US school system outdoes the French one concerns assistance to children coming from minority-language homes, but this assistance is under regular political attack. That these children are entitled to help in achieving equal educational opportunities was established by court decision, specifically the Supreme Court's *Lau v. Nichols* decision of 1974. However, what is deemed as required to create equal educational opportunity differs considerably across states and has changed over time. In terms of the goal of enabling minority-language students to participate fully in English-dominant classrooms, the effectiveness of the programs is highly variable (Gándara and Rumberger 2009; Goldenberg 2008; Slavin and Cheung 2005). Indeed, the term "bilingual education" has become more a political code word, reflecting polarized opinions over the appropriate policies for immigrant-origin and minority students, than a reference to a specific set of school policies. Thus, the practices encompassed by the term are quite varied, ranging from educating students for some of the school day in the minority language to placing them for limited periods of time in classes that teach English as a second language. In recent years, these policies have been constrained by referendum in some states. This process began in 1998 with the heavily financed campaign for Proposition 227 ("English for the Children"), which has severely restricted the period that students can be taught in bilingual programs in California, the state with by far the largest number of English-language learners (Olsen 2009). It appears that the number of California students in bilingual education has fallen precipitously as a result (Gándara and Rumberger 2009).

French schools have provided less in the way of assistance to ease students speaking languages other than French into mainstream classrooms. In some schools, classes of "reception" (*classes d'accueil* in the primary school) exist to help newly arriving immigrant students make the transition into regular classrooms (Lorcerie 1994). These classes were intended to provide only a few months of preparation, but several studies have shown that students have been relegated to them for long periods and that even some French students, coming from areas outside the metropole (e.g., the Antilles), have been placed in them. There were also attempts, especially during the 1970s, to provide courses in the language and culture of the countries of origin of students from immigrant families, taught by instructors sent by these countries. The purpose was more to cultivate the students' respect for the countries from which their parents came than it was to provide a transition to mainstream classes, but the success of the courses was disputed, in any event, and even some of immigrant parents were against them. The Berque Report of 1986 argued the policy was failing because of stigmatization of the students who were participating and of weak control over the teachers and what they were teaching. The children of immigrants are probably further disadvantaged by the relatively recent policy of introducing foreign-language instruction at early ages; it now begins in the *maternelles* (in affluent areas) or in the primary schools. Since the first foreign language is usually English, the children from immigrant families are confronted in the beginning school years with the need to learn two unfamiliar languages, the other of course being French.

Secondary-School Level

Middle school   The inequalities between native students and those of immigrant origins are already pronounced by the time the stage of secondary education begins. In the case of students in the United States, the already-cited differences among fourth-grade students measured by the National Report Card reveal these inequalities. They are also shown by similar tests taken by eighth-grade students, which indicate rather stable gaps between Anglo students and black and Hispanic ones in reading, writing, and mathematics. In France, the inequalities are revealed by grade repetitions, which are more common there than in the United States. (In the United States, by contrast, the criticism has been that unprepared students are pushed ahead by so-called social promotion.) The repetitions, which must be recommended by the teaching staff and can be appealed by parents, are concentrated especially at key transitional moments in the educational career, including the first and third years of primary school, along with the first and fourth years of middle school and the first year of high school. The children from immigrant families have been more likely than native French children to be required to repeat a school year. According to the analyses of the 1995 French Educational Panel by a member of our team, Yaël Brinbaum, about half of Maghrebin children have repeated at least one year of school by the time they reach the end of middle school (corresponding to the eighth grade in the US system), compared to about a quarter of native French children. This difference can be seen as due to social-class backgrounds, since the rate of grade repetition is almost as high, over 40 percent, among the native working-class (Brinbaum and Kieffer 2005). Nevertheless, it indicates that the children of Maghrebin immigrants are frequently older than their native French classmates at the moment of entry to the secondary level.

In both systems, the inequalities among students that have developed at the primary-school level are enhanced at the secondary level. The residential segregation by social class and ethno-racial origins means that there is substantial segregation among secondary schools, even though they generally have larger catchment areas than do primary schools; school segregation may be somewhat reduced by the larger areas, but it does not for that reason cease to be an important consideration. In the United States, there is, correlatively, inequality of resources, because of the role of local funding bases.

At the secondary-school level, moreover, segregation of students by social origins is also expressed frequently in more-formal ways through placements in different curricula or different tracks, placements that derive from school-relevant inequalities. Some of this segregation takes place within school buildings, as the diverse streams of students entering the buildings separate into different classrooms, where the teaching and subject matter channel students toward different academic destinations (e.g., Oakes 2005).

In France, the democratization of the system would seem to work against these tendencies. It has unified once-separate curricula (academic and vocational) and simultaneously limited the ability of parents to determine the *collège*, or middle school, of their children. However, the *collège* has therefore become the most problematic stage of the school system. In the suburbs with high concentrations of immigrant and poor families, the *collège* is the site of considerable violence beginning with the second year; and dropping out, which often takes the form of chronic absenteeism, becomes a common phenomenon at this point.

Moreover, since the 1980s there has been a growing decentralization of authority at this level that has widened differences among middle schools (Legrand 2000; Louis 1994). In the areas where students of immigrant origins are concentrated, the inner suburbs, the schools depend increasingly on municipal and regional governments that are themselves strapped for resources. Hence, the inequalities among the schools widen (Thomas 2005; Trancart 1998). The beneficial effects of the ZEP policy are too limited to offset the social and fiscal inequalities among them. The policy attempts to attract experienced teachers with bonuses and to avoid having schools in disadvantaged neighborhoods become mere transit stations for young teachers gaining classroom experience. However, its success in these ways has been disputed (Brizard 1995; Meuret 1994): since the bonuses for teachers are small, it continues to be the case that schools in ZEP areas are staffed with disproportionate numbers of less-experienced teachers. Recent studies have shown that the social homogeneity of the students in these schools has been increasing (Bénabou, Kramarz, and Prost 2005).

French parents who wish to avoid their children's attendance at a school that they view as problematic often resort to the private school system after the sixth and final year of primary school. Some of these children then reappear in the public system at the high school level. Another strategy pursued by some parents depends on the so-called hidden curricula (*curricula cachés*), which involve difficult modern or ancient languages (e.g., Japanese, Russian, ancient Greek) or unusual courses developed by principals to raise the prestige of their schools, such as the *classes européennes*, in which some of the instruction is in a foreign language such as English or German (Duru-Bellat and Van Zanten 1999). This sort of differentiation begins with the third year of middle school, when students start to study a second foreign language. The hidden curricula produce social segregation across schools, since not all middle schools can offer, for example, unusual languages such as Japanese, but also within school buildings, creating differences between classes similar to the effects of tracking in the United States (Duru-Bellat and Kieffer 1997).

Another divergence in the school careers of the immigrant working class and the native middle class occurs when children have problems in schools. Like their American counterparts, middle-class native French families then make use of tutoring; or they place their children in special courses given after school hours by regular teachers who are paid extra by the parents to instruct small groups of students, often in mathematics. Such instruction, which generally takes place off the school grounds, has become a common supplement at all levels of the school system. It appears that immigrant parents, even when they express very high educational aspirations for their children, do not take the same measures to support their children who are in difficulty in school (Brinbaum 2002). This difference then adds to the cumulative inequalities from which the children coming from immigrant families suffer throughout their time in school.

The Educational Goals and Orientations of Immigrant-Origin Students and Their Families   The middle-school stage is fateful for many students. By the time of middle school, a large number of the children from immigrant families are already having academic problems. An unresolved issue concerns how socially disadvantaged children, many from minority backgrounds, respond when they face the possibility of academic disappointment and even failure. One strand of theorizing and research posits that they are more likely to participate in oppositional subcultures and in this way their "failure" is crystallized. The idea that oppositional cultures appeal to minority youth because of their experiences and their fears of rejection is traceable to the work of John Ogbu and his collaborators (e.g., Fordham and Ogbu 1987).

While their formulation has been disputed, it seems unassailable that groups of alienated students form in secondary schools and engage in risky behavior (e.g., deviant acts, such as petty crime and drug use) while disengaging from academic work; this disengagement can be manifested in irregular attendance, refusal to do assignments, failure of courses, and eventual dropout. Students on these trajectories are usually supported socially and psychologically by similarly inclined peers. While some European-American students in the United States become involved in such oppositional subcultures, minority students are at greater risk because of their uncertainties about acceptance by mainstream teachers and educational institutions, if not outright experiences with discrimination, and greater anxieties about their futures (Kasinitz, Mollenkopf, Waters, and Holdaway 2008). Entry into oppositional subcultures is thought to be implicated in the higher dropout rates of Hispanics and African Americans, especially of boys. In France, qualitative studies have shown that the oppositional culture in evidence among the academically weaker children of minority origins, especially North African, emerges during the first years of middle school (Van Zanten 2001).

A very different line of thinking emphasizes the resilience of immigrant-origin youth. The immigrant optimism thesis of Kao and Tienda (1995) emphasizes the optimism of second-generation students, which may help them to weather initially unfavorable school experiences. In fact, the educational aspirations of immigrant-origin youth remain high through the middle-school years in both systems. These high aspirations suggest that the hold of oppositional culture remains limited.

Our best measurements of aspirations come from students who are at the end of middle school and/or the beginning of high school. For the United States, Yaël Brinbaum has analyzed data from the National Longitudinal Adolescent Health study;[2] for France, the data of the Educational Panel are employed. In the first case, the youngsters themselves are queried about their educational goals, in the second, the parents are.

The majority of children of Mexican immigrants aspire to a college education. For example, when asked how much they want to go to college, 59 percent of second-generation Mexican Americans in the ninth and tenth grades place themselves in the highest category on the survey. This percentage is only slightly below that for Anglo students (67 percent), who come in general from more advantaged families than the Mexican American students do. However, many fewer Mexican American students *expect* to go to college.

Only 29 percent of the second-generation students give the highest category when asked if they expect to attend college, and the difference from Anglo students, 52 percent of whom respond with this category, is thus much wider in this respect.

In France, when North African immigrant parents are asked what educational aspirations, they hold for their children, the great majority responds in terms of the *baccalauréat*, the indispensable credential for entry into higher education. Sixty-nine percent respond in this way, compared to 74 percent of native French parents. A high percentage of the immigrant parents—about two-thirds—hope to see their children earn an academic *baccalauréat*, the most prestigious secondary-school credential. The unusually high educational aspirations of the North African parents stand out when they are compared to working-class French parents and those of Portuguese immigrant origins. About twice as many North African parents aspire to the academic *bac* for their children as is the case for the others.

The expectation that their children will bring home prestigious academic credentials also is prominent in the interviews that Dalia Abdelhady conducted with second-generation North Africans in the suburbs around Paris. However, this picture becomes more nuanced by the frank statements by these young people about their parents' lack of knowledge about the French system. What emerges is a portrait in which immigrant parents strongly desire their children to earn academic credentials as proof of family success within the French system; however, the parents have little ability to assess what careers are likely to follow from particular academic outcomes. For example, Karim, a twenty-four-year-old youth councilor, describes his Algerian parents' lack of knowledge of the French educational system and the added importance they (especially the father) place on obtaining *le bac*. Karim has a technology high school degree and went to university for a year, and he describes how his father does not understand the different types of school-leaving options available through the French system:

> In the end they [the parents] are just not informed about the current educational options and all that. . . . I really belong to the first generation—that is, my father, he was born in Algeria and he participated in the war [for Algerian independence] and afterwards he came to France. His French is not great. . . . Yet like all Maghrebin families, it is the father who is the head, and he is involved, but he wants just the *bac* and doesn't give a damn

about anything else. Whether I do the *bac* S or the *bac* STI, or whatever, he is happy that I just got the *bac*. He is very happy about that. I have three sisters also, and he was more happy for me than for my sisters when they earned the *bac*.

The story was quite different for the Mexican American students Abdelhady interviewed. Their parents encouraged them to go finish high school, but rarely advised them to pursue a college degree. Javier, a twenty-year-old who just got a job at a furniture store, explained how his parents would have supported any of his decisions and pushed him to finish his high school:

> Right now, I am just trying to stay out of trouble. I want to go back to school, but not right now. My parents were never involved in any of my decisions. They just said that whatever I was going to do, they would support me, just like any parent would. They didn't push me to be anything that they wanted me to be, they just said, "find something that you like and go for it." . . . Of course they wanted me to graduate high school and I did, but now I don't know.

Similar to Javier's parents, many of the Mexican American respondents' parents were happy to see their children working and earning money and thus able to provide for their families.

High School   In France, matters become more complicated at the end of middle school and the beginning of high school (*lycée*) because of the complex menu of programs that students may choose from and that lead to different certificates, with different meanings for further education and eventual entry into the labor market. The complications are especially relevant to working-class students and those of immigrant origins because the great majority of middle-class native French students aim for the *baccalauréat*, followed by university education or, even better, acceptance into one of the *grandes écoles*, the Ivy League of the French system.

The *lycées* are comprised, on the one hand, of schools that provide a general academic and technological curriculum and, on the other, of those deemed "professional," which offer vocational training. This mix is a product of the unification policy of the 1980s, since previously there was a total separation between the general or academic *lycées* and those offering all other curricula. The partial unification is linked to the democratization initiative and was accompanied by the creation of the professional and technological *baccalauréats* alongside the academic one. At that point, a portion of the students who previously would have attended the vocational *lycées* began to attend the general ones, choosing their curricula at the end of the second year. A response to the unification has been increasing differentiation by prestige among the academic curricula themselves: students specialize along scientific, literary, or economic and social tracks, each of which has its own *baccalauréat*, but there is now a marked hierarchy among the different academic *baccalauréats*, with the highest status attached to the scientific one. The technological *baccalauréat* is, moreover, lower in general status than the academic ones though it still provides those who earn it with access to higher education, in specialized tracks that yield distinct university degrees (which in fact are often quite valuable in the labor market). These evolutions in the French *lycée* system appear to demonstrate that each attempt at unification for the purpose of greater equality of chances is counterbalanced by a further differentiation that preserves the privileges of the upper reaches of the system (Duru-Bellat and Kieffer 2000).

As a result of the democratization program, the professional *lycées* also now offer a credential, the *baccalauréat professionnel*, which does not automatically open the door to the postsecondary system. However, many of the students in these *lycées* do not obtain this credential. A portion of the students definitively leave the academic track at the end of middle school in order to earn vocational diplomas such as the CAP and BEP (the *certificat d'aptitude professionnelle* and the *brevet d'études professionnelles*, respectively) in programs that require two or three years. The vocationally oriented *lycées* are a major pathway for the separation of students with academic and other difficulties from their cohorts, and they are the sites of massive problems in the suburbs because of high rates of absenteeism and violence. At the end of the *collège*, about 40 percent of students enter a *lycée professionnel*, according to the data of the Educational Panel.

By comparison with native French students, the students of Maghrebin origins are overrepresented in technological and vocational curricula and thus underrepresented on the general, or academic, track, according to the analysis of the Educational Panel data by Yaël Brinbaum, whose results are presented in Table 5.2. However, their distribution across curricula is not at all remarkable when they are compared to working-class French students and those of immigrant Portuguese origins, as is done in the lower panel of the table.

Some of the vocational diplomas are very specialized and linked to a supposed future position on the labor market. Here also some degree of hierarchy is apparent (for instance, diplomas in electronics rank very high), depending on the return on the labor market. One problem is that, despite constant advertising to encourage students to choose vocational tracks, there are not enough places for the students who want them. This is a major source of frustration for immigrants' children, especially for the Maghrebins, as demonstrated by different surveys (Brinbaum and Kieffer 2005; Silberman and Fournier 1999). In some cases, a desired option is available only in a very distant *lycée*, a source of further discouragement for girls since their parents are reluctant to let them travel so far.

With such a complex menu of school options and families that are not well versed in their significance, the students of immigrant origins depend on the advice of school counselors. The interviews conducted by Dalia Abdelhady describe in many cases a process of academic orientation shaped by stereotypes and marked by misinformation. Najib, an eighteen-year-old coordinator (*animateur*) who dropped out of school after one year of BEP (and has no degree), complained that:

> Even the counselors, they didn't really counsel me, they criticized things . . . they criticized the choices I put down on the form that we have to fill out to indicate our wishes. They've criticized, they've said, that's a bit difficult, it's this, it's that. . . . They haven't given me advice, they've just criticized. That is, they haven't said, you should do this instead of that. . . . I don't know how to put it. . . . To analyze who I am and then to choose a good track. They have just criticized, that's all. They haven't helped to clarify things for me.

While Najib complained about the lack of orientation that he got in school, many second-generation Maghrebins complained about the inaccurate advice they received and viewed at times as discriminatory (Brinbaum and Kieffer 2005, 2009). Describing his educational trajectory, Farid, who worked part-time in public relations, explained the stereotypes that lead to inappropriate counseling and wrong choices:

> I was a normal student. . . . And afterwards I completed a BEP in electronics. Bad choice, bad guidance. This is precisely the problem for the newcomers in France, those from the suburbs—they are guided into a field they haven't chosen, rather it's imposed on them. Okay, so you are from the suburbs, therefore it's mechanics, it's electronics, it's social services for the

girls, it's plastics for the boys. That's it. We don't have possibilities to enter other fields. It's truly a shame. You do a BEP, that's all you do. You all wind up doing the same things.

Confronted by the crises of the immigrant suburbs, where many youths abandon school with no meaningful credential, the French government has recently attempted to reinstitute the pathway of apprenticeship (where work and classroom education are linked). However, a disadvantage of this pathway for Maghrebin youngsters is the requirement of an employment contract. Since the schools take no responsibility for these contracts, the requirement forces the North Africans to encounter the difficulties they will later face as prospective workers: the unwillingness of many employers to take them on. Research has shown that the employment contracts required by apprenticeship programs are often procured by students' relatives, and in this respect the family networks of the Maghrebins are less effective than those of other groups, such as the Portuguese, whose families can find places in the ethnic niches the group controls in, for example, construction (Silberman and Fournier 1999). The data of the Educational Panel, as shown in Table 5.2, reveal this inequality very clearly: very few of the Maghrebin youngsters (about 1 percent) are in apprenticeships despite their relatively high concentration in vocational curricula. Among working-class students, those from native French and Portuguese backgrounds are ten times more likely to have apprenticeships.

The complex system of secondary-school credentials in France marks an important difference from the United States. In the United States, the credential that matters is the high school diploma, which is the pathway to further education, almost regardless of the school and curriculum where it is earned. Indeed, the system even provides for the possibility of earning its equivalent outside of school, the GED (General Equivalency Development diploma), which is acquired by passing a test.

The French system offers a more complicated menu of diplomas and credentials at the secondary level. An important feature of the system is in fact that it offers relatively easy access to various tracks but a more rigorous selectivity when it comes to diplomas, which are unmistakably ranked. The new *baccalauréats*, the technological and professional (earned by 18 percent and 12 percent of the class of 2003, respectively), created as part of the democratization initiative, are ranked below the academic *baccalauréat*, which has itself separated

TABLE 5.2. 2002 Track Distribution of Students Who Entered the Sixth-year in France in 1995

All	General track	Technological Track	Vocational track	Apprenticeship	Drop out	Total
Native French	42.0	18.9	23.9	8.7	6.5	100
North-African origin	24.5	26.2	36.2	1.8	11.3	100
Portuguese origin	28.6	18.9	27.7	15.3	9.5	100
Working class						
Native French	23.0	18.7	33.9	12.8	11.5	100
North-African origin	22.7	26.7	38.0	1.3	11.5	100
Portuguese origin	28.3	19.1	28.7	14.2	9.6	100

Source: Educational Panel, 1995 (student panel and follow-up surveys: Family survey, 1998, Youth survey, 2002), MEN-DEP Yaël Brinbaum's calculations

according to subjects of specialization that are in turn ranked. Nevertheless, the new *baccalauréats* have opened roads to the tertiary level, especially to vocational tracks in the lower tertiary level. Yet the proportion of a cohort attaining the tertiary level remains lower than is the case in the United States.

Postsecondary Education

The proportions of cohorts entering the postsecondary system are different in France and the United States, but the students confront in both cases a differentiated and hierarchical system. In the US case, this internal stratification is much greater than exists at the secondary level and thus requires more knowledge on the part of students and their families about the nature and outcomes of different educational paths.

Both systems encompass relatively short paths that lead to vocational credentials. In the United States, the most important distinction in the system is between two- and four-year colleges. The two-year colleges generally feature a mix of curricula, with some providing vocational credentials, intended as the endpoints of the scholastic career and as direct links to jobs, while others offer a general academic preparation, allowing students to transfer to four-year colleges (Brint and Karabel 1989). In the French postsecondary sector, the vocational tracks have been an area of innovation and success. Thus, university institutes of technology (IUT) were created during the 1970s. In addition, a vocational credential that is earned at the *lycées* after the *baccalauréat* has been completed, the *Brevet de technicien supérieur* (BTS), now links to university programs. The technological/professional tracks that end in the BTS certificate are selective in their admissions, and the diploma is advantageous in the labor market. If students cross the bridges to the universities, they can earn university diplomas, the *licence* and masters. The universities are also developing more advanced tracks of this kind, leading to new credentials.

In both systems also, social origins correspond quite strongly with the tracks that students enter. In the American case, students of immigrant origins are more concentrated in the two-year schools (Fry 2003). This is a consequence undoubtedly of differences in academic careers prior to this branching point; on average, middle-class European-American students can present stronger academic records and test scores, qualifying them more easily for admission to four-year colleges. In addition to having weaker high school records, the children of working-class immigrants are constrained by the more limited economic resources of their families—typically, the two-year schools charge lower tuitions and students can live at home while attending the local community college. These students may feel less confident about their ability to complete a four-year academic program, if only because of the economic pressures they are under, and may also be uncertain about the wisdom of the choice between vocational and academic training given their circumstances. The correlation between social origins and college entered, along with the frequently slow progress of two-year college students and the high rates of failure at this level, have led some scholars to characterize the two-year colleges as a false promise of social advancement (Brint and Karabel 1989).

In France, the emergence of vocational tracks in postsecondary education, and especially at the universities, has benefited some students of immigrant origins, though students from Maghrebin families do not figure prominently in this group. Numerous in the vocational tracks in the *lycées*, students from immigrant backgrounds are able enter the postsecondary professional tracks thanks to the technological *baccalauréats*. This is notably the case for many second-generation Portuguese, but is much less true for the Maghrebins, who continue to prefer the academic curricula of the universities. In addition, the training for professions with a middling status in France (e.g., social workers and physician's assistants) is particularly in demand among young women from modest backgrounds, including many who come from immigrant families.

Apart from the vocational tracks, there is also, in each system, a pronounced hierarchy among the universities and institutions of professional training. In the United States, the distinctions evident among four-year colleges and universities are well known to almost all middle-class students applying for admission. The ranking of schools according to such criteria as the selectivity of their admissions correlates with the social origins and post-college trajectories of their students. The most selective schools can usually boast of the highest proportions of graduates who go on to receive further educational training.

Since most professional training is not provided through four-year college programs, the final educational stage for many students comes in postgraduate academic or professional programs. In this respect, the US system is different from European universities, where specialization begins at entry to the university. Postbaccalaureate programs can demand as many as four or more years of further education, and especially for students coming from weaker economic backgrounds must be balanced against considerations of expense and indebtedness, as well as against foregone earnings. By the postgraduate stage, there has been a rigorous prior selectivity, which has removed all but a small number of children of working-class immigrants.

In France, the most prominent feature of the system is the division between the *grandes écoles* and universities. The *grandes écoles* were founded in the Napoleonic era to educate civil servants and engineers (training the universities did not provide); several *grandes écoles* that train business elites were added later. The *grandes écoles* are the most selective branch of higher education and entry to them is strongly correlated with social origins (with a large proportion of entrants having parents who are university professors). Some recent studies reveal that the social homogeneity of their students has increased in recent decades, as entering classes have fewer and fewer children coming from the working class and other less-privileged strata (Albouy and Wanecq 2003). Preparation for entry, which is achieved through competitive examination for the strictly limited number of places, begins with the choice of a *lycée*. It continues after completion of the *lycée* years with "*classes préparatoires*," which are given in some of the best *lycées* of Paris and other large cities. Even these preparatory classes are highly selective: entrance to them is based on the student's dossier and takes into account the grades during the last two years of the *lycée* along with its reputation. The *classes préparatoires* provide a broad cultural education along with a training of high quality, and they are themselves stratified since several of the Parisian *lycées* produce the main group of students who will succeed in the entrance examinations for the *grandes écoles*. Success in the examinations requires therefore a risky multiyear strategy based on a sound grasp of the educational system and is consequently unthinkable for virtually all children from immigrant families. The top Parisian *lycée*, Henri IV, has recently proposed to institute a "preliminary" *classe préparatoire* to permit good students from the suburbs to attain this level. In fact, just a tiny number of these students currently succeed at the entrance examinations and can take advantage of the free education that ensues (some students in the *grandes écoles* are even treated as provisional civil servants and paid salaries during their training).

The attraction of the *grandes écoles* deprives the universities of a large part of the best students, at the same time as they are not adequately financed to educate the students they have. Except for their law and medical faculties, the French universities are widely considered to be undergoing a grave crisis, and the separation between them and the *grandes écoles* is regularly challenged but without much hope of achieving a true reform. Students from working-class and poor families, among them the great majority of the second generation of immigrant populations, enter then into a university system that is not well structured and can quickly find themselves disoriented and heading for failure (Beaud 2002). A new postsecondary tier that has emerged during recent decades is made up of less distinguished private universities that charge tuition and provide engineering and business education; they provide another outlet for children from middle-class families. The important reform that occurred under Sarkozy to bestow more autonomy on the state-supported universities will probably increase differentiation among them.

In the United States there are forces counteracting the social selection operating at the point of entry to higher education. Most important are policies of affirmative action instituted by many schools. They are, to be sure, contested by conservatives and have been overturned in some public universities, notably in California and Texas, by lawsuits or referendum. It is also hard to be sure how many students they affect. Yet research suggests that they can have powerful effects on the long-term opportunities of minority students (Alon and Tienda 2007; Bowen and Bok 1998; Massey et al. 2002).

In contrast to the United States, France has not developed policies of affirmative action and is, in principle, quite opposed to them. However, it is in the domain of higher education that the first initiative in this direction has been taken. Sciences Po (the Institute of Political Studies of Paris) has created an avenue of access specifically for the better students coming from the *lycées* of the immigrant suburbs. Despite the 2005 riots, such initiatives remain extremely limited and are contested by the adherents of the so-called Republican model. It is necessary to recognize in this context the rigidity of the French educational system: second chances are difficult to find, even though various reforms have attempted to open up the system. The direction of evolution has been more toward the validation by the university of vocational training than toward a veritable opening to allow students who left to return in order to complete advanced diplomas.

Part II: Entry to the Labor Market

Comparing Employment Disadvantages in the Two Systems

If the educational systems of France and the United States, despite their manifest differences, have produced roughly similar aggregate disadvantages for second-generation North Africans and Mexicans, that cannot be said of the labor markets of the two countries. Until the Great Recession in the United States that started in 2007, the two labor-market contexts were quite different, with levels of employment substantially lower in France (DiPrete, Goux, Maurin, and Quesnel-Vallee 2005; Estevão and Nargis 2005). For instance, according to the OECD, the male employment-to-population ratio in 2005–6 was 69 in France, but 9 points higher in the United States; however, by 2010, the US ratio had slumped to 71, while that in France was, at 68, essentially stable. The long-term, lower availability of employment in France has affected young workers especially. For instance, in 2005, the overall French unemployment rate was 9.8 percent, while unemployment for young people (ages fifteen to twenty-four) was 17.3 percent (INSEE 2007). Youth unemployment has risen also in the United States as a result of the Great Recession, but it is too early to say whether higher unemployment has become the new "normal."

Prior research has found that the French labor market provides a difficult transition from school to work for young people, and that the difficulties hit youth of immigrant origin harder than they do those of native French backgrounds. Richard (1997) observes that a surplus of young people in the French labor market may result in discriminatory hiring practices. Second-generation Maghrebins appear to be targets for this discrimination.

Silberman, Alba, and Fournier (2007) find that many second-generation North Africans feel that employers have discriminated against them, on the basis of their names or other distinguishing features of their person or application.

Unemployment is consequently higher among North African youth than among their native French counterparts. Richard (1997; also Simon 2003) finds that Algerian- and Moroccan-origin men and Algerian-origin women suffer, ceteris paribus, more often from long-term unemployment than do others. There is a gendered dimension to this situation. Brinbaum and Werquin (1999, 2004) note that women are more numerous among the unemployed and spend longer periods of time in unemployment than men. One estimate is that the probability of unemployment for young women of Maghrebin origin is double that for Maghrebin men. Maghrebin women thus face a "double handicap" in the labor market, by virtue of their ethnicity and gender (Frickey and Primon 2003, 178).

Amy Lutz's analysis of reasonably comparable data sets in the two countries reveals some of the differences that prevailed before the Great Recession. The US data are from the National Education Longitudinal Survey (NELS:88). NELS:88 is one of the few longitudinal, nationally representative datasets that follow the academic trajectories of youth from their pre–high school years through their mid-twenties. The French data used in this research are from *Génération 98* of CEREQ (Centre d'études et de recherches sur les qualifications) which began as a 2001 survey of those who left school in 1998. These data allow us to view what has happened three years later to members of a cohort of school leavers who benefited from the democratization of the school system. Both surveys included month-by-month calendars following departure from school, in which respondents were asked about their employment status. The periods involved are 1992–94 in the United States and 1998–2001 in France.

Since unemployment is less likely to be a problem for those children of immigrants with university credentials, we focus here on the labor-market entry of those without them, young people who have no more than a high school diploma in the United States and no more than the *baccalauréat* in France. The results are displayed in Figures 5.2 to 5.4.

The first two figures display the labor-market calendars. Both Mexicans and Maghrebins have an early labor-market disadvantage, though the levels of employment just after departure from school appear considerably higher in the United States. In France, the calendar in Figure 5.2 shows

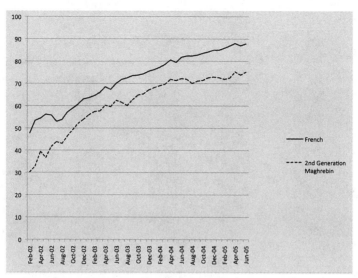

Figure 5.2. Percent of Young People without Post-Secondary Education Who Are Employed, France, 1998–2001

Source: Génération 98 and NELS:88

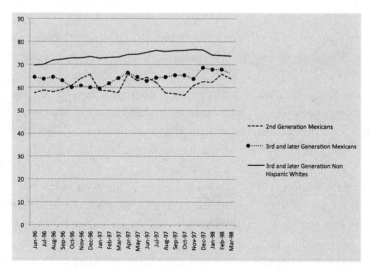

Figure 5.3. Percent of Young People without Post-Secondary Education Who Are Employed, United States, 1992–1994

Source: Génération 98 and NELS:88

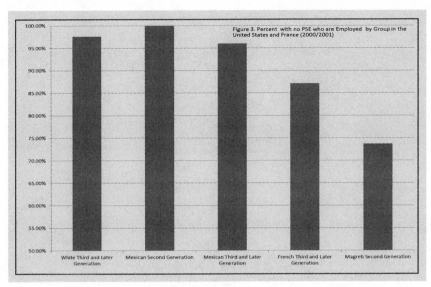

Figure 5.4. Percent without Post-Secondary Education Who Are Employed, by Group and Generation, France and the United States, 2000/2001

Source: Génération 98 and NELS:88

a steady increase in employment over time for all groups. However, both first- and second-generation Maghrebin are disadvantaged relative to the native French. For the United States, Figure 5.3 indicates trend lines that are quite flat. The members of the majority population, third- and later-generation non-Hispanic whites, have higher rates of employment than both second-generation and third- and later-generation Mexicans. The steeper slope in the French case reflects the greater difficulty that French young people initially experience in entering the labor market relative to American young people. This makes employment even more difficult for the second-generation Maghrebins in France than the second-generation Mexicans in the United States. Results of logistic regression indicate that young Maghrebins have significantly lower odds of having a job relative to the French natives, but second-generation Mexicans do not face significantly different odds of being employed relative to native-born non-Hispanic whites.

Disparities between the employment situations of the children of immigrants emerge over a longer period of time. Figure 5.4 shows the rate of employment by group in 2000 (United States) and 2001 (France). The rate calculations are limited to those who are active in the labor market and, as before, have no postsecondary credential. In the United States, Mexicans have overcome their initial labor-market disadvantages. In the case of second-generation Mexicans, they have caught up to, if not surpassed, third- and later-generation non-Hispanic whites. (The 100-percent employment figure should be understood as an estimate from a modest-sized sample, not as population data.) In 2001, which is fewer years from school completion than in the US case, the second-generation Maghrebins remain at a sizable disadvantage relative to the native-born French in their levels of employment.

It is not just that the Maghrebins are less likely to be employed. When they are employed, they are also less likely to be in full-time employment than are their native French peers, and they are more likely to hold positions below their level of qualifications (Dupray and Moullet 2004; Richard 1997; Silberman 1997). Lutz's analysis of the French data shows that, net of a set of control variables including whether or not the *bac* was completed, the Maghrebin youth who hold jobs are about 8 percentage points less likely to hold a full-time job. No similar disadvantage for Mexican Americans emerges from the analysis of American data. Analyses of the *Génération* data by Roxane Silberman and Irène Fournier (2006a) reveal, further, that Maghrebin youth are more likely than the native French to perceive their jobs as below their level of qualifications. This is true for nearly 40 percent of the young men and a third of the young women, compared to a quarter of native French youth. These perceptions, measured in 2001, gain credibility from the finding that they are predictive of the youth's labor-market situation two years later, in 2003.

The employment prospects of both groups have been affected by the financial crisis and recession in Europe and the United States late in the oughts decade. In France, the unemployment of the young people in France has dramatically increased, reaching the level of nearly 23 percent in 2010 for those between fifteen and twenty-four years old, among the higher rates in Europe. Beyond the immediate effect on the unemployment of the Maghrebin second generation, the impact may be strong in the long term as they eventually reenter the labor market with more difficulties than the mainstream population (Silberman and Fournier 2006a).

The employment of the Mexican American second generation has also been hurt, as has the employment of American youth of other backgrounds; and it appears from an analysis of census data through 2010 by Jeanne Batalova and Michael Fix (2011) that the impact on Mexicans has been somewhat harsher than that on native white youth. Batalova and Fix's data are for sec-ond-generation Hispanics, but Mexicans are the majority of this population, so we can reasonably infer their trends in the data. Between 2006 and 2010, the unemployment rate doubled among second-generation Hispanic young adults, going from 11 to 23 percent; however, it nearly doubled among their native white counterparts, rising from 8 to 14 percent.

The scarcity of good jobs for young adults has led many second-generation Hispanics into the postsecondary education system, in a search for credentials that would improve their labor-market chances. According to Batalova and Fix, among nineteen- to twenty-four-year-olds, second-generation Hispanic women have caught up to native white women in terms of enrollment at post-secondary institutions, and second-generation Hispanic men lag only slightly behind native white men. However, there are still large differences between Hispanics and whites when it comes to acquiring postsecondary credentials. Nevertheless, the surge in postsecondary education among the second gen-erations of Mexicans and other Hispanics could have large implications, as the most recent data show substantial earnings gains for more educated His-panics. Whether the credentialing differences between Hispanics and others will narrow over time remains to be seen.

Explaining the Greater Disadvantages of the Maghrebin Second Generation
Reasons for the relatively greater disadvantages of the Maghrebins emerge with clarity from the in-depth interviews conducted in the Paris and Dal-las, Texas, areas by Dalia Abdelhady. In a number of respects, the Mexican American and Maghrebin youth would seem to start their work lives with roughly equal disadvantages. Members of both groups come overwhelmingly from modest circumstances. Their parents had very low levels of education relative to the norms of the receiving societies and held jobs at the bottom of the labor market, involving limited skills and yielding low earnings. In nei-ther group was there a concentration of firms owned by coethnics that could provide employment on a sizable scale. In this respect, the Mexican situation is to be distinguished from the Cuban one in Miami,[3] and the North African situation from the Portuguese one (Silberman and Fournier 1999).

Nevertheless, the US labor market seems far more open to the conquest of niches by immigrant and ethnic groups, and at its lower end, at least, tol-erates far more hiring through informal channels, especially through per-sonal networks (Waldinger and Lichter 2003; Waldinger 1996). In a context where employment has been generally high, young people, even when leaving school with credentials of limited value, may be able find employment relatively quickly through their or their families' social networks. This is in fact the pattern that stands out from the interviews with second-generation Mexican Americans in the Dallas area. Many got their first jobs through close friends or older siblings who had found short-term employment and encouraged them to apply. For example, Javier: "My first job was at the restaurant. I was doing dishes and then worked my way up to being a waiter in two years. I knew a friend who was working at the restaurant, and he told me that I can apply so I did. I was in the back chopping onions and then I became a busboy, and then they made me a waiter. This is the business I know and I like it."

In other cases, family networks and neighborhood resources provided the means for finding the first job. Parents were often involved in the process of applying for jobs, offering specific help or advice that was strategic for the teenagers' first employment. For instance, those who started working before they turned sixteen, the legal minimum age of employment, were often told by their parents to lie about their age on the application form. Others found their first job by asking businesses in their neighborhood, especially ones that they and their family members frequented such as local grocery stores or bakeries. In general, it seems that strong-tie networks are the most important source for getting the first job for second-generation Mexican Americans. As they are likely to be surrounded by people who already work, they have been able easily to find out about available jobs and obtain "inside dope" about ways of landing them (Waldinger and Lichter 2003).

The Maghrebins have in the aggregate a different experience in seeking jobs. Very few of Abdelhady's interviewees ever found a job through the assistance of family members or friends. In fact, only two of twenty-five obtained jobs through their networks. A few other respondents benefited indirectly from knowledge obtained from family and friends. Nour, for example, after completing her BEP, started working as a sales associate in a clothing store at the mall. A number of her friends were already working for similar stores. One day, when she was shopping for herself, she decided to ask if the store management was recruiting, and in a week she was working there. Thus, Nour benefited from the general knowledge that her friends were working at the mall. But, unlike many Mexican Americans, she did not obtain knowledge about specific jobs or places to apply from friends and family.

Many of the Maghrebin interviewees stated that their siblings and close friends are not faring well in the labor market, and they perceived it to be difficult for someone of their background to find employment. With little or no help expected from their social networks, they are forced to rely on formal organizations for assistance in job searches. Organizations such as ANPE (Agence nationale pour l'emploi) and Mission Locale were their primary sources of knowledge about available job openings as well as of advice about the application process. The result is a job-search procedure that has a more formal character than that experienced by many young Mexican Americans:

Yusri: I had never registered at ANPE, this year is the first time that I registered. It's necessary to know that, even never having worked in my life, I hadn't registered at ANPE. Then I began to write letters of application, taking examples from RIJ. I took models for application letters, and I wrote my own. And I sent them at the beginning, when I didn't have the internet.

Q: So the RIJ, it's an organization that provides information for young people?

Yusri: Sure. There were some summer jobs, some small books of summer job announcements. That helped me a lot to write some application letters. Afterwards I took some resumes as models, so I had the framework but it was necessary to complete it. And I sent out, sent out, massive mailings all over. Even to those who weren't looking. To the banks, . . . It was a little difficult in the beginning because people were being let go. One is so all alone.

These organizations play a primary role in placing French Maghrebin youth in entry-level jobs. In many cases, personnel at the Mission Locale advised respondents to pursue specific internships and short-term courses that enabled them to find stable jobs shortly afterwards. Many of these respondents knew the administrators at the Mission Locale and drew on them in a manner similar to the way Mexican Americans got valuable information from their family and friends. However, there is a stigma attached to these organizations that some of the respondents referred to. Other than these organizations, many respondents utilized the internet (websites such Monster and Yahoo Jobs) to identify employment opportunities and sometimes apply for jobs. A few respondents had to send 100+ job applications before they could get an interview. This experience is a sharp contrast to that of the handful of Mexican American interviewees who resorted to mailing job applications, for they could only remember sending three to four applications during a job search.

Nearly universally, the respondents in both France and the United States believed that members of their ethnic groups are faced with prejudice and discrimination in their larger societies. However, the views of their personal experiences with discrimination were rather different. Almost all of the Mexican American men had some experience with discrimination, mostly in public settings. Stories of being asked to wait for forty-five minutes at restaurants where tables were visibly empty were common. A few respondents had been stopped by the police while they were driving and interrogated and searched for no apparent reason. But only a handful of respondents, all but one of them male, felt they had experienced unjust treatment at their workplace, and their explanations were not straightforwardly posed in terms of ethnic discrimination. For example, Gustavo, a twenty-seven-year-old manager at a popular restaurant in Dallas, explained the possible reasons for the negative treatment he experienced at the restaurant where he works: "Because I'm Mexican and that I'm young. That has something to do with it as well. I'm not surprised. They don't expect for someone as young as I am to be doing what I'm doing. Especially for a restaurant in this category, so they look down on you because of your age." The citing of youthfulness as a source of prejudice suggests an uncertainty about racialization in American society.

The Maghrebins, by contrast, regularly recounted experiences with discrimination in their job search as well as at their workplaces—in addition to the impersonal encounters in ordinary social life that the Mexican American respondents referred to. Many of them have had a hard time finding a job and pointed to the prejudice that individuals of North African origin face in the French labor market. Coupled with earlier experiences with prejudice and discrimination in school, these difficulties make the Maghrebins not very hopeful about their chances.

The discrimination against the Maghrebins often targets their names, and a number of respondents admitted to changing their names when applying for jobs. For example, Hayat, a nineteen-year-old woman with an Algerian father and French mother, takes on her sister's mainstream French name when applying for jobs and never includes a personal photograph with her resume: "Because the employers give too much attention to the photos.

If I were blonde with blue eyes, sure I would include my photo, but I have the head of an Arab, and therefore I will not include it." A common experience is one in which employers often show interest when approached over the phone before knowing the applicant's name. These employers appear to change their perception of the applicant as soon as a face-to-face interview takes place. Hayat described the often-bewildered reactions when potential employers meet her in person. Other respondents were successful in getting jobs by assuming French names. These were typically jobs that are not part of the regulated labor market—they involve payment in cash and do not require the young people to present official papers with their names on them.

Large-scale surveys are consistent with the perceptions of Abdelhady's Maghrebin interviewees that they face discrimination in the labor market. According to the Génération 98 survey, among the Maghrebins, some 40 percent of young men and 30 percent of young women believe they have been the victims of discrimination at the hands of employers. The comparable figures for native French youth, along with those from European immigrant backgrounds, are much lower.

Many North African interviewees believed that labor-market discrimination forced them into undesirable jobs. They asserted that while finding a job may not be easy in general, low-paying, contractual work that is neither interesting nor stable is more available to them. For example, Fatima, a twenty-seven-year-old who had quit the university after three years of studying law, works as a receptionist for a law firm. When asked about the possibilities of finding a job, she responded:

> Very easy. To have a job is very easy, as long as one doesn't insist on something great. If it's housecleaning, I will get the job, not a white. If it's a receptionist, I will get the job, not a white. But if I want a position that's a bit better, that's another matter. In fact, it isn't getting a job that's hard, it's getting a job that's stable and interesting. With a possibility of development, etc., that's where it gets hard, even impossible, if you don't have a connection. But if not that, an Arab who can work as cashier, as housecleaner, as conductor, etc., that's very, very easy. He will get priority because the superior who is hiring, he will always be able to find a justification for not promoting him, even to his own superiors. He's not exposing himself to any risk, it will be easy to justify that the person stays at the same salary,

in the same position, for 15 years, while a white person is going to complain because there isn't that barrier of, "I've got a job; it's alright."

Because they perceive themselves to have limited access to stable employment, many respondents took short-term contractual work in hopes of being able to go through the process of tenure and promotion at their workplaces. However, these hopes were often not fulfilled due to the rigidity of the system and, more importantly, the discriminatory behavior they experienced at the hands of superiors in the organizational hierarchy. Occasionally, work colleagues and immediate supervisors are interested in keeping them in their jobs and help them to figure out ways to stay on as permanent employees. Such inside help is rarely available to North African entry-level employees, which may explain some of the difficulties they face finding permanent positions or moving up organizational hierarchies.

In addition to their awareness of the general prejudice that individuals of North African origin face in French society, those living in an ethnic suburb agreed that their life chances are also limited due to their geographic location. For example, Fayez, who is twenty-one and unemployed, explained that peer pressure in the suburb where he grew up affected his performance at school so that he ended up with a BEP instead of a *bac*:

It's the ghetto here, it doesn't to do lie about it, even if we have the things that are necessary, there is the local mission, the mayor's office, but we live in the projects, and in the projects, it's a different world. No one goes there, the police don't go there. When they show up, it's because of a complaint. But they never come and see what's going on . . . because there's a lot of drugs, a lot of cocaine and that sort of thing. . . . You have to do like everyone else, you have to, you are in the projects. If you are not like everyone else, it's impossible. You leave school with your backpack, you run outside, and you do what you have to do outside, and afterwards you go back in. Yes, I think that if I had lived perhaps in Paris, I would have. . . . Perhaps I would have been a different student, I would have a different environment, it wouldn't have been the same, I wouldn't have seen the same things, I wouldn't have been in the same schools. Perhaps I would have been in less disruptive classes, then necessarily I would have been less disruptive, because I am not going to say to you that I was calm in class, it wouldn't be true because I also was like everyone else. But I think that if I had been in a calm class, I would have been calm. Of course if you are with the agitated, you are part of the group, you go along with the flock of sheep, you do the same. You are in middle school, you are seeking, you don't know who you are. That's for sure.

The awareness that the ethnic suburb is itself a product of discrimination against immigrants and their families was expressed by many respondents and related to their difficulties in the labor market. This contrasts sharply with Mexican Americans who lived in an ethnic neighborhood, who identified their location as an asset in their ability to find jobs and succeed financially.

Despite their different experiences with prejudice and discrimination, Mexican Americans and French Maghrebins deal with these injustices in somewhat similar ways.

Generally speaking, respondents were not likely to oppose discriminatory behavior or prejudiced views directly. When asked about their reactions, Mexican Americans typically gave such responses as: "I just ignore it. That's all I can do." "You just put things in perspective." "We don't live in a perfect world, and it's nobody fault."

The main reason that Mexican Americans were able to move beyond these experiences was their ability to find jobs and maintain a degree of financial success. All the Mexican American respondents believed that there were ample job opportunities for individuals with their qualifications and background. Even the ones who did not work or were employed part-time were confident of their ultimate chances of getting jobs that fit their qualifications and experience and were interesting and rewarding to them.

The Maghrebins also did not usually engage directly with discrimination or prejudice they encounter, but they seemed to have stronger reactions than did Mexican Americans. For example, one young man described the way his colleagues at work had to calm him down while he was being denied the long-term position at his work: "And, there, I felt a bit of discrimination. But I immediately turned the page because the people calmed me, told me, 'Don't get upset, you're going to stay. We're going to do everything to keep you here.' And I had confidence, and I did stay." Similar to Mexican American ambivalence about their racialized position in the United States was the Maghrebin ambivalence about their marginality in French society. But, while there was a general agreement that individuals of North-African descent faced various forms of prejudice and discrimination in France, many respondents refused a position of passive marginality. As Salime explained: "I do not know if that could be unjust. You have to go beyond that, the word 'unjust.' Because we are not victims, it's not true."

Conclusion

In both systems, the disparities between the native group and the children of immigrants are sizable, despite gains by the latter over time. In France, democratization has allowed the children of North African immigrants to improve their educational attainments: more now attain the *baccalauréat* and attend university. In the event, democratization has also benefited the native French group, and this fact has thwarted any large reduction in the overall gap between the two groups. A similar story could be told in the United States, where improvements in Mexican American educational attainments generally have been matched by improvements in the attainments of native-born whites. The disparity is quite large at the upper end of educational distribution, in the attainment of university degrees, which qualify individuals for the best-remunerated and most secure jobs. In both systems also, the children of low-status immigrants are much more likely than natives to leave the school system without any meaningful credential.

The most intriguing part of the educational comparison is that such superficially different systems produce such similar results. From the point of view of governance, the French and American systems appear to be opposites: The French system is mostly determined by policies and financing that emanate from the national state, whose basic thrust would seem to push in an egalitarian direction. By contrast, the US system is very much driven by centrifugal forces, with policies largely determined by states and financing coming heavily from localities and states, with the consequence of substantial inequalities among schools that correspond with the social compositions of their student populations. Moreover, the French system has instituted policies to overcome socially structured inequalities in educational opportunity. Yet the results are disputed; and the high proportion of students leaving school with no credential as well as the indifferent results of French schools according to the PISA study are increasingly issues for public debate. While the United States has attempted one major educational reform, the No Child

Left Behind policy, the benefits are uncertain and the policy is widely viewed as having pernicious effects (Ravitch 2010).

Of course, when one peers beneath the surface, there are some undeniable similarities: the most important is the way that social segregation, especially by race (in the United States) and social class and ethnic origin (in both France and the United States), shapes educational opportunity. In the United States, this shaping is very apparent and has been the subject of a lengthy literature, but it occurs in France too, both because local authorities and parents retain important influences on the resources of schools and on what happens within them and because schools that concentrate poor and immigrant-origin students are problematic in ways that schools that serve middle-class, native students are not. Another similarity lies in the stratification within schools that buttresses, and is buttressed by, the developing educational differences among students of different social origins. In France, this stratification is highly formalized in the ramified hierarchy of diplomas and certificates that can be earned at both the secondary and higher educational levels; but it also has less formal manifestations, as in the so-called hidden curricula, e.g., the study of unusual languages, that some schools have developed in order to attract better students and those from more privileged families. In the United States, tracking is less formal but it is nevertheless a highly developed feature of school systems, implemented in the early years through ability groupings that often occur within classrooms and later through subject-matter classes that proceed at different paces and to different depths, with the consequence that the mere possession of the high school diploma, the universal terminal secondary certificate, tells very little about the academic preparation of individuals.

That two such different systems produce such similar results is, however, also likely to be a consequence of the attempts of advantaged native families, from the middle class or more affluent circumstances, to retain privileges for their children in the face of the prospective competition with the children of recent immigrants, especially those from the most disfavored groups, such as the Mexicans in the United States and the Maghrebins in France. What the French case in particular demonstrates is a kind of Newtonian Third Law of Social Inequality: for every initiative to reduce inequality there is an opposing reaction to preserve it. Hence, in reaction to the initiatives of the state to promote greater equality of educational opportunity (e.g., the democratization of the access to the *baccalauréat*, the *carte scolaire*, and the ZEP policy), parents and to some degree local authorities have reacted by creating new mechanisms that give latitude for social inequalities to assert themselves in and through educational institutions: examples are the hidden curricula and the supplementary educational activities in schools for which families must bear the cost. In addition, the gap between principles and practices must not be underestimated, as demonstrated by the ZEP policy, which has suffered from inadequate resources since it was initiated in 1981.

Though the educational systems produce second-generation cohorts that in the aggregate show similar disadvantages, there have been subsequent sizable differences in labor-market outcomes. Until the Great Recession, the United States has had a substantially higher employment rate, according to OECD data, with little difference in employment between second-generation Mexican Americans and native whites. In France, where the employment rate has been depressed over an extended period, the labor-market differences between similarly qualified second-generation North Africans and native French are considerable (Silberman and Fournier 2006b).

In a context where older members of a group are generally employed, the reliance of employers on social networks to find prospective recruits to jobs at the lower end of the labor market assists younger members of the group to also find employment. Much research in the United States demonstrates the powerful role of social networks in the hiring for jobs with indefinite educational requirements. Waldinger and Lichter (2003) explain the power of networks on the grounds that, for low-skilled jobs where educational credentials and even prior experience may not give employers strong clues about the prospective value of an applicant, a reference from a known employee may in fact be more informative. Moreover, when an employee vouches for an applicant, he or she is taking on a degree of responsibility for ensuring that the new employee works out. Noteworthy here is that ethnic networks can control the access to many jobs even when the employers are not coethnics; the concept of labor-market "niches" covers such cases (Waldinger 1996). Waldinger and Lichter deploy this argument to explain precisely why immigrants and their children enjoy such high rates of employment in the US context (in contrast to African Americans).

Ethnically controlled niches, it must be pointed out, are not an unalloyed blessing. While they may make access to the labor market easier for the members of a group that controls them, the jobs involved are sometimes not very good ones. In this respect, niches can be as much a trap as an opportunity, anchoring young people to sectors of the labor market where working conditions are not good, pay is meager, and opportunities for career mobility are limited. Whether the Mexican niches work this way for the youthful members of the second generation we have studied for this project it is too early to say. Still, by comparison with the experiences of Maghrebin youth who are facing many difficulties in just getting started on a work career, the relatively smooth transition to employment for many Mexican Americans looks like good fortune.

Social networks do not have the same benefits for Maghrebin youth, in part because employment levels are lower in their family and friendship circles (Silberman and Fournier 1999). In a pattern that is found in other European countries as well, the older, immigrant generation is out of the labor market to a large degree. Instead of assistance, the Maghrebins appear to encounter discrimination at the hands of French employers—that is, they widely report experiencing such discrimination and, in our interviews, with a detail that seems convincing. For France, then, the evidence supports a conclusion that, when jobs for young people are scarce, employers tend to give preference to youth from native majority backgrounds and discriminate against those coming from immigrant minority ones. Ethnicity becomes the basis of a rationing system that ensures that the youth growing up in native families, especially middle-class ones, have a leg up.

The disparities in the French labor market could serve as an unfortunate augury for the United States. Should the scarcity of jobs for young people engendered in the United States by the Great Recession endure, then ethnicity and immigrant origins could come to play a larger role in labor-market rationing than they have in the recent past. The United States would then resemble France in this respect. In that case, the conclusion of chapter 3, that different systems can produce similar outcomes, will be extended.

Notes

The authors acknowledge the valuable research assistance provided in Paris by the Maurice Halbwachs Center at the Centre national de la recherche scientifique and in Albany, New York, by the Center for Social and Demographic Analysis at the University at Albany. Particular thanks go to Irène Fournier and Benoît Tudoux at the Halbwachs Center for help with data preparation and to Karim Mendil for invaluable support with interviewing around Paris; in Albany, Suzanne Macartney, Katy Schiller, and Hui-Shien Tsao played important supportive roles.

1. The great majority of French students obtain the BEPC, *Brevet d'études du premier cycle*, which is awarded based on an examination at the end of the *collège*, or middle school. However, unlike a US high school diploma, this diploma is neither a qualification for a university education nor a credential with value in the labor market.

2. This survey, known familiarly as "Add Health," is a major longitudinal study of American youth, with oversamples of important minority groups such as Mexican Americans, that began in 1994, when the sampled youngsters were in the seventh through twelfth grades. The latest wave of data is from 2008.

3. See Portes and Rumbaut (2001), however, for an account of the disadvantages for second-generation Cubans that flow from ready access to low-skill employment.

CHAPTER SIX

Promising Practices: Preparing Children of Immigrants in New York and Sweden

Carola Suárez-Orozco, Margary Martin, Mikael Alexandersson,

L. Janelle Dance, and Johannes Lunneblad

Immigrant-origin students bring to schools a variety of academic and linguistic challenges. Many of the schools that receive them provide far from optimal educational opportunities (Ruiz-de-Velasco and Fix 2001; Suárez-Orozco, Suárez-Orozco, and Todorova 2008; Valenzuela 1999). While it is not a challenge to critique the myriad of ways that schools fail to meet the needs of these students, it is decidedly more difficult to identify promising practices that serve them well (Lucas 1997; Walqui 2000). Although most studies focus upon the hidden curricula and agendas in schools that serve to marginalize students (Apple 2004a; Bowles and Gintis 1976, 2002; Loewen 2009; Orenstein 1995), in this study we seek to illuminate overt curricula and programs that prepare students from immigrant backgrounds to be active and empowered actors in the multicultural, global contexts of their receiving nations. This research sheds light on the strategies that teachers, students, and administrators develop as they attempt to meet the educational challenges of preparing immigrant-origin youth for this global era in two quite distinct social, political, and educational contexts—large cities in Sweden, and New York City (NYC) in the United States.

The United States, and New York City in particular, has a long-standing history of incorporating immigrants to its shores. Currently, half of the students in New York City public schools have an immigrant parent and nearly 10 percent arrived in the United States within the past three years (NYSED 2006). The vast majority of these students are poorly served; many are attending schools suffering from "savage inequalities" (Kozol 1991) between school contexts. While the 1954 US Supreme Court decision *Brown v. Board of Education* legislated equal access for students regardless of racial background, the requisite investments in schools serving different subpopulations have not been made (Heubert 1998).

Swedish schools make for an interesting point of comparison because of their explicit commitment to provide equal access to all students. The Swedish Education Act of the 1940s legislated that: "All children and youths shall have equal access to education." As a result, Swedes invest heavily in their schools and in their most challenged students. Hence, second-generation students in Sweden have significantly lower secondary-school dropout rates as well as higher rates of university participation than in other OECD nations (OECD 2006, 2008). However, once immigrant students graduate in Sweden, they encounter a low glass ceiling and find it difficult to enter the employment sector (OECD 2008). Sweden is relatively new to large numbers of immigrants from countries outside of Northern and Western Europe. It also has taken in a much higher proportion of refugees than has the United States. This population represents a significantly different set of incorporation challenges (Athey and Ahearn 1991; Lustig et al. 2004). Refugees face significant psychological trauma; while some are highly educated (e.g., Chileans), others suffer from high levels of illiteracy (e.g., Somalis); and many live in a liminal psychological space hoping to return to the homeland when 'things settle down.' Further, many of the new immigrants are of Muslim origin, which has resulted in a considerable degree of ambivalence, backlash, and social unrest (Cesari 2006).

Both the United States and Sweden share a contentious climate of debate over immigration (see Chavez 2001 for an example in the United States; see Mattsson and Tesfahuney 2002 for an example in Sweden). These two nations also share a similar pattern of low achievement by minority students from low-income backgrounds (Bunar 2001). Both countries exhibit the problem of a gender achievement gap—girls consistently outperform boys (Suárez-Orozco and Qin 2006; Öhrn 2002). Further, in both contexts, students of minority ethnic backgrounds are likely to be taught by teachers of mainstream backgrounds (Ingersoll 2003; Ingersoll and Smith 2003; Ljungberg 2005). Schools in both Swedish cities and New York are subject to marketplace-driven school reforms, which place high value on testing, performance, and accountability (Apple 2004b; Hargreaves 2003). This emphasis on "objective" measures does not take into account that second-language acquisition presents a unique set of challenges. The lack of consideration for these challenges takes a particularly high toll on immigrant-origin students and the schools that serve them (Menken 2008; Suárez-Orozco et al. 2008). Finally, while in most parts of the United States, students attend neighborhood high schools, in Swedish cities and New York alike, another market-based reform, "school choice," provides students with the option to "apply" to high schools. This process allows students to rank a number of schools and thereafter go through a selection process that can include entrance or standardized exams, interviews, audition, and/or lottery, and neighborhood demographics.

Methodological Strategy and Guiding Questions

The guiding questions for this research were:

What school-based practices are implemented in innovative, "promising" school settings to:

a—ease the transition and integration of immigrant-origin youth?
b—foster and enhance the academic performance of immigrant-origin youth?

We used a case study methodological strategy (Yin 2003) for this study in order to describe in detail each school context serving immigrant-origin youth. This approach allows us to illustrate findings in the lived experiences of diverse adolescent youth and to shed light on the processes and causal links that emerge from the data. The multiple-case study approach also provides the advantage of allowing analytical theoretical generalizations to emerge from empirical findings (Burawoy 1991; Stake 2005; Yin 2003) and provides insight into the "crucial role of pattern and context" (Yin 2003, x) in determining phenomena. The "replication logic" (Yin 2003, 4) of the multiple-case study approach allows for cross-case comparisons and conclusions.

In each context—New York City in the United States and large cities in Sweden—we identified two schools that were lauded locally as being particularly innovative in their approach to immigrant-origin students, providing this study with a total of four research sites (see below). Our research team used a variety of methodical strategies to gather data across sites. We conducted ethnographic fieldwork as the primary data collection strategy in order to gather information about innovative school practices, and assess the school ethos, teacher/student, teacher/teacher, and student/student relationships, school climate and intercultural understanding, as well as impediments to the implementation of innovative practices. Every school site included informants from three mixed cultural groups based on variation in: (1) demographic proportions in the school, (2) social status at each school, and (3) success in terms of grades and performance. The selected students were studied in *four different contexts* (classrooms during lessons, groups working on specific subjects, groups discussing general issues, and groups working together) for a period of twelve to twenty weeks (i.e., three to four months of data collection at each school). Semistructured interviews and focus groups with teachers and administrators were also conducted to learn about their perspectives on the implementation of innovative practices and the impediments that they encounter along the way. We examined the performance of schools on quantitative indicators gathered from school records and city education statistics, which included student retention and graduation rates, and university entry rates. Lastly, the team conducted structured *focus-group* interviews with students in order to contextualize emerging findings. The triangulated data from each site was coded according to innovative practices important for all immigrant students along with those specific to the needs of newcomers or second-language learners.[1] In addition, we examined theoretically relevant analytic themes (e.g., preparation vs. remedial agenda; significance of relationships; and priority of immigrant student needs) (Yin 2003).

We use several criteria to select our case-study "innovative" schools (see Table 6.1).

The schools had to serve a high proportion of immigrant-origin youth. They had to have a reputation within the broader educational community for being innovative and attaining superior outcomes on standard performance indicators in comparison to other schools with high proportions of "low-status" immigrant kids (e.g., student stability rates, teacher/student ratios, graduation rates, recruitment of highly qualified teachers, and retention of teachers). Also, three of the four schools were part of *networks* of innovative schools. We purposefully did not use standardized testing results as a criterion, since such tests underestimate the skills of second-language learners (Menken 2008). All schools had an institutional commitment to prepare students for the new global era by confronting core educational challenges. All of the selected schools claimed a grand narrative of providing engaging and relevant learning environments in order to foster personally meaningful

TABLE 6.1. School Site Characteristics

	New York High Schools		Swedish Gymnasiums	
	World Citizen	Progressive	Ekdalsskolan	Bergslunden
SCHOOL SITE INCLUSION CHARACTERISTICS				
Publicly recognized for its innovative approaches	✓	✓	✓	✓
Serves significant numbers of immigrant-origin youth	✓	✓	✓	✓
Does not have entrance exams	✓	✓	✓	✓
Academic relationship building narrative	✓	✓	✓	✓
Higher than average graduation rates compared to schools serving similar populations in the area	✓	✓	✓	✓
Higher than average results on performance indicators compared to schools serving similar populations in the area	✓	✓	✓	✓
Part of network	✓	✓	✓	
COMPARISONS TO OTHER CITYWIDE SCHOOLS ON PERFORMANCE INDICATORS				
Student Graduation Rates in 4 years[1,2]				
~City Rate	FB= 57.5% All=50.6%		74.5%[3]	73.1%
~Site Rate	64.8	95.5	85.2	67.0
Prepared to Enter University[4]				
~City Rate[1]	36.5%	36.5%	89.5%	86.4%
~Site Rate[5]	41.4	84	70.7	82.9

Sources: New York City—NYSED (2006). Sweden—Swedish Department of Education (Skolverket)
(Footnotes to Table 6.1)

relationships and constructive habits of work shown to contribute to academic performance. These schools also claimed to prepare youth to successfully navigate in a multicultural world.

The Educational Settings

New York City

According to the American Community Survey, as of 2007 over a third (36.7 percent) of the over 8.2 million people who reside in New York City are foreign born. Nearly half, 44.9 percent, of all households with children under eighteen years old have a foreign-born parent in the home. While there are no exact figures available, large numbers of children of immigrants can be found in New York City schools, and, in particular, its public school system. New York City is the largest public school district in the United States, serving close to 1.1 million students. It is a "minority-majority" school district; as of 2008 the majority of students come from nonwhite ethnic groupings, with 36.7 percent reported as Latino/Hispanic, 34.7 percent black/African American, 14.3 percent Asian, and 14.2 percent white. The district has one of the most diverse student populations in the country, and virtually every country on the globe is represented. Approximately 40 percent of its students live in households whose first language is not English, over half of whom are children of immigrants (NYCDOE 2008). Major languages are Spanish, Chinese, Urdu, Russian, Bengali, Haitian Creole, Korean, and Arabic. Almost one in seven students (13.4 percent) is classified as an English-language learner (ELL). Of

---

1 In Sweden, upper secondary education (i.e., high school) consists of three years instead of four. However, the statistics for students who have completed their upper secondary education are calculated within a four-year time frame.

2 In both the US and Sweden, students may remain in public secondary schools up to the age of 21. It is quite common for newcomer youth, and especially SIFE students to take longer to complete their high school education. In the US, graduation rates are typically reported in terms of both 4-year and 7-year rates; however, the cohorts of students participating in the study will not be at 7 years until 2011; therefore these data are not provided. Note that the 7-year graduation rate for the World Citizen Network is 90%.

3 So that we can have comparable statistics from the Swedish Department of Education (Skolverket), the rates reported are for the 07/08 school years. (Skolverket, Skolblad Avseende Ekdalsskolan och Bergslunden, 2007/08).

4 For NYC, we report the percent of students who passed the Regents Diploma—a comprehensive exam that represents college readiness. For Sweden, we report the percentage of students who, based on their performance in high school, *qualify* for entry into University.

5 Note that the World Citizen Network graduation rate is 90%.

the more than 200,000 ELL students in New York State, more than 70 percent (140,000) attend schools in New York City (NYCDOE 2008).

US and NYC School Reform and Its Impact on Children of Immigrants

New York is subject to high-stakes testing educational reform, both federal and local in origin, with particular implications for English-language learners. Standards-based reform is premised on the idea that the combination of setting high standards and establishing measurable goals can improve individual outcomes in education and reduce the achievement gap of underserved populations such as minority students, in particular black and Latino students, and "special populations," which include special education students and ELLs. The No Child Left Behind Act (NCLB) is a federally mandated standards-based education reform, first enacted in 2002. NCLB requires states to develop assessments of basic skills to be given to all students in certain grades, if those states are to receive federal funding. While NCLB has been instrumental in revealing subpopulations of students from different economic, racial/ethnic, and language backgrounds who are not well served in schools, it has at the same time narrowed the focus of concern to measurable outcomes based on the mastery of limited tasks not necessarily aligned with the skills one needs to be successful in college or the world beyond it (Goldrick-Rab and Mazzeo 2005).

Less well known is how NCLB changed the federal regulation of the education of English-language learners (Capps et al. 2005). Under NCLB the term "Limited English Proficient" is applied to students in elementary or secondary schools who have difficulty in speaking, reading, writing, or understanding English to the extent that it may affect their ability to participate fully in society and to succeed in school and on standardized tests. These students must be given a Home Language Survey that identifies bilinguals and provides a diagnostic assessment to determine English proficiency. NCLB requires annual English Language Proficiency (ELP) exams for ELL students.

All students are tested in math and science beginning in their first year of enrollment; however, accommodations can be made to provide the exams to ELL students in their mother tongue. More contentious is the federal regulation of English Language Arts (ELA) and reading assessments for these students. In particular, ELP and ELA are not supposed to be tested using the same exam; however, the regulations do not dictate to states the contents of the ELA exam.

Until 2007, New York State used its ELP exam, called the New York State English as a Second Language Achievement Test (NYSESLAT), to measure also ELA and reading performance. In the summer of 2006, for eighteen states, including New York, the US Department of Education questioned whether the alternative math and reading tests used for ELLs were comparable to the regular tests used for Adequate Yearly Progress (AYP) purposes. New York State's exams were determined to be "not comparable," and the state was ordered to be in compliance for the 2006–7 school year (NYSED 2006). Rather than create a new ELA exam, New York State mandated that all ELLs take the standard ELA exam after one year of enrollment. Given that research has consistently shown that no matter the age, developing academic English-language learning takes time, an impossible benchmark was set for schools, potentially hurting those schools with high numbers of ELLs and low-income students and placing them at risk of losing standing and funding under NCLB.

In 2002, the New York State legislature granted the mayor of New York City control over the New York City public schools. This action allowed the mayor to appoint the school system's chancellor and to restructure the administrative structure of the system, and set in notion a series of reforms beginning with the centralization of the system administration and the elimination of local community school boards. This broad accountability reform, known as Children First, was premised on market-based accountability innovations from the business world. Children First has led to a number of accountability reviews on top of what is required by NCLB. Teams of administrators visit schools midyear to conduct "quality reviews," and school performance is now measured in the form of progress reports, which assign schools A–F grades based upon a complicated mathematical equation that emphasizes improvements in performance exams but also includes perceptions of teachers, students, and parents of the "learning environment," measures of teacher quality, and allowances for special populations including ELLs. The progress reports have been highly controversial, and questions have been raised about how grades are calculated and their relevance. Further, at specific points in the elementary and middle school years, new retention policies have kept students who do not meet proficiency thresholds on standardized exams from advancing to the next grade. Given the Herculean task for ELLs of reaching high levels on the ELA and reading exams, these sanctions place them at a higher risk for grade retention. Taken together, the reforms place great pressures on administrators, teachers and, therefore, students alike. There is increased pressure for teachers to "teach to the test," in order to comply with accountability reforms at the school level as well as to prevent sanctions for individual students.

New York City Innovative School Sites

World Citizen High School   This school is a part of a New York City-based network of schools that serves exclusively newcomer immigrant youth, specifically youth who have been in the United States for less than four years and have limited proficiency in English. The formal network, a non-profit organization, was first established in 1985 through collaborative efforts between the city schools and a local community college and quickly evolved and expanded. The network of eleven World Citizen schools now includes eight small schools across the New York boroughs and three recently opened in California. With tremendous rates of success, the network serves 3500 overwhelmingly low-income, limited-English-proficient, recently arrived, adolescent students. While the New York City public school graduation rate for ELLs is a dismal 23.5 percent (NYSED 2006), the network sends 90 percent of its entirely first-generation student population to college within seven years of entrance; its exceptional success rate earned a national award from the Migration Policy Institute for "Exceptional Immigrant Integration Initiatives" (MPI 2009). The World Citizen High School featured in this chapter is one of the newest sites (established in 2004).

Central to the network's approach to teaching recent immigrant youth is the premise that language is learned best when embedded across the content areas. At the policy level this is expressed as: "Language skills are most effectively learned in context and emerge most naturally in purposeful, language-rich, experiential, interdisciplinary study" (school website). English-as-a-second-language curriculum is integrated in all content areas, including in electives and in all school activities and events. In addition, strategies are employed to provide students with opportunities to develop their mother-tongue skills through peer-mediated instructional activities and instructional materials and books in their native languages. Members of the network attribute their success partly to the diversity of the languages spoken by their students. English becomes the unavoidable common language, and diversity serves as a motivator to learn social English.

The school's educational program, designed and implemented by inter-disciplinary teams of teachers, incorporates innovative approaches to help students acquire academic English language skills as well as content knowledge. This curriculum is grounded in five core tenets: "Commitment to heterogeneity, language and content integration, autonomy and democracy, one model for all and schooling beyond the four walls." The curriculum is mirrored in the way the school is organized. The teachers play an active role in curriculum development and school decision-making. They meet regularly to plan lessons, discuss individual students' learning needs, develop instructional materials, and organize field trips that provide experiential learning opportunities. All classes are heterogeneous (i.e., students are not grouped by language level, achievement level, or age), and students work collaboratively in small groups on projects that provide opportunities to learn from each other. Students' progress and learning are assessed through performance-based tasks such as presentations and portfolios. These assessments are used to support students' mastery of state standards and skills they need to pass the standardized exams required for graduation. (See Table 6.2 for demographic details.)

Progressive High School   Progressive High School is one of the pioneers from the early small-schools progressive movement in New York City. The sixth-to-twelfth grade school is a member of the Progressive Coalition Network (PCN), a national network of schools dedicated to small class sizes and project-based, student-centered learning that has had both a major influence on progressive education and schools in the United States. In line with the PCN, the school is organized around a core set of guiding principles in the areas of school design, classroom practice, leadership, and community connections. At the center of the network's philosophy is building a curriculum, beginning with "essential questions." The school, along with other 1990s small-school pioneers in the city, is renowned for the use of portfolio assessment and student exhibition, which are similar to thesis defenses, and in the 1990s, students were allowed to substitute these alternative assessments for the state-required Regents exams.

The school prides itself on having demonstrated success via traditional assessment standards through the use of a "context-based" curriculum rather than through traditional preparation for standardized tests. This pride seems well founded. According to statistics for 2006–2007, 96 percent of its students met proficiency on the state ELA exam, compared to 88 percent in schools identified by the state as "similar"; these performance rates were comparable by gender and by racial background (ranging from

TABLE 6.2. School Populations

	New York High Schools		Swedish Gymnasiums	
	World Citizen	Progressive	Ekdalsskolan	Bergslunden
Grade level served (est. age)	9–11 (15–21)	6–12 (12–18)	11–13 (16–20)	10–13 (16–20)
# Students enrolled	330	697/ 398 grades 9–12	679	1050
# Teachers	20	42	46	110
% Male/females	55/45	48/52	42/58[1]	32/68
# Nationalities represented[2]	32+	16+	20+	26+
% Newcomer students[3]	56.1%	1.2%		
Foreign born (Sweden)			44%	25% (estimate)
% Children of immigrants/foreign background[4]	100%	43%[5]	87%	46%
% Students low income[6]	89.1%	34%	Not available	Not available

1 siris.skolverket.se, 2006/2007 Academic Year.

2 These numbers are based on best estimates from information supplied from the individual schools, or from student surveys (World Citizen, Progressive, & Ekdalsskolans)

3 New York City defines newcomer students as those who have been in the United States less than 4 years. Note that only newcomers are admitted to World Citizen but the school includes sophomores and juniors who are now technically beyond the 4 year newcomer delineation.

4 In the U.S. the term *children of immigrants* is used to include the foreign-born as well as having at least one parent born abroad while in Sweden the term *foreign background* refers to students with 1 or 2 parents born outside of Sweden

5 New York State does not require schools to report data on the immigration/generational status of students, with the exception of recently arrived immigrants; hence, the numbers reported are based on student reports in a survey administered to 10th and 11th graders (N=86). These numbers, when matched to census data, appear to be representative of the city. Language representation also comes from student reports from the survey. In Sweden, the percentages are based upon estimates provided by school officials.

6 Low income for participating New York City schools in the study is measured by the percentage of students who, according to the annual school report to the state, qualify for free or reduced-priced school lunch as this status is determined by family income. Given that Sweden provides general welfare support for all citizens, there is no official classification that differentiates students based upon income level.

Many of the students who attend Ekdalsskolan and Bergslunden High Schools come from communities where parents have a high likelihood of being blue-collar workers or unemployed. In 2006, the average disposable income was 129,650 Swedish Crowns. In both the Ekdalsskolan and Bergslunden communities, the disposable incomes were considerably lower. The average disposable income was approximately 79,000 Swedish Crowns in the Ekdalsskolan community and 66,000 in Bergslunden (Ungdomsstyrelsen, 2008:44–46).

81 to 100 percent). Graduation rates were consistently over 90 percent, with 95.5 percent of students graduating in four years compared to 50.4 percent of students citywide. Equally high percentages of students move onto the university, including to highly selective colleges. Given these outstanding outcomes, it is no surprise that in 2005, Progressive was chosen as a national mentor school of the Progressive Coalition Network as part of a Gates-Foundation-funded effort to improve schools nationwide with a small-schools initiative.

Located in an affluent neighborhood on the east side of Manhattan, Progressive Secondary School gives preference to students who live within the school's community district, but draws students from all five boroughs in New York City. The school has the luxury of being the only school in its building, which is increasingly rare in New York City as comprehensive high schools are being closed and multiple autonomous small high schools and charter schools are sharing the same building. The physical space, in addition to the school's location, contributes to its success at both generating a sense of community and establishing strong partnerships with neighborhood organizations, businesses, and residents. Situated at the intersection of two highly trafficked streets and sharing the block with a number of high-end restaurants, apartment buildings and small office buildings, Progressive occupies a historic turn-of-the-century building that originally served as the site of a trade school for girls. Once outside of the school doors, students have immediate access to the hustle and bustle of Manhattan.

The Swedish Context

Over the last fifty years, Sweden has changed from a largely homogenous society to one more and more defined by cultural, ethnic, religious, and other multicultural differences. The multicultural changes began with labor-market-driven immigration in the 1950s (largely from adjoining nations), and continued with the arrival of numerous groups of political refugees over the past three decades (Sawyer and Kamali 2006). Today, 13.8 percent of the people living in Sweden were born or have parents born outside of the country (Statistiska Centralbyrån 2009).

The 1960s and 70s were characterized by assimilation politics, some of which culminated in governmental policy related to immigrant children and the educational system. By the mid-1970s, assimilation was no longer

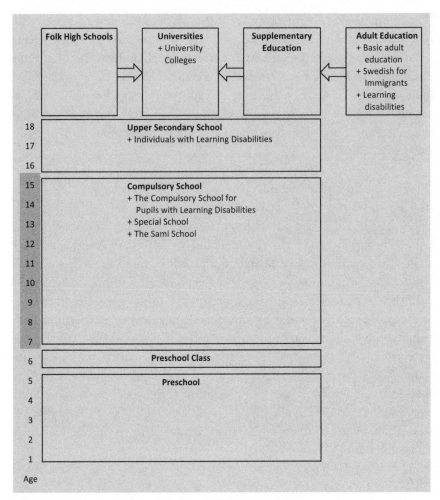

Figure 6.1. Structure of the Education System in Sweden
Created by: Mikael Alexandersson

the goal. Instead, new policies reflected three goals: (1) immigrants should have the same opportunities as Swedes and equal opportunities to develop their own cultural identity; (2) immigrants should have freedom to choose the degree to which they would develop a Swedish cultural identity; and (3) and there should be support, contact, and solidarity between the Swedish population and immigrants (Prop. 1975:26). These goals spurred educational reforms, which included adding teachers who could instruct in students' first languages and other supports for immigrant children. Also, during this period, developmental psychology was held in high regard in Sweden and affected the discourse on immigrant children. For example, this perspective engendered concerns about the difficulties immigrant children had in learning Swedish, the risks associated with losing their first languages, and the consequences that language difficulties could have upon children's cognitive development (Skolverket 2002).

From 1980–90, the country's policies with regard to immigrants were increasingly critiqued as too focused on cultural differences and ethnicity, resulting in a dichotomy between "Us" (the Swedes) and "Them" or the "Other" (the immigrants). By 1996, there was a call for a new policy—an "Integration Policy"—founded upon a broad concept of diversity. This new policy eschewed the concept "immigrant" and no longer explicitly focused upon the importance of maintaining first languages (Prop. 1997/98:16).

After compulsory schooling, almost all of native Swedish youth continue onto the upper secondary gymnasium (approximately 97 percent), whereas this rate is significantly lower for the children of immigrants (approximately 80 percent) (Skolverket 2002). Figure 6.1 shows the Swedish educational system. Instead of entering one of the seventeen national gymnasium programs, many immigrant-origin students begin an individualized preparatory program to ready them for upper secondary school (Skolverket 2002). In bigger cities such as Stockholm, Gothenburg, and Malmö, these programs are commonly referred to as the "Immigrant Program" because most of those children who leave the compulsory education system without the qualifications for upper secondary education have family histories of immigration.

The challenges associated with successful school outcomes for immigrant/ethnic minority children are not the only educational problems facing Sweden. Inequalities of social class and gender persist as well. To make matters worse, according to data from the PISA (2003), ethnicity and social class interact to impose the highest risk of school failure on children born in countries other than Sweden and coming from low-skilled, blue-collar families. Both the Swedish gymnasiums in our study confront these contentious sociopolitical debates regarding "immigrant" schools, low-income families, and marginalized suburban communities.

The Challenging Context of Swedish School Reform and Its Impact
on Children of Immigrants

National Reform Efforts: The Suburbs, The Million Program, and School Choice Reforms   In the 1960s, the Swedish government implemented a housing program called "Miljonprogrammet" or the "Million Program," which aimed to create one million apartments to remedy the rising housing shortage that accompanied urban industrial growth. At this time, there was a shortage of both adequate residential spaces in general, and modern spaces in particular, to meet the projected numbers of working-class residents that were relocating from rural areas to cities (Ericsson, Molina, and Ristilammi 2002). By the early 1970s, however, industrial growth slowed but not as many persons moved from rural areas to cities as was predicted, leaving many apartments empty. As immigrant populations began to increase, they were often relocated to these uninhabited apartments. Because of negative portrayals in the Swedish news media, the neighborhoods created by the Million Program, typically located in suburbs, were characterized as "unfriendly" and "uninviting" almost from the very beginning (Sernhede 2002).

In addition, since the mid-1980s, there has been a deregulation and a decentralization of the Swedish welfare system. Sweden has tried nevertheless to maintain the tradition of inclusive educational reforms, assuring access to equivalent education for everyone regardless of ethnicity, social class, or place of residence (Englund 1996). The economic crises of the 1990s contributed to cutbacks in the social welfare system and an increase in the privatization of the educational system. By 1992, the Swedish government mandated school-choice reform measures (Friskolreform[2]), thereby making it possible for parents and students to choose schools other than those in their communities (Schierup and Urban 2007).

School choice eventually led to new forms of educational governance, budget cuts, and increased competition between schools. This increased competition has had the by-product of school closings that are indirectly related to student performance on the National Tests. In suburban schools with disproportionately large numbers of immigrant students—who face the mainstream biases of the National Tests—more students fail them. Since the test outcomes are reported by the media, the schools run the risk of being labeled as "bad" or "low achieving." This creates a downward spiral as students leave the schools and fewer enroll the next year (Bunar 2001; Kallstenius 2007). Suburban schools then receive smaller amounts of funding because the money follows the students. Suburban schools struggle to draw new students from mainstream neighborhoods and to maintain enrollments of ethnic Swedish students and high-status immigrant students.

This legacy of neighborhood, social welfare, and school reforms impacts Ekdalsskolan and Bergslunden Gymnasiums, the two schools in our study. Suburban schools in Sweden are often stereotyped as "problem" schools with "immigrant students" who are "in the risk zone" (i.e., "at-risk" students in US terms). In 2006, the year we began our research, the foreign-born population in Sweden was 13 percent; during that same year, in both the communities in which Ekdalsskolan and Bergslunden are located, the percentage of foreign born was over 60 percent (Ungdomsstyrelsen 2008). It is against this backdrop of marginalization that our findings about innovations at the two Swedish schools should be considered. Both gymnasiums have adopted innovative strategies for serving their immigrant-origin students and attracting students from other neighborhoods in an era of school choice.

Swedish Innovative School Sites

Ekdalsskolan Gymnasium   Ekdalsskolan Gymnasium is located outside a large city in central Sweden, and serves almost exclusively immigrant-origin youth, most of whom are of refugee origin. Most students reside in the suburb where this upper secondary school is situated, or in nearby suburbs whose residents are also predominantly of immigrant origin. In fall 2003, the school launched its comprehensive school reform, which was modeled on a private American lab school in Long Island, New York. The fundamental idea at the center of the reform derives from Howard Gardner's theory of multiple intelligence (1983). History and integrated learning are emphasized across the curriculum and supplemented with integrated "units." Technology integration is at the center of the futuristic reform, and all students receive laptops to use during the school day. In addition, the school has growing mentorship and internship partnerships with local businesses and universities. With the individual learner at its center and a philosophy that focuses on the needs of the "whole child," both academic and nonacademic, the reform built a new school from the bottom up, designed to allow for maximum collaboration in lounges and group areas where students can socialize or work in individual study rooms. In addition, the school cafeteria was reorganized to serve only healthy food, and a sports program was put in place to support student learning. As part of its partnership with the Long Island school, Ekdalsskolan receives professional development and mentoring support from the lab school's newfound network to implement its program. Every year students from the Swedish school visit the host school in New York, as do teachers for the purpose of professional development. With much fanfare and support from the city's Central School District Office, this school reform has brought attention to the school (perhaps a bit prematurely, before the reform effort could be fully realized) in Sweden, Europe, and the United States. As with other high schools in Sweden, Ekdalsskolan houses several programs, similar to the education reform in the United States in the early 1990s that divided large schools into smaller "houses" where teams of teachers are responsible for teaching, advising, and supporting a smaller segment of the school population throughout its academic career. In addition, the school has a program for newcomer youth who are second-language learners.[3]

Bergslunden Gymnasium   Bergslunden Gymnasium is located outside one of Sweden's largest cities, in a suburban community made up of several neighborhoods, and the school sits among several important community resources, including a local transit station, a cultural center for musical and theatrical performances, and approximately, seventy different shops. It was created under Swedish social democratic policies, which call for high schools to provide equal opportunity for lower-income youths. Some teachers and other school officials joined the staff because they were dedicated to teaching working-class and immigrant students.

In 2005, Bergslunden reorganized its curriculum under two broad approaches referred to as "Passions" and "Problem-Based Learning" (PBL). Passions are attractive programs that resemble magnet-school activities in the United States. In addition to the traditional subject areas, students can choose special interests such as "Professional Dance," "Textiles, Fashion, and Design," "Computer-Based Game Development," and "Soccer" for a portion of the credits needed to graduate. Teachers at Bergslunden Gymnasium work in teams. The teachers meet regularly to develop instructional materials, organize the content and goals of Problem-Based Learning assignments, and discuss the academic challenges and successes of individual students along with their general welfare and social/peer interactions. Problem-Based Learning privileges an active, hands-on approach to learning instead of a reliance on textbooks alone. Students engaged in PBL assignments collaborate in small groups together with a teacher who acts as supervisor to answer questions. Bergslunden students work with topics that incorporate several subject areas into one project. This allows students to learn how different subjects are interrelated even if they receive different grades in the traditional subject areas.

Some demographic details of student enrollment are in Table 6.2. As a matter of policy, Swedish school districts do not keep counts of the ethnic backgrounds of students; therefore, we cannot provide the ethnic distribution of students' enrollment in various programs. However, our ethnographic data from Bergslunden reveal that the immigrant students tended to cluster in certain program areas such as the social science and business programs, while ethnic Swedish students tended to cluster in the theater and music programs. In addition, Bergslunden has a special program for students who have recently arrived (as voluntary immigrants or refugees) in Sweden. Teachers in this program work exclusively with newly arrived students to prepare them to pass the Swedish National Tests in Swedish, English, and math and transition into the formal high school programs.

School Practices Conducive to Positive Outcomes for Immigrant-Origin Youth

Across schools we sought to identify approaches and strategies implemented in the various school sites that would serve to ease the adaptation and meet the educational needs of immigrant-origin youth. We began with overarching conceptual categories based on previous research in the field. As part of the iterative process of fieldwork, we added new practices to our conceptual categories as we encountered them. We then sought to determine if these practices occurred in each site.

We found that some practices were sound, promising, or innovative for immigrant-origin students whether they were second generation, newcomers, or second-language learners. Arguably, some of these practices are simply sound for students in general, regardless of whether they are of immigrant origin. We organized the conceptual categories along the lines of: (1) curriculum; (2) pedagogical approaches; (3) school structures; (4) school climate; (5) assessment strategies; (6) educational supports and enrichment outside of class; and (7) preparation for higher education and the workplace. Other practices were very specific to the needs of newcomer students and second-language learners, serving to ease their negotiation of the cultural transition and learning a new language.

TABLE 6.3. Cross-Case Comparisons of Innovative Practices Important for *All* Immigrant-Origin Students

	New York High Schools		Swedish Gymnasiums	
	World Citizen	Progressive	Ekdalsskolan	Bergslunden
Curriculum				
Integrated curriculum	✓	✓	✓	✓
– Interdisciplinary	✓	✓	✓	✓
– Project-based learning	✓	✓	✓	✓
– Inquiry-based learning	✓	✓		
Relevant curriculum				
– Social justice teaching	✓	✓		
– Culturally responsive	✓	✓		✓
– Building on interests		✓	✓	✓
Pedagogical Approaches				
Multimodal instructional	✓	✓	✓	✓
Student-centered instruction	✓	✓	✓	✓
Differentiated instruction	✓	✓	✓	✓
Integration of technology			✓	✓
School Structures				
Shared teacher planning	✓		✓	✓
Teacher involvement in curricular decision making	✓	✓	✓	✓
Advisory program	✓	✓	✓	✓
Enhancing Positive School Climate				
Safe school environment	✓	✓	✓	✓
Caring & respectful relationships	✓	✓	✓	✓
Assessment Approaches				
Multimodal assessments	✓	✓	✓	✓
Dedicated exam preparation	✓	✓	✓	✓
Public presentation of competencies	✓	✓	✓	✓
Supports and Enrichment Outside of Class				
Tutoring & homework support	✓	✓	✓	✓
Extracurricular enrichment	✓	✓	✓	✓

	New York High Schools		Swedish Gymnasiums	
	World Citizen	Progressive	Ekdalsskolan	Bergslunden
Preparation for Higher Education and the Workplace				
Explicit college pathway instruction for students	✓	✓	✓	✓
College pathway information for parents	✓	✓		
Internships	✓	✓	✓	✓
Instruction in soft skills for success in the workplace	✓	✓	✓	✓

We will describe these sets of practices in separate sections. Below we provide a comparison between sites and then give some specific examples from the field to illustrate how practices were implemented and experienced in the everyday lives of students.

All four schools practice reforms founded on progressive multicultural education (Banks and Banks 2007; Nieto 2003). Interdisciplinary, project-based, and student-centered approaches to curriculum and instruction are central to teaching and learning across the schools. All four schools utilize an integrated curriculum in some form, and the two Swedish schools place particular emphasis on the integration of technology into the curriculum. The four schools have attempted to create curricula that are relevant to the lives of the diverse students they serve. To successfully deliver content, the schools use decentralized pedagogical strategies designed to place the student at the center of learning and move away from traditional teacher lectures for at least part of the time. In addition to rethinking content and delivery, the schools seek multiple strategies to assess their students as well as ways to prepare them for the high-stakes testing where immigrant origin youth are at a notorious disadvantage. All of the schools have implemented some kind of academic supports to help them to be successful. And finally, several of the schools place particular focus on the postsecondary school experience.

Curriculum

Numerous studies have shown that the rigor of curriculum is a critical contributor to the achievement gap (Bryk, Holland, and Lee 1993; Chubb and Moe 1990). In the United States, underrepresented racial, ethnic, and socioeconomic minorities typically are enrolled in the least rigorous courses (NCES 2001). Students who take algebra, geometry, trigonometry, chemistry, physics, higher-level English, and other challenging courses tend to have higher test scores than their peers (NCES 2000; Ford and Harris 1994; Frazier et al. 1995). In the schools we examined, providing access to rigorous curricula is an equity issue they have systematically addressed with their immigrant-origin students. Notably, consistent with recognized good practice (Gardner 2004; Gates 2006; Suárez-Orozco and Qin-Hilliard 2004), several of the administrators we spoke to explicitly told us that providing a curriculum that was rigorous and relevant to prepare their students to be educated citizens for the twenty-first century was central to their mission.

To accomplish the schools' goals, at the center of their strategic visions are student-centered, project-based strategies that are implemented and interpreted in multiple ways. All four schools have developed some form of Integrated Thematic Interdisciplinary Learning. At several sites, addressing particular issues, topics, or problems and integrating learning across disciplines and subjects are keys to the strategy for engaging students. As mentioned earlier, at Bergslunden, students participate in Problem-Based Learning; for example, during our period of observation, a social studies/history project that spanned six weeks focused on the "Metrocity: Then and Now."[4] This project had many, clearly stated functional and cultural literacy goals that included teaching students about how living conditions changed as their city developed from an agricultural society to an industrial metropolitan area. The assignment served to make students more aware of the influence of historical context. They also learned about the processes of doing field research and gathering information through site visits and from city officials. In addition, they developed new vocabulary and concepts related to the project's topic.

Similarly, Progressive High School utilizes a thematic, integrated approach to the curriculum. For example, the school has created a "Senior Institute" for all of its eleventh- and twelfth-grade students. Rather than take traditional English, history, and social science coursework, students at Progressive are offered courses based on a theme or topic such as "Philosophy of Life," "Ethics of Fear," or "Food" that integrates the humanities and social science material into a single course. Students thus learn their core subjects through a topic area. This inquiry-based approach encourages students to think deeply and fundamentally about real-life problems or concerns and examine problems from multiple standpoints and disciplines. For example, in the "Food" class, the teacher explained, the Senior Institute was designed to help students "notice things on a more fundamental level . . . notice things we are not usually conscious of" by using food as a way to provide insight into our own culture. We saw this approach in action during our classroom observations in the first week of the class as reflected in our field notes: "The teacher sliced up apples and distributed pieces to each student and asked students to draw what they saw. . . . During the next part of the activity students wrote eight questions related to the apple from the following list of categories of questions: phenomenological; gastronomical; historical; ecological; political; biological; economical; futuristic; technological; philosophical; spiritual; psychological; sociological, leading to a topical discussion." This example, from the Progressive High School's food class, points to another feature of the curriculum across the four schools—a focus on topics relevant to students' lives, even something as mundane as an apple.

At other times, the topic was more gripping. As noted by a teacher at Progressive High School, "I think that in other schools they spend way too much on the textbook and trying to make sure that students remember a whole bunch of facts from a textbook. And I'll sit here and tell you that as a thirty-year-old I don't remember most of what I learned in high school. These students, they're very conscious because we'll talk about genocide and the different areas in the world where there have been mass situations of genocide. That's something that they'll always remember." By taking theme- or topic-based courses, students have an opportunity to explore topics of interest to them as a vehicle to gain the humanities and social science knowledge they are expected to learn. In typical classes we observed across these schools, the teacher begins units with "essential questions" like "What is justice?" or "What is gender?" (see Wiggins and Tighe 2001). According to a group of seniors at World Citizen High Schools who spoke to us in a focus group, they often explore fundamental questions of life, interrogating their own views, the views of philosophers and literary figures from past to present, and media opinions, and actively discuss diverse perspectives in class, often in the form of formal debates.

Topics of social justice are a theme that often serves to engage the students in their learning. At Bergslunden Gymnasium, social studies and language teachers use media misrepresentations and stereotypes of the Bergslunden community as a starting point for discussions about social justice while simultaneously teaching social studies or language-based topics. An English teacher at World Citizen High used a recent shooting of an innocent black American by New York Police officers as a springboard for discussion about the current-day impact of past racist institutions like apartheid and American slavery. Debate is another means by which teachers introduce social justice topics. A debate coach at World Citizen High explained: "I know my team. They do a lot of research . . . and the material itself becomes inspiring to learn."

The debate format is used beyond the debate team. An English teacher interviewed at Ekdalsskolan mentioned that one of the barriers to improving her students' language abilities is their insecurity or "shyness" to speak the new language. Her primary goal for her students, she notes, is that they "feel secure speaking and writing." To encourage their speaking, she often uses debate as a tool to get her students going. Through debate, she explains, students

> have to speak and have an opinion. They have to take sides, because there is nothing wrong or right. . . . We looked at a dilemma involving a black nurse . . . in the 1960s . . . she came to a family and the daughter was having a baby . . . and they made her go to the back door. So she left and the baby died. Did she do the right thing? She was offended and insulted. Or should she have saved the baby? . . . We had a great conversation. And they really all had opinions and from every perspective from the left and the right. . . . Everyone was drawn into the discussion.

Across the four sites, we saw evidence of the schools providing rigorous curricula to their students. These schools are providing their immigrant students with an education meant to teach them to think and engage with the twenty-first-century marketplace.

Pedagogical Practices

Across school sites, the primary preference for instructional delivery was collaborative and cooperative learning. While not always consistently according to our observations, there was generally an ethos of collaboration and working together evinced by the students in each school; small-group work was the norm across school sites. In addition, each school developed innovative activities to improve the literacy and critical thinking skills of their students.

In the New York City sites, emphasis is placed on differentiated instruction. Differentiated instruction is based on the premise that instruction should vary according to the needs of students of differing abilities within the same class (Hall 2009). This approach to teaching provides students with multiple options for presenting knowledge as well as making sense of ideas, and requires teachers to present information in a variety of ways and to be flexible in modifying assignments (Hall 2009). A teacher at World Citizen High told us:

> I do assign more advanced kids the more challenging questions . . . [they can] organize everything, summarize everything, and they need to take it to the next step . . . whereas low level kids, . . . I have them just do things like find pictures. So it depends on the students. . . . And even though they don't do the same tasks, they will still need to bring back whatever they're supposed to do and explain it to the whole group. By explaining their parts, they *have* to understand it, and then, which will also help them to practice their speaking, which most of them need.

While technology is utilized across all four school sites, the two upper secondary schools in Sweden, with their superior facilities and access to technology, *integrate technology* in many aspects of their curriculum. At Ekdalsskolan Gymnasium, all students are given laptops. In a philosophy course in Ekdalsskolan, student debates were videotaped and then accessed through the school's virtual classroom server. Students could rewatch the debate and write a reflective critique on their performance. Through its Frontier server, students have full access to their classes. While not fully implemented during our time at the school, many teachers use their virtual classrooms as a place where students can see and upload assignments, communicate with teachers and other students, track their missing assignments and progress in a class, and access teacher-linked resources.

At Bergslunden, The Knowledge Portal is a technology support center. According to one of the school officials, an acronym for The Knowledge Portal could be HTOSLC: High Tech Open Space Learning Center. In this sense, teachers can use computers as tools or instruments of knowledge similar to the use of a pen or pencil. But this "tool" facilitates active pedagogical interaction. Furthermore, staff members of The Knowledge Portal are highly skilled and diverse in both their professional competencies and social/ethnic backgrounds. In terms of professional competencies, there are two teachers/pedagogues who are specialists in working with children/teens with special needs, one teacher who has a master's in modern language, and two who are working on doctoral degrees (one in pedagogy and literature and the other in science and civil engineering); additionally, there is a teacher who is a Spanish and didactics specialist, and a teacher who speaks and reads Arabic, Kurdish, Turkish, Swedish, and English. The ethnic/national/religious origins of The Knowledge Portal staff include the Middle East, Latin America, Sweden, as well as Christian, Jewish, and Muslim faiths. Though The Knowledge Portal was designed to accommodate students with learning disabilities, it is useful to a broad range of students, including immigrant-origin students and second-language learners.

School Structures: Facilitating Optimal Conditions for Learning

In order to implement school-wide academic reforms, schools also have to rethink the ways in which their structures affect the conditions in which innovation can occur. Many of these conditions—including everything from school staffing to the design and utilization of physical space—are often overlooked by social-science researchers, but are well known in the practitioner world to make or break innovation no matter how well intended (Balfanz, Jordan, McPartland, and Legters 2002; Comer 1995). Each of the schools in our study has experimented with structural ways of implementing curricular and instructional innovations while working explicitly to create a positive school climate inside the school. Three of the four schools were part of a larger network of schools that had experimented with many innovations: therefore, they were not reinventing the wheel and had the luxury of being mentored through the process.

While in both Swedish cities and New York City the content of teaching has largely become prescribed in order to prepare students for high-stakes tests, nonetheless, all the schools managed to find ways to allow for teachers to be part of the curriculum decision-making process. A teacher at World Citizen High School observed:

> My old school, it was just, we were treated in such a condescending way. . . . Here, the administration, we're just treated with respect. . . . They trust that we know our content, and we're motivated to teach our kids and

we have some ability to do that. And sure, we might need some professional development and we're always encouraged to learn more or learn from each other. . . . And we always help each other; we are expected to work together, to plan together, to develop curriculum, and we build binders of our curriculum so that next year there's something to work off of. So, there's accountability, but it's not like a McDonald's management style.

Although there were some big differences in the size, staffing, and resources available to the Swedish schools versus those in New York City, organizationally there is a surprising amount of similarity in how all four schools structure teaching and learning. All have interdisciplinary teacher teams responsible for small groups of students, with shared planning time to allow for collaborative curriculum planning. One teacher said of the interdisciplinary planning: "I love having to work in a team. It's definitely not easy, but I feel like I've learned so much from my co-workers. And also I don't know what I would do without my co-workers in terms of creating a curriculum. I work with the English department to create everything I do." The teams are also used as opportunities to discuss the individual needs of students. At Bergslunden Gymnasium, students are assigned both a base-group leader and a mentor; these two teachers coach students through projects and assignments. Both schools in New York City have advisory programs in place whereby small groups of students are assigned to a teacher who serves as a mentor and coach to students as they navigate through high school. An English teacher, expressing sentiments that existed across all four sites, described in detail the way in which the teams serve to deepen the understanding of students' learning challenges and to strategize solutions to better meet the needs of each student:

All the teachers in our team get together and we, you know, discuss students' behavior, academic improvement, and being there with their advisors and their teachers I really feel like it's a great way to combat, you know, problems that the kids have, and really kind of identify struggles that the kids have. And that's, to me, one of the most amazing things that we do. That the teachers really have a time every week when we sit down and talk about it. So, what we do in guidance, we bring up kids that we're having problems with usually. And we talk about what's going on and ask each other if anyone is more successful with them, like what they're doing. And so, we try to figure out ways to work with the kid.

A ninth/tenth-grade teacher at World Citizen High explained that the team meetings, along with the advisory program, play a critical role in the school's high graduation rate: "We need to know everything that has been done [and] want to make sure that the kids are getting all the help they need." The school structures are organized at these sites in such a way that teachers have time to systematically communicate about students and collaborate around curriculum development and teaching. This allows a spirit of collaboration between colleagues and a collective focus on the needs of the students.

Enhancing Positive School Climate

All the schools work intentionally to create a school climate where students feel welcome, respected, cared for, and safe. The advisory groups clearly help to foster a connection among students as well as between students and teachers. A twelfth-grade math teacher at World Citizen High School summed up the school's ethos by saying: "I think our school . . . it expects us to know our students, and push them. And to care about them." And another teacher echoed this sentiment: "One of the things that I love about this place, . . . it's so much based on relationships, your personal relationships with kids, building that relationship, and being there for the kids, I think it's really important. . . . I really think this school is very holistic in its approach." Students tended to report a positive climate at their schools. Students at both Bergslunden and World Citizen High Schools spoke highly of the learning environments of their respective schools. Second-language learners at Bergslunden felt that for the most part, their teachers were great at meeting students' needs. The second-language learners did not merely feel that their teachers were facilitating linguistic competencies but were also sensitive to how students were or were not adjusting to their new homeland. During interviews and conversations, students reported that they could approach their teachers not just for help with language improvement, but for other types of assistance. One female student enthusiastically explained, "When I have problems in my studies, I am free to go to my teachers and tell them. . . . I am free to go to the teachers, the nurse, everything. . . . I can talk to them and I feel comfortable." Generally speaking, second-language learners felt immersed in a supportive learning environment and were eager to follow the directives of teachers. At World Citizen High, similar to Bergslunden, the second-language learners expressed positive sentiments about teachers always being accessible to students. For example, students knew that they could get assistance from teachers during teachers' "down time" like lunch breaks, breaks between classes, and even after school. Our observations and interviews suggest a high degree of trust between teachers and students at both schools.

Likewise, during a focus group with ninth graders at World Citizen High, one student mentioned that she was motivated to do her work to please her teacher: "I like doing work for this class because I like my teacher. . . . I like [her] because although we all come from different countries she tries to explain so that we understand each other." To this, another participant added, "Yeah, some teachers, they always try to help you, and they respect you. They make you really want to come to school."

This climate of support extends to a philosophy of encouraging students to support one another. Students noted that they liked learning when there was a mix of levels so that the more advanced students could help the beginners. Teachers encouraged active collaboration. For example, at Progressive, we observed teachers advising their students to help one another through the rigorous exhibition process: "Identify someone in the advisory to check in with you later in the week . . . read your draft, give you feedback and encouragement."

Notably, unlike in many schools that serve diverse populations in the United States, students at these schools overwhelmingly reported feeling safe (Johnson, Arumi, and Ott 2006; Zeldin 2004). At Bergslunden, students spoke repeatedly about the amount of diversity, the lack of bullying, and how Calm Streets—a program within the school that uses youth workers from the community to maintain discipline—does a great job of preventing and mediating disputes and fights among students. A sentiment frequently expressed across student interviews was that the reputation of Bergslunden as a "bad school" with a lot of criminals and fighting is unjustified; in their view, there are few to no criminals and far more interactions based upon friendship than fighting. A second-language student in Bergslunden's program for newcomer immigrants explained that when she first got there, she asked to transfer because she had only known the school through its reputation. A few months later, she got a letter saying she could go to another school with fewer immigrants. At this point, however, she told us: "I didn't want to leave. . . . The reputation of [Bergslunden Gymnasium] is not true."

At Ekdalsskolan, the students were very proud of how their diverse population got along so well. For example, two friends from different backgrounds explained in an informal interview: "We have been best friends since third grade. We study Arabic together. We are different religions but it doesn't matter to us. The people at this school are really different, from all over the world, but they all get along really well. There are not many fights here. We are family here." Another student, whose family is from Sri Lanka, transferred from an elite school—where she was academically successful—to Ekdalsskolan even though she would be required to repeat her first year. Her reasons were based on a desire for a school that was, as she describes, "more than a school"—that is, somewhere where the relationships between teachers and students were personalized. As she explains, "You should be where you are comfortable . . . the environment and teachers are better at Ekdalsskolan . . . students have a more special connection with the teachers and students here, I feel." Positive student sentiments, like those presented above, were frequently expressed across all four sites.[5] The sense that teachers and administrators cared, served to keep students connected and engaged.

Assessment Approaches

Complementing progressive approaches to content and delivery is a corresponding approach to student assessment. The decisions about *what* to assess have been adapted to match instructional goals. Yet each school also recognizes that students are required to show certain forms of competency as demonstrated through high-stakes national (Sweden) or statewide (New York) exams in order to graduate. Consequently, the schools employ various ways of assessing students in line with their visions, while at the same time working to prepare students for standardized exams.

In day-to-day coursework, students have opportunities across all the school sites to be assessed in multiple ways intended to allow them to display competency and to accommodate different learning styles, or to be more representative of what students may find in the "twenty-first-century" world. These *multimodal assessments* have included student-created video documentaries, graphic novels or other multimedia representations (Progressive, World Citizen, and Bergslunden); classroom presentations using PowerPoint (all four schools); laboratory experiments; portfolios; and, of course, traditional papers and exams.

Several of the schools used portfolio assessments as a way to evaluate student progress. A chemistry teacher at World Citizen High told us:

We have a portfolio presentation at the end of the semester, where we have different panels. Each panel will have four students and the teacher for the advisory group. So each person will actually sit there and then defend him or herself . . . [and] explain what they did for the particular category. So, for example, for the research and reporting category, they have to put an entry sheet, . . . explaining why did I choose this work for this particular category. And what kind of work is that . . . basically explain their work . . . the rest of the students will be asking questions. Why did you choose this project for this category? What did you learn from this project, and so on and so forth.

Several of the schools also require each student to complete a culminating project that has been initiated and carried out entirely by him or her. In the natural-science research program at Ekdalsskolan, for example, students are mentored by doctoral students from the Karolinska Institute, an internationally renowned medical school and research center, as they work on self-initiated science projects that begin in their second year of the program and are completed in the fall of their final year. One of Ekdalsskolan's most highlighted job-work partnerships is in this program, where students have the opportunity to work with professionals in the science discipline of their choice.

Students at Progressive High School complete self-initiated projects known as exhibitions, which are designed to be akin to a "mini-thesis defense." At the end of each year, students write extensive papers to demonstrate both knowledge of a particular content area and the ability to think deeply about a selected topic using higher-order skills. The projects in Ekdalsskolan's science research program are similar, involving a thesis that is defended during the fall of the student's third (and final) year of school. The formal presentation takes place in a public forum at the Karolinska Institute's amphitheatre, where students present their research and, as at Progressive, then take questions from the audience of students, teachers, and Karolinska mentors and professors who participate in the partnership.

Ideally, high-stakes standardized exams are a way for students to show that they have mastery over required content. For a number of reasons, however, students who are in the process of acquiring a second language may not be able to demonstrate their knowledge on standardized tests though they may well understand the content knowledge. The reasons are varied and include issues related to lack of cultural familiarity with the testing format (Solano-Flores 2008), language acquisition, vocabulary knowledge, timed-testing (Amrein and Berliner 2002; Menken 2008; Solano-Flores 2008), and stereotype threat (Steele 1997). Second-language learners are particularly disadvantaged when taking standardized exams; hence, time spent explicitly in preparing students for exams can make a difference in how they perform, regardless of their knowledge of the content being tested (APA 2012; Menken 2008).

At World Citizen, for example, in a history class we observed, a quiz incorporated questions resembling the format of questions on the state-mandated Regents exam (multiple choice, studying a document and answering questions related to it, requiring the student to state an opinion with supporting evidence, etc.). At Progressive, portfolio assessment is privileged over standardized exams as a way to evaluate student competency. That said, teachers still set aside time to prepare students for exams, generally in the form of practice tests that are reviewed in class. Likewise, teachers at Bergslunden Gymnasium set aside time to give students assignments and pretests that will help prepare them for the National Tests.

While test preparation was viewed as instrumental and important, many teachers chafed at simply "teaching to the test." Two English teachers at World Citizen talked about how they tried to teach beyond the exams: "I think the two of us are here to give a real kind of steroid to their literacy, so that they can do well on all their exams. Not because all the exams are great but because they have to pass them to graduate from high school." Thus, the teachers in the schools were not happy about having to use precious teaching time to prepare their students for the high-stakes tests; nonetheless, they conscientiously took on the challenge, viewing it as another learning opportunity. In addition, they sought alternative assessment strategies and taught their students to present publicly—a skill that should serve their students well in the world of work.

Providing Academic Supports and Enrichment Outside of Class
All four schools provide supplementary academic support in some form for their students. In recent years, there has been a renewed interest in the role of after-school programming (Noam 2004). The students in several of the schools in this study were encouraged to participate in multiple after-school activities. The most common types of academic support provided by the

schools in our study are formal and informal homework support and tutoring; enrichment opportunities including field trips, arts-related programs with community partners, and discipline-related clubs such as a national science club, or author's club; and clubs related to students' ethnic or cultural backgrounds.

At World Citizen, for example, extracurricular activity clubs included Chinese language classes, Chinese calligraphy, and Brazilian martial arts. When these clubs hosted events such as a lunch celebrating Bengali Independence Day or Chinese New Year's Day, the guidelines were that everyone in the school is invited, and that the hosts/hostesses of the event share their cultural knowledge with others in the community. As a counselor at World Citizen noted: "I think the more students do outside of class, the more they'll be ready for college."

The school day alone rarely gives these students enough time to catch up with their peers; and immigrant parents dealing with language challenges are often unable to help their children academically. After-school academic programs, where immigrant students work individually or in small groups, represent a critical resource that may make all the difference in their academic trajectory. After-school activities provide immigrant-origin students the opportunity to receive personalized assistance with schoolwork and structure their time.

Preparation for Higher Education and the Workplace: Navigating Life-Stage Transitions

Explicit in the educational visions across the four school sites are the goals of preparing their students for the "twenty-first century" and a "global world." A social studies teacher at Progressive spoke of the school's focus on global consciousness and the students' keen interest in this area: "They're very current-event conscious and focused on the world and how to change it; how they can be an active participant in the world."

The goals of this preparation agenda are operationalized in specific strategies employed at each school, and are particular to the local and national contexts in which the schools reside. The processes of both applying to university and learning skills for the workplace in the host country require explicit and dedicated instruction by secondary schools. All four schools have programs to help students apply for the university and to gain the "soft skills," or workplace behaviors, that are culturally expected in each country and considered critical for the twenty-first century—such as the ability to work collaboratively with others. In the following paragraphs, we describe some of the practices the four schools employ to help their students navigate the transitions to university and the workplace.

Preparation for University Studies   In both the United States and in Sweden, there are specific processes to follow to apply and gain acceptance to the university. These processes require what is referred to in the US literature as "college pathway knowledge," or the tangible know-how to successfully navigate the process into the university. College-pathway knowledge is often seen among the privileged dominant group as something that is "self-evident" or "common sense," but schools that work with immigrant-origin youth or marginalized populations understand that for newcomer families, especially those with no experience with higher education, how to get into a university can be a mystery.

While both Sweden and the United States offer multiple pathways, full of "second chances," to higher education, the college-pathway process in Sweden is much more transparent and easier to follow than in the United States. It is based on a point system calculated in terms of courses completed in high school and performance in those classes as measured by the national exams. While the process is fairly straightforward, there are nonetheless a number of hurdles students must cross to get to a college or university. For example, immigrant-origin students might need to learn more about the kinds of options they have for higher education as well as about the schools themselves, have a clear understanding of the kinds of courses they need to take and the grades they will need to be accepted at the school of their choice, and get help completing the applications. Further, they need exposure to the expectations and culture of college/university life, which may be quite different from their personal experience.

At Ekdalsskolan Gymnasium, explicit preparation begins in the senior year. Each student meets with one of the college counselors to discuss options and the application process. At the beginning of the second semester, the school holds a university fair during the school day. Universities, technical colleges, and vocational schools from across the country send representatives to encourage application by immigrant-origin youth. After an initial presentation, the representatives disperse to classrooms, and students can choose three different schools to check out through question-and-answer sessions. In addition, the college counselor schedules campus visits for students. During our interviews with seniors, we asked them about the process for getting into a postsecondary school in Sweden. All appeared quite familiar with the online process and what they needed to do, even if they were less certain of their own plans.

At Berglunden, the process of providing information about college is also explicit and built into the curriculum. For example, in the social science program, teachers arrange for students to visit colleges. More generally, guidance counselors make themselves available to answer questions and work one-on-one with students interested in attending college. Also, Bergslunden provides a special college-pathway course for newcomer immigrant students who already have high school diplomas from their country of origin but need additional preparation to transition into the Swedish postsecondary system. Thus, promising students are provided with both advice and coursework needed to supplement their high school degree.

In the United States, students need to learn all of the above and more. Unlike Sweden, getting into the university is a much more complicated process, much of it "hidden" from view, especially for the elite universities. Beyond grades and performance on college-entry exams, students are expected to sell themselves to schools. For example, students can show they possess desirable soft skills such as personal responsibility and social skills associated with success (e.g., leadership, social responsibility, etc.) in the university or workplace as a result of the extracurricular or employment positions they have held outside of school. A wide range of activities displays "well-roundedness." In addition, students obtain recommendations from teachers and others who can attest to their abilities and personality traits, and provide personal statements or respond to prompts to attest to how they are uniquely qualified to attend certain institutions.

While marketing oneself, especially for elite universities, requires a lot of know-how on the part of students and their families, even more prohibitive is the cost of higher education. That is the biggest barrier to access to a postsecondary school in the United States; hence, knowledge about ways for paying for college, as well as tangible help in the process of obtaining financial assistance, must be provided by high schools to their immigrant-origin students.

Progressive High has a comprehensive college-pathway program designed to address all of these obstacles to college access. The college-pathway process at Progressive is publicly celebrated as evidenced by the bulletin board outside of the guidance counselors' office, which shows off photos and names of alumni according to the colleges they are attending. The school provides both group and individualized information, clearly articulating the college's access to the hidden "game."

All eleventh and twelfth graders are required to take a "college prep" class, which is run by the guidance counselors. In the class, students explore options for their university education and learn how to complete applications, including applications for loans and scholarships. During their junior year, the students take a class trip to a well-known test preparation company, where they complete surveys to identify what they are looking for in college. These interests, combined with performance information provided by the students (e.g., grade point average), are matched by the company to universities in tiers, ranging from "reaches," schools where students have only a modest chance of acceptance, to "safety schools," where they have a high probability of getting in. In addition, the guidance counselor gives students a list of summer programs where they can take college classes, explaining that this can enhance their resumes and college applications. Other examples of in-class activities include: practice filling out financial-aid applications, searching for universities, and lessons on deciding how many colleges to apply to, on writing application essays and statements, and on procuring recommendations. Acceptances and rejections are shared and discussed in the more intimate setting of the advisory program with their peers.

Formal instruction in college-pathway knowledge stands side by side with a structured approach to providing individual support not just to the student but to the parents as well, involving explicit instruction in college-pathway knowledge and tangible help while fully engaging them in the process. This approach also begins in junior year. A guidance counselor meets with every eleventh grade student and his/her parents for thirty minutes in the spring to discuss the application process/questions/next steps/how to choose a college. One guidance counselor we interviewed explained that immigrant parents often want their children to go to big-name schools. But he also noted that Hispanic parents probably knew less about the process and the names of schools than did Asian parents, who seemed to enjoy better exchange of college information across socioeconomic class lines (Louie 2004). Thus, he confided that he strove to focus particular energies to helping lower-income immigrant families. He also told us that while it was often difficult for immigrant parents to come in to see him during the workday, he estimated that, nonetheless, 85 percent of the parents managed to make a daytime meeting.

The costs for university entry start at the very beginning of the process with fees for standardized tests (SAT or ACT) and application costs. In addition, middle-class students in the United States often take expensive test preparation courses that give them an additional advantage on test day. To level the playing field, Progressive High School subsidizes SAT test preparation courses for its students.

Preparation for the Workplace

All four schools have specific programs or strategies designed to provide students with opportunities to gain practical skills in preparation for the workplace. Primary among these opportunities are internships and explicit connections to mentors that are arranged through university or community partnerships. At both World Citizen and Progressive High Schools, students are involved in internships that build on their interests. At the time of our data collection, Ekdalsskolan Gymnasium was piloting a mentorship program through a Stockholm business association, matching seniors in the economics program with Swedish business professionals. The school was planning to expand this program in the following year to all social science seniors. In its innovative entrepreneurial program, students are matched with community members in a school-to-work program that seeks to connect businesses with students who share compatible interests. As another example, a well-known commercial law firm provides up to three students from Bergslunden Gymnasium with: (1) scholarship funds of thirty-thousand SEK that they share; (2) mentors from the law firm; (3) funds to pay for textbooks while they attend law school; (4) summer jobs after their second year in law school; and (5) guaranteed internships (*praktikplats*) while in school. These innovative internships and practicums help to keep students academically motivated, serve to model the soft skills of the world of work, and provide crucial networks for connections to future positions.

School Factors Particularly Conducive to Better Outcomes for Newcomer Immigrant Youth and Second-Language Learners

In addition to the practices described above, newcomer immigrant youth and second-language learners have additional academic and socio-emotional needs, different from those of the typical second-generation immigrant student. At the forefront is the need to develop both the social and academic language of their new country while mastering the content knowledge necessary to be successful in the new society. Most graduation pathways are quite unforgiving of the five to seven years it takes for most students to develop the academic language to the point of competitiveness with native peers (Cummins 2000; Hakuta, Butler, and Witt 2000). This is the level of language competence required to be competitive on a timed multiple choice test, write a well argued essay, or confidently join in a class discussion. Thus, immigrant students often are tracked into non-college-bound courses, falter in confidence, and fall behind their nonimmigrant peers (Menken 2008; Ruiz-de-Valasco, Fix, and Clewell 1998; Suárez-Orozco et al. 2008).

Further, it is important to keep in mind that immigration is a stressful event (Falicov 1998; Suárez-Orozco 2001), which removes youth from predictable contexts while stripping them of significant social ties (Suárez-Orozco et al. 2008). Many have been separated from their parents for protracted periods of time and may face emotionally complex reunifications (Suárez-Orozco, Todorova, and Louie 2002). Immigrant children must contend with the particular acculturative challenges of navigating two worlds (Berry, Phinney, Sam, and Vedder 2006). They are often asked to take on responsibilities beyond their years, including sibling care, translation duties, and advocacy for their families (Faulstich-Orellana 2001), which at times undermine parental authority. These often highly gendered roles may have both positive and negative consequences for development (Smith 2002; Suárez-Orozco and Qin 2006). Children of immigrants also face the challenge of forging an identity and developing a sense of belonging to their new homeland while honoring their parental origins (Suárez-Orozco 2004). This acculturative stress has been linked both to psychological distress (APA 2012; García-Coll and Magnuson 1997) as well as to academic problems (Suárez-Orozco and Suárez-Orozco 1995).

Thus, we examined particularly innovative and promising practices that served to ease the emotional and linguistic transitions of newcomer and second-language learners at two school sites: World Citizen High School, which serves only newcomer immigrant youth, and Bergslunden, whose dedicated second-language-learners team gave the researchers full access to their work and their program. These schools employ the following innovative strategies to address both the academic needs of newcomer youth as well as their acclimation to their new environment: (1) support in helping students navigate the cultural transition to the new country; (2) support for students who had gaps in literacy or due to interrupted schooling; (3) language-intensive instruction across the curriculum; and (4) language-learning accommodations.

Negotiating Cultural Transitions

World Citizen High School is highly strategic in its approach to help newcomer youth adjust to their new environs. As new students come in, teacher teams meet to discuss each one, and a series of assessments are conducted and discussed in order to develop the best plan for him or her. The teachers try to meet with as many of the parents as possible. Parents are asked to bring in signed forms/health records at the beginning of the school year. Teachers also meet with parents sometime around the end of the first grading period in late October. This is when students first get to see their report cards, and it is an opportunity for teachers to get a sense of what their students' home and family situations are like. The information gleaned from these conferences is then shared when teachers meet across the teams working with each student.

The ongoing transition is primarily the responsibility of the advisory program, which helps students to adjust to their new school under the guidance of an advisor who is looking out for them. One of the guidelines for forming advisory groups is to have a newcomer/beginning learner of English in the same group as at least one student who shares the same native language and is also proficient in English so that the more advanced English speaker can translate. In advisory groups, students are encouraged to talk about anything they like. According to a mentor teacher, her advisees talk about anything from difficulties with a class, missing families and friends back home, to boyfriend/girlfriend issues:

> I think . . . that the culture of the classroom is very important. . . . At the beginning, it's a tradition in our school, you spend a lot of time on community-building activities, where they get to know each other as students. . . . Like background, and through that, what comes out is that some of them went to school so much longer . . . because of war or whatever. Some of them didn't get to go to school [at all]. So they start seeing and understanding much more about why some of them are more advanced than others. . . . Then the other kids help [each other because] they understand why. . . . It is very important that . . . you develop that trust and you make them comfortable.

TABLE 6.4. Cross-Case Comparisons of Two Schools with Innovative
Practices Specific to Newcomer or Second-Language Learners

	World Citizen	Bergslundens
Help in negotiating cultural transitions	✓	✓
Support for gaps in interrupted schooling & literacy	✓	✓
Language-based teaching across content areas	✓	✓
Language-learning accommodations	✓	✓

Further, aligned with the language-intensive and student-centered-learning approaches, instructional tasks, in particular writing tasks, encourage students to share their personal experiences both in their old and new countries and in the transition from one to the other. For example, in one English assignment, students were given the task of sharing their experiences of moving from their native country to the United States. They are encouraged to share their stories with each other. Such activities help them to recognize that they are not alone in the difficulties of transition.

Supports for Gaps in Interrupted Schooling and Literacy

Some students enter secondary school with limited prior education or significant interruptions in their schooling. These may occur for a variety of reasons including socio-economic or gender inequities in original educational access, political strife that could have interrupted schooling, or hiccups in the migratory process that may have led to a sustained period out of school before reentry in the new land. Whatever the cause of an interruption in schooling, the consequence is often students who are over-aged and under-skilled and have considerable catching up to do in the classroom. This takes significant creativity, flexibility, and sustained effort on the part of school administrators and teachers. Students with interrupted formal education (SIFE) are encouraged to use every learning opportunity: "I tell [SIFE students], if you are on the subway, and you are just sitting, do your onesies, twosies, and threesies in your head till you can say it . . . and I suppose that's a form of homework." Understanding is shown for these students' sensitivity about being over-aged. They are encouraged to be as independent as possible and to constructively seek help from peers. A math teacher at World Citizen High School said:

> When a kid comes to me with . . . asking for help, I'll say who have you asked to help you first? . . . I want them to be independent. . . . This SIFE student, for a long time, I couldn't get her to work with anyone else . . . and I think a part of it was that she was embarrassed of how much she didn't know, and I finally got her to a point where she is now reliant on two or three other people in the class that she relates to and can get assistance from.

SIFE students receive the same supports provided to other newcomer students and more. Particular emphasis is placed on literacy. Typically, these students take longer than the standard four years to graduate from high school—often stretching to seven years. With the right amount of scaffolding, the daunting tasks of learning a new language, acquiring literacy, mastering content knowledge of a new culture, accruing graduation credit courses, and passing high-stakes tests are achievable for many students who would have given up in another setting.

Second-Language Learning

While not all immigrant students are second-language learners, many if not most are; and, in some cases, immigration requires learning three or more languages. As noted earlier, learning a second language to a competent academic level takes considerable time (Christensen and Stanat 2007; Collier 1995; Cummins 2000; Cummins, Brown, and Sayers 2007; Hakuta, Butler, and Witt 2000; Thomas and Collier 2002). Students with limited literacy in their native language will need further time to solidify their academic skills in a new language. An English teacher at World Citizen High School voiced this as one of the challenges that teachers face on a regular basis:

> We have students who are reading at grade level in English and they have only been in the country for three or four years. And, we have students who still struggle with basic spelling and sentence composition issues. All in the same classroom, meeting their needs well with content that still is interesting and stimulating and kind of addressing all of these different issues; I think it is incredibly challenging.

A teacher in Bergslunden Gymnasium's newcomer program offered a similar observation:

> Some immigrant students succeed, but some need more time [to learn Swedish, English, or Math]. For example, those who come from Bosnia or China have usually been in educational systems of high quality that are comparable to Sweden and can be prepared in one or two years. But other students, like those from Afghanistan, who have grown up during wartimes when the schools were closed, come needing far more time to prepare to take the National Tests. . . . There is a general expectation that we can prepare all students in one base year. . . . [but] the needs of our students vary.

Thus, immigrant students entering upper secondary schools with little background in the language of instruction require systematic and effective long-term curriculum plans for language education. Unlike schools in Sweden, schools in the United States typically do not have systematic or consistent bilingual or second-language acquisition policies and practices; this lack places ELL students at a disadvantage.

Second-language instruction is most successful when learners are placed into a progressive and systematic program of instruction that first identifies their incoming literacy and academic skills (Christensen and Stanat 2007). Research shows that consistency of instruction is essential for students as frequent transitions place them at considerable disadvantage (Gándara and Contreras 2008). Second-language learning is most successful when high-quality second-language instruction is provided with continued transitional academic supports—like tutoring, homework help, and writing assistance—as the language learners integrate into mainstream programs (Christensen and Stanat 2007). In order to ensure a smooth transition between grades as well as the continual development of skills, teachers need to both understand and conform to the instructional model ascribed to by the school or district (Sugarman and Howard 2001). Further, assessment of skills growth should be done annually using portfolio assessment as well as testing in order to measure progress and adjust interventions (Christensen and Stanat 2007). In Sweden, these supports are consistent with government policy; we also found these supports available at World Citizen High School though they are certainly not the norm in US public schools.

Teaching across Content Areas

In addition to developing communicative proficiency in the language of their new country, second-language learners (SLLs) need to simultaneously build content literacies; many of them also have low cognitive academic-language proficiency skills (CALP). Second-language acquisition programs (e.g., bilingual education, self-contained SLL programs) primarily focus on literacy development in terms of language proficiency, with only limited attention to academic second-language acquisition in content areas (August and Hakuta 1997; Chamot and O'Malley 1994; García 1993). It is a challenge for students to learn content across the academic disciplines while at the same time acquiring new language and literacy skills, and it poses an instructional challenge to many teachers as well (August and Hakuta 1997; Chamot and O'Malley 1994; García 1993; NCES 1999). The teachers at World Citizen High in particular were able to draw on the rich experience of the network of World Citizen schools. The network had developed a well-thought-out, rigorous teaching approach with an excellent track record of success over its decade and a half of operation.

A mentor teacher at World Citizen High School explained the school's strategy to teach the new language across subjects to new second-language learners:

> You bring in articles about the topic you're covering. . . . Teach them explicitly how to summarize, and what it means to summarize, what it means to paraphrase. . . . We explicitly teach, what does it mean to analyze something. We go over the steps for different ways you can analyze in different content areas. Sometimes different teachers in the team would say they want to target this word . . . it's a skill, it's a process-type word, and they need to know what it means, so we'd all do it in our classes. . . . And we found that when we ALL do it, and we all show them how to use it in different content areas, in different content, they are able to get it better. But it has to be explicitly taught, like we are studying this now. And tell them how we're going to do it. And ALWAYS bring it into the lesson that particular word so they keep seeing it. . . . Tons of writing, tons of presenting.

All teachers in the World Citizen network receive extensive training in language-intensive curriculum, where language learning is embedded across the entire curriculum. Writing is not simply an activity for language-arts classes.

Students are pushed daily to write and use their developing language skills in every class.

A twelfth-grade math teacher stressed the importance of pushing the second-language learners to be constantly writing in every class as a way to develop their new language skills. Notably, teachers push kids to write in essay format in preparation for their transition to college. Thus, second-language instruction is embedded across every subject in every possible learning opportunity throughout the high school experience. In this way nothing is taken for granted, language learning is constantly reinforced, and students are explicitly prepared for college entry.

Language-Learning Accommodations

At World Citizen High School students are encouraged to use their first language to help them learn the second language, even if others don't know their mother tongue. Informally, students are encouraged to translate for the newest immigrants, read and write in their first language during silent reading times, and carry bilingual dictionaries, but gently prodded toward English over time. The mother tongue is thus used strategically to aid the development of the new one. As one teacher at World Citizen High explained: "We encourage our kids to continue to develop their native language. [We encourage this] because we believe it develops the second language and it [acknowledges that] the base is the native language, and . . . it becomes so much more difficult to build their second language if there is no foundation. So because we encourage our kids so much, our kids feel free to speak whatever language they speak." Examples of the use of first languages are commonplace at World Citizen and Bergslunden. At World Citizen, after one small-group assignment, students were told to assess their group with a twist; they had to answer questions such as "What worked well in your group?" and "Who made the group work particularly successful?" On one side of a sheet of paper, students first had to translate the questions into their native language; on the other side, they answered the questions in English. At Bergslunden, second-language learners are not only encouraged but expected, during Problem-Based Learning assignments, to write key concepts in both their first language and Swedish. Teachers encourage and expect individual students to maintain first-language fluency. The tolerant attitude facilitated by Bergslunden teachers has had an unanticipated, yet welcome consequence. The diversity of language backgrounds means that Swedish becomes the lingua franca, the language spoken in the hallway that allows students to converse with one another. In other words, speaking Swedish to friends becomes something that second-language learners do by choice instead of by force.

In addition to the use of first languages as a teaching/learning tool, a ninth/tenth-grade math teacher shared her strategy for making sure that every student is keeping up and understands: "I think it helps if I spend five minutes before the end of the class, reading the question, or the writing prompt, reading it to them . . . and have them talk amongst themselves to make sure that they understand it, and have other kids translate for the ones who may not understand English. So make sure they understand the homework, and . . . think about where kids are going to get stuck."

Assignments are continually modified to make them accessible to students. An eleventh-grade science teacher explained:

> We have team meetings where we sit down and talk. . . . You know, we'll talk about our students and we'd pick . . . we study five students. It's something that we do for each team, where each team will identify five students, where they have very, very low literacy skills and they pretty much struggle with every single class. And then we'll take out the work from each content area and then we'll put them together and we'll talk about the questions, the assignment itself, and also the way students respond, and we also talk about how could we modify this particular assignment, and then we'll set up a model of, in general, how we are going to modify this.

These accommodations provide the much-needed scaffolding to newcomer students as they make the transition to their new educational setting. They begin to gain confidence in themselves and take the necessary strides in their new language to gain the academic skills they will need to be successful in their new land.

Implications for Policy and Practice

Immigrant-origin students bring a myriad of challenges to the classroom, which are compounded by the late twentieth-century climate of school reforms (Meier and Wood 2004), which has had a series of unintended consequences for this population. Clearly there are no facile solutions to the complex problems facing many of these students. The four schools examined in this chapter, however, exemplify beacons of opportunity. Our multiple-case research strategy revealed a number of common denominators of promising practice.

Many of the principles essential to serve immigrant students, highlighted in this chapter, are simply sound educational practice. At the very core is a confluence of rigorous standards and high expectations coupled with a "pedagogy of care" (Noddings 2003). Rather than taking a remedial approach, this education is *preparatory* in nature. Rather than an education that is good enough for "other people's children" (Delpit 2006), it is an education that one would be happy to see provided to *one's own children*. Further, the education is framed within an ethical, relational, caring context. These principles, we would argue, are sound canons of pedagogy to serve all students, whether or not of immigrant origin. In addition, the schools described here provide an added layer of services that address the specific needs of students from immigrant families.

Preparing Students for the Twenty-First-Century Global Era

More than ever before, education in the twenty-first century requires the development of higher-order cognitive skills in order to be able to engage with the marketplace realities of our global era (Bloom 2004; Suárez-Orozco and Qin-Hilliard 2004). However, the educational practices we presented in this chapter are not limited to providing students with skills for the marketplace. Teachers diligently work to prepare students for life in general, regardless of whether they are interested in going on to college or taking other professional paths.

The four schools we studied are rich with innovations that allow youth to develop the ethics, skills, sensibilities, and competencies needed to identify, analyze, and solve problems from multiple perspectives. These schools nurture students to be curious and cognitively flexible, and to synthesize knowledge within and across disciplines (Gardner 2004; Schleicher and Tremley 2006; Suárez-Orozco and Sattin 2007). The schools have an explicit agenda to prepare their students to successfully navigate in a multicultural world and impart skills deemed essential not merely to survive but to thrive in the global era (Bloom 2004; Gardner 2004). These promising schools put rigor, relevance, and relationships (Gates 2006) at the core of their pedagogy. What we found in them was the standard of rigor that we would hope for our own children. Unfortunately, however, rather than featuring such a preparation agenda, all too many schools serving immigrant-origin youth, like schools that serve other disadvantaged students, are those that are relegated to teaching "other people's children" (Delpit 2006)—such suboptimal schools typically offer the very least to those who need the very most (Kozol 1998, 2006).

In all of the schools we examined, we found a commitment to marginalized and disadvantaged students. The schools offer a stimulating, rigorous, and relevant curriculum but also provide a number of supplemental resources (such as after-school programs, tutoring, high-stakes test preparation, homework help, explicit college entry information, and so forth) to at-risk students in order to ease their educational transition and ameliorate their outcomes. Teachers make their pedagogies transparent, and there is a wealth of initiatives taken from different levels in the school system as a whole. The schools promote an alignment of instructional methods, content, and assessments and foster collaborative efforts to raise students' achievement levels and reduce barriers to educational equity. Notably, these services are helpful not only for immigrant-origin students but for other at-risk youth as well.

Our findings reveal that the four schools are learning communities with regular, rich encounters of exchange between students and teachers, teachers and teachers, and students and students. Teachers meet frequently to discuss student well-being and encourage their students in managing their learning and personal development. Students are treated as valued members of the learning community. The preparation agenda emphasizes a "caring" approach to teaching (Noddings 2002), whereby teachers' concern about students transcends mere subject matter. Essential values that are often stressed as part of the schools' ethos include: openness, communication, trust, respect, empathy, truth, participation, and a sense of justice. These values are not simply encouraged in school but are to be carried into life as a basis for nurturing ethical relationships with others. Notably, these core values are consistent with the kinds of values endorsed by John Dewey a century ago as fundamental for a participatory democratic society soliciting the full civic engagement of all citizens (Dewey 1909/1975).

These promising schools place positive relationships at the very core of the educational enterprise. Relationships between the administration and the faculty are respectful and teachers work in collaborative teams, reducing the sense of isolation that so often plagues the classroom teacher. Students are encouraged to support one another's learning and develop collaborations as well. The class and school environments of collaborative learning play a critical role in sustaining effortful student learning (Pianta 1999; Suárez-Orozco,

Pimentel, and Martin 2009). The educational enterprise is characterized by reciprocal interactions between teachers and students, in which teachers see their own destinies linked to the success of their students (Dance 2002).

In the schools we have highlighted, we saw students reflected daily in the eyes of their teachers. In addition, these promising schools all have faced head-on the specific challenges that immigrant-origin students bring to schools that must operate within citywide and nationwide contexts of some-times-heedless school reform. In this chapter, we pointed to a number of fundamental ways by which accommodations were made for newcomer immigrant students and second-language learners, providing them the opportunity to catch up with their native-born peers. These efforts include assisting immigrant-origin students in making psycho-social and cultural adjustments during their initial transitions. They also involve tangible aid to make up gaps in interrupted schooling. Further, these schools provide a series of language-based accommodations while the academic language of the new land is being acquired.

Though we have found most teachers and other school officials at the four schools eagerly engaged in the implementation of the preparation agenda, there are still challenges and obstacles to be overcome. For example, the needs of immigrant students and the expertise of their teachers, which are central to the preparation agenda, are not the ultimate arbitrators of pedagogical practices and curriculum content. Instead, due to the requirement that schools conform to standardized and/or national test regulations, it is the state/nation-centered testing mandates that have the final word. Even worse, the tests are not designed with the unique needs of second-generation or newly arrived students who are second-language learners in mind (APA 2012; Menken 2008). The demands of these standardized tests interrupt and hinder teacher efforts to achieve the goals of the preparation agenda.

Successful schooling that encompasses a preparation agenda is not facilitated by standardized examinations, which privilege superficial knowledge, skills, and competencies. Successful schooling goes "beneath surface meaning, first impressions, dominant myths, official pronouncements . . . to understand the deep meaning, root causes, social context, ideology, and personal consequences of any action . . . text, subject matter, policy, mass media, or discourse" (Shor 1992, 129). A preparation agenda relies upon ethical and dialogical pedagogical processes between teachers and students that empower students (Delpit 2006; Freire 2000, 2004; Shor 1992).

The best efforts will be those that will take a systematic approach to incorporation. In Sweden, there is a clearer recognition of the importance of providing systematic services to those with greater need, with promising if somewhat uneven results, as policy alone cannot eradicate marketplace discrimination. Nonetheless, it is an important first step. In the United States, there is no systematic strategy to ease the transition of newcomer immigrant-origin youth into secondary schools or colleges or to the labor market. This current "non-policy" of integration in the United States fails our neediest immigrant-origin students; it also robs the economy and other important societal sectors of many promising future contributors (Bertelsmann Stiftung 2008). World Citizen High School (embedded within a network of such schools), however, provides a tangible example of a model school that takes a systematic approach with remarkable success, despite the national absence of policy (MPI 2009).

To best serve immigrant-origin students, policymakers and educators should work together to face head-on the challenges that have been created by a combination of structural barriers, cultural and linguistic challenges, schoolwide problems, and school reform efforts. Immigrant-origin students arrive with optimism and hope for the future that should be cultivated and treasured—they are the first to understand that schooling is their key to a better tomorrow (Kao and Tienda 1995; Suárez-Orozco et al. 2008). Harnessing their energy, optimism, and faith in the future is arguably one of the most important challenges to our countries' democratic promises. Providing the kinds of promising practices offered by the innovative schools highlighted in this chapter is essential to help immigrant youth become incorporated into the fabric of their new lands.

Notes

We would like to thank Hee Jin Bang for her insightful observations at World Citizen High School as well as Alexandra Cordero and Carolyn Sattin for their assistance at Progressive High. We would also like to thank Greta Gibson and Silvia Carrasco for their careful reading of our chapter and their suggestions for framing our conclusion.

1. In Sweden, these students are referred to as students with Swedish as a second language (S2 students) and in the United States as English-language learners (ELLs).

2. The Swedish Government mandated, via "Propositionen om valfrihet och fristående skolor (Prop. 1991/92:95)" that students had a right to choose elementary and secondary schools.

3. Due to language constraints and the school administrators' preference, this program was not included in this research study.

4. "Metrocity" is a pseudonym. We learned about this project while holding follow-up meetings at Bergslunden during the spring of 2008 and thought it typical of the effort that second-language teachers invest in integrating language and content.

5. We should note, however, that there were small groups of students to whom we did not gain adequate access—namely, those students who were frequently absent from class. Though they were a clear minority, their opinions and experiences are important, yet we have no data on how these students viewed their relationships with teachers.

CHAPTER SEVEN

The Children of Immigrants at School: Conclusions and Recommendations

Richard Alba and Jennifer Holdaway

In what follows, we outline the main conclusions and recommendations that we have drawn from our investigation over a four-year period of how receiving-society educational systems and processes impact on the children of immigrants. It must be noted at the outset that our research was not designed to test policies affecting the educational opportunities of the children of immigrants. Consequently, our recommendations should be understood as inferences about the amelioration of existing inequalities that we have drawn from observations concerning the impacts of current school systems on the children coming from immigrant homes. Our focus remains on children who face the greatest challenges because their parents have limited educations and occupy the position of low-wage workers or are unemployed in the receiving society and because they belong to groups that are ethnic, racial, or religious minorities there.

For greater clarity in this discussion, we use the examples of Britain, France, the Netherlands, and the United States to highlight system-level differences. This choice also reflects the fact that the research on these countries focused on institutional differences and used quantitative analysis to consider how they relate to differences in outcomes. We draw on the studies of schools in Catalonia and California and in Sweden and New York to consider what we can learn about how institutional differences and policies play out at the school level.

Achievements and Gaps: The Overall Situation of Students from Low-Status Immigrant Homes

In the introduction we reviewed data from the PISA program, which show significant differences in school-related skills between children of immigrant and native-born parents. While informative, the focus on skills has two drawbacks as a basis for assessing the effectiveness of education systems in educating children of immigrants.

The first is that the skills differences among children of a similar age arise not only from their different experiences in educational systems but also from their home and community environments, in particular the language at home and the educational background of parents. Few native-born parents speak a language different from the host society with their children, and those with similarly low educational levels are generally both few in number and challenged in other ways. At the same time, it is difficult to capture differences in the social and cultural capital of households and communities in ways that can be introduced into statistical models. For this reason, family and community effects cannot easily be controlled in analyses of skills. There is a risk therefore of attributing to schools inequalities that stem from other sources, and in particular to the selectivity or particular resources of different immigration streams.

Because educational credentials are necessary, if not always sufficient, for entry into the labor market and particularly the highly skilled occupations to which we have argued it is increasingly important for children of immigrants to have access, credentials are another important and often-neglected educational outcome. The importance of final credentials, especially for immigrant-origin students, has been demonstrated by the long-term outcomes of open-admissions systems in higher education in the United States. The most recent study of the City University of New York's open-admissions program (Attewell and Lavin 2007), which beginning in 1970 allowed many students to attend college who previously would have been excluded by their school records and test scores, shows that: (1) many of these "new" students eventually earned baccalaureates, though this process frequently took considerably longer than the normative four-year period; (2) these college degrees paid off by qualifying the graduates for jobs they would not otherwise have obtained; and (3) the degrees also brought benefits to the next generation, the children of the open-admissions students, whose aspirations and performance in school were in turn lifted as a consequence of their parents' educational experiences. That both credentials and skills contribute to the subsequent labor-market position of young people has also been shown with the data of the International Adult Literacy Survey (see OECD 2001, 20).

Table 7.1 presents a comparison of credentials earned by young adults for four of the countries in this study. Gathering data on educational outcomes is not a simple task because of the variations among systems, which imply that their stages and credentials are not precise equivalents, and because of differences in national statistical systems, especially in the ways they keep track of ethnic background and generational status. For the table, we have selected the second-generation groups on which the teams focused in their research, such as Moroccans in the Netherlands and Maghrebins in France. As a glance down its rows will reveal, the table was constructed with a strategy of capturing relevant data however we could, and numbers are not precisely comparable from one country to another. In two cases, notably Spain and Sweden, we could not find data that were consistent in format with those we report in the table for the other countries.

In all cases, some of the students coming from immigrant-origin families are doing remarkably well, at least in comparison to their parents. Not at all uncommon are young people from families in which immigrant parents have primary-school educations (or less) who themselves have earned university diplomas; and many students from such backgrounds have achieved some degree of postsecondary education.

Yet it is also true that in all of these systems immigrant-origin students are disadvantaged on average when compared with those coming from native families. Moreover, the rough magnitude of the immigrant-native gap is similar in some systems with very different structures and features. The credentials data indicate in general an advantage for the children from native families, though not with the consistency of the school-based skills as measured in the PISA data. These findings show the relevance of theories of persisting educational stratification by origin, such as maximally or effectively maintained inequality (Lucas 2001; Raftery and Hout 1993).

The advantage for native young adults appears most consistently at the lower end of the educational spectrum, in the departure from school without a final secondary credential. The young adults from immigrant families are generally more likely—and by a large margin—to have left school without any credential useful in the labor market. The margins of advantage for the offspring of native families frequently approach two to one, and in the case of Mexican American versus Anglo youth in the United States, they are larger. Typically, the dropout rates are higher for males than for females, with the consequence that many young immigrant-origin men are condemned to the bottom of the host-society labor market.

Though there is less consistency at the upper end, there is generally a visible advantage for young adults from native families. At an extreme like the differences between Mexicans and Anglos in the United States, the margin of that advantage is on the order of two to one when it comes to acquiring university credentials. (The advantage of Anglos over US-born Dominicans is smaller than this because the Dominicans are concentrated in and around New York City, where large public higher-educational systems offer an unusual degree of opportunity to pursue post-secondary education.) There is a sizable advantage also for native youth in France and the Netherlands. However, in Britain, it appears that the second generation of the most disadvantaged South Asian groups, exemplified in the table by the Pakistanis, has closed the gap in terms of rates of attending universities and earning university credentials (see chapter 4; also Modood 2011).

As noted in the chapter on Great Britain and the United States, the inequalities in quantitative educational attainment are typically amplified by differences in the quality of the institutions where members of majority and minority groups are concentrated. In the United States, Dominicans, for instance, are more concentrated than native whites and most other groups in the less selective colleges of the public-university system, whose credentials carry less value in the labor market (see chapter 2; also Kasinitz et al. 2008). Children of immigrants are also far less likely to obtain the postgraduate and professional qualifications that are increasingly required for entry into highly skilled occupations in the United States. In Great Britain, differences in favor of white natives appear when the status hierarchy of universities is considered because the children from immigrant families are relatively more concentrated in the newer and less prestigious universities

Note to Table 7.1 (opposite page): These data come from the analyses prepared for the various chapters of this volume, and readers should refer to the discussions there for the sources and descriptions of limitations. In the case of the British data, the figures are compiled from two different, not fully compatible, data sets—to avoid confusion, only the lowest and lightest categories are reported.

TABLE 7.1. Educational Outcomes for Native and Second-Generation Youth in Selected Countries

	No Secondary Credential	Basic Secondary Credential	Some Post-Secondary	University Degree
France (ages 26–35, 2008 Trajectoires et Origines survey)				
Males				
Native French	12.5	36.4	27.6	23.5
North Africans	27.4	30.1	26.4	16.1
Females				
Native French	12.2	31.9	30.1	25.7
North Africans	20.5	32.0	30.9	16.5
Great Britain (Youth Cohort and Longitudinal Studies [see note])				
White British	39.5	—	—	28.8
Afro-Caribbean	54.4	—	—	41.7
Pakistani	48.4	—	—	32.0
Netherlands (Amsterdam, TIES data)				
Native Dutch	9.5	10.0	14.7	65.8
Moroccans	29.1	15.5	24.3	31.1
United States (ages 26–35, 2005–09 American Community Survey)				
Males				
Anglo natives	8.0	28.2	31.4	32.5
U.S.-born Dominicans	14.0	34.0	35.5	16.5
U.S.-born Mexicans	20.5	34.3	31.9	13.0
Females				
Anglos	5.8	21.1	33.3	39.8
U.S.-born Dominicans	9.5	18.3	39.5	32.8
U.S.-born Mexicans	16.3	29.1	36.8	17.9

that have emerged from the former polytechnics. In less open systems such as the Netherlands, the percentage of children of immigrants entering university and the higher levels of vocational education is actually quite high and, given the greater selectivity of these systems, the quality and value of the education they receive is more likely to be similar to that of children of native-born parents. This suggests that where postsecondary education is more universally accessible, the locus of competition shifts in the direction of the "quality" of the credentials obtained, as the theory of effectively maintained inequality holds (Lucas 2001). Although we are not in a position to analyze the implications of this for labor-market participation, it seems likely that more open systems enable a large number of children of immigrants to enter paraprofessional and pink-collar occupations, while excluding them from the most prestigious and highly paid professions. At the same time, more-selective systems leave a greater number of children of immigrants in blue-collar and service industries, but enable a small number to enter elite occupations.

"Reactivity" of Educational Systems

Our in-depth analysis of educational systems in six different countries reveals that, in political and organizational terms, educational systems are "reactive"—they are not pliable, neutral materials that policymakers can simply shape to their ends. These are systems in which privileged groups—most notably, socially advantaged parents—seek to achieve their own ends, which include bestowing advantages on their children through education. Hence, these actors respond to attempts at reform, often in ways that weaken, if not undermine, their thrust. We believe that, borrowing from Newton, the reactivity of educational systems justifies a Third Law of Educational Inequality: for every initiative to reduce inequality, there is an opposing (but not necessarily equal) reaction to preserve it. In this respect, our research contributes to the theories of persisting educational stratification by sketching some of the mechanisms behind maximally and effectively maintained inequality. However, in our view, the Third Law does not mean that attempts to reduce the inequalities among students are hopeless. The ability of privileged actors to work against reforms may be constrained by law or ideology or, perhaps more important, these changes may also offer benefits to them. It does imply that policy cannot simply be made by imposing a reform intended to reduce inequality under the assumption that the system will otherwise remain the same.

This reactivity becomes clear in our analysis of the French system, where we noted the responses of middle-class parents and school administrators to the democratization efforts undertaken starting in the 1980s. In reaction to the initiatives of the state to promote greater equality of educational opportunity through, for instance, the ZEP policy, which offered additional funding to schools serving socially disadvantaged student populations, parents and to some degree local authorities reacted by creating new mechanisms that give more latitude for social inequalities to assert themselves in and through educational institutions. Examples are the hidden curricula, which offer difficult modern or ancient languages (e.g., Japanese, classical Greek) or other unusual courses that have been established by schools to attract middle-class students and create differentiation within and across schools; and the status hierarchy that has emerged, and continues to evolve, among the different types of *baccalauréat*, the high school credential that leads to the university.

The Netherlands and the United States also illustrate the challenges facing efforts to address the effect of residential segregation on schooling. The bussing of students in the United States and zoning policy that forced parents in the Netherlands to send their children to local schools both led to unintended consequences, with middle-class parents either moving out of the area or, in some instances in the United States, sending their children to private schools. It is worthy of note that in the British case, the native born seem to have been less successful in preserving their access to preparation that will enable their children to monopolize the higher echelons of the postsecondary system. Why this is would require a closer analysis of school reform in that country, as well as attention to the precise role of class inequalities in the native white population.

More generally, however, the Third Law of Inequality suggests that policies intended to ameliorate inequality must be carefully formulated with an eye to whether they will be perceived in a zero-sum manner (i.e., enhancing the opportunities of socially disadvantaged students at a cost to socially advantaged ones). Jennifer Hochschild and Nathan Scovronick (2003, 2) observe in their study of US education:

Many issues in educational policy have therefore come down to an apparent choice between the individual success of comparatively privileged students and the collective good of all students or the nation as a whole. Efforts to promote the collective goals of the American dream through public schooling have run up against almost insurmountable barriers when enough people believe (rightly or wrongly, with evidence or without) that those efforts will endanger the comparative advantage of their children or children like them.

Policies that are non–zero sum in character, that offer improvements to the educations of most or all children, while contributing relatively more to disadvantaged students, probably have the greatest chances for success. For instance, in countries where preschool education is not universal, a policy to create high-quality preschool education could offer something to families from a wide variety of backgrounds. Obviously, it will not always be possible to craft policies in this way, but in considering options for reform policymakers should attempt to anticipate the innovations that privileged parents and school administrators might introduce in reaction.

Factors That Affect the Educational Success of Immigrant-Origin Children

Our in-depth and comparative analysis of school systems has illuminated the importance of particular factors in facilitating or hindering the progress of children of immigrants.

The Balance of Responsibility among Schools, Communities, and Families

As we have seen, formal education in schools is always complemented by learning in the home and community. Immigrant parents with limited education and knowledge of the host language are often disadvantaged in their ability: to prepare children for starting school, for example by reading to them in the host language; to assist them during their school careers by help with homework or guidance on important decisions about schooling; and to pay for ongoing supplemental education such as tutoring, educational summer camps, or cultural trips and activities.

Immigrant-origin children in several countries are likely to benefit from a shift in the balance of educational responsibility among schools, families, and communities. There are a number of ways of moving this balance in a favorable direction:

1. In some countries, like the United States, more days in school each year would reduce the weight placed on families and communities and ameliorate the inequalities among students that stem from the variations in educational and cultural resources in homes and neighborhoods.

2. Schools need to reach out to parents whose native language is not that of the receiving society, to engage them in the educational process. Notices sent home from school, for example, should be translated into the main home languages of immigrant-origin students. For occasions when immigrant parents come to school for meetings, translators should be available to help them to follow and participate in the events.

3. Communities can be given more resources to help immigrant-origin students and relieve some of the weight on immigrant parents. Studies of some Asian communities in the United States have identified community institutions as playing a critical role in the educational mobility of children from working-class homes—they perform such tasks as teaching children how to study and disseminating information about educational opportunities (Zhou and Kim 2006; Zhou and Li 2003). Maurice Crul's (2011) research in the Netherlands indicates that those children who happen to have academically successful older siblings are in a better position to surmount their parents' lack of familiarity with education in the receiving society.

These findings suggest ways that communal organizations could come to the aid of families facing disadvantages in helping their children to do well in school. For instance, with the help of outside funding, after-school programs have been established in the Netherlands in which young people who come from the same groups and have been successful in school serve as mentors, assisting young people in doing homework and consulting with students and their parents about educational decisions. Since the advanced students from immigrant groups often need to work while they pursue their studies, such a program could satisfy multiple needs at once.

4. Another way to alter the overall balance of responsibility among schools, families, and communities is to enroll children from the age of two or three in preschool programs. An early entry into an educationally rich context can help to compensate for the school-relevant inequalities, in

language and other aspects of school readiness that children bring to school from their homes.

One of our researchers, Maurice Crul, has argued that the universal *maternelle* experience in France has helped Turkish youngsters there to improve their educational outcomes compared to their coethnics in other European countries (Crul and Vermeulen 2003). This experience undoubtedly also contributes to the high levels of fluency in French exhibited by the children of North African immigrants (Tribalat 1995). In the United States, attendance in preschool programs has been shown to narrow school-readiness gaps for minority children from low-income families. However, the inequalities among children from different backgrounds in preschool exposure are probably adding to those gaps, since Hispanic children are less likely than white and black children to be in preschool. One estimate is that universal preschooling could reduce the gap between Hispanic and white children at the beginning of graded schooling by a third (Magnuson and Waldfogel 2005).

To be sure, the quality of preschooling is a critical variable. Simply placing children into a collective child-care setting at an early age will not have a large impact on their school readiness. The quality dimension includes, at a minimum, a requirement that the adults in a preschool setting have appropriate in-depth training in the education and nurturance of young children, but this dimension needs more specification and empirical research. In the United States, projects with demonstrated success, such as Perry Preschool program in Ypsilanti, Michigan, and the Abecedarian project of Chapel Hill, North Carolina, offer models.

Research in the United States also indicates that the effectiveness of preschool programs can be enhanced by simultaneously working with parents to assure that their activities with their children support early learning—for example, by encouraging them to read more to their children.

Inequalities among Schools

There is substantial evidence that immigrant-origin children are concentrated in schools that are, in various ways, inferior to the schools attended by children from native families, especially those of the middle class. These differences probably exist in all countries with immigrant populations, but they are clearly worse in some than in others. Here we consider the implications of school financing, teacher quality, and class size.

The United States stands apart from the other countries we have studied because of its system of school financing, which is heavily dependent on local and state sources, with limited involvement by the federal government. This results in differences in funding of the order of two to one between the lowest and highest spending districts— differences that broadly correlate with the social origins of students, including whether they come from native versus immigrant backgrounds. The inequality of funding is being exacerbated by the dispersion of many immigrant families from central cities, which contain a diversity of income groups, to inner suburbs, smaller jurisdictions whose tax revenues may depend disproportionately on working-class families. Disparities are less marked in countries, such as France and the Netherlands, where funding is more centralized, but it is clear that wealthier areas nonetheless benefit from donations made by parents for additional facilities, trips, and activities. Better-trained teachers also gravitate toward schools in more affluent areas. Although more severe in some countries than in others, variation in school quality is underpinned in all cases by residential segregation, which results in children of immigrant origin, who have the most educational needs, being concentrated in schools that generally have fewer resources and less experienced teachers.

Issues of funding and "school choice" are of course thorny ones for which there is no easy solution. However, analysis of the countries in this study suggests that:

1. Efforts to desegregate schools either by bussing students to schools in other neighborhoods, as was done in the United States in the 1970s, or by zoning restrictions that require students to attend schools in their neighborhoods, as in France and the Netherlands, have not done much to reduce segregation, resulting instead in exit from public school systems or urban neighborhoods by more affluent native parents.

2. Increasing opportunities for parents to choose their children's schools have become the most common method of trying to reduce segregation, at least in France, the Netherlands, and the United States, but choice will only lead to improved educational opportunities for immigrant origin children if: (a) there are enough places in "good schools" to meet demand, which is rarely

the case; (b) those good schools are close enough to immigrant neighborhoods for families to be willing to allow their children to travel there; and (c) immigrant families have access to information and a sufficient understanding of the school system to make choice work to their advantage, a condition that is also not universally the case.

3. It therefore seems that efforts to improve the quality of education available to children of immigrants must start with existing schools. In countries like the United States where sizeable disparities exist in basic school funds, equalizing these through federal subsidies or by obliging states to ensure equal provision (as has already happened in a number of states) would be an obvious first step, and one that would benefit all students in the less-favored schools.

4. However, given that the needs of immigrant students in terms of language instruction and academic preparation are often greater than those of the native born, equal funding is unlikely to be sufficient. The experience of the Netherlands, which has made the greatest effort to invest in schools serving immigrant-origin students, gives an indication of the magnitude of the investment that might be necessary to level the playing field. Providing almost two–to-one funding for these students, as the Netherlands did for a time, allowed for smaller class sizes and additional teachers' aides, which were factors in the shrinking the gap in educational outcomes between native-born and immigrant-origin youth and were also reflected perhaps in the relatively high scores on the PISA assessments achieved by second-generation students from educationally disadvantaged homes (see Table 1.1 in chapter 1). Yet, even this policy was not enough to close the gap.

Whether similar schemes would be politically acceptable elsewhere is, of course, open to question given the strong reactions of middle-class, native parents to compensatory policies that might reduce the educational advantages of their children. The situation is particularly complicated in the United States, where the long history of the segregation of native-born black students, and the (largely failed) efforts to overcome it must also be considered. In this context, any efforts to assist children of immigrants would certainly have to be extended to native-born minority students.

5. Aside from targeted funding, which may not be politically feasible in many contexts, investing in teacher training is a strategy that would have

benefits for all students. It seems apparent that not only has teacher quality declined on average as the result of alternative employment options for women, but also that the strongest and most experienced teachers often gravitate to schools in more affluent districts. The evidence on teacher salaries from the United States suggests that large salary differentials may be required if the goal of policy is to alter the sorting process that moves better teachers to more advantaged schools. However, it does not speak to the question of whether stronger cadres of young people can be attracted to teaching by improvements in teacher earnings. Moreover, it may be that strong teachers will be as attracted by other features of their work situation—e.g., smaller classes, challenging curricula—as by monetary incentives.

6. Small class sizes also make a difference for learning. In the United States, this has been demonstrated by, for example, the Tennessee STAR experiment, and in France by the analysis of ZEP outcomes. It is not clear that immigrant-origin children are disadvantaged by comparison with children from native homes in terms of the sizes of the classes in which they are typically found, but because they often have greater needs than native-born students, reducing class size could be an effective way of helping them. The evidence in chapter 6 from the innovative schools in New York City and Sweden reveals the positive impact for both academic attainment and social integration of a low teacher-to-student ratio for youngsters from immigrant backgrounds.

Educating Students from Minority-Language Homes

Language education is one of the most controversial topics in the education of immigrant-origin students, raising as it does complex issues about the value and feasibility of bilingual education. But these issues aside, it is clear that many countries are struggling to meet the basic goal of enabling immigrant-origin students to acquire an academic level of competence in the mainstream language, the one that is taken for granted as the language of instruction in schools. This process can take as long as five to seven years.

Our research, particularly in chapter 3 on California and Catalonia, identifies some approaches that do not work. Segregating minority-language students for long periods of time in special classes has a negative impact, as does stigmatizing speech in their home language. Offering these students a watered-down curriculum in order to emphasize their acquisition of language skills also fails because they are then not engaged by their schoolwork.

Though it is clear that many common approaches fail these students, it is not apparent what approaches offer a general solution. The subject of educational programs for English-language learners has been the focus of a lengthy and too-often-tendentious literature in the United States. The persuasive conclusions to come from this literature have been few, although there is an emerging consensus from meta-analyses that some instruction in a child's home language is helpful and contributes to better learning of the mainstream language (e.g., Goldenberg 2008; Greene 1997; Slavin and Cheung 2005).

Translating this conclusion into specific programs for the classroom is not easy. For example, there is good evidence for the educational benefits of two-way bilingual schools, in which the school day is divided between two languages and students who speak each language at home are mixed in the classroom (Suárez-Orozco, Suárez-Orozco, and Todorova 2008). But such an approach is expensive because it requires fully bilingual teachers and can only be implemented for languages that native parents view as desirable for their children to learn and that are shared by a large enough student population.

The French experience with the *maternelle* system, which brings children by the age of three into a school-like setting where the mainstream language predominates, suggests that universal preschool education could ameliorate the mainstream-language handicaps of minority-language children in their primary-school years. But universal preschooling cannot solve the difficulties faced by 1.5-generation students who arrive in the receiving country after having spent their early childhoods elsewhere. Chapter 6 on promising practices identifies approaches—for example, mixing students from different immigrant backgrounds in the classroom and thus encouraging them to use the mainstream language as a lingua franca—that can help these students as well as those of the second generation. These approaches have been shown to work on a small scale, with innovative school leadership and a dedicated teachers corps. It is not clear, however, how well they would translate onto a larger scale. For instance, one would not want as a general strategy to segregate immigrant-origin students from other students, even though this can work under the right set of circumstances.

The main conclusion we draw from our research is that public policy should encourage innovation and small-scale experiments to improve educational opportunities for minority-language students. The enthusiasm and commitment of teachers and administrators appear to count for a lot when it comes to the engagement and learning of these students, and they should be actively involved in designing programs suited to the particular student populations with which they work. In addition, it is critical for teachers to be trained to meet the educational needs of mainstream-language learners; and they should be strongly encouraged by pay and other incentives to become competent in at least one language of the major immigrant groups.

Selection and Tracking Mechanisms

Other ways that systems vary concern the formality—and rigidity—of the differences between educational tracks and the age at which students are selected into them. At one extreme is the United States, where, generally speaking, little formal selection takes place prior to college entrance, and postsecondary education of some kind is open to all students who successfully complete high school, regardless of the age at which they do it. At the other end of the spectrum, at least among the countries we have studied, is the Netherlands, where at the age of twelve, students are sorted into vocational and academic tracks that separate them into different schools with distinct programs and educational endpoints.

Tracking has been rightly criticized as a practice that requires premature judgments about students' abilities on the basis of unfair criteria and that curtails their expectations and therefore their potential to achieve, but there are rationales for it that should be taken seriously. Tracking is a response to the reality of highly differentiated labor markets, in which diverse occupations require different lengths and kinds of training. Given this, educational policy makers need to consider how tracking processes can be made more transparent and fair. This would include consideration of the best age at which specialization should begin, the selection mechanisms that determine which children end up on which trajectory, the educational means to ensure that children with different combinations of abilities and interests can thrive, and the provision of sufficient second chances to students who start out on lower tracks to allow them to move up when they have the ability. The last is particularly relevant to children from immigrant homes who may have linguistic and cultural knowledge not recognized in regular curricula, and who may also need more time to catch up with native-born children in many subjects.

The need for some occupational specialization within the educational system is almost universally accepted, but the timing of it has been a major subject of debate and of educational reform in most countries, which have seen a general trend toward later specialization as the total length of the educational pipeline has extended into the mid-twenties and beyond. A source of deeper tensions has been the fatefulness of tracking with respect to ultimate labor-market position, between, for example, tracks that lead through postsecondary education to high-status, well-paid jobs or those that lead through earlier school credentials to lesser-skilled and lower-paid work. The implications of holding a low-wage job do vary across countries depending on the degree of overall variation in income and the provision of public services that can make earned income less determinative of quality of life; however, returns to education have increased over time in all countries, linking it more closely with both lifetime income and social status. This means that currently privileged families have a greater incentive to preserve their grip on higher educational credentials, and disadvantaged families suffer more from their lack of them.

In fact, tracking still takes place even within very open educational systems. In the countries we studied, the nature of tracking varied from the formal and quite rigid test-based process in place in the Netherlands, to more subtle and informal processes at work in France, Britain, and the United States, where education is ostensibly comprehensive for most students, but differences in the prestige of different credentials and schools in fact lead to very different opportunities in further education and the labor market.

Regardless of the mechanisms at work, tracking continues to work to the disadvantage of less advantaged groups, despite efforts to reduce inequality. As a consequence in part of tracking mechanisms, in none of the countries we studied were children from disadvantaged immigrant families receiving access to a similar average quality of education as those from native families. Effectively maintained inequality appears to be in operation in this respect, so that efforts to secure greater equality of educational outcomes are thwarted as privileged families find ways to circumvent them. If one considers the successful completion of a secondary-education credential that allows the option of proceeding into the tertiary system to be the minimum bar for achieving "the essential prerequisites for adult participation in society," then none of these systems is succeeding in bringing the students from low-status immigrant families up to the mainstream norm.

How can the disadvantages created for immigrant-origin students be reduced? For formalized systems of tracking, one set of recommendations is appropriate:

1. Postponing the Point of Selection   The case of the Netherlands shows the disadvantages of early, rigid tracking, which involves segregating students in different schools. The young age of this tracking puts children of immigrants at a clear disadvantage because they have not had enough time to catch up to native peers in terms of language preparation and familiarity with the mainstream institutions, norms, and practices that govern school processes. Once placed in second- and third-tier tracks and schools, immigrant-origin students are exposed to low expectations that are tacitly if not overtly associated with their class and ethnic backgrounds, and to an uninspiring curriculum. Understandably, many become alienated from school. If children of immigrants are to have an equal chance, selection needs to take place later in the educational career.

2. Improved Preparation for Selection Processes   Immigrant-origin children and their families also need to be prepared for any crucial fork in the educational pipeline. Because the parents usually have less familiarity with host-society educational institutions than do the parents from native families, they need to be made aware of the implications of a selection process in terms of later career opportunities, and they need to have as much support as possible in preparing their children for testing. Additional funds and support for community and school-based mentoring and other supplemental education programs seem to have been a factor in narrowing the gap in the Netherlands between natives and children of immigrants, although more rigorous evaluation would be needed to determine the precise impact of different kinds of programs.

3. Second Chances for Students to Enter Higher Tracks   One of the most disturbing aspects of formal tracking is that decisions made when children are young hold such potential fatefulness for their adult status. Those students who, in early grades, academically mature more slowly than their peers can be placed at a permanent disadvantage regardless of their talents, and the risk of underplacement is especially severe for immigrant-origin students because they come from non-mainstream homes and communities. Tracking systems need to provide escape hatches that allow later-maturing students to transition into higher tracks.

4. Scaffolding the Transition from School to Work Even within the vocational tracks in which they are disproportionately found, the children of immigrants appear to be at a disadvantage in relation to native students. In the Netherlands and France, children of immigrants have less chance to gain those apprenticeships that provide the best bridges to secure, well-remunerated employment. In addition, vocational programs often are not sufficiently sensitive to changing labor market needs, and the children of immigrants are at greater risk of consignment to dead-end vocational training. Greater efforts need to be made to ensure that children of immigrants in vocational programs can gain meaningful work experience that will prepare them for adult employment. Otherwise, it might be preferable to provide more general education and leave training to employers, as has been the norm in the United States.

Informal tracking has the advantage of being less rigid than institutionalized systems but is not without its disadvantages. Informing children at the age of twelve that they are destined for no more than a blue- or pink-collar job may be harsh, and underestimate their potential in many cases, but at least such a clear turning point can focus students and families on what they need to do, and on the implications of success or failure. This clarity has also enabled reforms in the Netherlands to prepare students for the key test, with measurable improvements. In the United States, students are rarely told explicitly that they are on a low track and often have unrealistic expectations about their future. They may be unaware that although there is no one decisive test, key turning points do exist—for example, they need to take certain courses in order to prepare for college-level study. There also are few programs to prepare young people who cannot or do not want to attend college for work, and those who leave before the end of compulsory education do so without meaningful qualifications (Rosenbaum 2001). Hence, the following points are in order:

1. **Better Information about Educational Qualifications and Career Options** Immigrant parents are rarely in a good position to navigate the complexities of informal tracking processes. Schools should provide more information about the different programs and opportunities that may be available, including the types of early preparation that are necessary if their children wish to pursue certain careers. As much information as possible should be provided in the parents' language. The Dutch case suggests that mentoring programs can be helpful not just in assisting immigrant students

with academic preparation but also in informing them about educational and career options.

2. Better Preparation for Employment   The rhetoric of equal opportunity and the possibility of college for all should not preclude encouraging young people to think seriously about alternatives to postsecondary education. And, even though much job-specific training may take place in the workplace, more provision should be made in high school to prepare young people for employment, perhaps through the kinds of cooperative education programs that are run at certain US community colleges, which offer internships and exposure to the workplace.

3. Strengthening Relationships between Communities and Schools   In some countries, community-based organizations already play an important role in providing services for immigrant families and their children, including educational support, counseling, and other programs. In the Netherlands, in particular, state investment in these programs seems to have been quite effective in improving educational outcomes. It seems that these links could be strengthened so that community-based organizations could serve as more comprehensive liaisons between schools and immigrant families, offering advice to teachers and school administrators on how best to organize cultural activities for immigrant students, mediating disputes, and perhaps working with the classroom assistants to help to make immigrant students feel more welcome. This would help to compensate for the fact that immigrant parents often find it difficult to take time away from work to participate in the life of the school and may have different conceptions of the division of labor between families and schools.

Postsecondary Education

Higher-education systems in the countries we studied vary in terms of the barriers to entry, the degree of differentiation between vocational and academic training, the timing of specialization, and the quality of institutions. Broadly speaking, the US system can be characterized as having a low barrier to entry, in the sense that all students who graduate high school can enter some kind of university or postsecondary institution. However, there are large differences in the quality of institutions and the kinds of opportunities the credentials they offer will lead to. European systems are generally more selective at the point of entry, but the quality of the education varies less. In general, specialization takes place earlier in Europe than in the United States. Finally, systems differ in terms of cost, with university fees being much higher in the United States than elsewhere, with the consequence that some students from poorer families are unable to afford their academic aspirations, though they have demonstrated the ability to do so (Goldin and Katz 2008).

The implications of these various arrangements for children of immigrants are complex. In the United States, immigrant-origin students tend to be concentrated within public two-year or local colleges, where rates of dropout are frequently high and the chances of ultimately gaining a baccalaureate or a professional degree are low. The labor-market returns to credentials from these institutions are also unlikely to be equivalent to degrees from more-prestigious four-year colleges and universities. Meanwhile, college remains a serious financial investment that often strains the resources of immigrant families. However, the system offers a lot of flexibility in terms of transferring across different institutions and of opportunities to reenter education or pursue degree programs part time while working that are not available in other systems.

By contrast, in the Netherlands, direct entry into university is possible only to students who have attended academic high schools (VWO). As few youth from immigrant backgrounds are able to test into this track, they are often obliged to take what has become known as the long route to university, completing four years of lower vocational education (VMBO) followed by four years of middle vocational education (MBO) and one year of higher vocational education (HBO). Once there, however, the quality of universities is more uniform. Higher-level vocational education also provides training for many careers that would be accessed through four-year degree programs in the United States, including teaching, social work, and many technical occupations. In the Netherlands, postsecondary education is free, and the financial penalty for students who take the long route is not heavy.

The situations in France and Britain fall somewhere between these two poles. In Britain, earlier distinctions between universities and technical colleges have blurred, but there remains clear stratification across institutions, and children of immigrants are overrepresented in the newer, generally less prestigious institutions (see chapter 4). In this respect, Britain resembles the United States, and the recent lifting of the ceiling on university tuition fees has increased the similarity, but it differs (and more resembles European systems) in also offering a range of occupation-specific qualifications—for example, Higher National Diplomas. In France, by comparison, the quality of the universities is more uniform, but a critical distinction lies between the university sector and the *grandes écoles*, which provide an elite form of training. Few children from immigrant homes enter the *grandes écoles*.

Given the variations among, and the complexities of, these systems, it is perhaps less easy than with secondary-education systems to identify all the implications of these arrangements for immigrant-origin children and to develop recommendations for ameliorating the disadvantages they face. What can be said with certainty is that in all of them, children of immigrants are clustered at the lower end of the spectrum, and their career opportunities are therefore limited compared with those of native youth. To a considerable extent, this clustering should be viewed as the accumulation of numerous disadvantages that accrue to immigrant-origin youth on their way through the prior stages of education.

It is also clear that students from immigrant homes who do manage to get to university often take longer to complete their degrees—for example, the Dutch students who of necessity pursue the long route through middle and higher vocational education to reach the university, and the US students who pass first through community college or must work while attending school. In the United States, the percentage of immigrant-origin youth from low-status backgrounds who complete the postgraduate programs necessary to enter the highest-paid professions (such as law and medicine) is low. In Europe, the second generation tends to cluster in law, medicine, and economics, which lead to financially secure careers, rather than the social sciences and humanities.

What can be done? We see several ways to improve the chances of immigrant-origin children:

1. The longer time it generally takes immigrant-origin students to acquire university credentials needs to be addressed. Some American research indicates that financial considerations, along with the difficulties in balancing school and work, play a role here (Kasinitz, Mollenkopf, Waters, and Holdaway 2008). Obviously, this is especially true in the United States because of the costs associated with postsecondary education, but it can also apply to low-cost European systems such as that in Sweden, where there are no tuition costs, because of the wages families must forego while their adult, unmarried children are studying.

Increasing the financial support available to low-income students would make it easier for children of immigrants to attend and complete higher levels of postsecondary education.

2. The poorer secondary-school preparation of immigrant-origin students (as shown for example by the PISA studies) is a major barrier to their entering and completing postsecondary education. In postsecondary systems that are quite open, like those in France and the United States, many children of immigrants enter colleges and universities but fail to finish. Research on student attrition in general (for example, Tinto 1994), and on immigrant students in New York City (Kasinitz et al. 2008) has found that many of these students struggle with college-level work and must either waste time (and money) taking remedial classes or drop out. Until high school preparation improves, students who are admitted with marginal preparation need to be given more academic support through tutoring or other supplementary programs to improve retention and completion rates.

3. In a context where educational opportunities along the educational pipeline are likely to remain unequal for some time, the disproportionate concentration of immigrant-origin students in the lower strata of differentiated systems can be ameliorated by programs of positive discrimination that provide opportunities to students from poor and/or minority families to gain more elite forms of education and the careers that ensue from them. Affirmative action in US higher education, though it is under legal attack and in some states has been dismantled in publicly funded universities, has demonstrated that minority students make very good use of these opportunities (Bowen and Bok 1998; Massey, Charles, Lundy, and Fischer 2002). However, such programs need to go hand in hand with initiatives to level the playing field and, over the longer term, enable children of immigrants to compete for university places on their own terms. Otherwise, these programs will draw increasing hostility on the grounds that they unfairly displace other students.

Successful Practices within Schools

So far we have discussed the ways in which national-level differences in educational systems and policies affect immigrant students. But whatever policies are in place, their impact is mediated by the way in which they are implemented in the classroom. In this process, teachers and school administrators play a crucial role. In this section we discuss what we have learned from the in-depth study of a number of schools in California, Catalonia, Sweden, and New York.

Chapter 3 compared six high schools and found remarkably similar processes at work. Although all the schools espoused a rhetoric of inclusion and high expectations for all students, the reality was disappointing, both in terms of academic preparation and the degree to which students felt included in the school community. Teachers and administrators were in most cases well meaning, but they knew little about the challenges their students faced in terms of language and social adjustment and in many cases did not see them as entitled to, or as able to benefit from, an education equal to the one the teachers would want for their own children. As a result, they failed to recognize the skills and potential of their students and tended to approach education as a process of remediation rather than preparation. Not infrequently, they assumed that their students were suited only to vocational education. Although multiculturalism was described as a goal, schools' efforts to be culturally inclusive were clumsy and tended either to ignore students' ethnic backgrounds or to organize events and activities that were tokenistic or essentializing (i.e., assuming that all students from the same background held similar religious beliefs and practiced similar ethnic customs). In too many ways, these schools ended up reinforcing cultural and linguistic boundaries and hierarchies present in the larger society.

The result of these subtle and not-so-subtle forms of discrimination was that immigrant students were marginalized socially and received educational support only in the form of segregated classes for ESL or with less rigorous curricula. They felt excluded and in some cases highly stigmatized, internalizing the low expectations they encountered from adults. Most reported feeling uncomfortable at school and with their native peers, and many had come to feel that they were less able than other students.

The study of innovative schools in Sweden and New York focused on the other side of the picture and considered four schools that have been quite effective in enabling children of immigrants to succeed academically. They sum up the approach as an emphasis on "preparation practices" that teach students strategies for learning and living, rather than just content knowledge, and that stress the three Rs of "rigor, relevance, and relationships."

This includes second-language learning that is embedded in content and geared toward enabling students to express themselves in real-life situations;

assessment techniques that enable immigrant students to show their strengths through cross-disciplinary research projects rather than standardized tests; and teacher-student relationships that involve small groups and mentoring rather than didactic interactions. Teachers and administrators made an effort to find out about the backgrounds and family circumstances of their students, and encouraged engagement with the local community through volunteering and participatory research projects.

While the authors stress that many of these approaches are beneficial to all students, their flexibility and responsiveness to the needs and aptitudes of different students make them particularly effective in bringing out the potential of immigrant students, who are very diverse in their levels of preparation and needs. All of the schools achieved very high rates of graduation and college entry, and enthusiastic endorsements by students and teachers, who clearly felt a strong sense of commitment and respect for each other.

But these schools were also the beneficiaries of programs that provided funding for low student-teacher ratios and innovative curriculum development. Replicating this kind of success would require investment, particularly in teacher training, on an order of magnitude that has not been considered in any of the countries in this study.

Final Thoughts

One of the great challenges to be faced in this century by the wealthy societies of the West involves the impending, demographically driven transition to increasing diversity. Broadly put, because of the shrinking numbers of the native majority in young age groups, these societies will almost certainly have to depend increasingly on young people from immigrant backgrounds to assume positions of leadership, in the labor force and elsewhere. During the next several decades, this transition will manifest itself acutely for an additional reason: the retirement of very large post–World War II birth cohorts, dominated by the native majority. If these societies are to avoid economic, political, and cultural sclerosis, they must successfully integrate the second generation.

This situation places an obvious spotlight on the performance of educational systems in their role as integrative institutions. Our review of the success of the children of immigrants in six quite different educational systems appears to indicate that schools are failing to bring immigrant-origin students to parity. Indeed, with occasional exceptions, such as the South Asians of Great Britain, the general conclusion could be summarized as "different systems, similar results."

One response to these findings could be that they are unsurprising: after all, the immigrant students on whom we have focused come from low-status backgrounds and from families where the parents have little or no education and work at jobs at the bottom of the labor force. One of the most consistent findings from the literature on education, and on social and economic inequalities more broadly, concerns the large impacts of social-class background on outcomes.

Yet we think that this response is not satisfactory. As this comparative study has revealed, the social reproduction of inequality does not proceed in the same way or to the same degree in all societies, and experience shows that there are windows of opportunity for educational reforms that can improve opportunities for disadvantaged groups. Nor does social reproduction proceed in similar fashion for all disadvantaged groups: the children from immigrant homes, even low-status ones, usually possess optimism and ambition to an uncommon degree; these characteristics, under the right circumstances, can enable them to succeed to an extent that is surprising given their low starting points. Since the rich societies' future vitality, in all senses of the word, seems to depend on a better integration of young people from immigrant families than their schools are now achieving, the price of a mistakenly fatalistic attitude toward existing inequalities will be exceedingly high.

Another way of understanding the near universality of unequal outcomes is to see the institutional arrangements of school systems as reflecting broader power inequalities in society. Certainly, hypotheses such as maximally or effectively maintained inequality (Lucas 2001; Raftery and Hout 1993), which depict educational systems as resistant to opportunity-enhancing changes, capture a fundamental truth. The explanation is not hard to grasp—namely, that in democratic societies, middle-class and upper-middle-class native parents have the potential to influence educational policy and institutions, a potential that remains invisible as long as those institutions function in expected ways to give cumulative advantages to their children. Where the advantages of these children are threatened—for example, by egalitarian reforms—their parents will intervene politically.

But all may not be as hopeless as this formulation implies. The coming demographic changes, and in particular the shrinkage of the youth group from the most advantaged populations, suggests that opportunities to alter the balance of power in these societies will arise. These opportunities could come about through what Alba (2009) has called "non-zero-sum mobility": chances for the children of disadvantaged groups to move up without appearing to threaten the position of the children of advantaged ones. The reduction in threat could allow a relaxation of the boundary-protective mechanisms that normally rule in ethno-racially diverse societies, like the United States, where a huge literature documents them. Alba points to the mass assimilation in post–World War II United States of previously excluded white groups, Catholics and Jews of Southern and Eastern European origins, as an historical instance of the potency of non-zero-sum mobility.

Non-zero-sum mobility, engendered by the demographic shrinkage of the native majorities of Western societies, is highly likely to enhance the educational life chances of immigrant-origin groups to some degree. At the postsecondary level, most importantly, institutions are likely to experience difficulty recruiting sufficient students as their traditional pools subside. This may lead them to make more-intensive efforts to recruit students from nontraditional groups. In the event, it should lead to more places at universities that are accessible to the children of immigrants. However, unless these young people from immigrant homes are better prepared by the earlier stages of the educational system, this seeming opening up will engender more sorting by social origin among the tracks and institutions in postsecondary education, with an increased emphasis on the "quality" of the school attended and the degree attained, just as the theory of effectively maintained inequality suggests. In short, Western societies cannot afford to stand pat, under the assumption that future non-zero-sum mobility will more or less remedy current educational inequalities. These inequalities must be addressed by public policy and educational reform.

To be sure, one cannot expect wholesale reorganization of educational systems to facilitate the success of immigrant-origin children. But much more modest policies promise some amelioration. For instance, the Dutch policy of giving schools additional funding for every immigrant-origin student in attendance seems to have yielded beneficial results, in terms of narrowing test score gaps (Crul and Holdaway 2009). Granted, the apparent inefficacy of the ZEP policy in France, which also involves extra funding for schools, shows that money is not a magic formula. Additional analysis is required to determine appropriate levels and delivery mechanisms of such funding. Also intriguing is the Dutch policy of subsidizing community organizations to help immigrant-origin students with homework and educational guidance. Since the weakness of mainstream cultural capital in immigrant homes is a major source of disadvantage for these students, this policy suggests ways of providing counterweights.

The coming period is one where the different educational systems can profit by adopting opportunity-enhancing innovations from each other. Each has features that tend to disadvantage the students coming from low-status immigrant families. But these are students who will be as critical to the labor forces of the advanced economies as any others. All of these systems will have to meet the challenge of integrating them.

Bibliography

Alba, Richard. 2005. "Bright vs. Blurred Boundaries: Second-Generation Assimilation and Exclusion in France, Germany, and the United States." *Ethnic and Racial Studies* 28: 20–49.

———. 2009. *Blurring the Color Line: The New Chance for a More Integrated America*. Cambridge, MA: Harvard University Press.

———. 2011. "Schools and the Diversity Transition in the Wealthy Societies of the West." *American Behavioral Scientist* 55: 1616–34.

Alba, Richard, Nancy Denton, Donald Hernandez, Ilir Disha, Brian McKenzie, and Jeffrey Napierala. 2009. "Nowhere near the Same: The Neighborhoods of Latino Children." In *Growing Up Hispanic: Health and Development of Children of Immigrants*, edited by Nancy Landale, Susan McHale, and Alan Booth, 3–48. Washington, DC: The Urban Institute.

Alba, Richard, and Roxane Silberman. 2002. "Decolonization Immigrations and the Social Origins of the Second Generation: The Case of North Africans in France." *International Migration Review* 36: 1169–93.

Alba, Richard, Jennifer Sloan, and Jessica Sperling. 2011. "The Integration Imperative: The Children of Low-Status Immigrants in the Schools of Wealthy Societies." *Annual Review of Sociology* 37: 395–415.

Albouy, Valérie, and Thomas Wanecq. 2003. "Les inégalités sociales d'accès aux grandes écoles." *Économie et statistiques* 361: 27–52.

Alon, Sigal. 2009. "The Evolution of Class Inequality in Higher Education: Competition, Exclusion, and Adaptation." *American Sociological Review* 74: 731–55.

Alon, Sigal, and Marta Tienda. 2007. "Diversity, Opportunity and the Shifting Meritocracy in Higher Education." *American Sociological Review* 72: 487–511.

Amrein, Audrey L., and David C. Berliner. 2002. *An Analysis of Some Unintended and Negative Consequences of High-Stakes Testing.* Tempe, AZ: Arizona University Education Policy Research Unit.

Anyon, Jean. 1997. *Ghetto Schooling: A Political Economy of Urban Education Reform.* New York: Teachers College Press.

American Psychological Association. 2012. *Crossroads: The Report of the Presidential Task Force on Immigration.* Washington, DC: American Psychological Association.

Apple, Michael. 2004a. *Ideology and Curriculum.* New York: Routledge.

———. 2004b. "Creating Difference: Neo-Liberalism, Neo-Conservatism, and the Politics of Educational Reform." *Educational Policy* 18: 12–44.

Arango, Joaquín, and Maia Jachimowicz. 2005. "Regularizing Immigrants in Spain: A New Approach." Migration Information Source. http://www.migrationinformation.org/Feature/display.cfm?ID=331.

Athey, Jean L., and Frederick L. Ahearn. 1991. *Refugee Children: Theory, Research, and Services.* Baltimore, MD: John Hopkins University Press.

Attewell, Paul, and David Lavin. 2007. *Passing the Torch: Does Higher Education for the Disadvantaged Pay Off across the Generations?* New York: Russell Sage Foundation.

August, Diane, and Kenji Hakuta, eds. 1997. *Improving Schooling for Language-Minority Children: A Research Agenda.* Washington, DC: National Academy Press.

Bade, Klaus. 1994. *Ausländer, Aussiedler, Asyl: eine Bestandsaufnahme.* Munich: C. H. Beck.

Balfanz Robert, and Nettie Legters. 2004. "Locating the Dropout Crisis: Which High Schools Produce the Nation's Dropouts? Where Are They Located? Who Attends Them?" Baltimore, MD: Johns Hopkins University Center for Research on the Education of Students Placed at Risk (CRESPAR).

Balfanz, Robert, W. J. Jordan, James M. McPartland, and Nettie E. Legters, eds. 2002. *Comprehensive Reform for Urban High Schools: A Talent Development Approach.* New York: Teachers College Press.

Banks, James, and Cherry Banks. 2007. *Multicultural Education: Issues and Perspectives,* 6th ed. New York: Wiley and Sons.

Barth, Fredrik. 1969. *Ethnic Groups and Boundaries.* Boston: Little Brown.

Batalova, Jeanne, and Michael Fix. 2011. "Up for Grabs: The Gains and Prospects of First- and Second-Generation Young Adults." Washington, DC: Migration Policy Institute.

Bean, Frank D., and Gillian Stevens. 2003. *America's Newcomers and the Dynamics of Diversity*. New York: Russell Sage Foundation.

Beaud, Stéphane. 2002. *80 % au bac? Et après? Les enfants de la démocratisation scolaire*. Paris: Éditions La Découverte.

Bénabou, Roland, Francis Kramarz, and Corinne Prost. 2005. "Zones d'éducation prioritaires: quels moyens pour quels résultats." *Économie et statistique* 380: 3–34.

Berry, J. W., Jean S. Phinney, David L. Sam, and Paul Vedder, eds. 2006. *Immigrant Youth in Cultural Transition: Acculturation, Identity, and Adaptation across National Contexts*. Mahwah, NJ: Lawrence Erlbaum Associates.

Bertelsmann Stiftung. 2008. "The Toronto District School Board Wins the Carl Bertelsmann Prize 2008." http://www.bertelsmann-stiftung.de/cps/rde/xchg/SID-0A000F0A-7A205618/bst_engl/hs.xsl/nachrichten_89487.htm.

Black, Dan A., and Jeffrey A. Smith. 2006. "Estimating the Returns to College Quality with Multiple Proxies for Quality." *Journal of Labor Economics* 24: 701–28.

Blau, Francine D., and Lawrence M. Kahn. 2002. *At Home and Abroad: US Labor Market Performance in International Perspective*. New York: Russell Sage Foundation.

Bloom, David E. 2004. "Globalization and Education: An Economic Perspective." In *Globalization: Culture and Education in the New Millennium*, edited by Marcelo Suárez-Orozco and Desirée Qin-Hilliard, 56–77. Berkeley: University of California Press.

Boliver, Vikki. 2004. "Widening Participation and Fair Access at the University of Oxford." Working Paper No. 2004–02, Sociology Department, Oxford University.

Boog, I., J. Donselaar, D. Houtzager, P. Rodrigues, and R. Schriemer. 2006. *MonitorRassendiscriminatie 2005*. Leiden, The Netherlands: Universiteit van Leiden.

Boudon, Raymond. 1974. *Education, Opportunity and Social Inequality: Changing Prospects in Western Society*. New York: Wiley.

Bowen, William, and Derek Bok. 1998. *The Shape of the River: Long-Term Consequences of Considering Race in College and University Admissions*. Princeton, NJ: Princeton University Press.

Bowles, Samuel, and Herbert Gintis. 1976. *Schooling in Capitalist America: Educational Reform and the Contradictions of Economic Life*. New York: Basic Books.

———. 2002. "Schooling in Capitalist American Revisited." *Sociology of Education* 75: 1–18.

Brand, Jennie, and Yu Xie. 2010. "Who Benefits Most from College? Evidence for Negative Selection in Heterogeneous Economic Returns to Higher Education." *American Sociological Review* 75: 273–302.

Breen, Richard, and Jan Jonsson. 2005. "Inequality of Opportunity in Comparative Perspective: Recent Research on Educational Attainment and Social Mobility." *Annual Review of Sociology* 31: 223–43.

Brinbaum, Yaël. 2002. "Au cœur des parcours migratoires, les investissements éducatifs des familles immigrées: attentes et désilluisions." PhD diss., Université Paris Descartes.

Brinbaum, Yaël, and Annick Kieffer. 2005. "D'une génération à l'autre, les aspirations éducatives des familles immigrées: ambition et persévérance." *Éducation & formations* 72: 53–75.

———. 2009. "Trajectories of Immigrants' Children in Secondary Education in France: Differentiation and Polarization." INED. *Population-E* 64: 507–54.

Brinbaum, Yaël, and Patrick Werquin. 2004. "Des parcours semés d'embûches: l'insertion professionnelle de jeunes d'origine maghrébine en France." In *Marché du travail et genre Maghreb-Europe*, edited by Lachen Achy, Jérôme De Henau, Danièle Meulders, and Catherine Sofer, 145–66. Brussels: Brussels Economic Series.

Brint, Steven, and Jerome Karabel. 1989. *The Diverted Dream: Community Colleges and the Promise of Educational Opportunity, 1900–1985.* New York: Oxford University Press.

Brizard, Agnès. 1995. "Comparaisons des performances des élèves scolarisés en ZEP et hors ZEP." *Éducation et formations* 41: 1–4.

Brown, Susan K., and Charles Hirschman. 2006. "The End of Affirmative Action in Washington State and Its Impact on the Transition from High School to College." *Sociology of Education* 79: 106–30.

Brubaker, Rogers. 1992. *Citizenship and Nationhood in France and Germany.* Cambridge, MA: Harvard University Press.

Bryk, Anthony, Peter Holland, and Valerie Lee. 1993. *Catholic Schools and the Common Good.* Cambridge, MA: Harvard University Press.

Buchmann, Claudia, and Emilio Parrado. 2006. "Educational Achievement of Immigrant-Origin and Native Students: A Comparative Analysis

Informed by Institutional Theory." *International Perspectives on Education and Society* 7: 345–77.

Bunar, Nihad. 2001. *Skolan mitt i förorten: fyra studier om skola, segregation, integration och multikulturalism.* Symposion. Eslöv, Sweden: B. Östlings bokförl.

Burawoy, Michael. 1991. *Ethnography Unbound: Power and Resistance in the Modern Metropolis.* Berkeley: University of California Press.

California Department of Education. 2006. "Fact Book 2006: Handbook of Education Information." www.cde.ca.gov.

———. 2008a. "Ed-Data—Fiscal, Demographic, and Performance Data on California's K–12 Schools. Students by Ethnicity: State of California, 2007–08." http://www.ed-data.k12.ca.us/Navigation/fsTwoPanel.asp?bottom =%2Fprofile.asp%3Flevel%3D04%26reportNumber%3D16.

———. 2008b. "Ed-Data—Fiscal, Demographic, and Performance Data on California K–12 Schools. Number of Students in Private Schools: State of California, 2007–08." http://www.ed-data.k12.ca.us/Navigation/fsTwo Panel.asp?bottom=%2Fprofile.asp%3Flevel%3D04%26reportNumber %3D16.

———. 2008c. "Ed-Data—Fiscal, Demographic, and Performance Data on California K–12 Schools. Comparing California." http://www.eddata.k12 .ca.us/Navigation/fsTwo Panel.asp?bottom=%2FArticles%2FArticle%2 Easp%3Ftitle%3DHow%2520California%2520Compares.

———. 2008d. "Achievement Gap Fact Sheet." http://www.cde.ca.gov/eo/ in/se/agfactsheet.asp.

———. 2008e. "Closing the Achievement Gap: Report of Superintendent Jack O'Connell's California P-16 Council." http://www .closingtheachievementgap.org/downloads/ p16_ctag_report.pdf.

Cameron, Stephen, and James J. Heckman. 1998. "Life Cycle Schooling and Dynamic Selection Bias: Models and Evidence for Five Cohorts of American Males." *The Journal of Political Economy* 106: 262–333.

Capps, Randolph, Michael E. Fix, Julie Murray, Jason Ost, Jeffery S. Passel, and Shinta Herwantoro Hernandez. 2005. *The New Demography of America's Schools: Immigration and the No Child Left Behind Act.* Washington, DC: The Urban Institute.

Carbonell, Jaume, Nuria Simó, and Antoni Tort. 2005. *Magribins a l'escola. El model de Vic a debat.* Barcelona: EUMO.

Carrasco, Silvia. 2001. "La llengua en les relacions interculturals a l'escola." *Articles de Didàctica de la Llengua i la Literatura* 23: 29–40.

———. 2008. "Segregació escolar i immigració: repensant debats i alternatives." *Revista Nous Horitzons* 190: 31–40.

Carrasco, Silvia, Beatriz Ballestín, and A. Borison. 2005. "Infància i immigració: Tendències, relacions, polítiques, Vol. II." *Informe Infància, Famílies i Canvis Socials a Catalunya*, Barcelona: CIIMU. http://www.ciimu.org.

Carrasco, Silvia, Marta Bertran, Carme Gómez-Granell. 2005. *La infància i les famílies al districte d'Horta-Guinardó*. Monogràfics, vol. 7. Barcelona: CIIMU.

Carrasco, Silvia, Jordi Pàmies, and Marta Bertran. 2009. "Familias inmigrantes y escuela: desencuentros, estrategias y capital social." *Revista Complutense de Educación* 30: 55–78.

Carrasco, Silvia, Jordi Pàmies, Maribel Ponferrada, Beatriz Ballestín, and Marta Bertran. 2009. "Segregación escolar e inmigración: aproximaciones etnográficas." In *Investigaciones en educación e inmigración en España: homenaje a Eduardo Terrén Lalana,* edited by Francisco Javier García Castaño and Silvia Carrasco, 367–400. Madrid: CIDE.

Casciani, Dominic. 2006. "An illegal immigration amnesty?" BBC News Wednesday June 16, 2006. http://news.bbc.co.uk/2/hi/uk_news/politics/4989874.stm.

Castles, Stephen, and Mark Miller. 2009. *The Age of Migration*, 4th ed. New York: Guilford Press.

Cesari, Jocelyne. 2006. "Securitization and Religious Divides in Europe: Muslims in Europe After 9/11: Why the Term Islamophobia Is More a Predicament Than an Explanation." Paper presented at the Changing Landscape of Citizenship and Security, 6th PCRD of European Commission, June. http://www.libertysecurity.org/IMG/pdf_Challenge_Project_report.pdf.

Chavez, Leo. 2001. *Covering Immigration: Popular Images and the Politics of the Nation*. Berkeley: University of California Press.

Children Now. 2007. "2006–07 California Report Card: The State of the State's Children." Oakland, CA. http://publications.childrennow.org/publications/invest/reportcard _2007.cfm.

Christensen, Gayle, and Petra Stanat. 2007. "Language Policies and Practices for Helping Immigrants and Second-Generation Students Succeed." Washington, DC: Migration Policy Institute and Bertelsmann Stiftung.

Chubb, John E., and Terry M. Moe. 1990. "America's Public Schools: Choice Is a Panacea." *The Brookings Review* 8: 4–12.

Civil Rights Project. 2008. *Preserving Integration Options for Latino Children: A Manual for Educators, Civil Rights Leaders, and the Community*. Los Angeles: UCLA Civil Rights Project.

Coleman, David. 2006. "Immigration and Ethnic Change in Low-Fertility Countries: A Third Demographic Transition." *Population and Development Review* 32: 401–46.

College Board. 2010. "The College Completion Agenda: 2010 Progress Report." http://completionagenda.collegeboard.org/reports.

Collier, Virginia P. 1995. "Acquiring a Second Language for School." *Directions in Language and Education* 1: 1–14.

Condron, Dennis J., and Vincent J. Roscigno. 2003. "Disparities Within: Unequal Spending and Achievement in an Urban School District." *Sociology of Education* 76: 18–36.

Connolly, Paul. 2006. "The Effects of Social Class and Ethnicity on Gender Differences in GCSE Attainment: A Secondary Analysis of the Youth Cohort Study of England and Wales 1997–2001." *British Educational Research Journal* 32: 3–21.

Connor, Helen. 2001. "Deciding for or against Participation in Higher Education: The Views of Young People from Lower Social Backgrounds." *Higher Education Quarterly* 55: 202–24.

Cookson, Peter W., and Charlotte S. Lucks. 1995. "School Choice in New York City: Preliminary Observations." In *Restructuring Schools: Promising Practices and Policies*, edited by Maureen T. Hallman, 99–110. New York: Plenum Press.

Cordero-Guzmán, Héctor. 2005. "Community-Based Organisations and Migration in New York City." *Journal of Ethnic and Migration Studies* 3: 889–909.

Covello, Leonard. 1972. *The Social Background of the Italo-American School Child*. Totowa: Rowman & Littlefield.

Crawley, Heaven. 2009. "The Situation of Children in Immigrant Families in the United Kingdom." Working Paper 18, Special Series on Children in Immigrant Families in Affluent Societies. Florence: UNICEF Innocenti Research Centre.

Crok, S, J. Slot, T. Fedorova, M. Janssen, and L. ten Broeke. 2004. *Naar Burgerschap in Amsterdam*. Amsterdam: Bestuursdienst Amsterdam.

Crul, Maurice. 2000. *De sleutel tot succes. Over hulp, keuzes en kansen in de schoolloopbanen van Turkse en Marokkaanse jongeren van de tweede generatie.* Amsterdam: Het Spinhuis.

———. 2001. *Succes maakt succesvol. Leerlingbegeleiding door Turkse en Marokkaanse studenten in het voortgezet onderwijs.* Amsterdam: Het Spinhuis.

———. 2003. "Student mentoring onder allochtone leerlingen. Een methodiek in ontwikkeling." *Pedagogiek* 1: 21–39.

———. 2011. "How Do Educational Systems Integrate? Integration of Second Generation Turks in Germany, France, The Netherlands, and Austria." In *The New Generation: The Children of Immigrants in Comparative Perspective*, edited by Richard Alba and Mary Waters, 269–82. New York: NYU Press.

Crul, Maurice, and Ahmet Akdeniz. 1997. *Het hidswerkbegeleidingsproject van SOEBA.* Amsterdam: SOEBA.

Crul, Maurice, and Jeroen Doomernik. 2003. "The Turkish and Moroccan Second Generation in the Netherlands: Divergent Trends between and Polarization within the Two Groups." *International Migration Review* 37: 1039–64.

Crul, Maurice, and Karen Kraal. 2004. *Evaluatie Landelijk Ondersteunings Programma Mentoring.* Amsterdam: IMES.

Crul, Maurice, Adel Pasztor, Frans Lelie, Jonathan Mijs, and Philipp Schnell. 2009. *De lange route in internationaal vergelijkend perspectief: Tweede generatie Turkse jongeren in het onderwijs in Nederland, België, Duitsland, Frankrijk, Oostenrijk, Zwitserland en Zweden* (report for the Dutch Ministry of Education). Amsterdam: IMES/UvA.

Crul, Maurice, and Jens Schneider. 2009. "Integration of Turkish Second-Generation Men and Women in Germany and the Netherlands: The Impact of Differences in Vocational and Academic Tracking Systems." *Teachers College Record* 111: 1508–27.

Crul, Maurice, Jens Schneider, and Frans Lelie (eds.). 2012. *The European Second Generation Compared: Does the Integration Context Matter?* Amsterdam: Amsterdam University Press.

Crul, Maurice, and Hans Vermeulen. 2003. "The Second Generation in Europe." *International Migration Review* 37: 965–86.

Cummins, Jim. 2000. *Language, Power, and Pedagogy.* Clevedon, UK: Multilingual Matters.

Cummins, Jim, Kristin Brown, and Dennis Sayers. 2007. *Literacy, Technology, and Diversity: Teaching for Success in Changing Times.* Boston: Pearson.

Dale, Stacy, and Alan B. Krueger. 2011. "Estimating the Return to College Selectivity over the Career Using Administrative Earning Data." Working Paper #563, Princeton University. http://www.krueger.princeton.edu/working_papers.html.

Dance, L. Janelle. 2002. *Tough Fronts: The Impact of Street Culture on Schooling*. New York: Routledge.

DDAA. 2008. *Avance del Padrón Municipal a 1 de enero de 2008*. Madrid: Instituto Nacional de Estadística. http://www.ine.es/prensa/np503 .pdf.

De Jong, Lammert. 2010. *Being Dutch, More or Less*. Amsterdam: Rozenberg.

De Valk, Helga A. G., and Gülseli Baysu. 2011. "Onderwijstrajecten van de tweede generatie: een vergelijkende sequentieanalyse." In *Goede bedoelingen in het onderwijs: kansen en missers*. Boekaflevering Mens & Maatschappij 86, edited by Jaap Dronkers, 51–80. Amsterdam: Amsterdam University Press.

De Valk, Helga A. G., and Maurice Crul. 2008. "Education." In *The Position of the Turkish and Moroccan Second Generation in Amsterdam and Rotterdam*, edited by Maurice Crul and L. Heering, 63–85. Amsterdam: Amsterdam University Press.

Del Barrio, Ana. 2007. "España es ya el país que recibe más inmigrantes después de Estados Unidos." *El Mundo* March 22. http://medios.mugak .eu/noticias/noticia/93013.

Delpit, Lisa. 2006. *Other People's Children: Cultural Conflict in the Classroom*, updated ed. New York: New Press.

Departament d'Educació de la Generalitat de Catalunya. 2008. "Estadística d'educació." http://www20.gencat.cat/portal/site/Educacio.

Dewey, John. [1909] 1975. *Moral Principles in Education*. Carbondale, IL: Southern Illinois University Press.

DfES. 2005. "Ethnicity and Education: the Evidence on Minority Ethnic Pupils Aged 5–16." https://www.education.gov.uk/publications//eOrderingDownload/DFES-0208–2006.pdf.

DiPrete, Thomas, Dominique Goux, Eric Maurin, and Amelie Quesnel-Vallee. 2005. "Work and Pay in Flexible and Regulated Labor Markets: A Generalized Perspective on Institutional Evolution and Inequality Trends in Europe and the US." Unpublished paper.

Dobbin, Frank, and Alexandra Kalev. 2007. "The Architecture of Inclusion: Evidence from Corporate Diversity Programs." *Harvard Journal of Law and Gender* 30: 279–301.

Dougherty, Kevin. 2002. "The Evolving Role of Community College: Policy Issues and Research Questions." In *Higher Education: Handbook of Theory and Research*. vol. 17, edited by John Smart and William Tierney, 295–348. New York: Kluwer Press.

DuBois, W.E.B. 1903. *The Souls of Black Folk*. Chicago : A.C. McLurg and Co.

Dupray, Arnaud, and Stéphanie Moullet. 2004. "L'insertion des jeunes d'origine maghrébine en France: Des différences plus marquées dans l'accès à l'emploi qu'en matière salariale." www.cereq.fr.

Duru-Bellat, Marie, and Annick Kieffer. 2000. "Inequalities in Educational Opportunities in France: Educational Openness, Democratization or Shifting Barriers?" *Journal of Education Policy* 15: 333–52.

———. 1997. "La constitution de classes de niveau dans les collèges: les effets pervers d'une pratique à visée égalisatrice." *Revue française de sociologie* 28: 759–89.

Duru-Bellat, Marie, and Agnès Van Zanten. 1999. *Sociologie de l'école*, 2nd ed. Paris: Colin.

Dutercq, Yves. 2000. *Politiques éducatives et évaluation: Querelles de territories*. Paris: PUF.

Economist, The. 2009. "The Underworked American." June 11.

Englund, Tomas. 1996. *Utbildningspolitiskt systemskifte?* Stockholm: HLS.

Entwisle, Doris, and Karl Alexander. 1992. "Summer Setback: Race, Poverty, School Composition, and Mathematics Achievement in the First Two Years of School." *American Sociological Review* 57: 72–84.

Erickson, Frederick D. 1987. "Transformation and School Success: The Politics and Culture of Educational Achievement." *Anthropology and Education Quarterly* 18: 335–56.

Ericsson, Urban, Irene Molina, and Per-Markku Ristilammi. 2002. *Miljonprogram och media: föreställningar om människor och förorter*. Stockholm Norrköping: Riksantikvarieämbetet: Integrationsverket.

Estevão, Marcello, and Nigar Nargis. 2005. "Structural Labor Market Changes in France." Discussion Paper no.1621. Bonn, Germany: Forschungsinstitut zur Zukunft der Arbeit, June.

European Monitoring Centre on Racism and Xenophobia. 2006. "Muslims in the European Union: Discrimination and Islamophobia." http://eumc.europa.eu/eumc/material/pub/ muslim/Manifestations_EN.pdf.

Farley, Reynolds, and Richard Alba. 2002. "The New Second Generation in the United States." *International Migration Review* 36: 669–701.

Favell, Adrian. 2001. *Philosophy of Integration: Immigration and the Idea of Citizenship in France and Britain.* London: Palgrave.

Feliciano, Cynthia. 2005. "Does Selective Migration Matter? Explaining Ethnic Disparities in Educational Attainment among Immigrants' Children." *International Migration Review* 39: 841–71.

Felouzis, Georges. 2005. "Performances et 'valeur ajoutée' des lycées: Le marché scolaire fait des différences." *Revue Française de Sociologie* 46: 3–36.

Ferguson, Ronald F. 2002. "What Doesn't Meet the Eye: Understanding and Addressing Racial Disparities in High-Achieving Suburban Schools." Oak Brook, IL: North Central Regional Educational Laboratory (NCREL). http://www.ncrel.org/gap/ferg/.

Ferrer, Ferran, Oscar Valiente, and José Luis Castel. 2008. "Equitat, eficiència i excel·lència a Catalunya. Una anàlisi comparada." Barcelona: Fundació Bofill. www.fbofill.cat/intra/fbofill/documents/.

Fine, Michelle, Lois Weis, and Linda C. Powell. 1997. "Communities of Difference: A Critical Look at Desegregated Spaces Created for and by Youth." *Harvard Educational Review* 67: 247–84.

Fishkin, James. 1997. "Liberty versus Equal Opportunity." In *Equality: Selected Readings*, edited by Louis P. Pojman and Robert Westmoreland, 148–57. New York: Oxford University Press.

Foley, Douglas. 1996. "The Cultural Production of the Silent Indian." In *The Cultural Production of the Educated Person: Critical Ethnographies of Schooling and Local Practice*, edited by Bradley Levinson, Douglas Foley, and Dorothy Holland, 79–91. Albany: State University of New York Press.

Foner, Nancy, and George M. Fredrickson, eds. 2004. *Not Just Black and White: Historical and Contemporary Perspectives on Immigration, Race, and Ethnicity in the United States.* New York: Russell Sage Foundation.

Ford, Donna Y., and J. John Harris. 1994. *Multicultural Gifted Education.* New York: Teachers College Press.

Fordham, Signithia, and John Ogbu. 1987. "Black Students' School Success: Coping with the Burden of Acting White." *Urban Review* 18: 176–206.

Freeman, Gary. 2004. "Immigrant Incorporation in Western Democracies." *International Migration Review* 38: 945–69.

Freire, Paulo. 2000. *Pedagogy of the Oppressed.* New York: Continuum.

————. 2004. *Pedagogy of Hope: Reliving Pedagogy of the Oppressed.* New York: Continuum.

Frickey, Alain, and Jean-Luc Primon. 2004. "L'insertion professionnelle après des études supérieures des jeunes femmes issues des familles d'immigrés des pays du Maghreb: une inégalité redoublée." In *Marché du travail et genre Maghreb-Europe*, edited by Lachen Archy, Jérôme De Henau, Danièle Meulders, and Catherine Sofer, 167–82. Brussels: Brussels Economic Series.

Fry, Richard. 2003. "Hispanics in College: Participation and Degree Attainment." ERIC Clearinghouse on Urban Education, Institute for Urban and Minority Education. http://www.ericdigests.org/2004-2/hispanics.html.

Fuentes-Mayorga, Norma. 2011. "Sorting Black and Brown Latino Service Workers in Gentrifying New York Neighborhoods." *Latino Studies* 9: 106–25.

Galindo, René, and Jami Vigil. 2006. "Are Anti-Immigrant Statements Racist or Nativist? What Difference Does It Make?" *Latino Studies* 6: 419–47.

Gándara, Patricia. 1995. *Over the Ivy Walls, the Educational Mobility of Low Income Chicanos.* Albany: State University of New York Press.

Gándara, Patricia, and Frances Contreras. 2008. *Understanding the Latino Education Gap—Why Latinos Don't Go to College.* Cambridge, MA: Harvard University Press.

Gándara, Patricia, and Russel Rumberger. 2006. "Resource Needs for California's English learners." UC LMRI Paper. http://lmri.ucsb.edu/publications/07_gandara-rumberger.pdf.

————. 2009. "Immigration, Language, and Education: How Does Language Policy Structure Opportunity?" *Teachers College Record* 111: 750–82.

Gans, Herbert. 1999. "The Possibility of a New Racial Hierarchy in the Twenty-First Century United States." In *The Cultural Territories of Race: Black and White Boundaries*, edited by Michele Lamont, 371–90. Chicago: University of Chicago Press.

Garces, Liliana M. 2012. "Necessary But Not Sufficient: The Impact of Grutter v. Bollinger on Student of Color Enrollment in Graduate and Professional Schools in Texas." *The Journal of Higher Education* 83, no. 4: 497–534.

Garcia, Ofelia, Jo Ann Kleifgen, and Lorraine Falchi. 2008. "From English Language Learners to Emergent Bilinguals." Equity Matters: Research Review 1. http://www.tcequity.org/i/a/document/6468_Ofelia_ELL__Final.pdf.

García-Coll, Cynthia, and Katherine Magnuson. 1997. "The Psychological Experience of Immigration: A Developmental Perspective." In Immigration and the Family, edited by Alan Booth, Ann C. Crouter and Nancy Landale, 91-132. Mahwah: Lawrence Erlbaum.

García Sánchez, Inmaculada. 2009. "Moroccan Immigrant Children in a Time of Surveillance: Navigating Sameness and Difference in Contemporary Spain." PhD diss., University of California, Los Angeles.

Gardner, Howard. 1983. *Frames of Mind: The Theory of Multiple Intelligences.* New York: Basic Books.

———. 2004. "How Education Changes: Considerations of History, Science, and Values." In *Globalization: Culture and Education in the New Millennium*, edited by Marcelo M. Suárez-Orozco and Desirée B. Qin-Hilliard, 235–58. Berkeley: University of California Press.

Gates, William H., Sr. 2006. "Remarks." Speech presented at Bennett College Founder's Day. http://www.gatesfoundation.org/speeches-commentary/Pages/bill-gates-sr-2006–bennett-college.aspx.

Gautié, Jérôme, and John Schmitt. 2010. *Low-Wage Work in the Wealthy World.* New York: Russell Sage Foundation.

Gibson, Margaret. 1988. *Accommodation without Assimilation: Sikh Immigrants in an American High School.* Ithaca, NY: Cornell University Press.

———. 1995. "Additive Acculturation as a Strategy for School Improvement." In *California's Immigrant Children: Theory, Research, and Implications for Educational Policy*, edited by Ruben G. Rumbaut and Wayne A. Cornelius, 77–105. La Jolla, CA: Center for US-Mexican Studies.

Gibson, Margaret, and Livier Bejínez. 2002. "Dropout Prevention: How Migrant Education Supports Mexican Youth." *Journal of Latinos and Education* 1: 155–75.

Gibson, Margaret, and Anne Ríos-Rojas. 2006. "Globalization, Immigration, and the Education of 'New' Immigrants in the 21st Century." *Current Issues in Comparative Education* 9: 69–75.

Gijsberts, Mérove, and Marijke Hartgers. 2005. "Minderheden in het Onderwijs." In *Jaarrapport Integratie 2005*, 57–79. Rijswijk: SCP.

Gitlin, Andrew, Edward Buendía, Kristin Crosland, and Fode Doumbia. 2003. "The Production of Margin and Center: Welcoming-Unwelcoming of Immigrant Students." *American Educational Research Journal* 40: 91–122.

Glasman, Dominique. 2001. *L'accompagnement scolaire: Sociologie d'une marge de l'école.* Paris: PUF.

Goldenberg, Claude. 2008. "Teaching English Language Learners: What the Research Does—and Does Not—Say." *American Educator* 32: 8–23, 42–44.

Goldin, Claudia, and Lawrence Katz. 2008. *The Race between Education and Technology*. Cambridge, MA: Harvard University Press.

Goldrick-Rab, Sara, and Christopher Mazzeo. 2005. "What No Child Left Behind Means for College Access." *Review of Research in Education* 29: 107–29.

Goodenough, Ward. 1976. "Multiculturalism as the Normal Human Experience." *Anthropology and Education Quarterly* 7: 4–6.

Grasmuck, Sherri, and Patricia R. Pessar. 1991. *Between Two Islands: Dominican International Migration*. Berkeley: University of California Press.

Greene, Jay P. 1997. "A Meta-Analysis of the Rossell and Baker Review of Bilingual Education Research." *Bilingual Research Journal* 21: 103–22.

Grutter v. Bollinger, 539 US 306 (2003).

Guarnizo, Luis. 1994. "Los Dominicanyorks: The Making of a Binational Society (Trends in US-Caribbean Relations)." *Annals of the American Academy of Political and Social Science* 533: 70–86.

Guillon, Michelle. 1990. "Français et étrangers en Ile de France: dynamiques de localisation divergentes." In *Stratégies résidentielles*, edited by Catharine Bonvallet and Anne-Marie Fribourg, 419–40. Paris: INED.

Hakuta, Kenji, Yuko Goto Butler, and Daria Witt. 2000. *How Long Does It Take English Learners to Attain Proficiency?* University of California Linguistic Minority Research Institute Policy Report.

Hall, Tracey. 2009. "Differentiated Instruction." Cast Universal Design for Learning. http://www.cast.org/publications/ncac/ncac_diffinstruc.html.

Halsey, A. H., Anthony Heath, and John M. Ridge. 1980. *Origins and Destinations: Family, Class and Education in Modern Britain*. Oxford: Clarendon Press.

Harris, Kathleen Mullan, Carolyn Tucker Halpern, Pamela Entzel, Joyce Tabor, Peter S. Bearman, and J. Richard Udry. 2008. "The National Longitudinal Study of Adolescent Health: Research Design." http://www.cpc.unc.edu/projects/addhealth/design.

Heath, Anthony, Catherine Rothon, and Elina Kilpi. 2008. "The Second Generation in Western Europe: Education, Unemployment, and Occupational Attainment." *Annual Review of Sociology* 34: 211–35.

Heath, Anthony, and Yaël Brinbaum. 2007. "Explaining Ethnic Inequalities in Educational Attainment." *Ethnicities* 7: 291–304.

Heath, Anthony, and Sin Yi Cheung, eds. 2007. *Unequal Chances: Ethnic Minorities in Western Labour Markets*. Oxford: Oxford University Press for the British Academy.

Heath, Anthony, and Anna Zimdars. 2005. "Social Factors in Admission to the University of Oxford." Department of Sociology working papers 2005–01. www.sociology.ox.ac.uk/index.php/working-papers/2005.html.

Heckmann, Friedrich. 2008. *Education and Migration: Strategies for the Successful Integration of Migrant Children in European Schools and Societies*. Bamberg, Germany: European Forum for Migration Studies.

Heckmann, Friedrich, and Dominique Schnapper. 2003. *The Integration of Immigrants in European Societies: National Differences and Trends of Convergence*. Stuttgart: Lucius und Lucius.

Helmsley-Brown, Jane. 1999. "College Choice: Perceptions and Priorities." *Educational Management and Administration* 27: 85–98.

Henriot-Van Zanten, Agnès. 1990. *L'école et l'espace local*. Lyon: PUL.

Héran, François. 1995. "École publique, école privée, qui peut choisir?" *Économie et statistique* 293: 17–40.

Hernandez, Donald, Nancy Denton, and Suzanne McCartney. 2006. "Children in Newcomer and Native Families." State University of New York Center for Social and Demographic Analysis, The University at Albany. http://mumford.albany.edu/children/.

———. 2011. "Early Childhood Education Programs: Accounting for Low Enrollment in Immigrant and Minority Families." In *The New Generation: The Children of Immigrants in Comparative Perspective*, edited by Richard Alba and Mary Waters, 46–66. New York: New York University Press.

Herwijer, Lex. 2003. "Voortgezet Onderwijs, beroepsonderwijs en hoger onderwijs." In *Rapportage Minderheden*, edited by Jaco Dagevos, Mérove Gijsberts, and Carlo van Praag, 111–42. Rijswijk, The Netherlands: SCP.

Heubert, Jay, ed. 1998. *Law and School Reform: Six Strategies for Promoting Equity in Education*. New Haven, CT: Yale University Press.

Heyns, Barbara. 1979. *Summer Learning and the Effects of Schooling*. New York: Academic Press.

Hinrichs, Peter L. 2012. "The Effects of Affirmative Action Bans on College Enrollment, Educational Attainment, and the Demographic Composition of Universities." *The Review of Economics and Statistics* 94, no. 3: 712–22.

Hochschild, Jennifer, and Nathan Scovronick. 2003. *The American Dream and the Public Schools.* New York: Oxford University Press.

Holdaway, Jennifer, and Richard Alba. 2009. "Introduction: Educating Immigrant Youth: The Role of Institutions and Agency." *Teachers College Record* III, no. 3: 597–615.

Holdaway, Jennifer, Maurice Crul, and Catrin Roberts. 2009. "Cross-National Comparison of Provision and Outcomes for the Education of the Second Generation." *Teachers College Record* III, no. 6: 1381–403.

Hout, Michael. 2012. "The Social and Economic Returns to College Education in the United States." *Annual Review of Sociology* 38: 379-400.

Hoxby, Caroline. 2009. "The Changing Selectivity of American Colleges." *Journal of Economic Perspectives* 23: 95-118.

Hurd, Clayton. 2004. "'Acting Out' and Being a 'Schoolboy': Performance in an ELD Classroom." In *School Connections: US Mexican Youth, Peers, and School Achievement*, edited by Margaret Gibson, Patricia Gándara, and Jill Koyama, 63–86. New York: Teachers College Press.

———. 2008. "Cinco de Mayo, Normative Whiteness, and the Marginalization of Mexican-Descent Students." *Anthropology & Education Quarterly* 39: 293–313.

INE (Instituto Nacional de Estadística). 2008. Notas de prensa. June 20. http://www.ine.es/prensa/np503.pdf.

———. 2010. "Movimiento natural de la población. Resultados provisionales 2009." http://www.ine.es/jaxi/menu.do?type=pcaxis&path=/t20/e301/ provi&file=pcaxis.

Ingersoll, Richard M. 2003. "The Teacher Shortage: Myth or Reality?" *Educational Horizons* 81: 146–52.

Ingersoll, Richard M., and Thomas M. Smith. 2003. "The Wrong Solution to the Teacher Shortage." *Keeping Good Teachers* 60: 30–33.

Inglis, Christine. 2004. "Australia's Continuing Transformation." Migration Information Source. http://www.migrationinformation.org/Profiles/display.cfm?ID=242.

Innocenti Insight. 2009. *Children in Immigrant Families in Eight Affluent Countries: Their Family, National and International Context.* Florence: Innocenti Research Centre.

INSEE National Institute for Statistics and Economic Studies. 2007. "Statut et type de contrat en 2010." http://www.insee.fr/unemployment_statistics .html.

Itzigsohn, Jose, and Carlos Dore-Cabral. 2000. "Competing Identities? Race, Ethnicity and Panethnicity among Dominicans in the United States." *Sociological Forum* 15: 225–47.

Jackson, Michelle, Robert Erikson, John H. Goldthorpe, and Meir Yaish. 2007. "Primary and Secondary Effects in Class Differentials in Educational Attainment: The Transition to A-Level Courses in England and Wales." *Acta Sociologica* 50: 211–29.

Jackson, Michelle, Jan Jonsson, and Frida Rudolphi. 2012. "Ethnic Inequality and Choice-Driven Educational Systems: A Longitudinal Study of Performance and Choice in England and Sweden." *Sociology of Education* 85: 158-78.

Johnson, Jean, Anna Maria Arumi, and Amber Ott. 2006. "How Black and Hispanic Families Rate Their Schools." Reality Check 2006. http://www.publicagenda.org/research/pdfs/ rc0602.pdf.

Jong, Wiebe de. 1986. *Interetnische verhoudingen in een oude stadswijk.* Delft, The Netherlands: Eburon.

———. 1997. "De taak van het onderwijs en de volwasseneneducatie binnen een actief inburgeringsbeleid." In *Nieuwe burgers in de samenleving?*, edited by Marie-Claire Foblets and Bernard Hubeau, 155–71. Leuven, Belgium: Acco.

Joppke, Christian. 1999. *Immigration and the Nation State.* Oxford: Oxford University Press.

Junger-Tas, Josine, M. J. L. F. Cruyff, P. van de Looij-Jansen, and F. Reelick. 2003. *Etnische Minderheden en het belang van binding.* The Hague, The Netherlands: Sdu.

Kallstenius, Jenny. 2007. "Är en svensk skola bättre? Om skolval som strategi för bättre karriär." In *Utbildning arbete medborgarskap*, edited by Magnus Dahlstedt, Fredrik Hertzberg, Susanne Urban, and Aleksandra Ålund, 111–28. Umeå, Sweden: Boréa.

Kao, Grace, and Jennifer Thompson. 2003. "Racial and Ethnic Stratification in Educational Achievement and Attainment." *Annual Review of Sociology* 29: 417–42.

Kao, Grace, and Marta Tienda. 1995. "Optimism and Achievement: The Educational Performance of Immigrant Youth." *Social Science Quarterly* 76: 1–19.

Karabel, Jerome. 2006. *The Chosen: The Hidden History of Admission and Exclusion at Harvard, Yale, and Princeton.* New York: Houghton Mifflin.

Kasinitz, Philip. 2004. "Race, Assimilation and 'Second Generations,' Past and Present." In *Not Just Black and White: Historical and Contemporary Perspectives on Immigration, Race, and Ethnicity in the United States*, edited by Nancy Foner and George M. Fredrickson, 278–98. New York: Russell Sage Foundation.

Kasinitz, Philip, John Mollenkopf, Mary Waters, and Jennifer Holdaway. 2008. *Inheriting the City: The Second Generation Comes of Age*. Cambridge, MA: Harvard University Press Russell Sage Foundation.

Keller, Morton, and Phyllis Keller. 2001. *Making Harvard Modern: The Rise of America's University*. Oxford: Oxford University Press.

Kerckhoff, Alan C. 1995. "Reforming Education: A Critical Overlooked Component." In *Restructuring Schools: Promising Practices and Policies*, edited by Maureen Hallinan, 199–231. New York: Plenum Press.

Kirszbaum, Thomas, Yaël Brinbaum, and Patrick Simon. 2009. *The Children of Immigrants in France: The Emergence of a Second Generation*. Special Series on Children in Immigrant Families in Affluent Societies. Florence: Innocenti Research Centre.

Komen, Mieke. 2002. "Dangerous Children: Juvenile Delinquency and Judicial Intervention in the Netherlands, 1960–1995." *Crime, Law and Social Change* 37: 379–401.

Koyama, Jill, and Margaret Gibson. 2007. "Marginalization and Membership." In *Late to Class: Social Class and Schooling in the New Economy*, edited by Jane Van Galen and George Noblit, 87–111. Albany, NY: State University of New York Press.

Kozol, Jonathan. 1991. *Savage Inequalities: Children in America's Schools*. New York: Crown.

———. 2006. *The Shame of the Nation: The Restoration of Apartheid Schooling in America*. New York: Three Rivers Press.

Langouët, Gabriel, and Alain Léger. 1997. *Le choix des familles: École publique ou école privée*. Paris: Fabert.

Legrand, André. 2000. "Décentralisation et déconcentration." In *L'école, l'état des savoirs*, edited by Angès Van Zanten, 94–102. Paris: Éditions La Découverte.

Leonhardt, David. 2010. "The Case for $320,000 Kindergarten Teachers." *The New York Times*, July 27, A1.

Levels, Mark, Jaap Dronkers, and Gerbert Kraaykamp. 2008. "Immigrant Children's Educational Achievement in Western Countries: Origin,

Destination, and Community Effects on Mathematical Performance." *American Sociological Review* 73: 835–53.

Levitt, Peggy. 1991. *The Transnational Villagers.* Berkeley: University of California Press.

Lewin, Tamar. 2010. "Once a Leader, US Lags in College Degrees." *The New York Times,* July 23, A11.

Lipsit, Mia. 2003. "Newcomers Left Behind: Immigrant Parents Lack Equal Access to New York City's Schools." New York: Center for New York City Affairs, Milano Graduate School of Management and Urban Policy, New School University.

Liptak, Adam. 2012. "Race and College Admissions, Facing a New Test by Justices." *The New York Times,* October 9, A1.

Ljungberg, Caroline. 2005. *Den svenska skolan och det mångkulturella—en paradox?* Malmö Linköping, Sweden. IMER Malmö högskola: Tema Etnicitet University.

Loewen, James. 2009. *Teaching What Really Happened: How to Avoid the Tyranny of Textbooks and Get Students Excited about Doing History.* New York: Teachers College Press.

Logan, John R. 2001. "The New Latinos: Who They Are, Where They Are." Albany, NY: Lewis Mumford Center for Comparative Urban and Regional Research.

———. 2002. "Hispanic Populations and Their Residential Patterns in the Metropolis." Albany, NY: Lewis Mumford Center for Comparative Urban and Regional Research.

Logan, John, Deirdre Oakley, and Jacob Stowell. 2008. "School Segregation in Metropolitan Regions 1970–2000: The Impacts of Policy Choices on Public Education." *American Journal of Sociology* 113: 1611–44.

Lopez, Nancy. 2003. *Hopeful Girls, Troubled Boys: Race and Gender Disparity in Urban Education.* New York: Routledge.

Lorcerie, Françoise. 1994. "L'Islam dans les cours de langue et culture d'origine: le procès." *Revue européenne des migrations internationales* 10: 5–43.

Louie, Vivian. 2004. *Compelled to Excel: Immigration, Education, and Opportunity among Chinese Americans.* Palo Alto, CA: Stanford University Press.

Louie, Vivian, and Jennifer Holdaway. 2009. "Catholic Schools and Immigrant Students: A New Generation." *Teachers College Record* 111: 783–816.

Louis, Françoise. 1994. *Décentralisation et autonomie des établissements: La mutation du système éducatif.* Paris: Hachette.

Lucas, Samuel. 2001. "Effectively Maintained Inequality: Education Transitions, Track Mobility, and Social Background Effects." *American Journal of Sociology* 106: 1642–90.

Lucas, Tamara. 1997. *Into, through, and beyond Secondary School: Critical Transitions for Immigrant Youths*. Washinton, D.C.: Center for Applied Linguistics.

Lucassen, Leo. 2005. *The Immigrant Threat: The Integration of Old and New Migrants in Europe since 1850*. Urbana: University of Illinois Press.

Luckie, Mark. 2009. "INTERACTIVE: Comparing Student-to-Teacher Ratio Nationwide." California Watch. http://californiawatch.org/k-12/interactive-comparing-student-teacher-ratio-nationwide.

Lustig, Stuart L., Maryam Kia-Keating, Wanda Grant-Knight, Paul Geltman, Heidi Ellis, J. David Kinzie, Terence Keane, and Glenn Saxe. 2004. "Review of Child and Adolescent Refugee Mental Health." *Journal of American Academy of Child and Adolescent Psychiatry* 43: 24–36.

Lutz, Amy. 2007. "Barriers to High-School Completion among Immigrant and Later-Generation Latinos in the USA: Language, Ethnicity and Socioeconomic Status." *Ethnicities* 7: 323–42.

Magnuson, Katherine, and Jane Waldfogel. 2005. "Early Childhood Care and Education: Effects on Ethnic and Racial Gaps in School Readiness." *The Future of Children* 15: 169–96.

Maira, Sunaina, and Elisabeth Soep. 2005. *Youthscapes: The Popular, the National, the Global*. Philadelphia: University of Pennsylvania Press.

Mare, Robert. 1980. "Social Background and School Continuation Decisions." *Journal of the American Statistical Association* 75: 295–305.

Marks, Gary. 2005. "Cross-National Differences and Accounting for Social Class Inequalities in Education." *International Sociology* 20: 483–505.

Martin Rojo, Luisa, ed. 2003. *¿Asimilar o integrar? Dilemas ante el multilingüismo en las aulas*. Madrid: CIDE.

Martineau, Erin M. 2006. "'Too Much Tolerance': Hang-Around Youth, Public Space, and the Problem of Freedom in the Netherlands." PhD diss, Graduate Center of the City University of New York.

Massey, Douglas, Camille Charles, Garvey Lundy, and Mary Fischer. 2002. *The Source of the River: The Social Origins of Freshmen at America's Selective Colleges and Universities*. Princeton, NJ: Princeton University Press.

Massey, Douglas, Jorge Durand, and Nolan Malone. 2003. *Beyond Smoke and Mirrors: Mexican Immigration in an Era of Economic Integration.* New York: Russell Sage Foundation.

Mattsson, Katarina, and Mekonnen Tesfahuney. 2002. "Rasism i vardagen." In *Det slutna folkhemmet. Om etniska klyftor och blågul självbild*, edited by Samir Amin, Ingemar Lindberg, and Magnus Dahlstedt,. Stockholm: Agora.

McAndrew, Marie, 2009. "Ensuring Proper Competency in the Host Language: Contrasting Formulas and the Place of Heritage Languages." *Teachers College Record* 111: 1528–54.

McCrudden, Christopher, Raya Muttarak, Heather Hamill, and Anthony Heath. 2009. "Affirmative Action without Quotas in Northern Ireland." *The Equal Rights Review* 4: 7–14.

McGrath, Susan, and Peter Millen. 2004. "Getting Them In: An Investigation of Factors Affecting Progression to Higher Education of 16–19-Year-Olds in Full-Time Education." Manchester Metropolitan University and the Learning Skills and Development Agency. http://www.guidance-research.org/EG/benefits/other-studies/ldsastudy/gettingthemin.

Mei, Lori, Jennifer Bell-Ellwanger, and Ron Miller. 2002. "An Examination of Four-Year Cohort Graduation and Dropout Rates for the New York City School's Class of 2001 and Final School Completion Outcomes for the Class of 1990." Paper presented at the annual meeting of the American Education Research Association, New Orleans, April.

Meier, Deborah, and George Wood. 2004. *Many Children Left Behind: How the No Child Left Behind Act Is Damaging Our Children and Our Schools.* Boston: Beacon Press.

Mendoza-Denton, Norma. 2008. *Homegirls: Language and Cultural Practice among Latina Youth Gangs.* Malden, MA: Blackwell Publishing.

Menken, Kate. 2008. *English Language Learners Left Behind: Standardized Testing as Language Policy.* Clevedon, UK: Multilingual Matters.

Merle, Pierre. 2002. *La démocratisation de l'enseignement.* Paris: La Découverte.

Meuret, Denis. 1994. "L'efficacité de la politique des zones d'éducation prioritaires dans les collèges." *Revue française de pédagogie* 109: 41–64.

MPI (Migration Policy Institute). 2000. "New York-based Internationals Network for Public Schools Earns National Award for Exceptional Immigrant Integration Initiatives." http://www.migrationinformation.org/integrationawards/winners-inps.cfms.

———. 2009. *Exceptional Immigrant Integration Initiatives*. Available from http://www.migrationpolicy.org/news/2009_5_20.php.

———. 2010. "2010 American Community Survey and Census Data on the Foreign Born by State." http://www.migrationinformation.org/datahub/ acscensus.cfm.

Modood, Tariq. 2011. "Capitals, Ethnic Identity, and Educational Qualifications." In *The Next Generation: Immigrant Youth in Comparative Perspective*, edited by Richard Alba and Mary C. Waters, 185-206. New York: New York University Press.

Moll, Luis, Cathy Amanti, Deborah Neff, and Norma Gonzalez. 1992. "Funds of Knowledge for Teaching: Using a Qualitative Approach to Connect Homes and Classrooms." *Theory into Practice* 31: 132–41.

Morgan, Stephen. 2005. *On the Edge of Commitment: Educational Attainment and Race in the United States*. Palo Alto, CA: Stanford University Press.

Musterd, Sako, and Rinus Deurloo. 2002. "Unstable Immigrant Concentration in Amsterdam: Spatial Segregation and Integration of Newcomers." *Housing Studies* 17: 487–503.

Muttarak, Raya, and Anthony Heath. 2010. "Who Intermarries in Britain? Explaining Ethnic Diversity in Intermarriage Patterns." *British Journal of Sociology* 61, no. 2: 275–305.

Myers, Dowell. 2007. *Immigrants and Boomers: Forging a New Social Contract for the Future of America*. New York: Russell Sage Foundation.

NCES (National Center for Education Statistics). 2000. "High School Dropouts by Race/Ethnicity and Recency of Migration. NCES 2001– 602." *Education Statistics Quarterly* 2: 25–27.

———. 2001. *The Condition of Education 2001 (NCES 2001–072)*. Washington, DC: US Department of Education.

———. 2005. "The Nation's Report Card." http://nces.ed.gov/nationsreport card/pdf/main2005/ 2006451.pdf.

Nettles, Saundra. 1991. "Community Involvement and Disadvantaged Students: A Review." *Review of Educational Research,* 61: 379–406. New York City Board of Education. 2001. "Regulation of the Chancellor." http://docs .nycenet.edu/docushare/dsweb/Get/Document-22/A-443.pdf.

NYCDOE (New York City Department of Education). 2008. "New York City's English Language Learners: Demographics." http://schools.nyc .gov/Academics/ELL/default.htm.

NYSED (New York State Education Department). 2006. "New York State of Learning: A Report to the Governor and the Legislature on the Educational Status of the State's Schools." http://www.regents.nysed .gov/meetings/2006Meetings/October2006/1006bra3a.pdf.

———. 2011a. "Graduation Rates: Students Who Started 9th Grade in 2001, 2002, 2003, 2004, 2005, and 2006." http://www.p12.nysed.gov/irs/statistics/hsgrads/2011/GradRateSlides-final.PPT.

———. 2011b. "School Improvement Scenarios for Washington Irving High School." http://schools.nyc.gov/community/planning/changes/manhattan/Irving.

Nieto, Sonia. 2003. *Affirming Diversity: The Sociopolitical Context of Multicultural Education.* 4th ed. Boston: Pearson/Allyn and Bacon.

Noam, Gil, ed. 2004. *After-School Worlds: Creating a New Social Space for Development and Learning,* vol. 101. New York: Jossey-Bass.

Noam, Gil, and Jodi Rosenbaum Tillinger. 2004. "After-School as Intermediary Space: Theory and Typology of Partnerships." *New Directions for Youth Development* 101: 75–113.

Noddings, Nel. 2002. *Educating Moral People: A Caring Alternative to Character Education.* New York: Teachers College Press.

Nussbaum, Luci, and Virginia Unamuno. 2006. *Usos i competències multilingües entre escolars d'origen immigrant.* Barcelona: UAB.

Oakes, Jeannie. 2005. *Keeping Track: How Schools Structure Equality.* New Haven, CT: Yale University Press.

———. 2002. Education Inadequacy, Inequality, and Failed State Policy: A Synthesis of Expert Reports Prepared for *Williams v. State of California.* Document wws-rr016–1002. Los Angeles: UCLA Institute for Democracy, Education, and Access.

OECD. 2001. *Knowledge and Skills for Life: First Results from the OECD Programme for International Student Assessment (PISA) 2000.* Paris: Organization for Economic Co-operation and Development.

———. 2004. *Learning for Tomorrow's World: First Results from PISA 2003.* Paris: Organization for Economic Co-operation and Development.

———. 2006. *Where Immigrant Students Succeed—A Comparative Review of Performance and Engagement from PISA 2003.* Paris: Organization for Economic Co-operation and Development.

———. 2007. *Science Competencies for Tomorrow's World:* vol. 1: *Analysis from PISA 2006.* Paris: Organization for Economic Co-operation and Development.

————. 2008. *Labor Market Report*. Paris: Organization for Economic Co-operation and Development.

Oeuvrard Françoise. 2000. "La construction des inégalités de la scolarisation de la maternelle au lycée." In *L'école, l'état des savoirs*, edited by Angès Van Zanten. Paris: Éditions La Découverte.

Öhrn, Elisabet. 2002. "Könsmönster i förändring: en kunskapsöversikt om unga i skolan." Stockholm: Skolverket Fritz förlag.

Olsen, Laurie. 2009. "The Role of Advocacy in Shaping Immigrant Education: A California Case Study." *Teachers College Record* 111: 817–50.

Opotow, Susan. 2005. "Hate, Conflict, and Moral Exclusion." In *The Psychology of Hate*, edited by Robert J. Sternberg, 121–53. Washington, DC: American Psychological Association.

Orenstein, Peggy. 1995. *Schoolgirls: Young Women, Self-Esteem, and the Confidence Gap*. New York: Anchor Books.

Orfield, Gary. 2001. "Schools More Separate: Consequences of a Decade of Resegregation." Harvard University: The Civil Rights Project. http://www.civilrightsproject.harvard.edu/research/deseg/separate_schools01.php.

Orfield, Gary, and Chungmei Lee. 2006. "Racial Transformation and the Changing Nature of Segregation." Cambridge, MA: Civil Rights Project, Harvard University.

Orfield, Gary, and John T. Yun. 1999. "Resegregation in American Schools." Cambridge, MA: Civil Rights Project, Harvard University.

Pàmies, Jordi. 2004. "Entre la Yebala marroquí y las aulas de un instituto de la periferia de Barcelona." *Actas I Congreso Etnografía y Educación*. Valencia, Spain: Editorial Germania.

————. 2006. "Dinámicas escolares y comunitarias de los hijos e hijas de familias inmigradas marroquíes de la Yebala en la periferia de Barcelona." PhD diss., Departament d'Anthropologia Social i Cultural, Universitat Autonoma de Barcelona. http://www.tdx.cat.

Passel, Jeffrey. 2006. "Size and Characteristics of the Unauthorized Migrant Population in the US: Estimates Based on the March 2005 Current Population Survey." Pew Hispanic Center Report. http://pewhispanic.org/reports/report.php?ReportID=61.

————. 2011. "Demography of Immigrant Youth: Past, Present, and Future." *The Future of Children* 21: 19–41.

Passel, Jeffrey, and D'Vera Cohn. 2008. *Trends in Unauthorized Immigration: Undocumented Inflow Now Trails Legal Inflow*. Washington, DC: Pew Hispanic Center.

Peach, Ceri. 1996. "Does Britain Have Ghettos?" *Transactions of the Institute of British Geographers* 21, no. 1: 216–35.

Perreira, Krista, Kathleen Mullan Harris, and Dohoon Lee. 2006. "Making It in America: High School Completion by Immigrant and Native Youth." *Demography* 43: 1–26.

Pessar, Patricia. 1995. *Visa for a Dream: Dominicans in the United States*. Boston: Allyn and Bacon.

Pettit, Becky, and Bruce Western. 2004. "Mass Imprisonment and the Life Course: Race and Class Inequality in US Incarceration." *American Sociological Review* 69:151–69.

Phelan, Patricia, Ann Davidson, and Hanh Yu. 1997. *Adolescents' Worlds: Negotiating Family, Peers, and School*. New York: Teachers College Press.

Phillips, Meredith, and Tiffani Chin. 2004. "School Inequality: What Do We Know?" In *Social Inequality*, edited by Kathryn Neckerman, 467–519. New York: Russell Sage Foundation.

Pianta, Robert C. 1999. *Enhancing Relationships between Children and Teachers*. Washington, DC: American Psychological Association.

Piketty, Thomas, and Mathieu Valdenaire. 2006. "L'impact de la taille des classes sur la réussite scolaire dans les écoles collèges et lycées français: une estimation à partir du panel primaire 1997 et du panel secondaire 1995." Les dossiers Evaluation et statistiques, no 173. Paris: Ministère de l'éducation nationale.

Ponferrada, Maribel. 2008. "Chicas y poder en la escuela. Identidades académicas, sociales y de género entre jóvenes de la periferia." PhD diss., Departament d'Anthropologia Social i Cultural, Universitat Autonoma de Barcelona. http://www.tdx.cat.

Portes, Alejandro, and Rubén Rumbaut. 2001. *Legacies: The Story of the Immigrant Second Generation*. Berkeley: University of California Press.

———. 2006. *Immigrant America: A Portrait*, 3rd ed. Berkeley: University of California Press.

Portes, Alejandro, and Alex Stepick. 1993. *City on the Edge: The Transformation of Miami*. Berkeley: University of California Press.

Portes, Alejandro, and Min Zhou. 1993. "The New Second Generation: Segmented Assimilation and Its Variants." *The Annals* 530: 74–96.

Préteceille, Edmond. 2009. "La ségrégation ethno-raciale a-t-elle augmenté dans la métropole parisienne?" *Revue française de sociologie* 50: 489–519.

Prop. 1975: 26 *Riktlinjer för invandrar- och minoritetspolitiken m m.* Regeringskansliet. Stockholm.

Prop. 1997/98:16 *Sverige, framtiden och mångfalden.* Regeringskansliet. Stockholm.

Prost, Antoine. 1968. *Histoire de l'enseignement en France 1800–1967.* Paris: Colin.

Public Policy Institute of California. 2008. "Just the Facts: Immigrants in California." http://www.ppic.org/content/pubs/jtf/JTF_ImmigrantsJTF .pdf.

Raftery, Adrian, and Michael Hout. 1993. "Maximally Maintained Inequality: Expansion, Reform, and Opportunity in Irish Education, 1921–75." *Sociology of Education* 66: 41–62.

Ravitch, Diane. 2010. *The Death and Life of the Great American School System: How Testing and Choice Are Undermining Education.* New York: Basic Books.

Reitz, Jeffrey and Ye Zhang. 2011. "National and Urban Contexts for the Integration of the Immigrant Second Generation in the United States and Canada." In *The Next Generation: Immigrant Youth in a Comparative Perspective*, edited by Richard Alba and Mary C. Waters, 207-28. New York: New York University Press..

Richard, Jean-Luc. 1997. *Dynamics démographiques et socio-économiques de l'intégration des jeunes generations d'origine immigrée en France.* Institut d'Études Politiques de Paris.

Rogers, John, Veronica Terriquez, Siomara Valladares, and Jeannie Oakes. 2006. "California Educational Opportunity Report 2006: Roadblocks to College." Los Angeles: UCLA Institute for Democracy, Education, and Access. http://www.idea.gseis.ucla.edu/publications/eor07/state/pdf/ StateEOR2007.pdf.

Rosenbaum, James. 2001. *Beyond College for All: Career Paths for the Forgotten Half.* New York: Russell Sage Foundation.

Rothon, Catherine. 2007. "Can Achievement Differentials Be Explained by Social Class Alone? An Examination of Minority Ethnic Educational Performance in England and Wales at the End of Compulsory Schooling." *Ethnicities* 7: 306–22.

Rothon, Catherine, Anthony Heath, and Laurence Lessard-Phillips. 2009. "The Educational Attainment of the 'Second Generation': A Comparative Study of Britain, Canada and the United States." *Teachers College Record* 111 (6): 1404-43.

Ruiz-de-Velasco, Jorge, Michael Fix, and Beatriz Clewell. 1998. *Overlooked and Underserved: Immigrant Students in US Secondary Schools.* Washington, DC: The Urban Institute.

San Miguel, Guadalupe, and Richard Valencia. 1998. "From the Treaty of Guadalupe Hidalgo to Hopwood: The Educational Plight and Struggle of Mexican Americans in the Southwest." *Harvard Educational Review* 68: 353–412.

Sawyer, Lena, and Masoud Kamali. 2006. *Utbildningens Dilemma: Demokratiska Ideal och Andrafierande Praxis.* Stockholm: Statens Offentliga Utredningar.

Schierup, Carl-Ulrik, and Susanne Urban. 2007. "Svensk välfärdsstat i omvandling: Medborgarskap arbete utbildning." In *Utbildning arbete medborgarskap,* edited by Magnus Dahlstedt, Fredrik Hertzberg, Susanne Urban, and Aleksandra Ålund, 27–56. Umeå, Sweden: Boréa.

Schleicher, Andreas, and Karine Tremley. 2006. "Education and the Knowledge Economy in Europe and Asia." *Challenge Europe* 15: 24–36.

Schneider, Silke. 2008. "The International Standard Classification of Education (ISCED 97). An Evaluation of Content and Criterion Validity for 15 European Countries." Mannheim, Germany: MZES (Mannheimer Zentrum für Europäische Sozialforschung).

Schweder, Richard. 2008. "After Just Schools: The Equality-Difference Paradox and Conflicting Varieties of Liberal Hope." In *Just Schools: Pursuing Equality in Societies of Difference,* edited by Martha Minow, Richard Schweder, and Hazel Rose Markus, 254–90. New York: Russell Sage Foundation.

Sen, Amartya. 1999. *Development as Freedom.* New York: Knopf.

Sernhede, Ove. 2002. *AlieNation Is My Nation: hiphop och unga mäns utanförskap i Det nya Sverige.* Stockholm: Ordfront.

Serra, Carles, and Josep Miquel Palaudàries. 2007. "L'alumnat de nacionalitat estrangera en els estudis postobligtoris." In *L'estat de la immigració a Catalunya. Anuari 2006,* edited by Jesus Larios and Monica Nadal, 301–34. Barcelona: Mediterrània.

Shor, Ira. 1992. *Empowering Education: Critical Teaching for Social Change.* Chicago: University of Chicago Press.

Silberman Roxane, 1997, "L'insertion professionnelle des enfants d'immigrés." In *La scolarisation de la France. Critique de l'état des lieux,* edited by J-P Terrail, 193-207. Paris: La dispute.

Silberman, Roxane. 2011. "The Employment of Second Generations in France: The Republican Model and the November 2005 Riots." In *The New Generation: The Children of Immigrants in Comparative Perspective,* edited by Richard Alba and Mary Waters, 283–315. New York: New York University Press.

Silberman, Roxane, Richard Alba, and Irène Fournier. 2007. "Segmented Assimilation in France: Discrimination in the Labour Market against the Second Generation." *Ethnic and Racial Studies* 30: 1–27.

Silberman, Roxane, and Irène Fournier. 1999. "Les enfants d'immigrés sur le marché du travail. Les mécanismes d'une discrimination selective." *Formation Emploi* 65: 31–55.

———. 2006a. "Les secondes générations sur le marché du travail en France: une pénalité ethnique ancrée dans le temps. Contribution à la théorie de l'assimilation segmentée." *Revue française de sociologie* 47: 243–92. (Published in English: 2008. "Second Generations on the Job Market in France: A Persistent Ethnic Penalty. A Contribution to Segmented Assimilation Theory." *Revue française de sociologie,* Sélection anglaise vol. Supplément 49: 45–94).

———. 2006b. "Is French Society Truly Assimilative? Immigrant Parents and Offspring on the French Labour Market." In *Unequal Chances. Ethnic Minorities in Western Labour Markets,* edited by Anthony Heath, and Sin Cheung, 221–70. Oxford: Oxford University Press.

Simon, Patrick. 2003. "France and the Unknown Second Generation: Preliminary Results on Social Mobility." *International Migration Review* 37: 1091–119.

Síndic de Greuges. 2008. *Informe sobre segregación escolar a Catalunya.* Barcelona: Generalitat de Catalunya.

Skolverket. 2002. *Flera språk- flera möjligheter. Utveckling av modersmålsstödet och modersmålsundervisningen.* Skolverket rapport 2002: 28. Stockholm.

Slavin, Robert, and Alan Cheung. 2005. "A Synthesis of Research on Language of Reading Instruction for English Language Learners." *Review of Educational Research* 75: 247–84.

Solano-Flores, Guillermo. 2008. "Who Is Given Tests in What Language by Whom, When, and Where? The Need for Probabilistic Views of Language in the Testing of English Language Learners." *English Education Researcher* 37: 189–99.

Spivak, Gayatri. 1990. *The Post-Colonial Critic: Interviews, Strategies, Dialogues.* London: Routledge.

Stake, Robert. 2005. "Qualitative Case Studies." In *The Sage Handbook of Qualitative Research*, 3rd ed, edited by Norman Denzin and Yvonna Lincoln, 443–66. Thousand Oaks, CA: Sage Publications.

Statistics Netherlands. 2009. "Population, Generation, Sex, Age and Origin." http://www.cbs.nl/en-GB/menu/themas/bevolking/cijfers/default. htm.

Statistiska Centralbyrån, 2009. "Sveriges Framtida Befolkning Demogrfiska rapporter: 2009–2060." Örebro:SCB-Tryck. http://www.scb.se/statistik/_ publikationer/BE0401_2009I6Q_BR_BE51BR0901.pdf.

Steele, Claude. 1997. "A Threat in the Air: How Stereotypes Shape Intellectual Identity and Performance." *American Psychologist* 52: 613-29.

Suárez-Orozco, Carola. 2004. "Formulating Identity in a Globalized World." In *Globalization: Culture and Education in the New Millennium*, edited by Marcelo Suárez-Orozco and Desirée Qin-Hilliard, 173–202. Berkeley: University of California Press and the Ross Institute.

Suárez-Orozco, Carola, Allyson Pimentel, and Margary Martin. 2009. "The Significance of Relationships: Academic Engagement and Achievement among Newcomer Immigrant Youth." *Teachers College Record* 111: 712–49.

Suárez-Orozco, Carola, and Desirée Baolian Qin. 2006. "Gendered Perspectives in Psychology: Immigrant Origin Youth." *International Migration Review* 40: 165–98.

Suárez-Orozco, Carola, and Marcelo Suárez-Orozco. 1995. *Transformations: Immigration, Family Life, and Achievement Motivation among Latino Adolescents.* Palo Alto, CA: Stanford University Press.

Suárez-Orozco, Carola, Marcelo Suárez-Orozco, and Irina Todorova. 2008. *Learning in a New Land: Immigrant Students in American Society.* Cambridge, MA: Harvard University Press.

Suárez-Orozco, Carola, Irina Todorova, and Josephine Louie. 2002. "'Making Up for Lost Time': The Experience of Separation and Reunification among Immigrant Families." *Family Process* 41: 625–43.

Suárez-Orozco, Marcelo, and Carolyn Sattin. 2007. "Introduction: Learning in the Global Era." In *Learning in the Global Era; International Perspectives on Globalization and Education*, edited by Marcello Suárez-Orozco, 1–45. Berkeley: University of California Press.

Suárez-Orozco, Marcelo, and Desirée Qin-Hilliard. 2004. *Globalization: Culture and Education in the New Millennium*. Berkeley: University of California Press.

Sugarman, Julie, and Elizabeth Howard. 2001. "Development and Maintenance of Two-Way Immersion Programs: Advice from Practitioners." http://www.cal.org/resources/digest/ PracBrief2.html.

Tanguy, Lucy, ed. 1986. *L'introuvable relation formation/emploi. Un état des recherches en France*. Paris: La Documentation française.

Telles, Edward, and Vilma Ortiz. 2008. *Generations of Exclusion: Mexican Americans, Assimilation, and Race*. New York: Russell Sage Foundation.

Teske, Paul, Mark Schneider, Christine Roch, and Melissa Marschall. 2000. "Public School Choice: A Status Report." In *City Schools: Lessons from New York*, edited by Diane Ravitch and Joseph Viteritti, 313–38. Baltimore, MD: Johns Hopkins University Press.

Tesser, Paulus, Johanna Merens, and Carlo van Praag. 1999. *Rapportage minderheden 1999*. Rijswijk, The Netherlands: Social and Cultural Planning Office (SCP).

Thomas, Fanny. 2005. "Typologie des collèges publics. Disparités entre collèges publics en 2003–2004." *Éducation et formations* 71: 117–35.

Thomas, Wayne, and Virginia Collier. 2002. *A National Study of School Effectiveness for Language Minority Students' Long-Term Academic Achievement*. Berkeley: UC Berkeley Center for Research on Education, Diversity & Excellence.

Tinto, Vincent. 1994. *Leaving College: The Causes and Cures of Student Attrition*. Chicago: University of Chicago Press.

Trancart, Danièle. 1998. "L'évolution des disparités entre collèges publics." *Revue française de pédagogie* 124: 43–53.

Tribalat, Michèle. 1995. *Faire France: Une enquête sur les immigrés et leurs enfants*. Paris: Éditions La Découverte.

UCLA/IDEA & UC/ACCORD. 2007. "Latino Educational Opportunity Report: California's Latino Opportunity Gap." Los Angeles: UCLA Institute for Democracy, Education, and Access. http://www.idea.gseis.ucla.edu/publications/eor07/index.html.

Ungdomsstyrelsen. 2008. Fokus 08: En analys av ungas utanförskap. Stockholm: Elanders Sverige AB.

US Census Bureau. 2008. *The 2008 Statistical Abstract of the United States.* Washington, DC: Department of Commerce.

Valdés, Guadalupe. 1998. "The World Outside and Inside Schools: Language and Immigrant Children." *Educational Researcher* 27: 4–18.

———. 2004. "Between Support and Marginalization: The Development of Academic Language in Linguistic Minority Children." In *Bilingualism and Language Pedagogy*, edited by Janina Brutt-Griffler and Manka Varghese, 10–35. Buffalo, NY: Multilingual Matters.

Valenzuela, Angela. 1999. *Subtractive Schooling: US—Mexican Youth and the Politics of Caring.* Albany: State University of New York Press.

Van de Werfhorst, Herman G., and Jonathan J. B. Mijs. 2010. "Achievement Inequality and the Institutional Structure of Educational Systems: A Comparative Perspective." *Annual Review of Sociology* 36: 407–28.

Van Zanten, Agnès. 2001. *L'école de la périphérie. Scolarité et ségrégation en banlieue.* Paris: Presses universitaires de France.

Vasagar, Jeevan. 2011. "Oxford University and David Cameron Clash over Black Student Numbers." *The Guardian*, April 11. http://www.guardian.co.uk/education/2011/apr/11/ oxford-cameron-black-students.

Vertovec, Steven. 2007. "New Complexities of Cohesion in Britain: Super Diversity, Transnationalism and Civil-Integration." *Ethnic and Racial Studies* 29: 1024–54.

Vigil, James Diego. 2004. "Gangs and Group Membership: Implications for Schooling." In *School Connections: Peers, Schools, and the Achievement of U.S. Mexican Youth*, edited by Margaret Gibson, Patricia Gándara, and Jill Koyama, 87–106. New York: Teachers College Press.

Vila, Ignasi. 2006. "Lengua, escuela e inmigración." *Cultura y educación* 18: 127–42.

Waldinger, Roger. 1996. *Still the Promised City? African-Americans and New Immigrants in Postindustrial New York.* Cambridge, MA: Harvard University Press.

Waldinger, Roger, and Michael Lichter. 2003. *How the Other Half Works: Immigration and the Social Organization of Labor.* Berkeley: University of California.

Walqui, Aída. 2000. *Access and Engagement: Program Design and Instructional Approaches for Immigrant Students in Secondary School.* Brooklyn, NY: Delta Publishing Group.

Waters, Mary. 2008. "Counting and Classifying by Race: The American Debate." *The Tocqueville Review* 29: 1–21.

Weil, Patrick. 2002. *Qu'est-ce que un Français? Histoire de la nationalité française depuis la Révolution.* Paris: Grasset.

Westin, Charles. 2003. "Young People of Migrant Origin in Sweden." *International Migration Review* 37: 987–1010.

———. 2006. "Sweden: Restrictive Immigration Policy and Multiculturalism." Migration Information Source. http://www.migrationinformation. org/Profiles/display.cfm?ID=406.

White, Michael and Jennifer Glick. 2009. Achieving Anew: How New Immigrants Do in American Schools, Jobs, and Neighborhoods. New York: Russell Sage Foundation.

Wiggins, Grant, and Jay McTighe. 1998. *Understanding by Design.* Upper Saddle River, NJ: Merill Prentice Hall.

Williams, Juliet. 2009. "Schools Chief: California Education System 'Precarious.'" *The Union*, February 3. http://www.theunion.com/article/20090203/ WEBUPDATE/902039972/-1/rss02.

Woodland, Malcolm. 2008. "Whatcha Doin' after School?: A Review of the Literature on the Influence of After-School Programs on Young Black Males." *Urban Education* 43: 537–60.

Wyner, Joshua, John Bridgeland, and John DiIulio. 2007. "Achievement Trap: How America Is Failing Millions of High-Achieving Students from Lower-Income Families." A Report by the Jack Kent Cooke Foundation & Civic Enterprises. http://www.civicenterprises.net/pdfs/jkc.pdf.

Yin, Robert. 2003. *Case Study Research: Design and Method*, 3rd ed. Thousand Oaks, CA: Sage Press.

Zapata-Barrero, Ricard. 2010. "Dynamics of Diversity in Spain: Old Questions, New Challenges." In *The Multiculturalism Backlash: European Discourses, Policies, and Practices,* edited by Steve Vertovec and Susanne Wessendorf, 170–89. London: Routledge.

Zeldin, Shepherd. 2004. "Preventing Youth Violence through the Promotion of Community Engagement and Membership." *Journal of Community Psychology* 32: 623–41.

Zhou, Min, and Susan Kim. 2006. "Community Forces, Social Capital, and Educational Achievement: The Case of Supplementary Education in the Chinese and Korean Immigrant Communities." *Harvard Educational Review* 76: 1–29.

Zhou, Min, and Xiyuan Li. 2003. "Ethnic Language Schools and the Development of Supplementary Education in the Immigrant Chinese Community in the United States." In *New Directions for Youth Development: Understanding the Social Worlds of Immigrant Youth*, edited by Carola Suárez-Orozco and Irina Todorova, 57–73. San Francisco: Jossey-Bass.

Zimdars, Anna, Alice Sullivan, and Anthony Heath. 2009. "Elite Higher Education Admissions in the Arts and Sciences: Is Cultural Capital the Key?" *Sociology* 43: 648–66.

Zimmer, Ron, Brian Gill, Paula Razquin, Kevin Booker, J. R. Lockwood, Georges Vernez, Beatrice Birman, Michael Garet, and Jennifer O'Day. 2007. "Do Title I School Choice and Supplemental Educational Services Affect Student Achievement?" RAND Report. http://www.rand.org/pubs/research_briefs/RB9273/.

Contributors

DALIA ABDELHADY is senior researcher at the Center for Middle Eastern Studies at Lund University in Sweden.

RICHARD ALBA is distinguished professor of sociology at the Graduate Center of the City University of New York.

MIKAEL ALEXANDERSSON is vice chancellor and professor of education at Halmstad University in Sweden.

VIKKI BOLIVER is a lecturer in sociology in the School of Applied Social Sciences at Durham University in England.

YAËL BRINBAUM is a sociologist and researcher at the Centre d'études de l'emploi (CEE), and is associated with the Institut national d'études démographiques (INED) and at the Institut de recherche sur l'éducation (IREDU, CNRS).

SILVIA CARRASCO PONS is a professor of social anthropology, Universitat Autònoma de Barcelona.

MAURICE CRUL is a professor of organizational sciences at the Free University in Amsterdam and also working in the sociology department at Erasmus University in Rotterdam.

L. JANELLE DANCE is an associate professor of sociology and ethnic studies at the University of Nebraska and a senior researcher at CMES, Lund University in Sweden.

HELGA A.G. DE VALK is a professor of demography at the Interface Demography, Free University in Brussels and also working at the Netherlands Interdisciplinary Demographic Institute in The Hague.

JOSH DEWIND is director of the Migration Program and Dissertation Proposal Development Fellowship Program at the Social Science Research Council.

NORMA FUENTES-MAYORGA is a visiting research fellow at the Center for Migration and Development, Princeton University in New Jersey.

MARGARET GIBSON is professor emerita of education and anthropology, University of California, Santa Cruz.

ANTHONY HEATH, FBA, is emeritus professor of sociology at the University of Oxford and professor of sociology at the Institute for Social Change at the University of Manchester.

JENNIFER HOLDAWAY is a program director and China representative at the Social Science Research Council.

JOHANNES LUNNEBLAD is an associate professor in the Department of Education, Communication and Learning at the University of Gothenburg.

AMY LUTZ is an associate professor of sociology in the Maxwell School of Citizenship and Public Affairs at Syracuse University in New York.

MARGARY MARTIN is a research scientist at the NYU Steinhardt School of Culture, Education and Human Development.

JORDI PÀMIES ROVIRA is an associate professor of education, migration, and diversity, Universitat Autònoma de Barcelona.

MARIBEL PONFERRADA ARTEAGA is a postdoctoral fellow, Department of Cultural Anthropology and History of America and Africa, University of Barcelona.

ANNE RÍOS-ROJAS is an assistant professor of comparative and international education, Department of Educational Studies, Colgate University in Hamilton, New York.

ROXANE SILBERMAN is senior researcher (directeur de recherches) at the Centre National de la Recherche Scientifique (CNRS) and member of Paris School of Economics (PSE), Paris.

CAROLA SUÁREZ-OROZCO is a professor of psychological studies in education at the University of California, Los Angeles.

VAN C. TRAN is an assistant professor of sociology at Columbia University.

MARY C. WATERS is the M. E. Zukerman Professor of Sociology at Harvard University.

MAYIDA ZAAL is an assistant professor in the Department of Secondary and Special Education of the College of Education and Human Services at Montclair State University, New Jersey.

Index

Page numbers with *fig* indicate a figure; those with a *t* indicate a table.

after-school and enrichment programs:
in California, 117; in France, 172; in
the Netherlands, 261; in New York,
59, 79–80, 82; practices conducive to
positive outcomes for immigrant-origin
youth, 221, 234–35

After School Corporation (TASC; New
York City), 80

Agence nationale pour l'emploi (ANPE;
France), 194–95

Alba, Richard, ix, 85–86, 188, 278

Algerians in France, 6, 9, 168. *See also*
North Africans

Allianza Dominicana (New York City), 59

American Community Survey, 166–67,
209

Amsterdam: Amsterdam-West district,
42–43; mentoring programs, 56, 76–79,
82, 270–71; Moroccan immigrants'
children in, 32–33, 39–83; school
districts and school choice, 54–56, 259;
school system characteristics, 49–51;
second-generation immigrants in, 4

apprenticeships, 19, 182, 183*t*, 270

Argentinians in Spain, 107

Asians in France, 5

Asians in the U.S.: "color line" concept
and, 125; community institutions
and, 261; demographics, 5; parents'
knowledge of postsecondary education
process, 238

associate's degree in the U.S., 167

Australia, immigrants to, viii, 19, 126–27

baby boomers, 1–2

baccalaureate degree in the U.S., 168, 254

baccalauréat (bac) in France: attainment

rates, 199; immigrant parents' lack of
knowledge about, 178–79; importance
of, 179–80; new types of, 16, 35, 162,
179–83, 184, 200, 259; peer pressure
and, 197–98; system of, 27, 30, 161–62;
unemployment and, 188

Bangladeshis in the U.K.: demographics,
5; educational catch-up by, 34, 122,
277; immigration of, 127; performance
scores, 134, 135*t*, 136; performance scores
at age sixteen correlated with school
completion, 140*t*, 142*t*; postsecondary
education completion rates, 143–46,
144*t*; primary and secondary effects of
ethnicity on education, 122

Barcelona: Catalan as primary language
in, 85, 91, 101, 105–7, 110, 113, 114;
cultural diversity in schools, 101–3;
exchange students in, 107; high schools
in study, 95–98; Moroccan immigrants'
children study, 33–34, 84–119, 265–66,
275; percentage of immigrant children
as students, 89; racial stereotyping in,
101–3, 104–5, 275; school segregation,
91; schools selected for study, 87;
student demographics for schools in
study, 97–98, 98*t*; teacher-to-student
ratio, 95; welcome classes for minority-
language students, 110–11

Batalova, Jeanne, 191–92

Batxillerat program in Catalonia, 89, 92,
95, 111

Bergslunden Gymnasium (Sweden):
about, 220–21; Calm Streets
disciplinary program, 231;
collaborative/cooperative learning
approach, 227; demographics, 221;

U.K., 153–54; overcoming racism in, 59; performance scores at age sixteen, 134–37, 135*t*, 141, 143; performance scores at age sixteen correlated with school completion, 140*t*, 142*t;* PISA study scores, 13–14, 132; postsecondary education, 28–29, 34–35, 122–23, 147–52, 183–87; postsecondary education completion rates, 143–46, 144*t*, 156, 254–55; preschool in, 21, 262; primary schools, inequalities in, 168–74, 255–56; private school system in, 27, 162–63; race and inequality factors compared with the U.K., 123–26, 151–53; racial policies in, 124–25, 154; refugees as immigrants in, 9–10, 41–42; residential segregation in, 23, 35–36, 46, 51–52, 128, 161, 168–70, 174–75, 200; school choice in, 27, 171, 206, 263–64; school dropout rates, 61, 62, 177, 255–56; school financing system, 12, 22, 56–57, 161, 263, 264; school inequalities compared with France, 160–203; school system structure, 53*fig,* 156–57, 182–83, 199; school-to-labor market transition, 35–36, 52, 187–99, 256; school-year length in, 21, 261; secondary education completion rates, 131, 137–43, 138*t*, 153; secondary schools, inequalities in, 174–83; second-generation attainment and inequality, 120–59; second-generation immigrant demographics, 4–5, 276–79; students with interrupted education in, 242–43; testing and inequality, 154–55; tracking schemes, 3, 12, 27, 35–36, 52, 124, 176, 267, 268; U.K. social models compared with, 123–24; undocumented

immigrants in, 8, 42, 125; universities' status differences, 17; zero-sum educational policies and, 259–60. *See also* California; Dominicans; Mexicans; New York City
University of California, 94
University of Michigan Law School case, 154–55

VBO track in the Netherlands, 50
Vietnamese in the U.S., 5
Vigil, Jami, 109
VMBO track in the Netherlands, 50, 61, 272
VMO track in the Netherlands, 50
voucher programs, 27
VWO track in the Netherlands, 30, 56, 61, 74, 76, 272

Waldinger, Roger, 201
Washington Irving High School (New York), 64
Waters, Mary, 143
Werquin, Patrick, 188
West Indians. *See* Afro-Caribbeans in the U.K.; Caribbeans in the U.S.
"whole child" learning concept, 219–20
World Citizen High School (New York City): about, 212–13; collaborative/cooperative learning approach, 227; cultural transition support at, 241–42; debates at, 226; extracurricular activities, 235; interdisciplinary teacher team structure, 229–30, 245–46; language-learning accommodations, 246, 250; newcomers and second-language learners at, 240, 243–44, 251;